THE PORTABLE WORLD

A
COMPLETE
POCKET
ATLAS

——— EDITED BY ———

B.M. WILLETT, DAVID GAYLARD
AND LILLA PRINCE-SMITH

AVON BOOKS ◆ NEW YORK

World

Europe

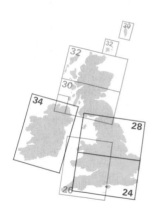

Originally published in Great Britain as *Philips' Small World Atlas*

Maps prepared by Cox Cartographic, Ltd., and George Philip Cartographic Services, Ltd., London, under the direction of Alan Poynter.

AVON BOOKS
A division of
The Hearst Corporation
105 Madison Avenue
New York, New York 10016

First Avon Books Trade Printing:
September 1990

AVON TRADEMARK REG. U.S. PAT. OFF. AND IN OTHER COUNTRIES, MARCA REGISTRADA.

10   9   8   7   6   5   4   3   2   1

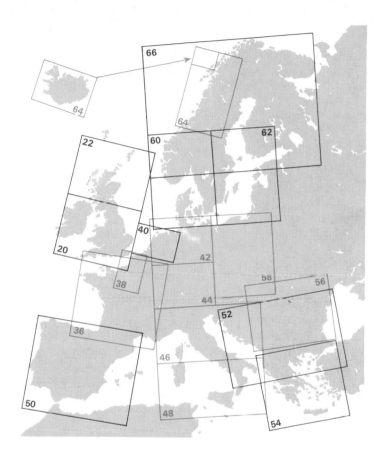

Asia

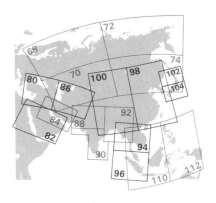

68-75 **U.S.S.R.**
  68-69 West
  70-71 South West
  72-73 North East
  74-75 South East and Mongolia

76-77 **Asia: Physical**
78-79 **Asia: Political**
80-81 **Turkey and the Middle East**
82-83 **Arabian Peninsula**
84-85 **The Gulf**
86-87 **Central Asia and Afghanistan**
88-89 **Pakistan and North West India**

90-91 **Central and Southern India, Sri Lanka**
92-93 **Eastern India, Bangladesh and Burma**
94-95 **Mainland South East Asia**
96-97 **The Malay Peninsula**
98-99 **China: East**
100-101 **China: West**

102-109 **Japan**
  102-103 North
  104-105 South
  106-107 Tokyo, Kyoto, Osaka
      108 Kyushu
      109 West Honshu and Shikoku

110-111 **Indonesia: West**
112-113 **Indonesia: East**

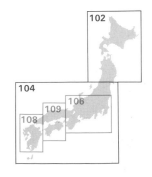

Australasia

114-115   **Australia, New Zealand and Papua New Guinea**

116-121   **Australia**
116-117   Brisbane, Sydney, Melbourne
118-119   Adelaide, Melbourne,
          Tasmania
      120   Perth
      121   North East Queensland

122-123   **New Zealand, Central and South West Pacific**

Africa

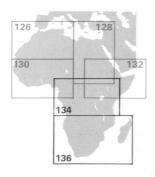

124-137   **Africa**
      124   Physical
      125   Political
126-127   North West
128-129   North East
130-131   West
132-133   East
134-135   Central
136-137   South

North America

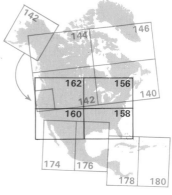

138   **North America: Physical**
139   **North America: Political**

140-155   **Canada**
  140-141 South East
  142-143 South West and Alaska
  144-145 North West
  146-147 North East
  148-149 Saint Lawrence Estuary
  150-151 The Great Lakes
  152-153 Southern Saskatchewan and
            Manitoba
  154-155 Southern British Columbia and
            Alberta

156-173   **U.S.A.**
  156-157 North East
  158-159 South East
  160-161 South West
  162-163 North West
     164 Boston, New York,
           Washington
     165 Washington, Atlanta
  166-167 Upper Mississippi
  168-169 Lower Mississippi and Gulf
           Coast
     170 Florida
     171 Columbia Basin
  172-173 California

174-175   **Mexico: West**
176-177   **Mexico: East**
178-179   **Caribbean: West**
180-181   **Caribbean: East**

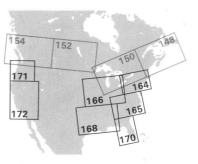

South America

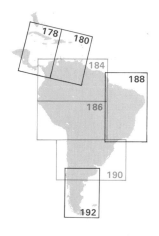

182-192 South America

182 Physical
183 Political
184-185 North West
186-187 West
188-189 East
190-191 Central
192 South

Index

Map Symbols

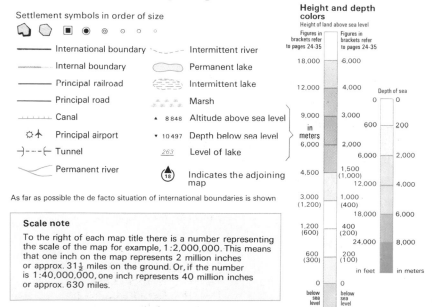

Settlement symbols in order of size

─────── International boundary
─────── Internal boundary
─────── Principal railroad
─────── Principal road
┼┼┼┼┼┼ Canal
☼✈ Principal airport
─┤---├─ Tunnel
～～ Permanent river

⌇‒‒‒⌇ Intermittent river
⬭ Permanent lake
⬭ Intermittent lake
⁂ Marsh
▲ 8848 Altitude above sea level
▼ 10497 Depth below sea level
263 Level of lake
(18) Indicates the adjoining map

As far as possible the de facto situation of international boundaries is shown

Height and depth colors

Height of land above sea level

Figures in brackets refer to pages 24-35

18,000
12,000
9,000
in meters
6,000
4,500
3,000 (1,200)
1,200 (600)
600 (300)
0
below sea level
in feet

Figures in brackets refer to pages 24-35

-6,000
4,000
3,000
2,000
1,500 (1,000)
1,000 (400)
400 (200)
200 (100)
0
below sea level
in meters

Depth of sea

0   0
600   200
6,000   2,000
12,000   4,000
18,000   6,000
24,000   8,000
in feet   in meters

Scale note

To the right of each map title there is a number representing the scale of the map for example, 1 : 2,000,000. This means that one inch on the map represents 2 million inches or approx. 31½ miles on the ground. Or, if the number is 1 : 40,000,000, one inch represents 40 million inches or approx. 630 miles.

World: Northern Part

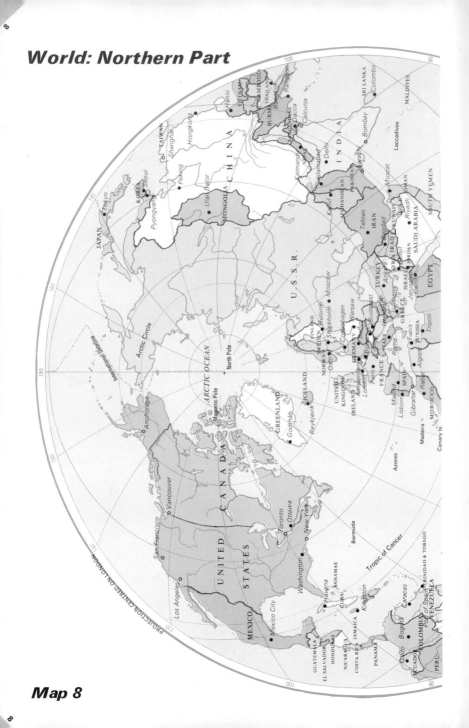

Map 8

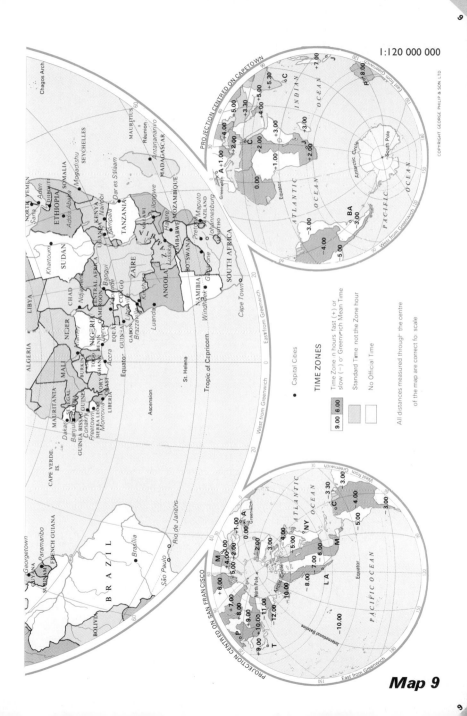

Map 9

1:120 000 000

PROJECTION CENTRED ON CAPETOWN

PROJECTION CENTRED ON SAN FRANCISCO

TIME ZONES

- Capital Cities

Time Zone n hours fast (+) or slow (−) or Greenwich Mean Time

Standard Time not the Zone hour

No Official Time

All distances measured through the centre of the map are correct to scale

COPYRIGHT GEORGE PHILIP & SON LTD

Chagos Arch.

NORTH YEMEN
ALGERIA
LIBYA
MALI
NIGER
CHAD
SUDAN
ETHIOPIA
SOMALIA
DJIBOUTI
SEYCHELLES
MAURITANIA
SENEGAL
GUINEA BISSAU
GUINEA
SIERRA LEONE
LIBERIA
IVORY COAST
GHANA
TOGO
BENIN
NIGERIA
CAMEROON
CENTRAL AFRICA
EQUAT. GUINEA
GABON
CONGO
ZAIRE
UGANDA
KENYA
TANZANIA
ANGOLA
ZAMBIA
MALAWI
MOZAMBIQUE
ZIMBABWE
NAMIBIA
BOTSWANA
SWAZILAND
LESOTHO
SOUTH AFRICA
MADAGASCAR
MAURITIUS
Réunion
BURKINA

Sana
Aden
Mogadishu
Addis Ababa
Khartoum
Ndjamena
Bangui
Niamey
Dakar
Banjul
Conakry
Freetown
Monrovia
Accra
Yaoundé
Libreville
Kinshasa
Brazzaville
Luanda
Kampala
Nairobi
Dar es Salaam
Lusaka
Lilongwe
Harare
Maputo
Pretoria
Johannesburg
Gaborone
Windhoek
Antananarivo
Cape Town

BRAZIL
BOLIVIA
GUYANA
SURINAM
FRENCH GUIANA
Georgetown
Paramaribo
Brasília
Rio de Janeiro
São Paulo

St. Helena
Ascension

Tropic of Capricorn
Equator
East from Greenwich
West from Greenwich

Capital Cities

INDIAN OCEAN
ATLANTIC OCEAN
PACIFIC OCEAN

Greenwich
Equator
Antarctic Circle
South Pole

A +1.00
0.00
+2.00
+3.00
+4.00
+5.00
+5.30
+3.30
−2.00
−3.00
−4.00
−5.00
+1.00
+2.00
+7.00
+8.00

East from Greenwich
West from Greenwich

North Pole
Arctic Circle
International Dateline
Equator

ATLANTIC OCEAN
PACIFIC OCEAN

+1.00
0.00
Greenwich
−2.00
−3.00
+4.00
+5.00
+6.00
+7.00
+8.00
+9.00
+10.00
+11.00
−12.00
−10.00
−8.00
−7.00
−6.00
−5.00
−4.00
−3.00
3.00

9.00 6.00

World: Southern Part

PROJECTION CENTRED ON THE ANTIPODES OF LONDON

West from Greenwich

East from Greenwich

International Dateline

Galapagos Is.

Easter I.

PACIFIC OCEAN

Marquesas Is.

Tuamotu Arch.

Tropic of Capricorn

Pitcairn I.

FRENCH POLYNESIA

Tahiti

Kiritimati

PACIFIC OCEAN

Cook Is.

Hawaiian Is.

Tropic of Cancer

SAMOA

Equator

TONGA

Auckland

Wellington

Antipodes I.

NEW ZEALAND

Antarctic Circle

Victoria Land

Midway I.

KIRIBATI

FIJI

Auckland I.

Macquarie I.

Adélie Land

Wake I.

Marshall Is.

TUVALU

New Caledonia

Auckland Is.

SOLOMON IS.

VANUATU

Sydney

Canberra

Bonin I.

Northern
Marianas

Guam

Caroline Is.

PAPUA

Port Moresby

NEW GUINEA

AUSTRALIA

Perth

PHILIPPINES

Manila

INDIAN OCEAN

VIETNAM

BRUNEI

Ho Chi Minh City

INDONESIA

MALAYSIA

Singapore

Jakarta

Kuala Lumpur

Map 10

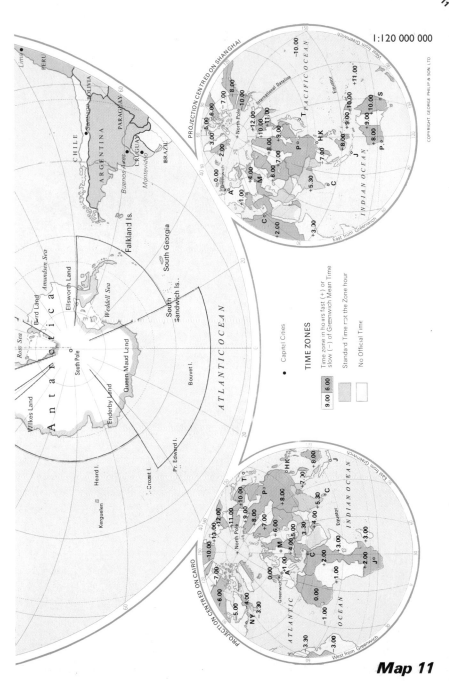

PROJECTION CENTRED ON SHANGHAI

1:120 000 000

West from Greenwich

COPYRIGHT GEORGE PHILIP & SON LTD

PERU
Lima

BOLIVIA
PARAGUAY

CHILE

ARGENTINA

Santiago
Buenos Aires
URUGUAY
Montevideo
BRAZIL

Falkland Is.

South Georgia

South
Sandwich Is.

Amundsen Sea

Byrd Land

Ellsworth Land

A n t a r c t i c a

Weddell Sea

Ross Sea

Wilkes Land

South Pole

Queen Maud Land

Enderby Land

Bouvet I.

ATLANTIC OCEAN

Pr. Edward I.

Crozet I.

Heard I.

Kerguelen

PACIFIC OCEAN

International Dateline

North Pole

Equator

INDIAN OCEAN

East from Greenwich

• Capital Cities

TIME ZONES

Time zone in hours fast (+) or
slow (−) of Greenwich Mean Time

| 9.00 | 6.00 | Standard Time ½ past the Zone hour |

No Official Time

PROJECTION CENTRED ON CAIRO

East from Greenwich

North Pole

Equator

INDIAN OCEAN

Greenwich

ATLANTIC OCEAN

West from Greenwich

Map 11

Arctic

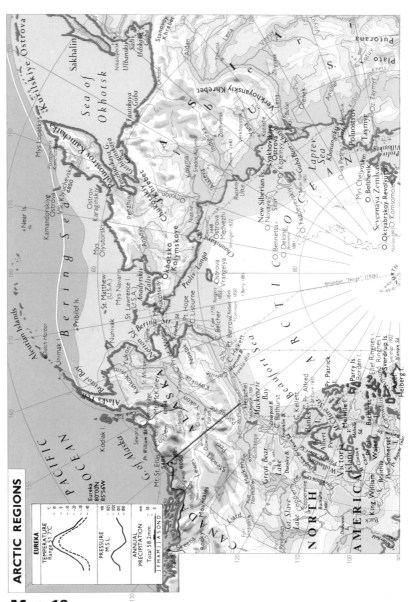

ARCTIC REGIONS

EUREKA
TEMPERATURE
Range 51.7°C

Eureka
80°00N
85°56W

PRESSURE
M.S.L.

ANNUAL
PRECIPITATION
Total 58.2mm.

J F M A M J J A S O N D

Map 12

1:42 000 000

Map 13

Antarctic

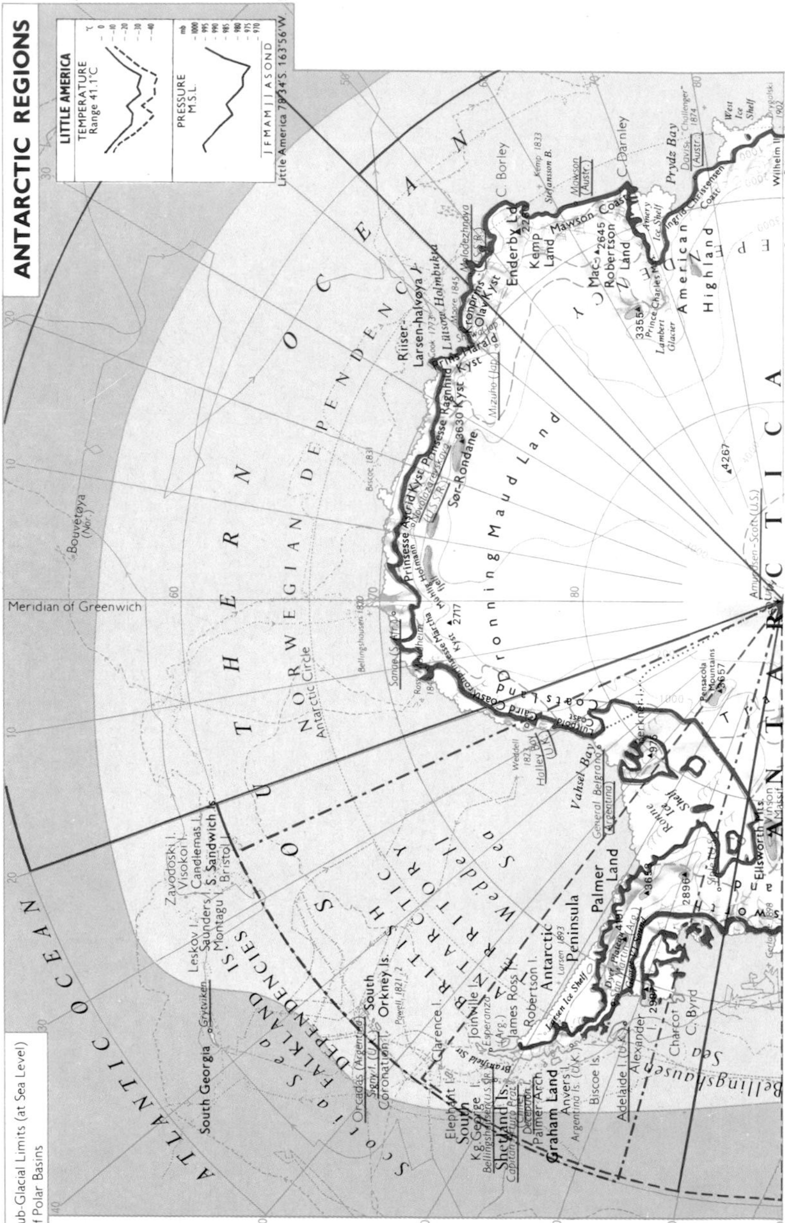

ANTARCTIC REGIONS

LITTLE AMERICA

TEMPERATURE
Range 41.1°C

PRESSURE
M.S.L.

Little America 78°34'S 163°56'W

J F M A M J J A S O N D

--- Sub-Glacial Limits (at Sea Level)
of Polar Basins

Map 14

SOUTHERN OCEAN

ATLANTIC OCEAN

INDIAN OCEAN

NORWEGIAN DEPENDENCY

BRITISH ANTARCTIC TERRITORY

AUSTRALIAN ANTARCTIC DEPENDENCY

ANTARCTICA

Meridian of Greenwich

Antarctic Circle

Dronning Maud Land

Coats Land

Palmer Land

Antarctic Peninsula

Graham Land

Ellsworth Mountains

Weddell Sea

Ross Sea

Bellingshausen Sea

Amundsen Sea (U.S.)

Ronne Ice Shelf

Filchner Ice Shelf

American Highland

Prydz Bay

Kemp Land

Enderby Land

Robertson Land

Mac-Robertson Land

Prince Charles Mountains

Lambert Glacier

Wilhelm II Coast

Mawson Coast

Bouvetøya (Nor.)

South Georgia

South Sandwich Is.

Zavodovski I.
Visokoi I.
Candlemas I.
Leskov I.
Saunders I.
Montagu I.
Bristol I.

South Orkney Is.
Coronation I.
Signy I.
Orcadas (Argentina)

South Shetland Is.
Elephant I.
Clarence I.
King George I.
Livingston I.
Deception I.
Smith I.
Snow I.

Anvers I.
Palmer Arch.
Biscoe Is.
Adelaide I.
Alexander I.
Charcot I.

Falkland Dependencies

James Ross I.

C. Boriey
C. Darnley
Riiser-Larsen Halvøya

Larsen-halvøya

Princess Astrid Coast

Sør-Rondane

West Ice Shelf

5139

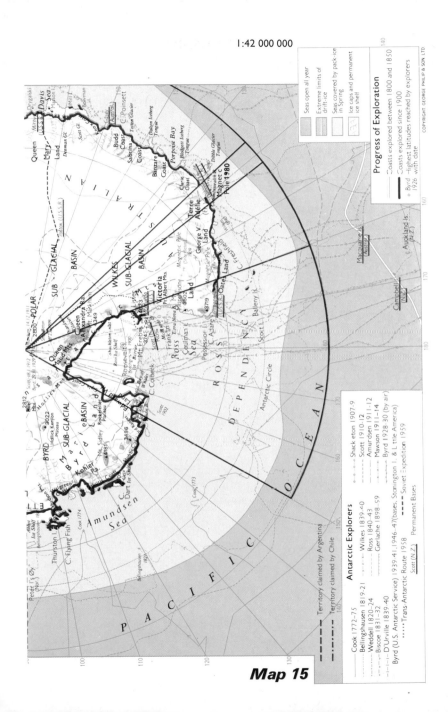

1:42 000 000

Map 15

Progress of Exploration

Seas open all year

Extreme limits of
drift-ice

Seas covered by pack-ice
in Spring

Ice caps and permanent
ice shelf

———— Coasts explored between 1800 and 1850

———— Coasts explored since 1900

+ Byrd +Highest latitudes reached by explorers
1926 with date

COPYRIGHT GEORGE PHILIP & SON LTD

Antarctic Explorers

———— Cook 1772–75
·····— Bellingshausen 1819–21
–··–··– Weddell 1820–24
———— Biscoe 1831–32
–·—·—· D'Urville 1839–40
·—·—·— Shackleton 1907–9
···—···— Wilkes 1839–40
———— Ross 1840–43
———— Gerlache 1898–59
·····— Scott 1910–12
———— Amundsen 1911–12
———— Mawson 1911–14
———— Byrd 1928–30 (by air)
———— Byrd (U.S. Antarctic Service) 1939-41, 1946-47(bases, Stanington I. & L'ttle America)
·····Trans-Antarctic Route 1958
Scott (N.Z.)
Soviet Expedition 1959
Permanent Bases

– – – Territory claimed by Argentina
–··–··– Territory claimed by Chile

Europe: Physical

Iceland
Hekla 1491
Oraefa Jokull 2119

NORWEGIAN SEA

Arctic Circle

Vesteralen
Lofoten
2123 Kebnekaise

Scandinavia

G. of

Faroe Is.

Fisher Bank

Shetland Is.

Galdhopiggen 2469

Rockall

Umi
Inda

Hebrides

Orkney Is.

Malaren

ATLANTIC

British Isles

Ben Nevis 1344

Lindesnes

Skagerrak

Kattegat

Vanern

Gotland

Vattern

BALTIC

Valentia I.

Ireland

Irish Sea

Snowdon 1085

Great Britain

NORTH SEA

Dogger Bank

Heligoland

Jutland

North

C. Clear

Land's End

Thames

Netherlands

Elbe

Weser

Odra (Oder)

Wisła (Vistula)

OCEAN

English Channel

Meuse

Rhine

Harz 1142

Sudetes

C

Brittany

Seine

Ardennes

Eifel

Wester wald

Taunus

Erz Geb.

Moravian Heights

Bay of Biscay 4861

Loire

Gironde

Vosges

Black For.

Jura

Danube

Inn

Bohemian For.

Hunsruck

Bakony For.

Drava

Sava

C. Finisterre

Garonne

Central 1886 Mt. Dore

Massif

Rhone

Cevennes

Mt. Blanc 4807

ALPS

Po

Apennines

Dinaric Alps

ADRIATIC SEA

Cantabrian Mts.

Pyrenees

Pico de Aneto 3404

G. of Lions

Ligurian Sea

Ouro

Old Castile

Sa. de Guadarrama

Iberian

New Castile

Corsica

Tiber

Gran Sasso 2914

C. da Roca

Tejo (Tagus)

Sa. da Estrela

Peninsula

Balearic Is.

Str. of Bonifacio

Vesuvius 1277

Str. of Otranto

C. St. Vincent

Sierra Morena

Guadalquivir

Andalusia

Sa. Nevada

Mulhacen 3478

Sardinia

Tyrrhenian Sea

Calabria

Ionian

C. Trafalgar

C. Spartel

Str. of Gibraltar

Er Rif

MEDITERRANEAN

C. Blanco

Str. of Messina

Etna 3263

Sicily

Ionian Sea

Maritime Atlas

West from Greenwich   0   East from Greenwich   10

C. Bon

Malta

SEA

Map 16

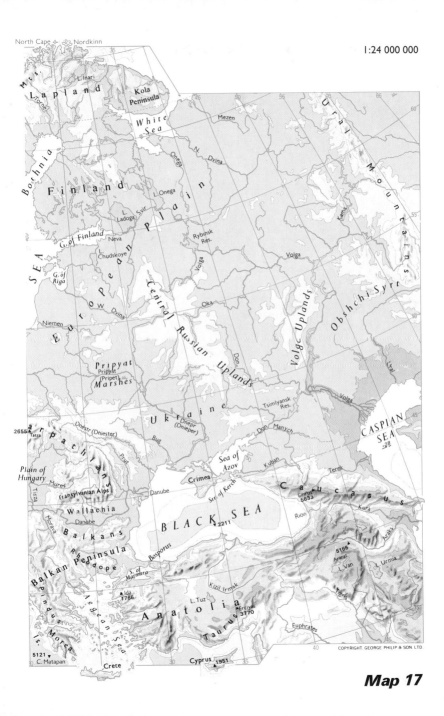

1:24 000 000

North Cape ✧ ⇠⇢ Nordkinn

Mts.
Lapland
L. Torne
L. Inari
Kola
Peninsula

White
Sea

Mezen

Bothnia

Onega
N. Dvina

Finland

L. Onega

L.
Ladoga
Svir

European Plain

Kama

Ural Mountains

G. of Finland
Neva
Rybinsk
Res.

SEA

L.
Chudskoye

Volga

G. of
Riga

Central Russian Uplands

Niemen

Europow

W. Dvina

Oka

Volga

Volga Uplands

Obshchi Syrt

Pripyat
Pripyat
(Pripet)
Marshes

Don

Tsimlyansk
Res.

Ural

2655
Tatra

Ukraine

Dnepr
(Dnieper)

Carpathians

Onestr (Dniester)

Bug

Don
Manych

Volga

CASPIAN
SEA
-28

Plain of
Hungary

Mures

Prut

Sea of
Azov

Kuban

Terek

45

Tisza

Transylvanian Alps

Danube

Crimea

Str. of Kerch

Elbrus
5633

Caucasus

Wallachia

Morava

Danube

BLACK SEA

▼2211

Rion

Kura

40

Balkans

Kizil Irmak

Araks

Rhodope

Bosporus

5166
Ararat

L. Van

L. Urmia

Balkan Peninsula

S. of
Marmara

Tigris

Pindus

Aegean Sea

▲ Ida
1766

Taurus

L. Tuz

Erciyas
3770

Euphrates

Is.

Morea

Anatolia

Taurus

40

5121 ▼
C. Matapan

Crete

Cyprus ▲1951

COPYRIGHT GEORGE PHILIP & SON. LTD.

Map 17

Europe: *Political*

Map 18

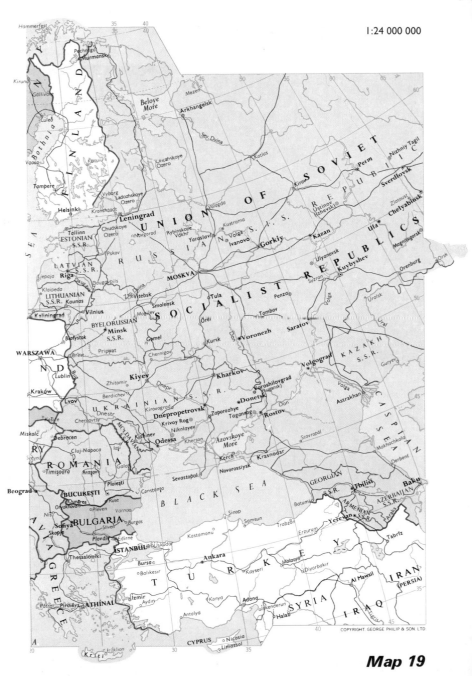

1:24 000 000

Hammerfest

Pechengo
Kiruna
Gallivare
Luleå
Vaasa
Bothnia
Tampere
Helsinki

Murmansk
Beloye
More
Arkhangelsk
Sev. Dvina
Mezen
Kotlas
Perm
Nizhniy Tagil
Sverdlovsk
Zlatoust
Ustinov
(Izhevsk)
Ufa
Chelyabinsk
Magnitogorsk
Orsk

SEA

Kronstadt
Leningrad
Vyborg
Ladozhskoye
Ozero
Tallinn
ESTONIAN
S.S.R.
Chudskoye
Ozero
Novgorod
Rybinskoye
Vdkhr.
Yaroslavl
Ivanovo
Gorkiy
Kazan
Ulyanovsk
Kuybyshev
Orenburg
Uralsk

UNION
OF
SOVIET
REPUBLIC

Pskov
RUSSIAN
S.F.S.
Volga
Syzran
Ural
Uralsk

LATVIAN
S.S.R.
Liepaja
Riga
Daugavpils
MOSKVA
SOCIALIST
REPUBLICS
Penza

Klaipeda
LITHUANIAN
S.S.R. Kaunas
Vitebsk
Smolensk
Tula
Örel
Tambov
Saratov

Kaliningrad
Vilnius
Mogilev
Don
Voronezh
Volga
KAZAKH
S.S.R.
Guryev

BYELORUSSIAN
Minsk
S.S.R.
Gomel
Kursk
Volgograd
Astrakhan
CASPIAN

WARSZAWA
Białystok
Brest
Pripyat
Chernigov
Don

N D
Lublin
Zhitomir
Kiyev
Dnepr
UKRAINIAN S.S.R.
Kharkov
Voroshilovgrad
(Lugansk)
Donetsk
Rostov
Makhachkala

Kraków
Lvov
Berdichev
Kirovograd
Dnepropetrovsk
Zaporozhye
Taganrog
Derbent

Przemyśl
Chernovtsy
Dnestr
Krivoy Rog
Nikolayev
Azovskoye
More
Stavropol
SEA

Miskolc
Debrecen
Kishinev
MOLDAVIAN
Odessa
Kherson
Kerch
Krasnodar

RY
Cluj-Napoca
Iași
Novorossiysk
Batumi
GEORGIAN
S.S.R.
Tbilisi
Baku

ROMANIA
Timișoara
Argeș
Galați
Sevastopol
Novorossiysk
AZERBAIJAN
S.S.R.

Sibiu
ARMENIAN
S.S.R.
Yerevan
Araks

Beograd
BUCUREȘTI
Dunărea
Pleven
Ruse
BLACK SEA
Sinop
Samsun
Trabzon
Erzurum
Tabrīz

Niš
Oltul
Varna
Burgas
IRAN
(PERSIA)

AVIA
Sofiya
BULGARIA
Skopje
Plovdiv
Sliven
Edirne
Kastamonu
Ankara
Kayseri
Malatya
Diyarbakır
Al Mawsil

Thessaloníki
ISTANBUL
Üsküdar
Bursa
T U R K E Y
SYRIA
IRAQ

GREECE
Balıkesir
İzmir
Aydın
Konya
Adana
İskenderun
Halab

Pátrai
Piraiévs
ATHÍNAI
Antalya

A
KRÍTI
CYPRUS
Nicosia
Limassol

Iráklion

Map 19

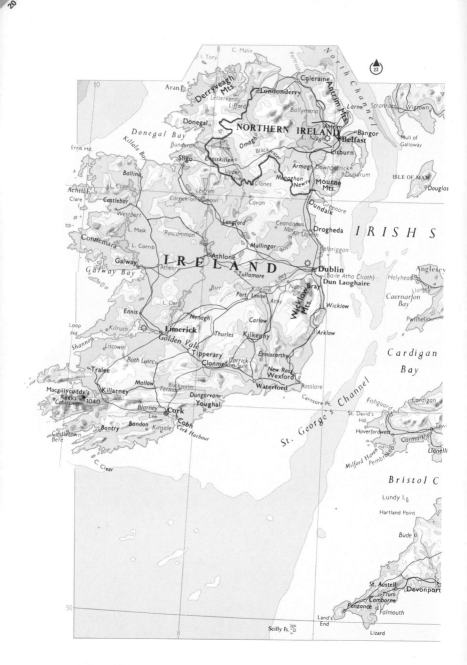

Map 20

British Isles: South

1:4 000 000

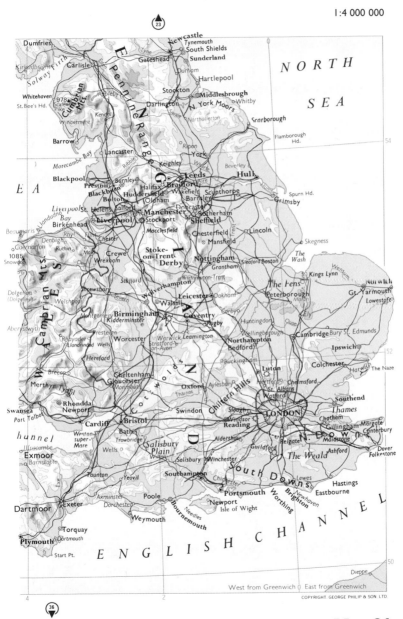

Map 21

British Isles: North

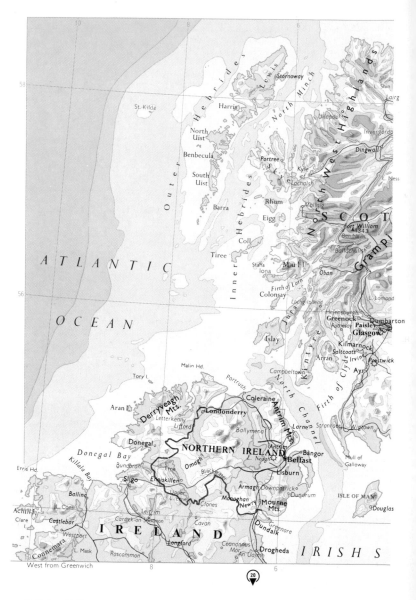

Map 22

1:4 000 000

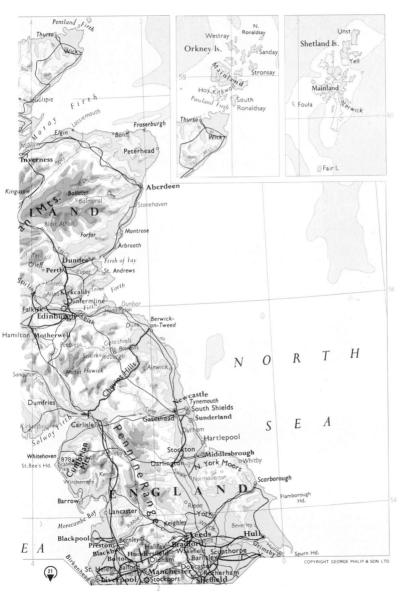

Map 23

Southern England

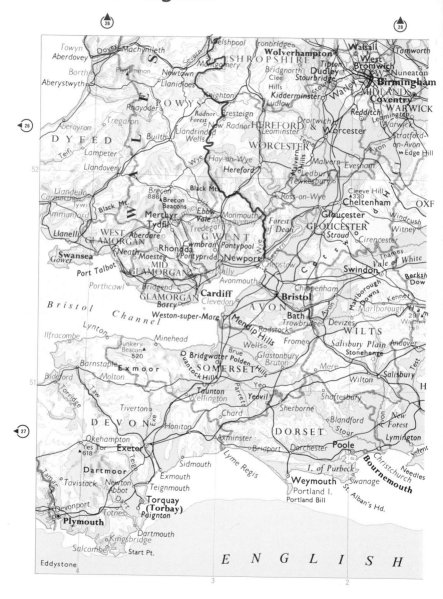

Map 24

1:2 000 000

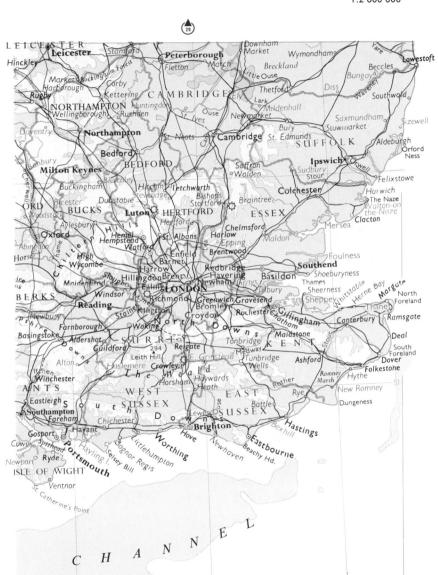

West from Greenwich   0   East from Greenwich

Map 25

Wales and South West England

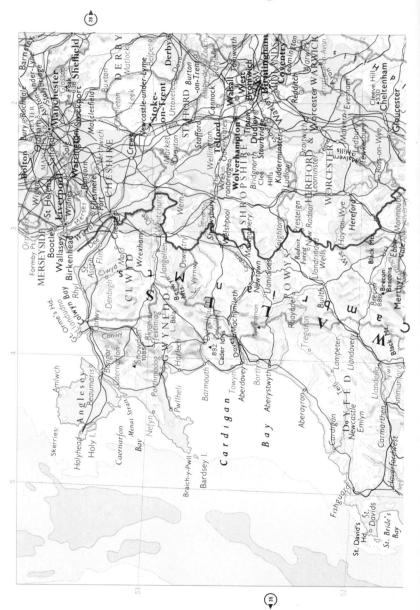

Map 26

1:2 000 000

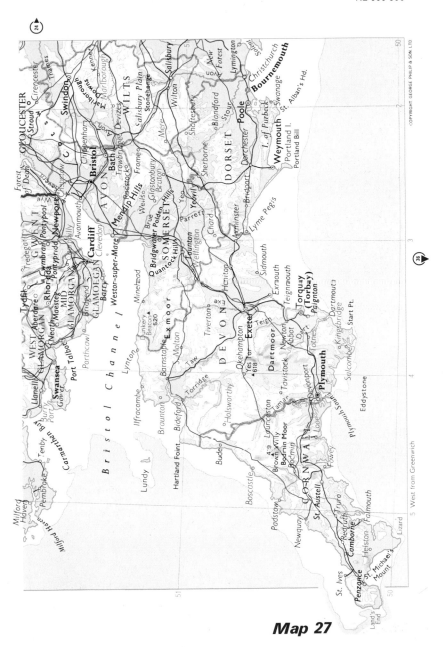

Map 27

Northern England

Map 28

1:2 000 000

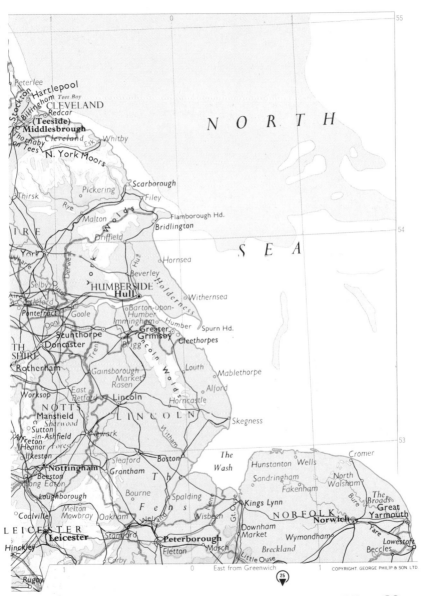

N O R T H

Peterlee
Hartlepool
Stockton
Billingham Tees Bay
CLEVELAND
Redcar
(Teeside)
Middlesbrough
Thornaby
on Tees
Cleveland   Whitby
N. York Moors
Esk

Thirsk
Pickering   Scarborough
Rye   Filey
Malton   Wolds
Driffield   Flamborough Hd.
Bridlington

S E A

IRE
York
Wharfe   Derwent   Hull   Hornsea
Selby   Beverley
Ouse   HUMBERSIDE
Aire   Hull   Holderness
Castleford   Goole   Withernsea
Pontefract   Barton-upon-Humber
Don   Immingham
Scunthorpe   Humber   Spurn Hd.
Doncaster   Greater   Grimsby   Cleethorpes
Brigg   Trent
TH
SHIRE
Rotherham   Gainsborough   Louth   Mablethorpe
Market
Rasen   Lincoln   Alford
Worksop   East   Wolds
Retford   Lincoln   Horncastle
NOTTS
Mansfield   L I N C O L N   Skegness
Sherwood
Sutton
-in-Ashfield   Newark
Heanor   Forest
Ilkeston   Witham
Sleaford   Boston   The
Nottingham   Grantham   Wash
Beeston
Long Eaton   Hunstanton   Wells   Cromer
Bourne   Spalding   Sandringham   North
Loughborough   Fens   Fakenham   Walsham
Melton   Oakham   The
Coalville   Mowbray   Welland   Kings Lynn   Broads
Nene   Great
Wisbech   NORFOLK   Yarmouth
LEICESTER   Downham   Norwich   Yare
Leicester   Stamford   Market   Wymondham   Lowestoft
Hinckley   Peterborough   March   Beccles
Fletton   Breckland
Corby   Little Ouse
Rugby

East from Greenwich
25

Map 29

Southern Scotland

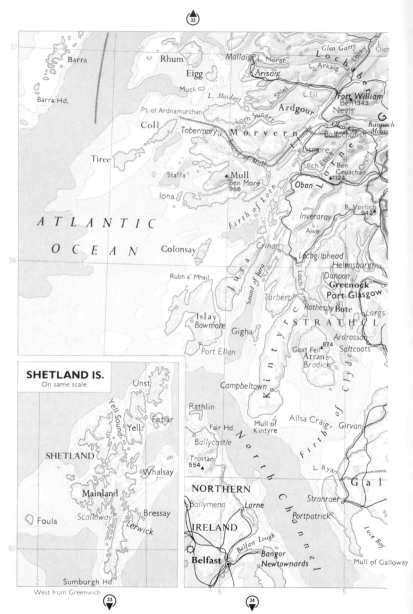

32

57

Barra

Rhum

Mallaig L. Morar

Loch aber

Glen Garry L. Oich

Eigg

Arisaig

L. Arkaig

Muck

L. Moidart

L. Shiel

L. Eil

Fort William

Ben 1343

Nevis

Pt. of Ardnamurchan

Loch Sunart

Ardgour

Coll

Tobermory

M o r v e r n

Loch Linnhe

Glen Coe

Rannoch Moor

Ballachulish

Tiree

Sound of Mull

Lismore

Loch Etive

Ben Cruachan

Loch Awe

Staffa

Mull

Ben More

966

Oban

Ben 1124

Iona

Firth of Lorn

B. Vorlich 942

A T L A N T I C

Inveraray

L. Awe

O C E A N

Colonsay

Crinan

Lochgilphead

Helensburgh

56

Rubh a' Mhail

Dunoon

Greenock

Port Glasgow

Jura

Sound of Jura

Tarbert

Loch Fyne

Rothesay Bute

Largs

Islay

Bowmore

Gigha

S T R A T H C L

Port Ellen

Kintyre

Goat Fell 874

Ardrossan

Saltcoats

Arran

Brodick

Firth of Clyde

On same scale

Unst

Campbeltown

Rathlin

Fair Hd.

Mull of Kintyre

Ailsa Craig

Girvan

Yell Sound

Fetlar

Yell

Ballycastle

North Channel

SHETLAND

Whalsay

Trostan 554

L. Ryan

G a l

Mainland

Bressay

NORTHERN

Stranraer

Foula

Scalloway

Lerwick

Ballymena

Larne

Portpatrick

Luce Bay

IRELAND

Belfast Lough

Mull of Galloway

60

Belfast

Bangor

Newtownards

Sumburgh Hd.

West from Greenwich

33

6

34

5

Map 30

1:2 000 000

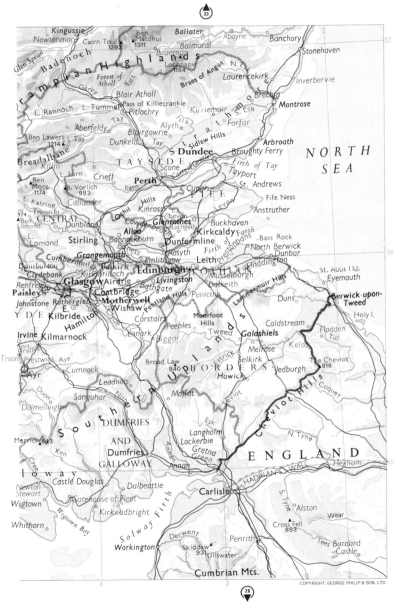

NORTH
SEA

ENGLAND

Map 31

Northern Scotland

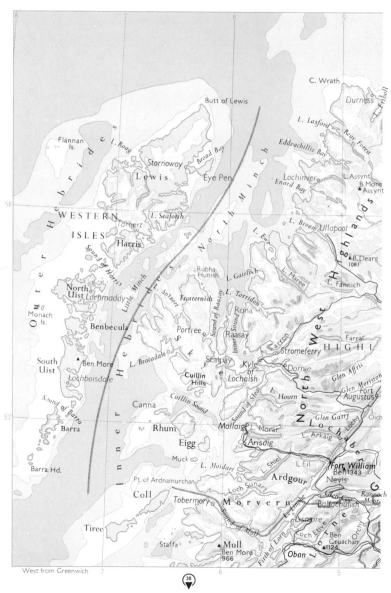

C. Wrath
Durness
L. Eriboll
Butt of Lewis
L. Laxford
Reay Forest
Eddrachillis Bay
Flannan Is.
L. Roag
Broad Bay
Stornoway
Lochinver
L. Assynt
B More
Enard Bay
Assynt
Lewis
Eye Pen.
WESTERN
Eye Pen.
North Minch
L. Broom Ullapool
58
L. Seaforth
ISLES
Tarbert
Harris
L. Ewe
B. Dearg
1081
L. Maree
North
L. Fannich
WEST
HIGHLANDS
Sound of Harris
Outer Hebrides
Little Minch
Rubha Hunish
L. Gairloch
North
Uist
Lochmaddy
Sollas
Trotternish
L. Torridon
Monach
Is.
Benbecula
Portree
Rona
Raasay
Sound of Raasay
Inner Sound
Carron
Farrac
Stromeferry
HIGHL
South
Uist
Ben More
L. Bracadale
Scalpay
Kyle
of
Lochalsh
Dornie
Glen Affric
Glen Moriston
Lochboisdale
Cuillin
Hills
Skye
L. Hourn
North West
Fort
Augustus
Sound of Barra
Canna
Cuillin Sound
Sound of Sleat
Glen Garry
L. Lochy
Oich
57
Barra
Rhum
Mallaig
L. Morar
Lochaber
L. Arkaig
Eigg
Arisaig
Barra Hd.
Muck
L. Moidart
L. Shiel
L. Eil
Fort William
Ben 1343
Pt. of Ardnamurchan
Ardgour
Nevis
Coll
Loch Sunart
Glen Coe
Rannoch Moor
Tobermory
Morvern
Ballachulish
Sound of Mull
Lismore
Linnhe
Tiree
Loch Etive
Ben
Cruachan
1124
Staffa
Mull
Ben More
966
Firth of Lorn
Oban
L. Orch

Map 32

1:2 000 000

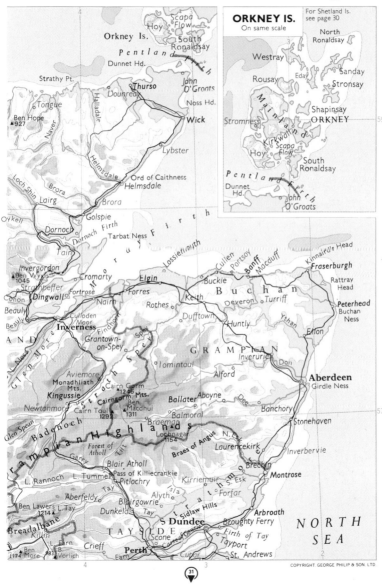

ORKNEY IS.
On same scale

For Shetland Is.
see page 30

North Ronaldsay

Westray

Rousay   Eday   Sanday

Stronsay

Stromness   Mainland   Shapinsay

Kirkwall   ORKNEY

Hoy   Scapa Flow

South Ronaldsay

Pentland Firth

Dunnet Hd.

John O'Groats

Orkney Is.

Hoy   Scapa Flow

South Ronaldsay

Pentland Firth

Dunnet Hd.

Strathy Pt.

Thurso

Dounreay

John O'Groats

Noss Hd.

Tongue

Ben Hope ▲927

Naver   Halladale   Wick

Helmsdale   Lybster

Loch Shin   Ord of Caithness   Helmsdale

Lairg   Brora   Brora

Oykell   Golspie

Dornoch   Dornoch Firth   Tarbat Ness

Tain

Invergordon   Murray Firth   Lossiemouth   Cullen   Portsoy   Banff   Macduff   Kinnaird's Head

Ben Wyvis ▲1045   Cromarty   Elgin   Buckie   Fraserburgh

Strathpeffer   Fortrose   Forres   Keith   Rattray Head

Conon   Dingwall   Nairn   Rothes   Deveron   Turriff   Peterhead

Beauly   Dufftown   Huntly   Ythan   Buchan Ness

Beauly   Culloden Moor   Findhorn   BUCHAN

Inverness   Grantown-on-Spey   Spey   Ellon

Glen More   GRAMPIAN   Inverurie   Don

Tomintoul   Alford   Aberdeen

Aviemore   Girdle Ness

Monadhliath Mts.   Cairn Gorm ▲1245

Kingussie   Cairngorm Mts.   Ballater   Aboyne   Dee   Banchory

Newtonmore   Cairn Toul ▲1293   Ben Macdhui 1311   Balmoral   Stonehaven

Glen Spean   Braemar   Lochnagar 1154   N. Esk

Badenoch   Grampian Highlands   Braes of Angus   Laurencekirk

Garry   Forest of Atholl   Tilt   Inverbervie

Blair Atholl   Brechin

L. Rannoch   L. Tummel   Pass of Killiecrankie   Kirriemuir   S. Esk   Montrose

Pitlochry

Aberfeldy   Alyth   Forfar

Ben Lawers 1214 ▲   L. Tay   Blairgowrie   Isla   Strathmore

Breadalbane   Tay   Dunkeld   Tay   Sidlaw Hills   Arbroath

Killin   Dundee   Broughty Ferry

Ben More 1174   L. Earn   Crieff   Scone   Firth of Tay   NORTH SEA

Vorlich 985   Perth   Earn   Tayport

Cupar   St. Andrews

Map 33

Ireland

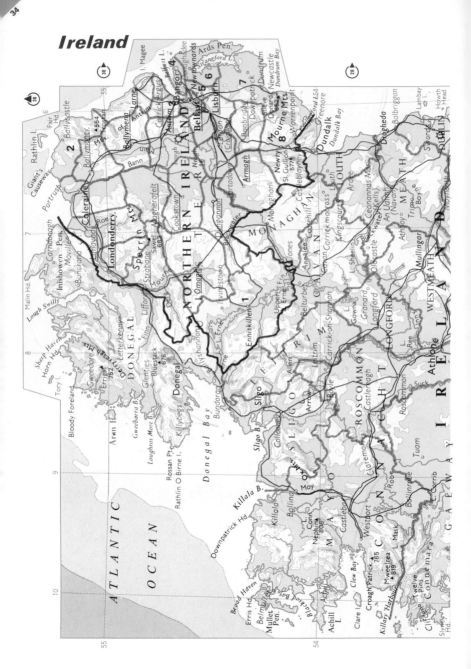

Map 34

1:2 000 000

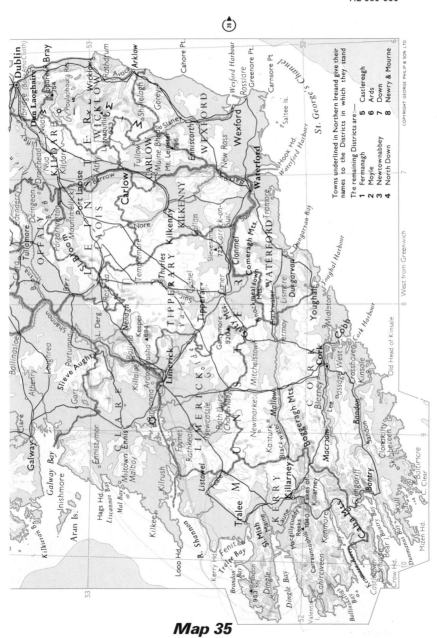

Towns underlined in Northern Ireland give their
names to the Districts in which they stand

The remaining Districts are:—

1	Fermanagh	5	Castlereagh
2	Moyle	6	Ards
3	Newtownabbey	7	Down
4	North Down	8	Newry & Mourne

COPYRIGHT GEORGE PHILIP & SON LTD

Map 35

France

Map 36

West from Greenwich

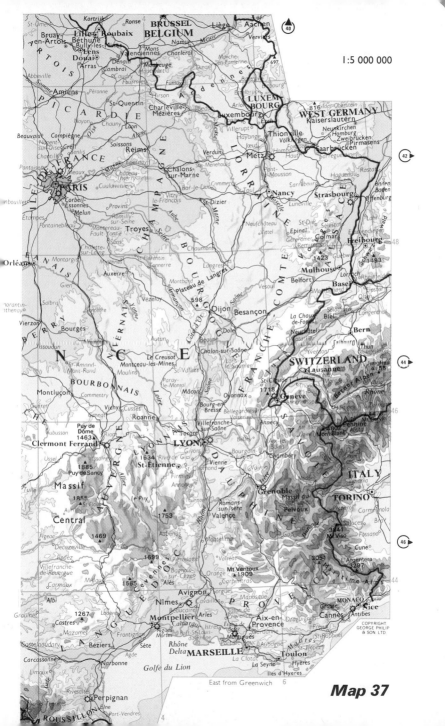

1:5 000 000

42 ▶

48

44 ▶

46

46 ▶

44

COPYRIGHT
GEORGE PHILIP
& SON. LTD.

East from Greenwich

Map 37

Northern France

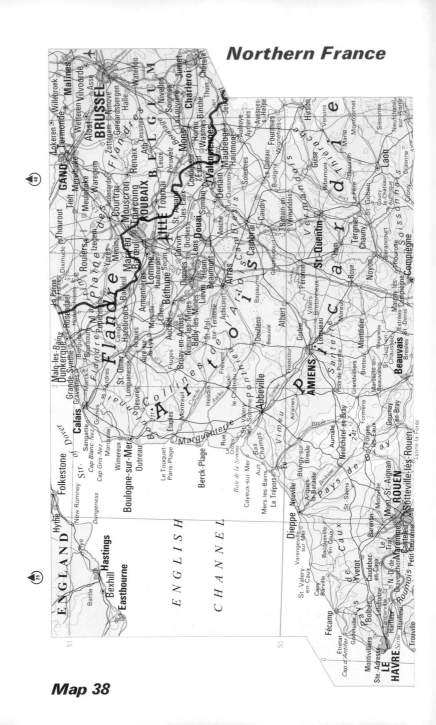

Map 38

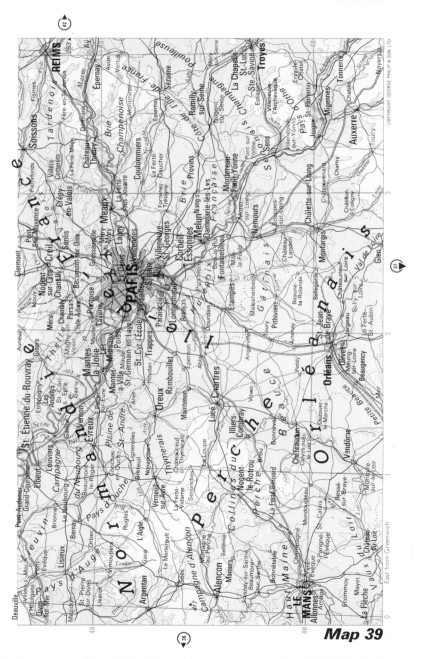

1:2 000 000

Map 39

East from Greenwich

Netherlands

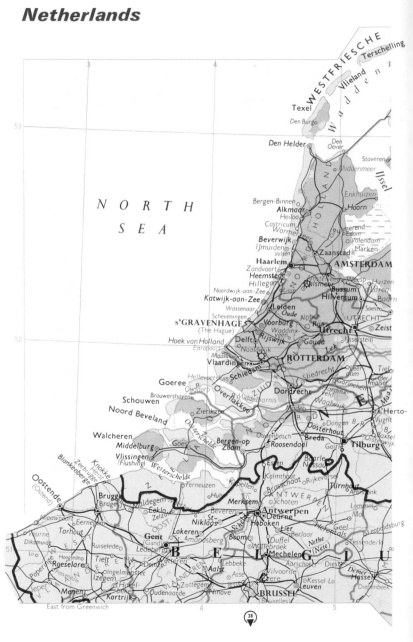

NORTH SEA

WESTFRIESCHE
Terschelling
Vlieland
Texel
Den Burgo
Den Helder
Den Oever
Staveren
Middenmeer
Ijssel
Bergen-Binnen
Alkmaar
Heiloo
Enkhuizen
Hoorn
Castricum
Wormer
Purmerend
Edam
Beverwijk
IJmuiden
Velsen
Volendam
Zaanstad
Marken
Haarlem
AMSTERDAM
Zandvoort
Heemstede
Weesp Huizen
Hillegom
Bussum Laren
Noordwijk-aan-Zee
Aalsmeer
Hilversum
Baarn
Katwijk-aan-Zee
Lisse
Soest
Wassenaar
Leiden
UTRECHT
Scheveningen
Oude
Voorburg
Alphen
Rijn
s'GRAVENHAGE
Waddin
Veen
Utrecht
Zeist
(The Hague)
Rijswijk
Gouda
Hoek van Holland
Delft
Naaldwijk
Eemnort
Lek
Maassluis
Tiel
Vlaardingen
Schiedam
ROTTERDAM
Oleen
dam
Sliedrecht
Gorinchem
Goeree
Hellevoetsluis
Gardinx
Imalse
Brouwershaven
Overflakkee
Dordrecht
Veld
Maas
Schouwen
Oudorp
Middelharnis
Waalwijk
Noord Beveland
Zienkzee
Dongen
Herto-
R
Vught
Walcheren
Oosterschelde
Oudenbosch
Oosterhout
B.
Boxtel
Middelburg
Goes
Bergen-op-
Breda
Goes
Zoom
Roosendaal
Tilburg
Vlissingen
Westerschelde
Baarle
(Flushing)
Nassau
Oostende
Zeebrugge
Esen
Kalmthout
(Ostend)
Knokke
Terneuzen
Rijkevorsel
Blankenberge
Zellen
Brasschaat
Turnhout
Nieuwpoort
Brugge
Hulst
Schoten
Lommel
Veurne
(Bruges)
Moldegem
Merksem
ANTWERPEN
Mol
Diksmuide
Eeklo
Beveren
Antwerpen
Geel
Leopoldsburg
Torhout
Zelzate
St-
Deurne
Lo
Eernegem
Lokeren
Niklaas
Haboken
Lier
Berlaar
Tessenderlo
Ruiselede
St. Amandsberg
Boom
Nethe
Hoogledoo
Gent
Mechelen
Demer
Roeselare
Tielt
(Gand)
Duffel
Hasselt
Izegem
Ledeberg
Wetteren
Willebroek
Leuven
Dieperbeek
Ingelmunster
Demze
Vilvoorde
Kessel-Lo
BELGIE
Ieper
Hotel
Aalst
Asse
Menen
Oudenaarde
Zottegem
Ninove
BRUSSEL
Kortrijk
(Bruxelles)

Map 40

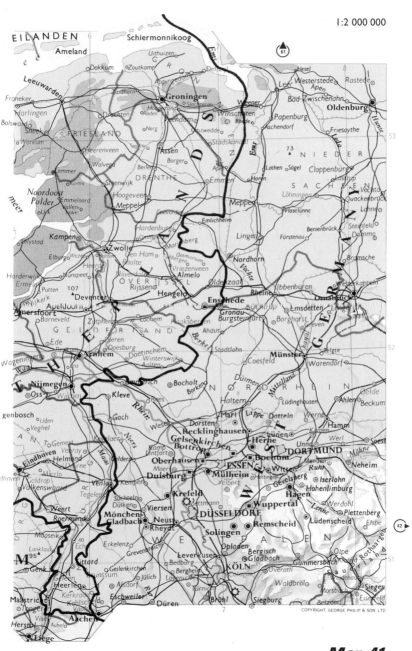

1:2 000 000

Map 41

Germany and the Low Countries

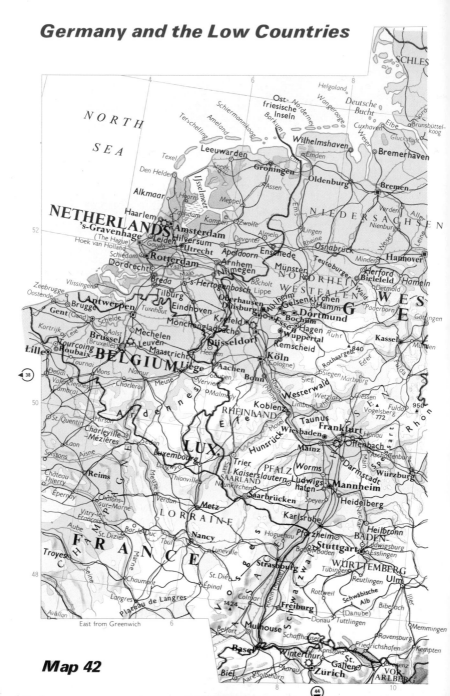

Map 42

42

1:5 000 000

BALTIC SEA

Map 43

COPYRIGHT GEORGE PHILIP & SON, LTD

Alpine Lands

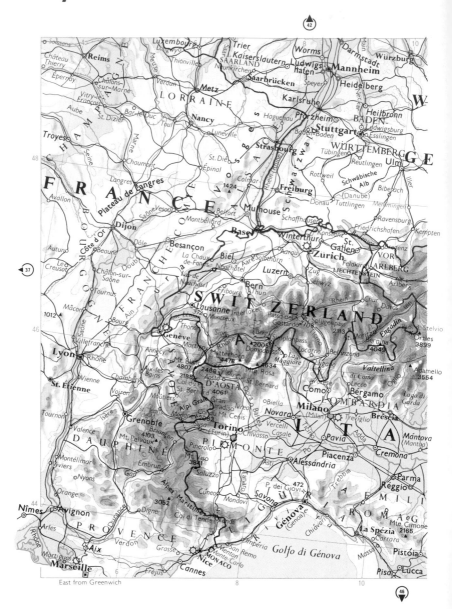

Map 44

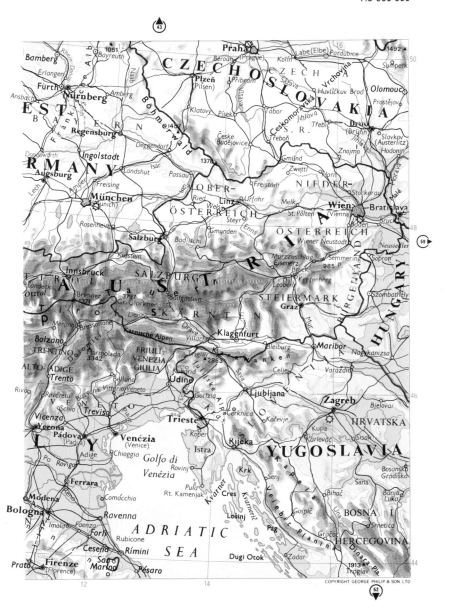

1:5 000 000

Map 45

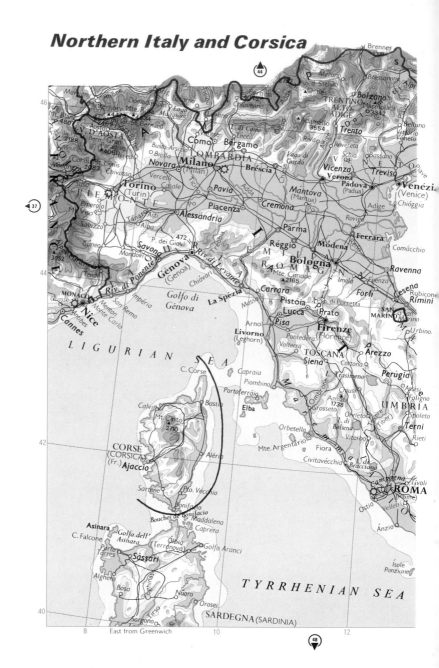

Northern Italy and Corsica

Map 46

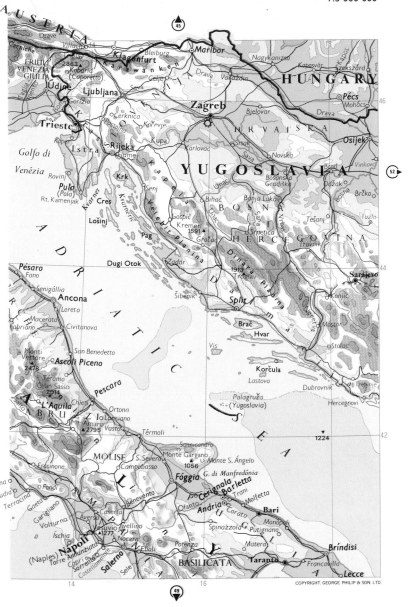

1:5 000 000

Map 47

Southern Italy and Sardinia

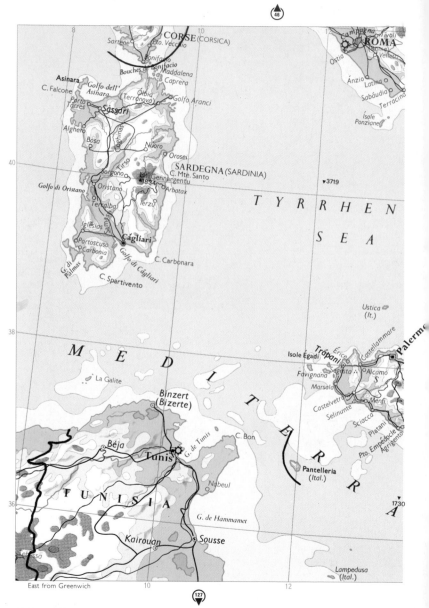

Map 48

1:5 000 000

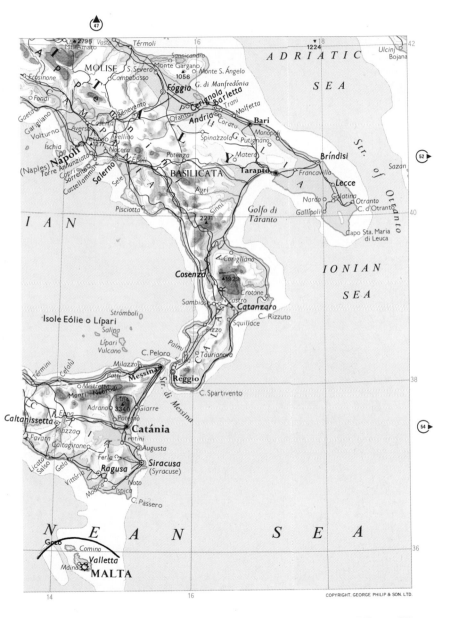

Map 49

Spain and Portugal

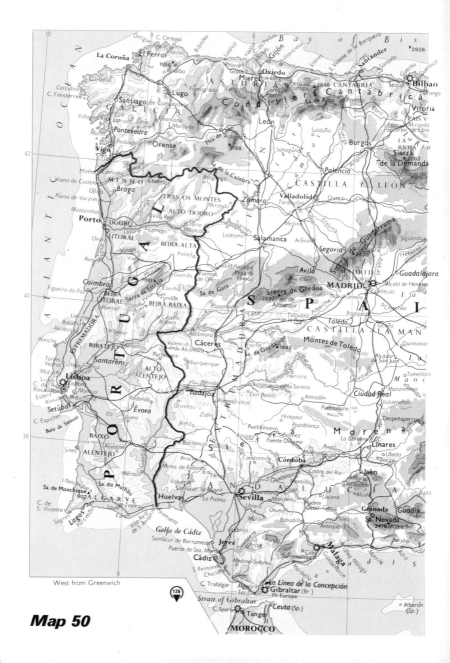

West from Greenwich

126

Map 50

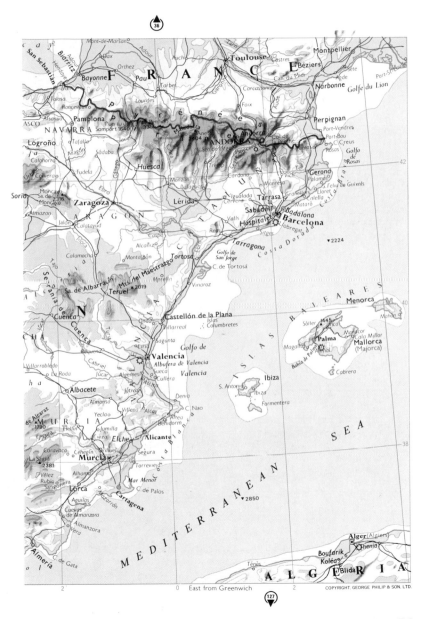

1:6 000 000

East from Greenwich

COPYRIGHT. GEORGE PHILIP & SON. LTD.

Map 51

Danube Lands

East from Greenwich

Map 52

1:6 000 000

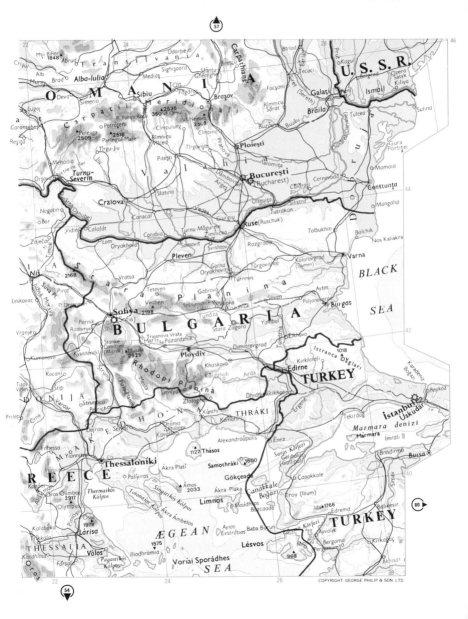

Map 53

Greece   *and Albania*

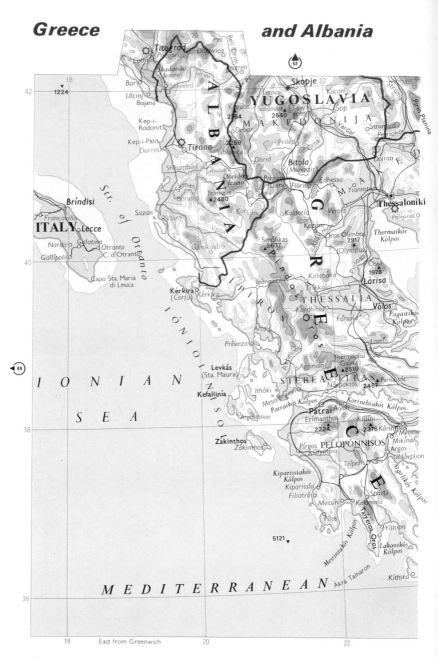

Map 54

East from Greenwich

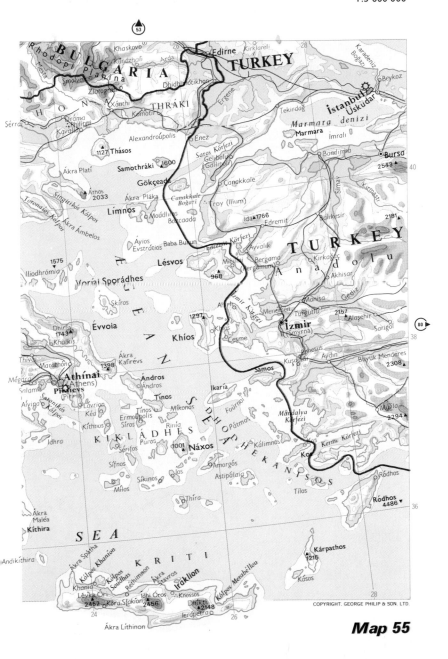

1:5 000 000

Map 55

COPYRIGHT. GEORGE PHILIP & SON. LTD.

Romania

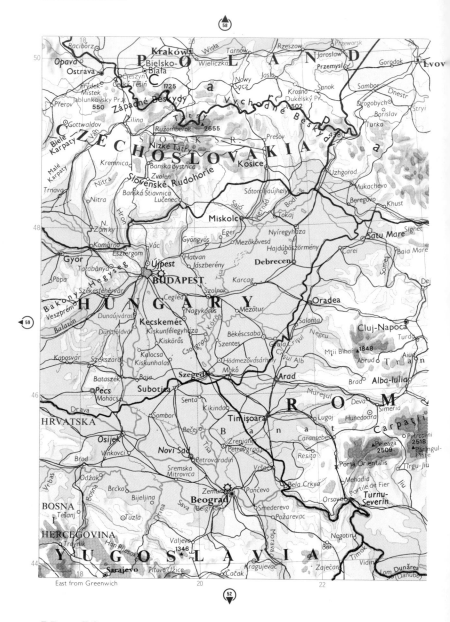

East from Greenwich

Map 56

1:5 000 000

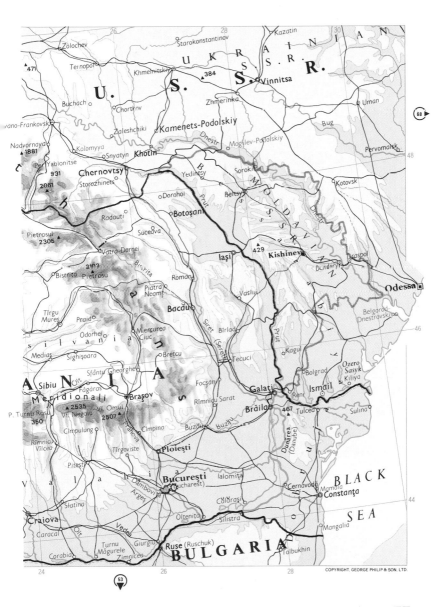

Map 57

Central Europe

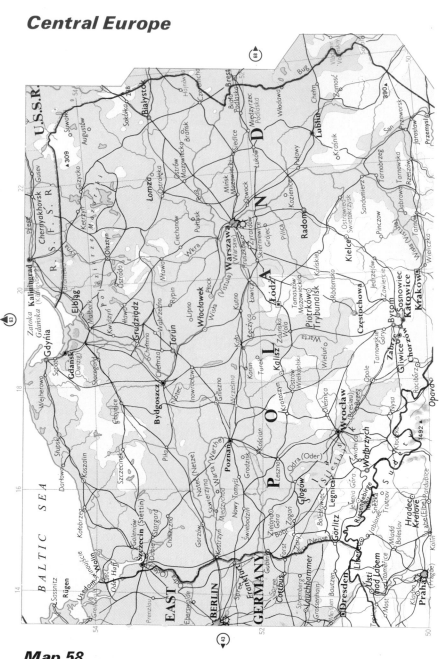

Map 58

1:5 000 000

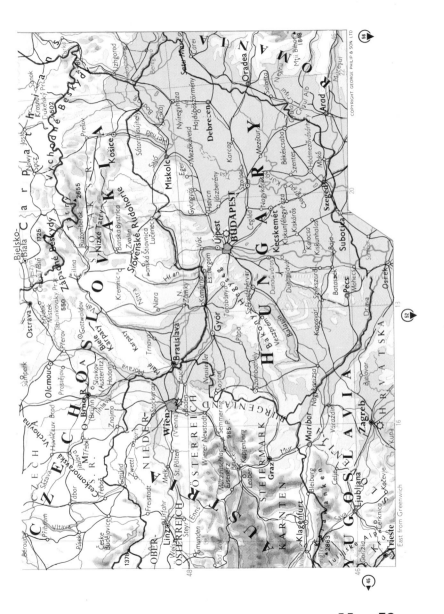

East from Greenwich

COPYRIGHT GEORGE PHILIP & SON LTD

Map 59

Southern Scandinavia

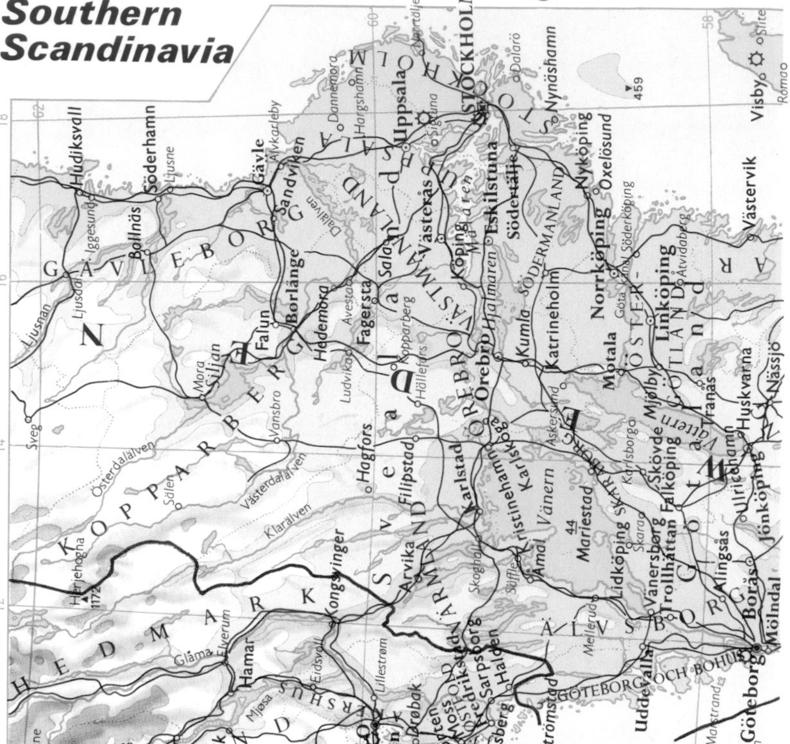

Map 60

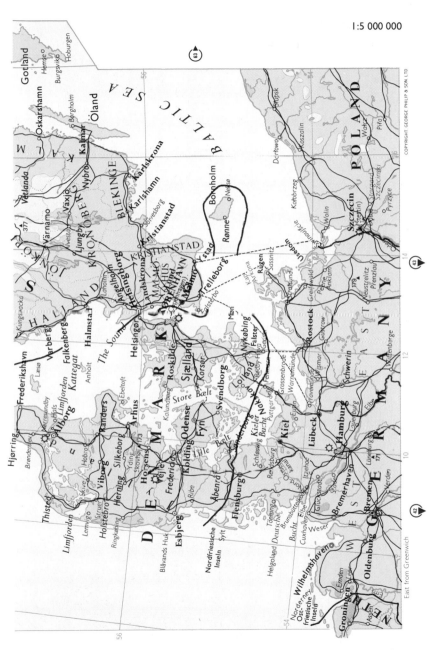

1:5 000 000

Map 61

61

Baltic Lands

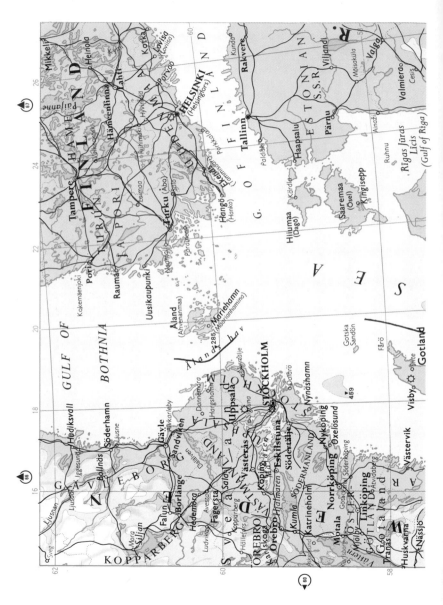

Map 62

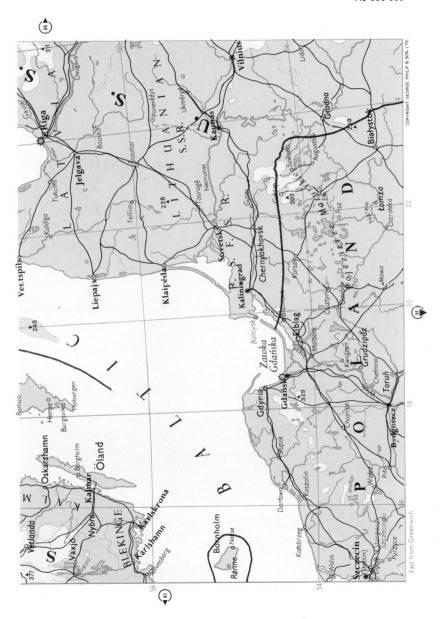

East from Greenwich

COPYRIGHT GEORGE PHILIP & SON. LTD.

Map 63

North West Scandinavia and Iceland

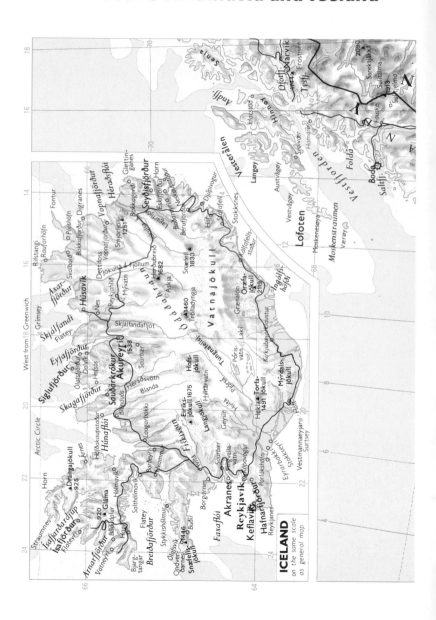

ICELAND
on the same scale
as general map

Map 64

64

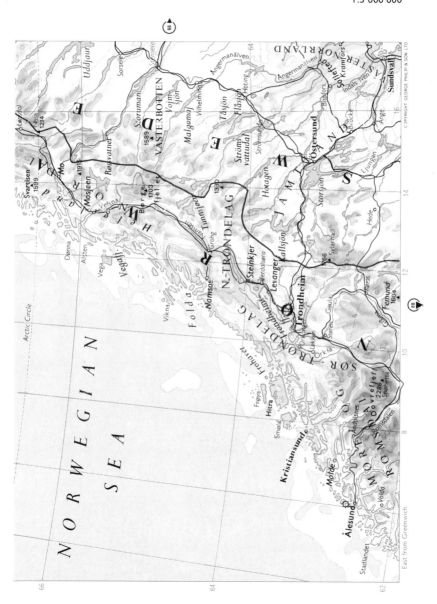

1:5 000 000

Map 65

Northern Scandinavia

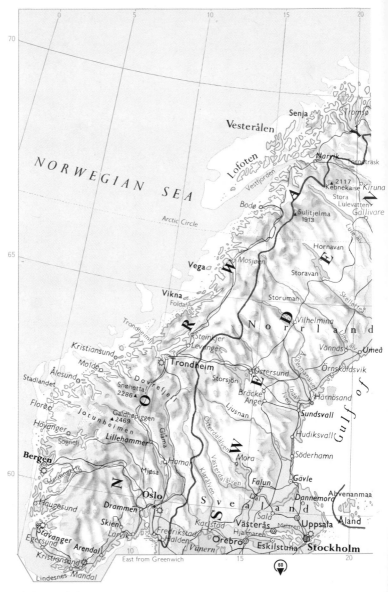

Map 66

1:10 000 000

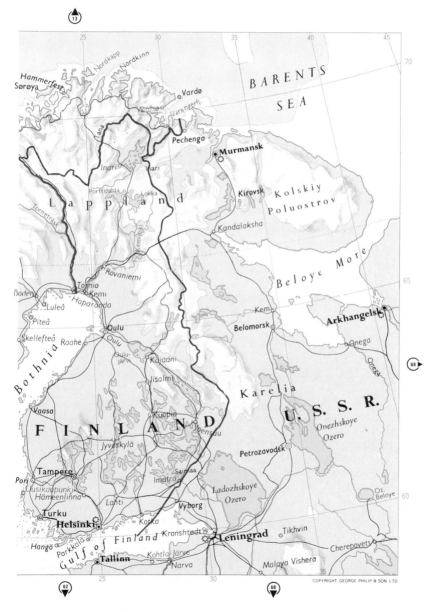

Map 67

U.S.S.R.: West

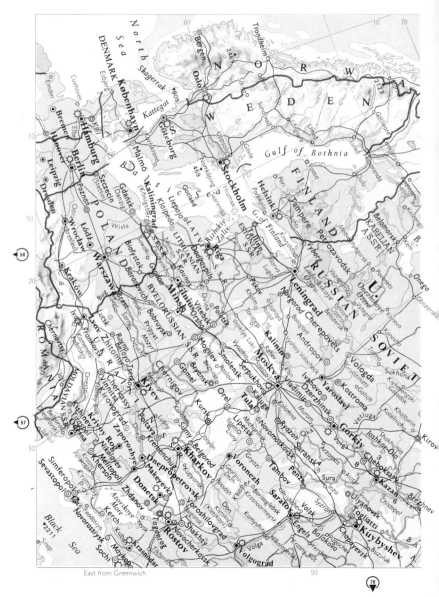

East from Greenwich

Map 68

1:20 000 000

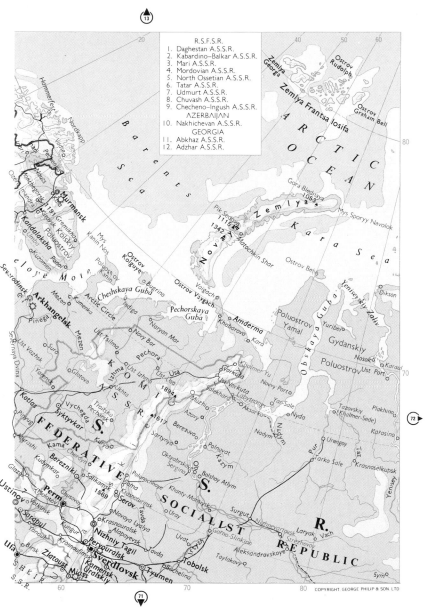

R.S.F.S.R.
1. Daghestan A.S.S.R.
2. Kabardino–Balkar A.S.S.R.
3. Mari A.S.S.R.
4. Mordovian A.S.S.R.
5. North Ossetian A.S.S.R.
6. Tatar A.S.S.R.
7. Udmurt A.S.S.R.
8. Chuvash A.S.S.R.
9. Checheno–Ingush A.S.S.R.
AZERBAIJAN
10. Nakhichevan A.S.S.R.
GEORGIA
11. Abkhaz A.S.S.R.
12. Adzhar A.S.S.R.

COPYRIGHT GEORGE PHILIP & SON LTD

Map 69

U.S.S.R.:
South West

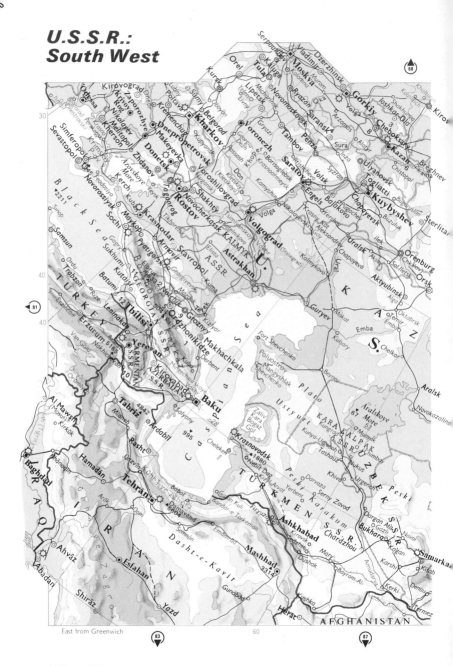

Map 70

1:20 000 000

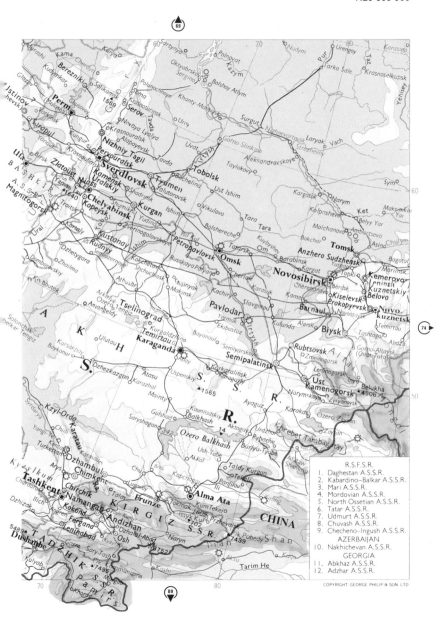

R.S.F.S.R.
1. Daghestan A.S.S.R.
2. Kabardino–Balkar A.S.S.R.
3. Mari A.S.S.R.
4. Mordovian A.S.S.R.
5. North Ossetian A.S.S.R.
6. Tatar A.S.S.R.
7. Udmurt A.S.S.R.
8. Chuvash A.S.S.R.
9. Checheno–Ingush A.S.S.R.
AZERBAIJAN
10. Nakhichevan A.S.S.R.
GEORGIA
11. Abkhaz A.S.S.R.
12. Adzhar A.S.S.R.

COPYRIGHT GEORGE PHILIP & SON LTD

Map 71

U.S.S.R.: North East

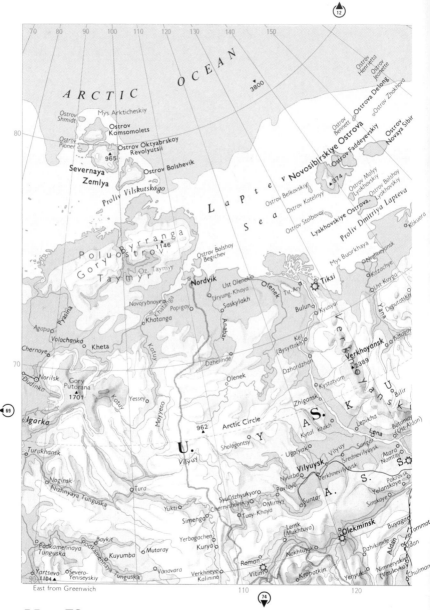

ARCTIC OCEAN

3800

Ostrov Henrietta
Ostrov Jeanette
Ostrova Delong
Ostrov Zhokhova

Ostrov Shmidt
Mys Arkticheskiy
Ostrov Komsomolets
Ostrov Pioner
Ostrov Oktyabrskoy Revolyutsii
965
Severnaya Zemlya
Ostrov Bolshevik
Proliv Vilskutskogo

Ostrov Bennett
Ostrova Novosibirskiye Ostrova
Ostrov Faddeyevskiy
Ostrov Novaya Sibir
Ostrov Belkovskiy
Ostrov Kotelnyy
Ostrov Molvy Lyakhovskiy
Ostrov Bolshoy Lyakhovskiy

L a p t e v   S e a
Ostrov Stolbovoy
Lyakhovskiye Ostrova
Proliv Dmitriya Lapteva
Kokuora

Poluostrov Goryo Byrranga Taymyr
1146
Oz. Taymyr
Ostrov Bolshoy Begichev
Nordvik
Ust Olenek
Uryung-Khaya
Saskylakh
Olenek
Tit-Ary
Tiksi
Mys Buorkhaya
Nizhneyansk
Kuzachye
Ust Kuyga

Novorybnoye
Popigay
Khatanga
Anabar
Bulun
Kyusyur
Ust Deputatskiy
Yana

Agapa
Pyasina
Volochanka
Kheta
Chernoye
Norilsk
Dudinka
Gory Putorana
1701
Yessey
Kotuy
Mayyero
Dzhelinde
Olenek
Kel (Bysyttakh)
Dzhardzhan
Kystatyam
Zhigansk
Verkhoyansk
2389
Bilir
Botuoy (Ust-Aldan)

Igarka
Turukhansk
962
Arctic Circle
Sholgontsy
Vilyuy
U. Y. A. S. S. R.
Kytyl-Kitakh
Kytal
Ugolyak
Srednevilyuysk
Lepikha
Lena
Atara
Nomtoy
S.

Noginsk
Nizhnyaya Tunguska
Tura
Syultdzhyukyoro
Chernyshevskiy
Tuoy-Khaya
Mirnyy
Vilyuy
Vilyuysk
Nyurba
Verkhnevilyuysk
Pavlovo
Suntar
Sangar
Pokrovsk
Yelanskoye
Singskoye

Yukti
Simenga
Lensk (Mukhtuya)
Olekminsk
Buyaga
Tommot

Podkamennaya Tunguska
Baykit
Kuyumba
Mutaray
Kurya
Yerbogachen
Nakhtuysk
Roman
Dzhikimde
Aldan
Aldan

Yartsevo
1104
Severo-Teniseyskiy
Tunguska
Vanavara
Verkhneye Kalinino
Vitim
Krobotkin
Yenyuka
Nimneryakina (Vosileyka)
Chulman

East from Greenwich

Map 72

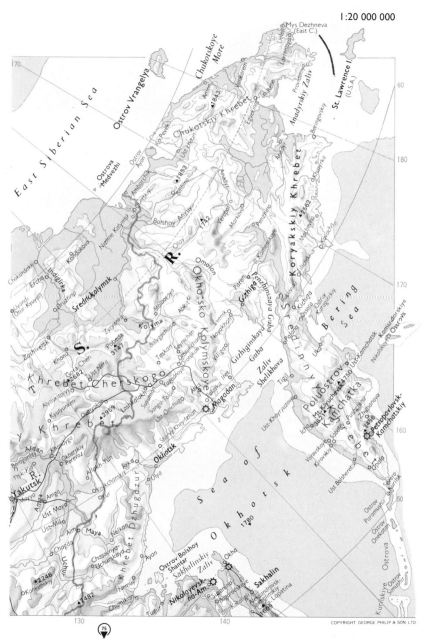

Map 73

U.S.S.R.: South East and Mongolia

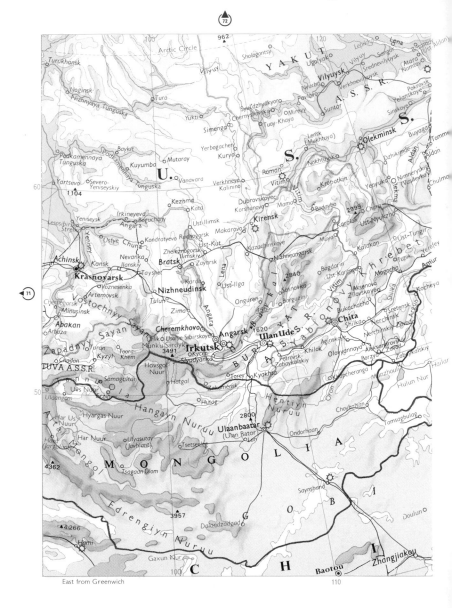

Map 74

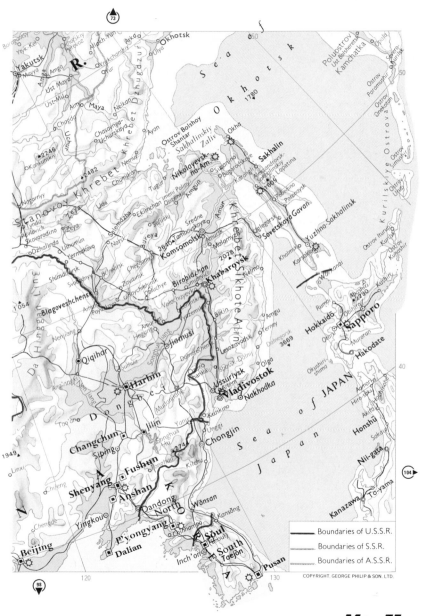

1:20 000 000

Map 75

Boundaries of U.S.S.R.
Boundaries of S.S.R.
Boundaries of A.S.S.R.

Asia: Physical

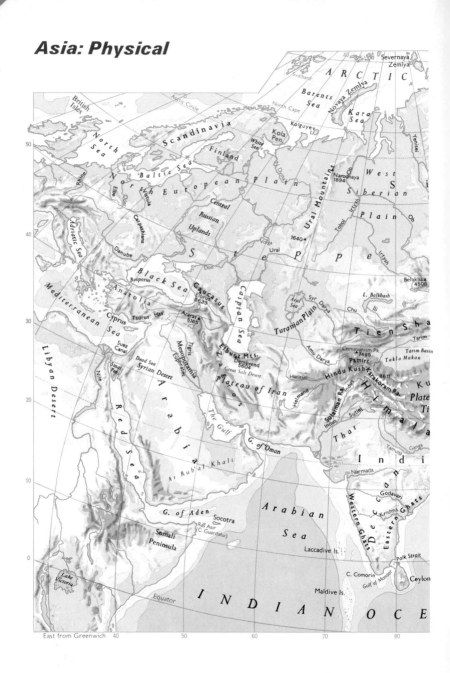

ARCTIC

British Isles

Svalbard

Arctic Circle

North Cape

Barents Sea

Severnaya Zemlya

Novaya Zemlya

Kara Sea

North Sea

Scandinavia

Kola Pen.

White Sea

Kolguyev I.

Yenisei

50

North European Plain

Finland

Baltic Sea

Ob

Narodnaya 1894

Ural Mountains

West Siberian

Plain

Rhine

Elbe

Oder

Vistula

Carpathians

Central Russian Uplands

Dnepr

Don

Volga

Ural

1640

Tobol

Irtysh

Ob

40

Adriatic Sea

Danube

S t e P P e

Belokha 4506

Black Sea

Bosporus

Caucasus

Elbrus 5633

Caspian Sea

Aral Sea

Syr Darya

L. Balkhash

Chu

Ili

Anatolia

Taurus Mts

Ararat 5165

Turanian Plain

Amu Darya

Tien Sha

Tarim

Mediterranean Sea

Cyprus

Elburz Mts.

Demavend 5604

Communism Pk. 7495

Pamirs

Tarim Basin

Takla Makan

Suez Canal

Dead Sea

Syrian Desert

Tigris

Mesopotamia

Euphrates

Great Salt Desert

Plateau of Iran

Zagros

Harirud

Hindu Kush

Karakoram Ra.

8611

Ku

Plate

Ti

Libyan Desert

Sinai Pen.

Nile

A r a b i a

Red Sea

The Gulf

G. of Oman

Helmand

Sulaiman Range

Indus

Sutlej

H i m a l a

Thar

I n d i

30

20

Narmada

Yamuna

Ganga

Ar Rub'al Khali

Godavari

Western Ghats

Eastern Ghats

10

G. of Aden

Socotra

Ras Asir (C. Guardafui)

Somali Peninsula

A r a b i a n

Sea

Krishna

Laccadive Is.

Polk Strait

Ceylon

0

Lake Victoria

C. Comorin

Gulf of Manaar

Maldive Is.

Equator

I N D I A N   O C E

East from Greenwich   40   50   60   70   80

Map 76

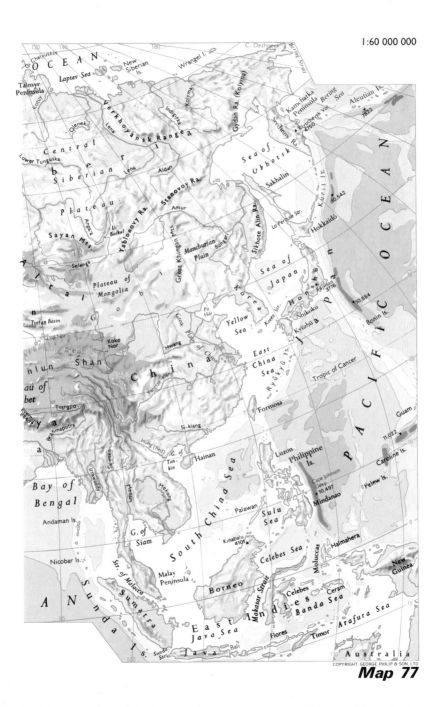

1:60 000 000

O C E A N

Chelyuskin
Taimyr Peninsula
Lapter Sea
New Siberian Is.
Wrangel I.
C. Dezhneva
Bering Strait

Kotuy
Olenek
Verkhoyansk Range
Indigirka
Kolyma
Gydan Ra. (Kolyma)
Kamchatka Peninsula
Srednniy Ra.
Klyuchevsk Vol. 4750
Bering Sea
Aleutian Is. 7822

Central
Lower Tunguska
Lena
Siberian
Lena
Aldan
Sea of Okhotsk
Sakhalin
Kuril Is.
40,542

Plateau
Angara
L. Baikal
Yablonovy Ra.
Stanovoy Ra.
Amur
Sikhote Alin Ra.
La Perouse Str.
Hokkaidō

Sayan Mts.
Selenga
Plateau of Mongolia
Great Khingan Mts.
Manchurian Plain
Sungari
Sea of Japan
Honshū
Fuji 3776

P A C I F I C   O C E A N

Altai
G o b i
Korea
Korea Str.
Shikoku
Kyūshū
10,554
Bonin Is.

Turfan Basin
Lop Nor
Koko Nor
Hwang
Great Plain of China
Pa Hai
Yellow Sea
East China Sea
Tropic of Cancer

nlun
Shan
C h i n a
Yangtze-kiang
Ryūkyū Is.

au of
bet
Tsangpo
Everest 8882
Brahmaputra
Si-kiang
Formosa
Guam
11,022

y a
Hong (Red)
G. of Tonkin
Hainan
Luzon
Philippine Is.
Caroline Is.

a
Irrawaddy
Salween
Menam
Mekong
Cape Johnson Deep 10,497
Mindanao
Pelew Is.

Bay of Bengal
South China Sea
Palawan
Sulu Sea

Andaman Is.
G. of Siam
Kinabalu 4101
Celebes Sea
Halmahera

Nicobar Is.
Str. of Malacca
Malay Peninsula
Borneo
Makassar Strait
Celebes
Moluccas
Ceram
New Guinea

A N
Sumatra
East Indies
Banda Sea

S u n d a Is.
Java Sea
Java
Flores
Timor
Arafura Sea

Sunda Str.
Bali
Australia

Map 77

Asia: Political

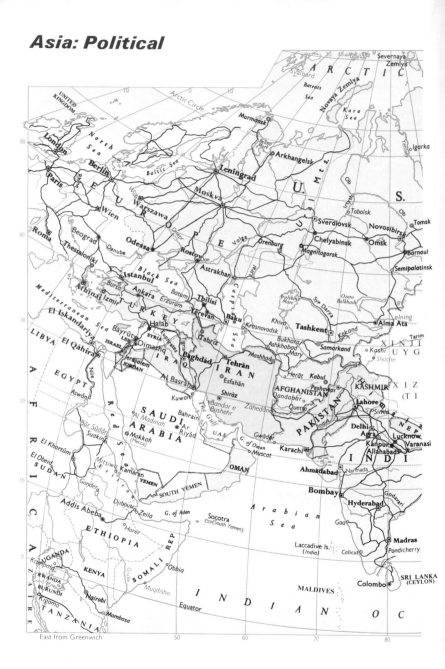

1:60 000 000

Map 79

Turkey and the Middle East

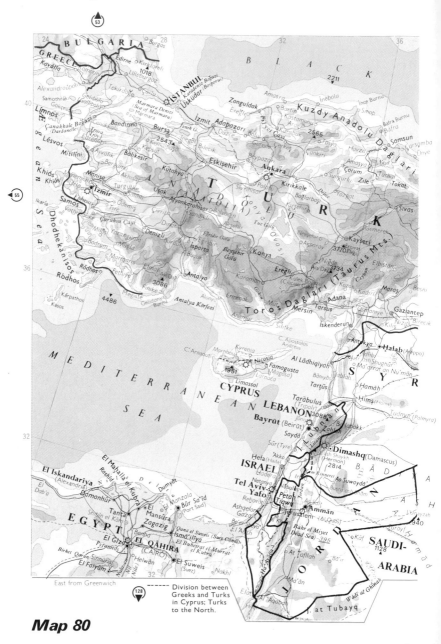

East from Greenwich

----- Division between
Greeks and Turks
in Cyprus; Turks
to the North.

Map 80

1:10 000 000

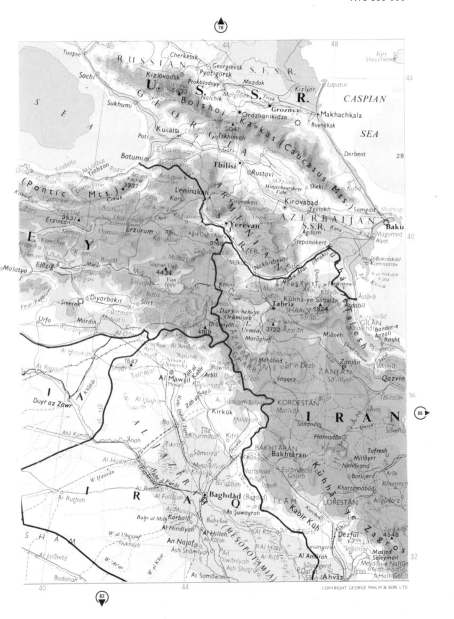

COPYRIGHT GEORGE PHILIP & SON LTD

Map 81

Arabian Peninsula

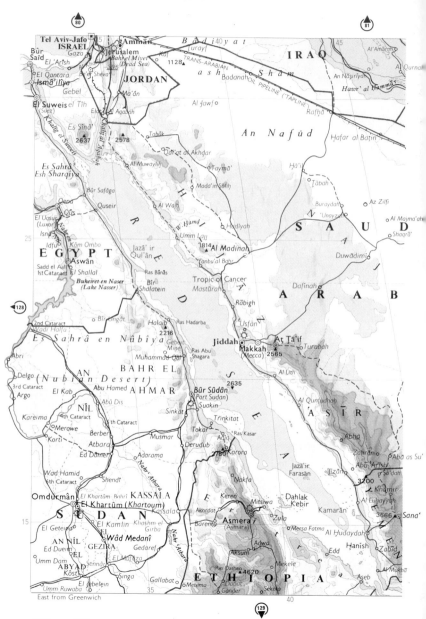

Map 82

1:15 000 000

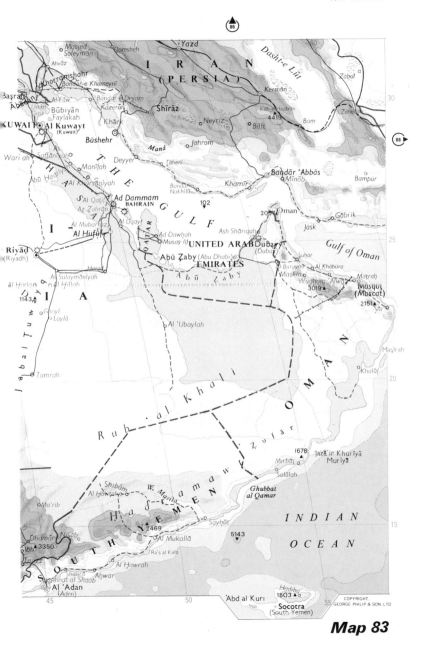

Map 83

The Gulf

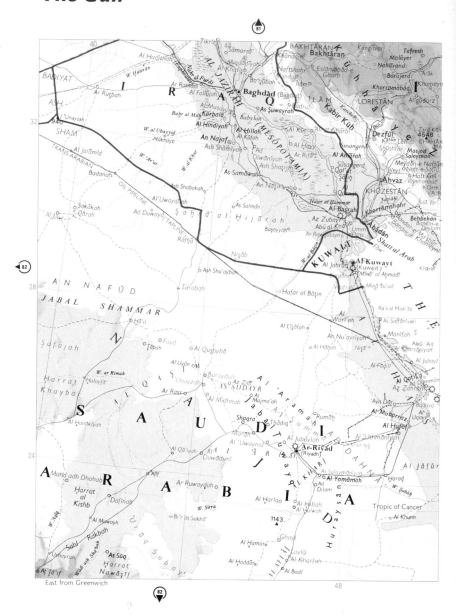

East from Greenwich

Map 84

1:10 000 000

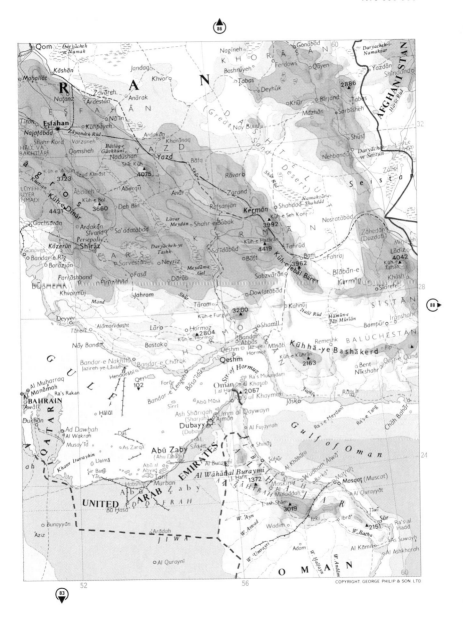

Map 85

Central Asia and Afghanistan

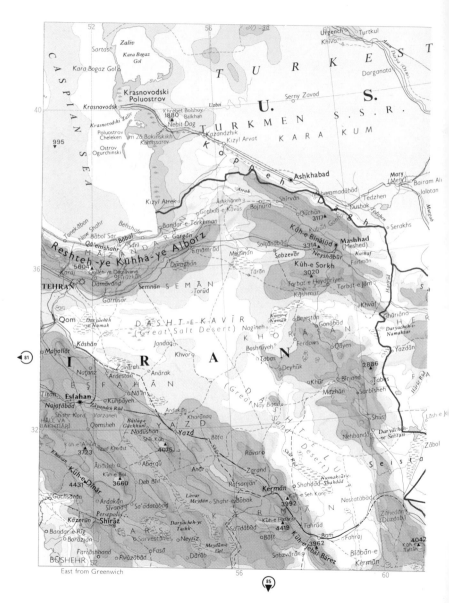

East from Greenwich

Map 86

1:10 000 000

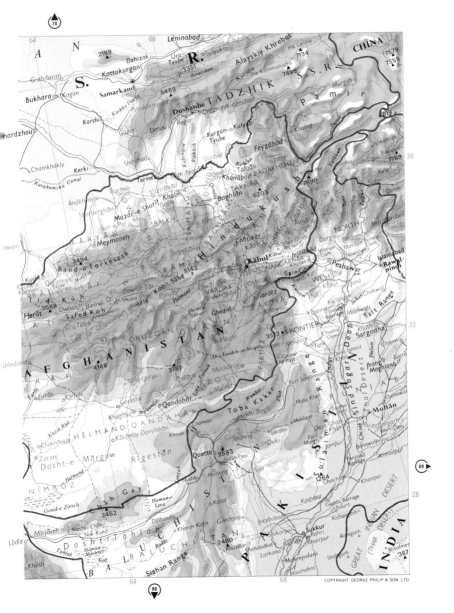

COPYRIGHT GEORGE PHILIP & SON LTD

Map 87

Pakistan and North West India

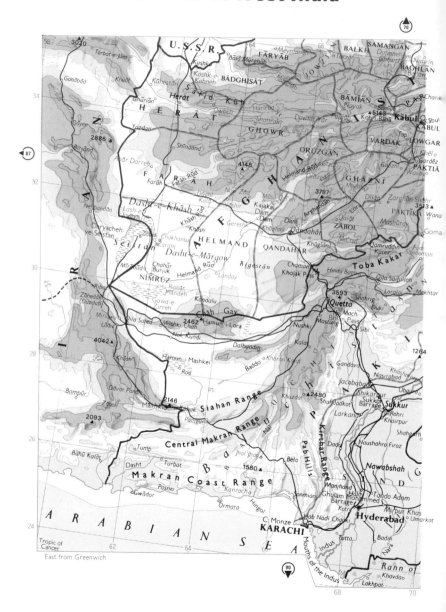

Map 88

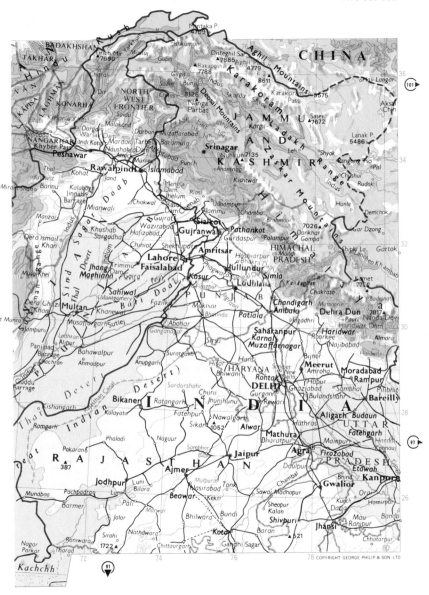

1:10 000 000

Map 89

Central and Southern India, Sri Lanka

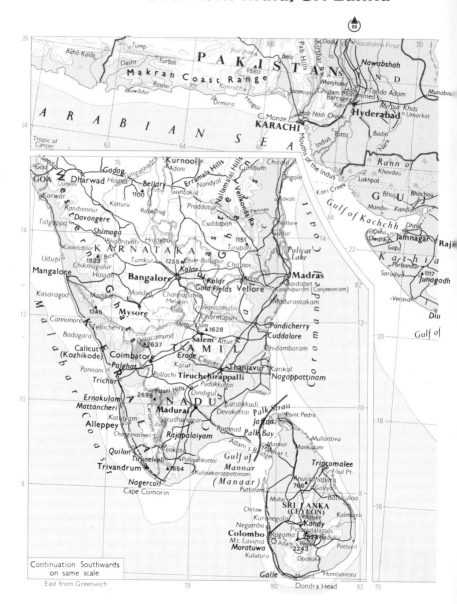

Continuation Southwards
on same scale

East from Greenwich

Map 90

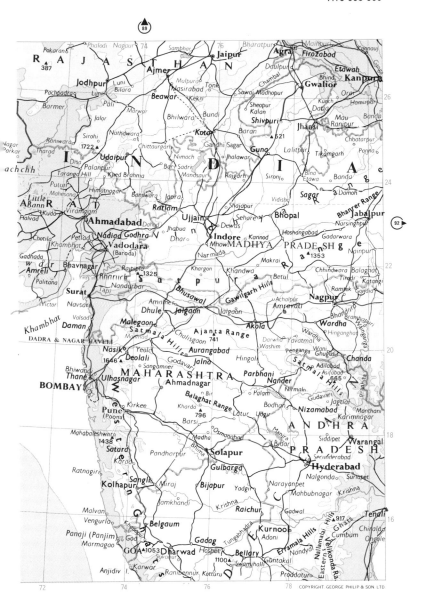

1:10 000 000

Map 91

COPYRIGHT GEORGE PHILIP & SON LTD

Eastern India, Bangladesh and Burma

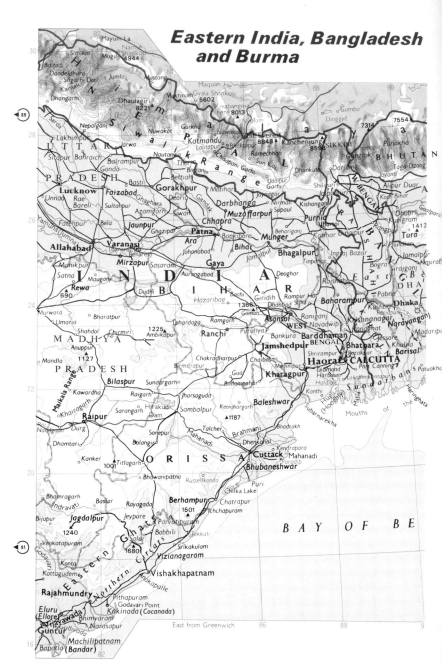

Map 92

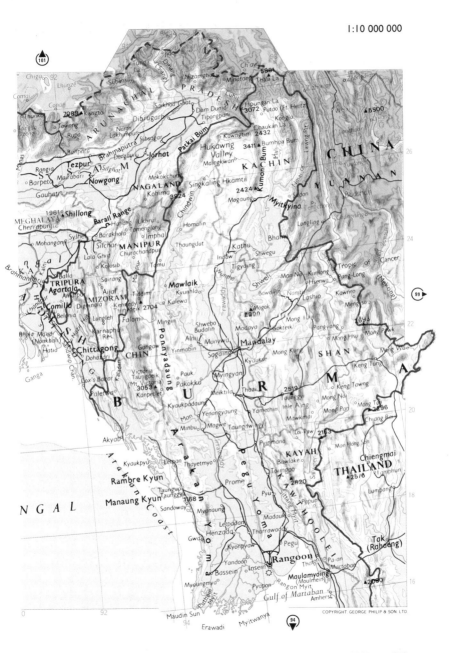

1:10 000 000

COPYRIGHT GEORGE PHILIP & SON LTD

Map 93

Mainland South East Asia

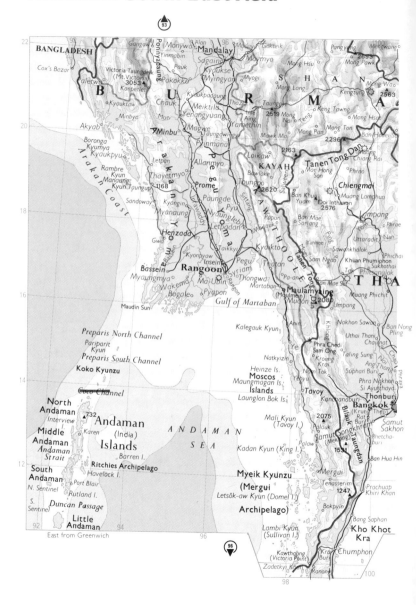

Map 94

1:10 000 000

Map 95

The Malay Peninsula

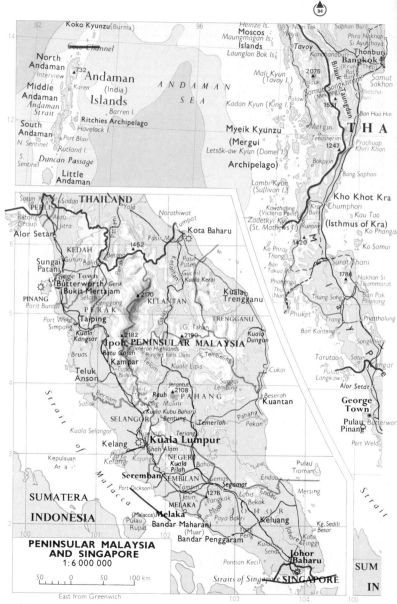

PENINSULAR MALAYSIA AND SINGAPORE
1:6 000 000

50   0   50   100 km

East from Greenwich

Map 96

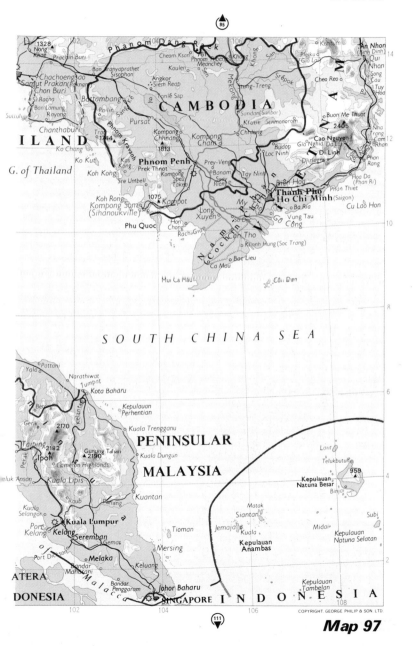

1:10 000 000

Map 97

South China Sea map showing Cambodia, Vietnam, Thailand, Peninsular Malaysia, Singapore, and Indonesia.

Cambodia region labels:
Phanom Dang Rek
1328 Nong Khae
Prachin-Buri
Cheom Ksan
Phnom Meanchey
Khong, San
Kontum
An Nhon (Binh Dinh)
Qui Nhon
Pleiku
Gia Lai
Chachoengsao
Ban Aranyaprathet Sisophon
Koulen
Song Cau
Tuy Hoa
Samut Prakan
Paknam
Chon Buri
Si Racha
Angkor
Siem Reap
Tonlé Sap
Stung-Treng
Srépok
Cheo Reo
Ban Lomung
Rayong
Battambang
Pailin
CAMBODIA
Sandan (Sanbor)
Buon Me Thuot
2405
Nha Trang
Cam Rhan
Chanthaburi
Trat
1744
Phnom Kravanh
Pursat
Kompong Chhnang
Kompong Cham
Chhlong
Kratie
Senmonorom
Gia Nghia
Cao Nguyen
Da Lat
Di Linh
ILAND
Ko Chang
1813
Budop
Loc Ninh
Djiringe
Phan Rang
G. of Thailand
Ko Kut
Kas Kong
Phnom Penh
Prek Thnot
Kompong Speu
Prey-Veng
Banam
Sa Dec
Tay Ninh
Bien Hoa
Hoa Da (Phan Ri)
Phan Thiet
Koh Kong
Sre Umbell
Kompong Takeo
Svay Rieng
Thanh Pho Ho Chi Minh (Saigon)
Koh Rong
1075
Kampot
Long Xuyen
My Tho
Ba Ria
Cu Lao Hon
Kompong Som (Sihanoukville)
Hon Chong
Rach Gia
Can Tho
Go Cong
Vung Tau
VIETNAM
Phu Quoc
Ca Mau
Khanh Hung (Soc Trang)
Cochinchina
Bac Lieu
Mui Ca Mau
Con Dao

SOUTH CHINA SEA

Yala
Pattani
Narathiwat
Tumpat
Kota Baharu
Kelantan
Kepulauan Perhentian
Betong
Gerik
2170
Kuala Trengganu
PENINSULAR
Laut
Telukbutung
Taiping
2182
Ipoh
Gunung Talan
2190
Cameron Highlands
Kuala Dungun
Perak
959
Kuala Lipis
MALAYSIA
Kuala
Kepulauan Natuna Besar
Binjai
Teluk Anson
Pahang
Kuantan
Matak
Siantan
Kuala Selangor
Port Kelang
Kelong
Kuala Lumpur
Seremban
Gemas
Raub
Tioman
Jemaja
Kuala
Midai
Kepulauan Natuna Selatan
Subi
Melaka
Mersing
Kepulauan Anambas
Port Dickson
SUMATERA
Bandar Maharani
Keluang
Malacca
INDONESIA
Bandar Penggaram
Johor Baharu
SINGAPORE
INDONESIA
Kepulauan Tambelan

China: East

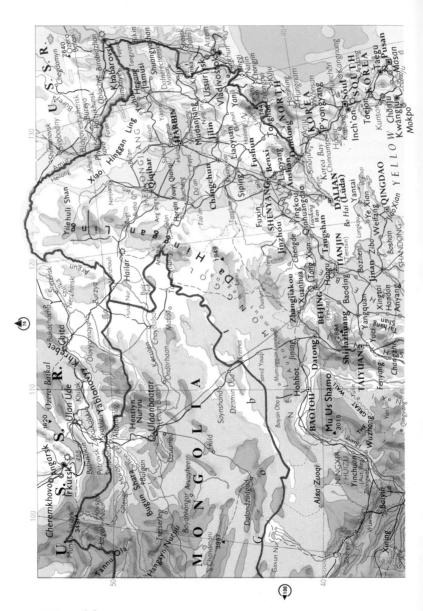

Map 98

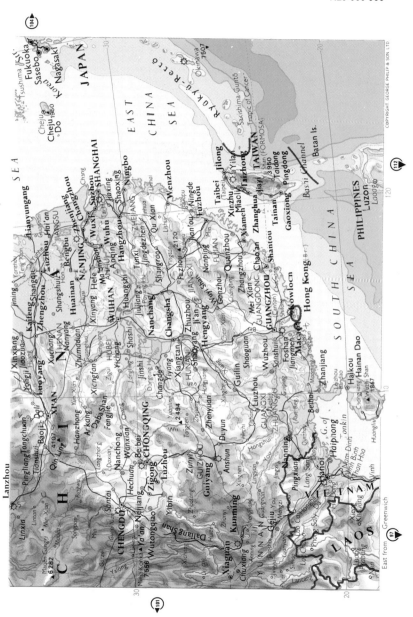

1:20 000 000

Map 99

China: West

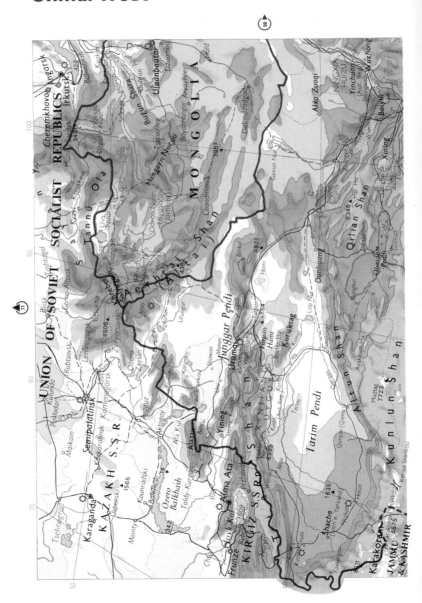

Map 100

1:20 000 000

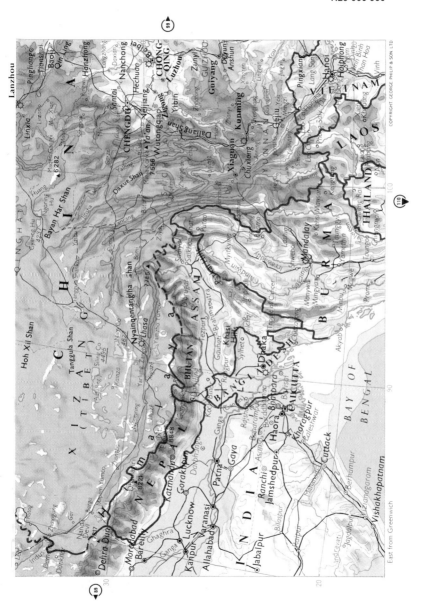

East from Greenwich

COPYRIGHT GEORGE PHILIP & SON LTD

Map 101

Japan: North

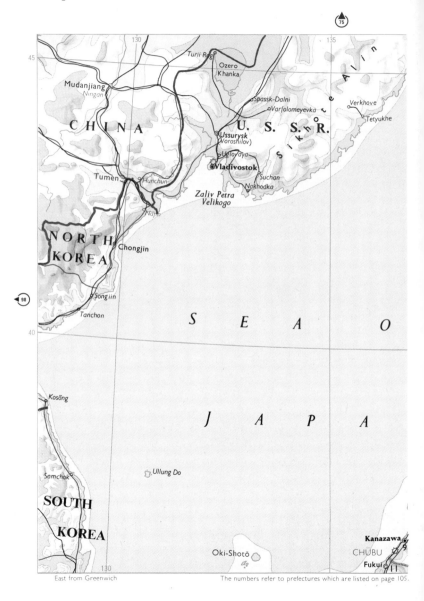

45

130

135

Turii Rog

Ozero
Khanka

Mudanjiang
Ningan

Spassk-Dalni
Varfolomeyevka

Verkhove

Tetyukhe

CHINA

U. S. S. R.

Sikhote

Alin

Ussursk
(Voroshilov)

Ugloyaya

Vladivostok

Suchan

Nakhodka

Tumen

Hunchun

Zaliv Petra
Velikogo

Najin

NORTH
KOREA

Chongjin

98

Songjin

Tanchon

40

S E A

O

Kosŏng

J A P A

Samchok

Ullung Do

SOUTH

KOREA

Kanazawa

CHUBU

Oki-Shotō

Fukui

11

130

East from Greenwich

The numbers refer to prefectures which are listed on page 105.

Map 102

1:7 500 000

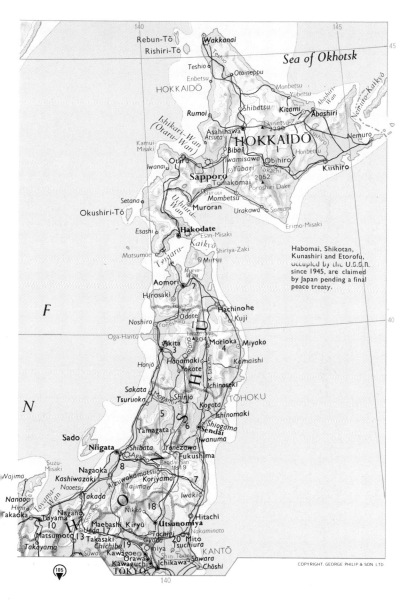

Habomai, Shikotan,
Kunashiri and Etorofu,
occupied by the U.S.S.R.
since 1945, are claimed
by Japan pending a final
peace treaty.

Map 103

Japan: South

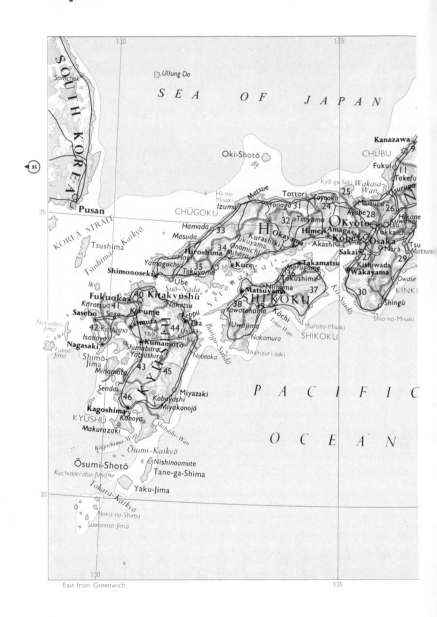

Map 104

1:7 500 000

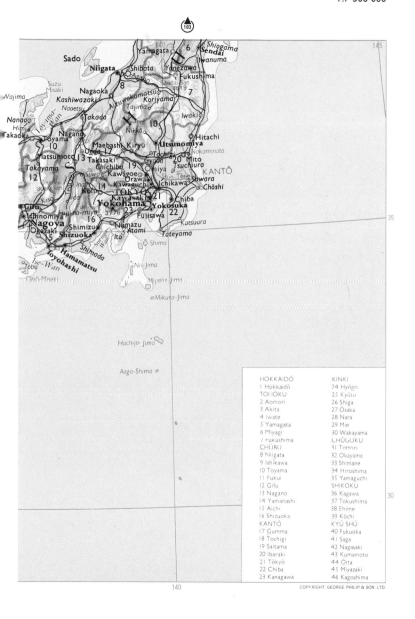

HOKKAIDŌ	KINKI
I Hokkaidō	24 Hyōgo
TŌHOKU	25 Kyōto
2 Aomori	26 Shiga
3 Akita	27 Ōsaka
4 Iwate	28 Nara
5 Yamagata	29 Mie
6 Miyagi	30 Wakayama
7 Fukushima	CHŪGOKU
CHŪBU	31 Tottori
8 Niigata	32 Okayama
9 Ishikawa	33 Shimane
10 Toyama	34 Hiroshima
11 Fukui	35 Yamaguchi
12 Gifu	SHIKOKU
13 Nagano	36 Kagawa
14 Yamanashi	37 Tokushima
15 Aichi	38 Ehime
16 Shizuoka	39 Kōchi
KANTŌ	KYŪ SHŪ
17 Gumma	40 Fukuoka
18 Tochigi	41 Saga
19 Saitama	42 Nagasaki
20 Ibaraki	43 Kumamoto
21 Tōkyō	44 Ōita
22 Chiba	45 Miyazaki
23 Kanagawa	46 Kagoshima

140

Map 105

Japan: Tokyo, Kyoto, Osaka

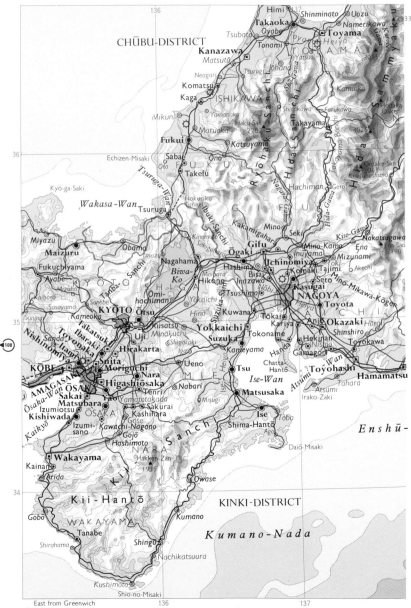

Map 106

1:2 500 000

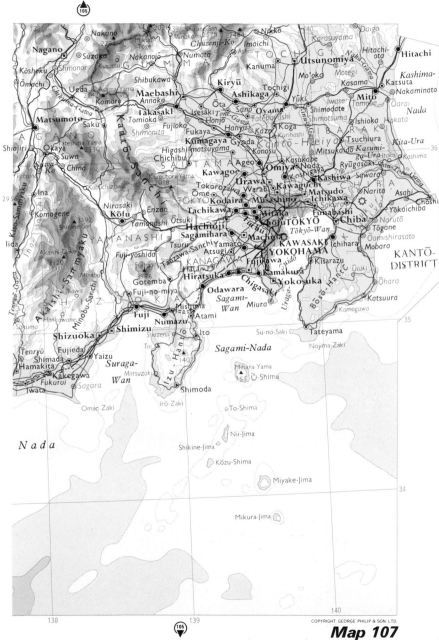

COPYRIGHT. GEORGE PHILIP & SON. LTD.

Map 107

Japan: Kyushu

1:2 500 000

Map 108

COPYRIGHT GEORGE PHILIP & SON LTD.

East from Greenwich 131

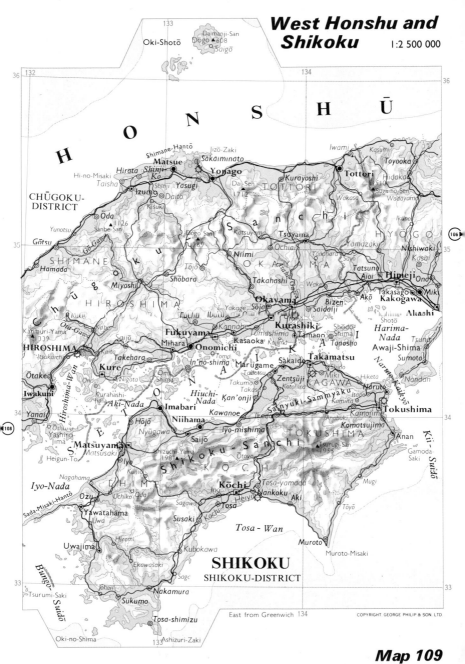

West Honshu and Shikoku

1:2 500 000

SHIKOKU
SHIKOKU-DISTRICT

East from Greenwich 134

COPYRIGHT GEORGE PHILIP & SON LTD.

Map 109

109

Indonesia: West

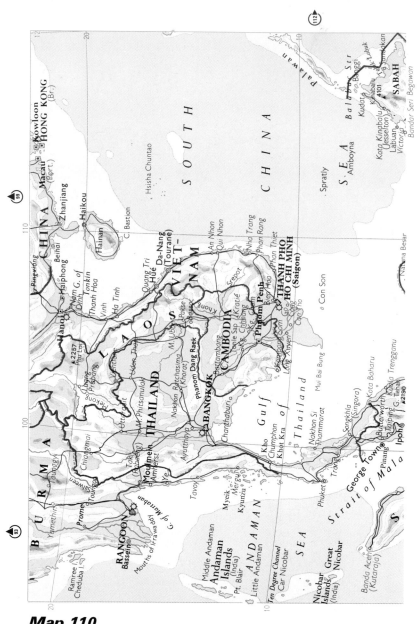

Map 110

1:20 000 000

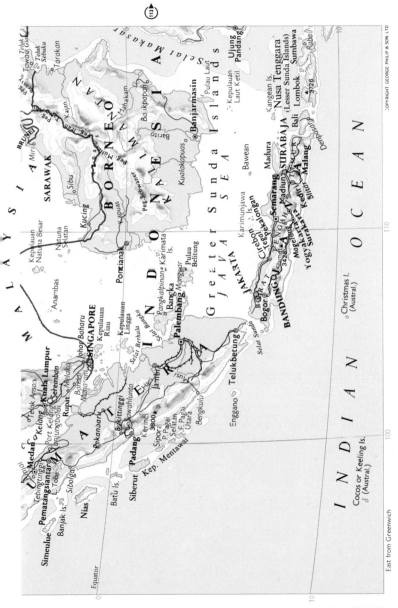

East from Greenwich

Map 111

Indonesia: East

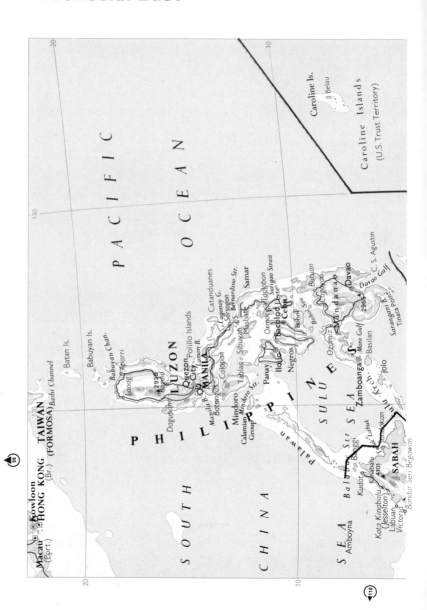

Map 112

1:20 000 000

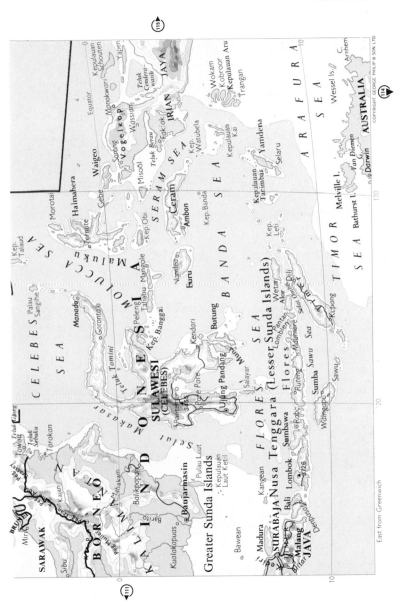

East from Greenwich

COPYRIGHT GEORGE PHILIP & SON LTD

Map 113

Australia, New Zealand and Papua New Guinea

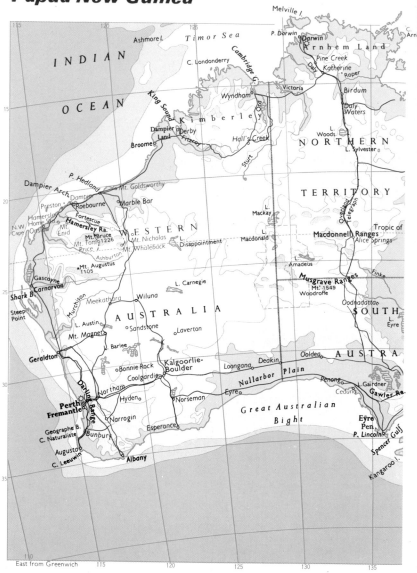

Map labels (Western Australia, Northern Territory, South Australia):

INDIAN OCEAN

Timor Sea

Melville I.
Ashmore I.
C. Londonderry
P. Darwin
Darwin
Arnhem Land
Arnh
Pine Creek
Katherine
Daly
Roper
Victoria
Birdum
Daly Waters
Wyndham
King Sound
KIMBERLEY
Dampier Land
Derby
Fitzroy
Hall's Creek
Sturt
L. Woods
NORTHERN
L. Sylvester
Broome
P. Hedland
Dampier Arch.
Dampier
Mt. Goldsworthy
Preston
Roebourne
Marble Bar
TERRITORY
Hamersley
N.W. Home I.
Cape Onslow
Mt. Enid
Hamersley Ra.
Fortescue
WESTERN
L. Mackay
Overland Telegraph
Tropic of
Mt. Bruce
Mt. Tom 1226
Price J.
Ashburton
Mt. Nicholas
Mt. Whaleback
L. Disappointment
L. Macdonald
Macdonnell Ranges
Alice Springs
Mt. Augustus 1105
L. Amadeus
Gascoyne
Carnarvon
Shark B.
L. Carnegie
Musgrave Ranges
Mt. 1549
Woodroffe
Finke
Steep Point
Murchison
Meekatharra
Wiluna
AUSTRALIA
Oodnadatta
SOUTH
L. Austin
Mt. Magnet
Sandstone
Laverton
L. Eyre
Geraldton
L. Barlee
Bonnie Rock
Coolgardie
Kalgoorlie-Boulder
Loongana
Deakin
Ooldea
AUSTRA
Northam
Hyden
Norseman
Eyre
Nullarbor Plain
Penong
L. Gairdner
Gawler Ra.
Perth
Fremantle
Darling Range
Narrogin
Esperance
Ceduna
Great Australian Bight
Eyre Pen.
P. Lincoln
Geographe B.
C. Naturaliste
Bunbury
Spencer Gulf
Augusta
C. Leeuwin
Albany
Kangaroo I.

Map 114

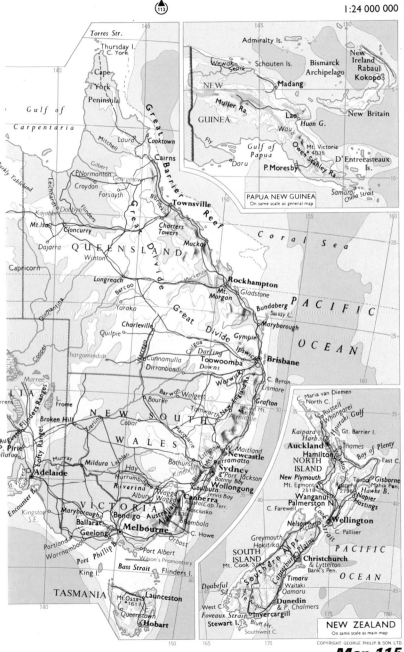

1:24 000 000

115

PAPUA NEW GUINEA
On same scale as general map

Torres Str.

Thursday I.
C. York

Cape
York
Peninsula

Gulf of

Carpentaria

Admiralty Is.

New
Ireland
Rabaul
Kokopo

Schouten Is.

Bismarck
Archipelago

Wewak
Sepik

NEW
GUINEA

Madang

Muller Ra.

Lae

Wau

Huon G.

New Britain

Mt. Victoria
4035

Owen Stanley Ra.

Fly

Daru

Gulf of
Papua

P. Moresby

D'Entrecasteaux
Is.

Samarai
China Strait

Cooktown

Cairns

Laura

Mitchell

Gilbert

P.Normanton

Georgetown

Croydon

Forsayth

Townsville

Great Barrier Reef

Charters
Towers

Mackay

Mt. Isa

Cloncurry

Burketown

Karabba

Dajarra

Dobbyn

Flinders

Leichhardt

Burke Tableland

QUEENSLAND

Winton

Longreach

Barcoo

Yaraka

Charleville

Quilpie

Thargomindah

Cooper

Marree

L. Frome

Flinders Ranges

Torrens

Broken Hill

Cobar

Bourke

Walgett

Barwon

Darling

Cunnamulla

Dirranbandi

Toowoomba
Downs

Warwick

Rockhampton

Mt.
Morgan

Gladstone

Bundaberg

Maryborough

Gympie

Ipswich

Brisbane

C. Byron

Lismore

Grafton

C O R A L   S E A

P A C I F I C

O C E A N

Capricorn

Great Divide

Barcoo

Mackenzie

Dawson

Barwon

Warrego

Culgoa

Dalby C.

Maria van Diemen
North C.

Russell
Whangarei

Kaipara
Harb.

Hauraki Gulf

Gt. Barrier I.

Auckland

Thames

Bay of Plenty

East C.

Hamilton

NORTH
ISLAND

New Plymouth
Mt. Egmont
2518

Wanganui

Taupo

Ruapehu
2796

Gisborne

Mahia Pen.

Napier

Hawke B.

Palmerston N.

Hastings

C. Farewell

Nelson

Picton

Cook Strait

Wellington

C. Palliser

Greymouth

Hokitika

SOUTH
ISLAND

Mt. Cook 3764

Southern Alps

Canterbury Plains

Christchurch
& Lyttelton
Bank's Pen.

P A C I F I C

O C E A N

Timaru

Waitaki

Oamaru

Doubtful
Sd.

West C.

Foveaux Strait

Stewart I.

Waikato

Dunedin
& P. Chalmers

Invercargill

Bluff Hr.

Southwest C.

NEW ZEALAND
On same scale as main map

LIA

P. Augusta

P. Pirie

Wallaroo

Adelaide

Encounter B.

St. Vincent G.

Kingston
S.E.

Quamantina

Eyre

Murray

Lachlan

Darling

NEW   SOUTH

WALES

Macquarie

Tamworth

Armidale

New England

Round Mt.
1616

Grafton

30

Mildura

Hay

Riverina

Murrumbidgee

Wagga
Wagga

Albury

Goulburn

Bathurst

Katoomba

Lithgow

Maitland

Newcastle

Parramatta

Sydney
Port Jackson
Botany Bay

Wollongong

Jervis Bay

Canberra
Austral.Cap.Terr.

Kosciusko

Bombala

C. Howe

VICTORIA

Bendigo

Melbourne

Geelong

Ballarat

Maryborough

Murray

Portland

Warrnambool

Port Phillip B.

Port Albert

Orbost

Wilson's Promontory

Bass Strait

Flinders I.

King I.

TASMANIA

Mt.Ossa
1617

Launceston

Queenstown

Hobart

Rocky Ranges

Murrumbidgee

COPYRIGHT. GEORGE PHILIP & SON. LTD.

Map 115

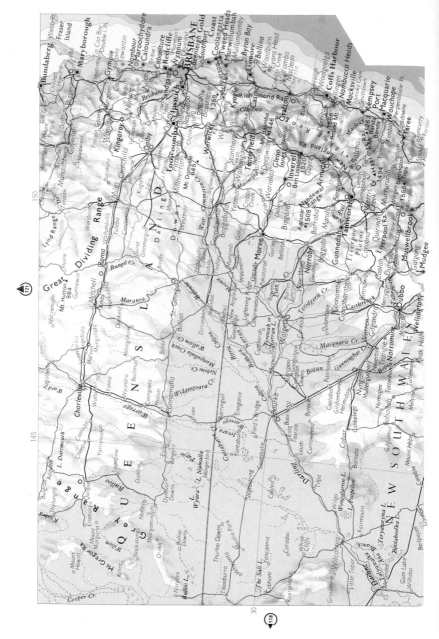

Map 116

Australia: Brisbane, Sydney, Melbourne

1:8 000 000

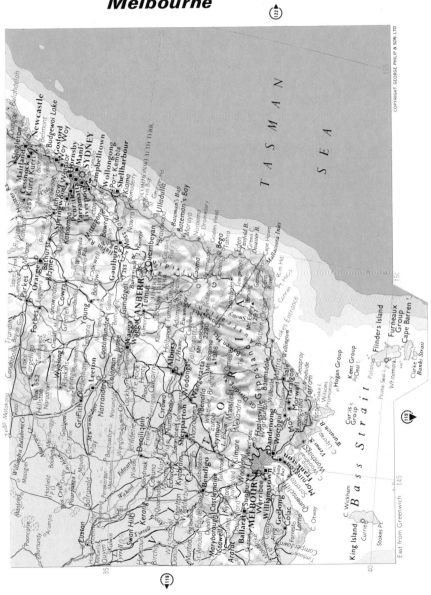

Map 117

Australia: Adelaide, Melbourne, Tasmania

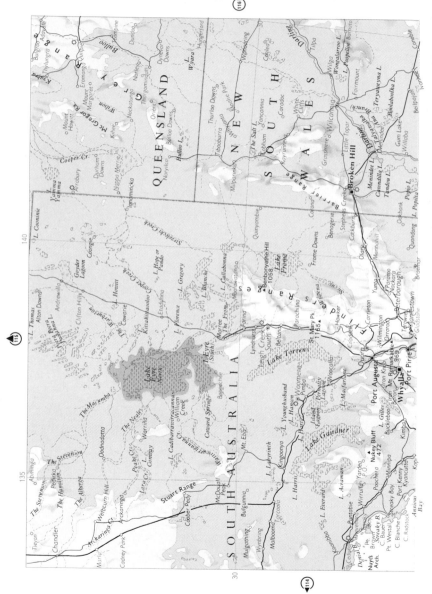

Map 118

1:8 000 000

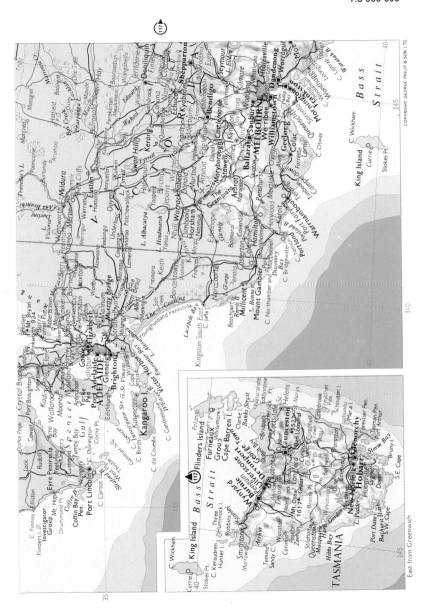

Bass Strait

C. Wickham
King Island
Currie
Stokes Pt.

COPYRIGHT GEORGE PHILIP & SON. LTD

East from Greenwich

Map 119

119

Australia: Perth

1:8 000 000

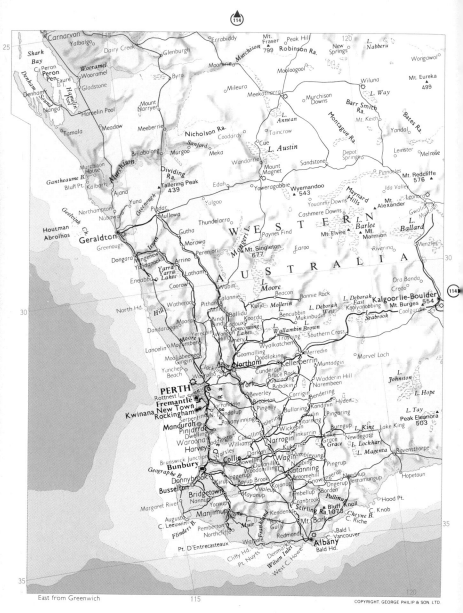

East from Greenwich

Map 120

Australia: North East Queensland

1:8 000 000

115

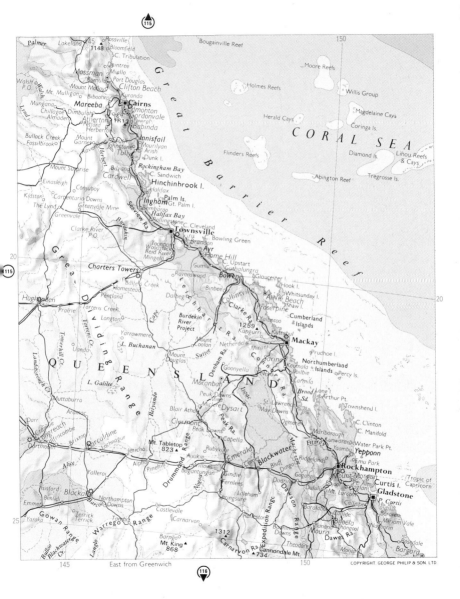

Bougainville Reef

150

Palmer Lakeland 145 Rossville
1148 Bloomfield
Cointree C. Tribulation
Mossman Miallo
Kumula Port Douglas
Walsh Mt. Mulligan Mount McCloud Clifton Beach
P.O. Kuranda
Mungana Biboohra
Chillagoe Dimbulah Mareeba **Cairns**
Almaden Atherton Edmonton
Yalga Gordonvale
Herberton Deeral
Babinda

Moore Reefs

Holmes Reefs

Willis Group

Magdelaine Cays

Herald Cays

Coringa Is.

C O R A L   S E A

Bullock Creek
Fossilbrook Mount
Garnet
Johnstone Mourilyan
Tully Arish
Dunk I.
Mount Surprise Bilyana Rockingham Bay
Cardwell C. Sandwich
Einasleigh Conjuboy Hinchinbrook I.
Halifax
Kidston Carpentaria Downs Palm Is.
The Lynd Greenvale Mine Gt. Palm I.
Ingham Bambaroo
Greenvale Halifax Bay
Clarke River Rollingstone
P.O. Cleveland
Yuru **Townsville**
Toonpan Brandon Bowling Green
Woodstock Reid River **Ayr**
Mingela Home Hill
Charters Towers Gumlu Upstart
Ravenswood Southalungra
Homestead Binbee
Hughenden Pentland Dalbeg Collinsville Hook I.
Prairie Torrens Creek Annie Beach
Longton Clarke Ra. Shaw I.
Proserpine Whitsunday. I.
Yarrowmere Burdekin Cumberland
River Yalleroi Islands
Uando Project Kangurri Kuttabul
L. Buchanan Netherdale **Mackay**
Mount Sutton
Coolon Prudhoe I.
Mount Denham Ra. Sarina
Landsborough Cr. **Q U E E N S L A N D** Douglas Kounala Northumberland
Goonyella Dbilbie Islands Percy Is.
L. Galilee Moranbah Larmila
Muttaburra Peak Downs Broad Long Arthur Pt.
Blair Athol St. Lawrence Sd. Townshend I.
Aramac May Downs
Darr Clermont Ogmore C. Clinton
Barcaldine Peak Ra. Marlborough C. Manifold
Brixton Capella Kunwarara Water Park Pt.
Dartmouth Lochnagar Mt. Tabletop Ruby vale Pitardi Yaamba **Yeppoon**
823 Anakie Emerald Emu Park
Alice Jericho **Blackwater** Ridgelands **Rockhampton**
Yalleroi Alpha Willow Bluff Dingo Mount Morgan Tropic of
Pinehill Bogantungan Comet Gogango Capricorn
Isisford Ngawa Duaringa Mt. Alma **Curtis I.**
Benlidi Gindie Dululu Raglan **Gladstone**
Blackall Fernlees Mt. Larcom Calliope P. Curtis
Emmet Northampton Lotcham Baralaba
Terrick Downs Springsure Jambin
Terrick Costlevale Tambo Carnarvon Biloela Miriam Vale
Yaraka Gowan Range 1312 Rolleston Moura Nagoorin
Bullee Mt. King Cannondale Mt. Banana Rosedale
Blackwater 868 734 Theodore Monto Bargara

145 East from Greenwich 150 COPYRIGHT GEORGE PHILIP & SON LTD

116

Map 121

New Zealand, Central and South West Pacific

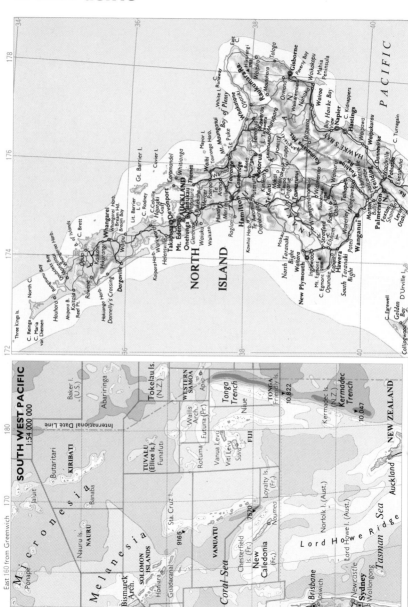

Map 122

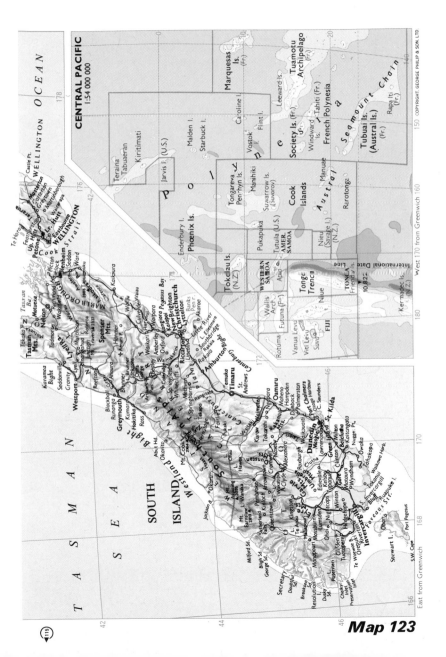

1:7 000 000

CENTRAL PACIFIC
1:54 000 000

Map 123

123

150 COPYRIGHT GEORGE PHILIP & SON LTD.

Africa: Physical

1:70 000 000

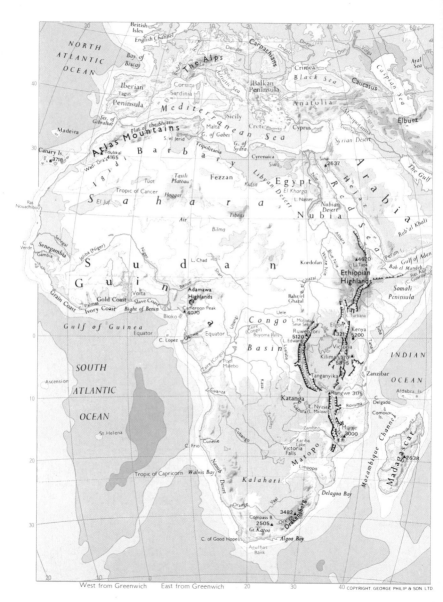

Map 124

Africa: Political

1 : 70 000 000

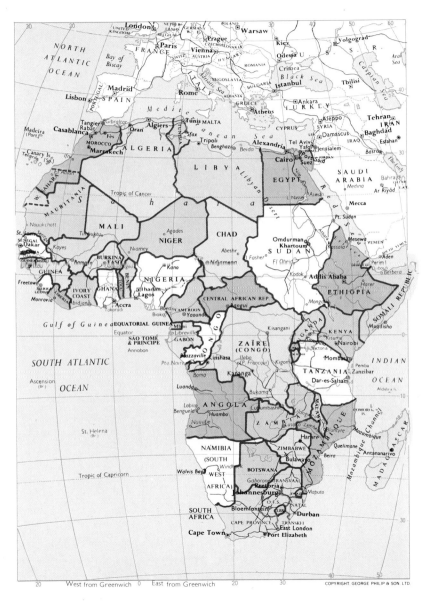

Map 125

Africa: North West

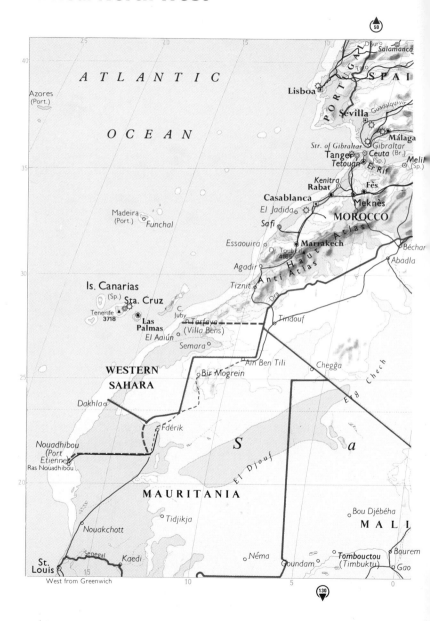

ATLANTIC

OCEAN

Azores
(Port.)

Madeira
(Port.) Funchal

Is. Canarias
(Sp.)
Sta. Cruz
Tenerife
3718
Las
Palmas
El Aaiún
C.
Juby

WESTERN
SAHARA

Dakhla

Nouadhibou
(Port
Etienne)
Ras Nouadhibou

MAURITANIA

Nouakchott

Senegal Kaedi

St.
Louis

Doúro Salamanca
PORTUGAL SPAI
Lisboa Tajo
Sevilla Guadalquivir
Málaga
Str. of Gibraltar Gibraltar
Tanger Ceuta (Br.)
Tetouan (Sp.) Meli
Er Rif (Sp.)
Kenitra
Rabat Fès
Casablanca Meknès
El Jadida MOROCCO
Safi
Essaouira Marrakech Béchar
Dj. Toubkal Abadla
4165
Agadir Haut Atlas
Tiznit Anti Atlas
Dra Tindouf
Tarfaya
(Villa Bens)
Semara
Aïn Ben Tili
Bir Mogrein Chegga Erg Chech
S a
Fdérik
El Djouf
Tidjikja Bou Djébéha
MALI
Néma Tombouctou Bourem
Goundam (Timbuktu) Gao

West from Greenwich

Map 126

126

1:20 000 000

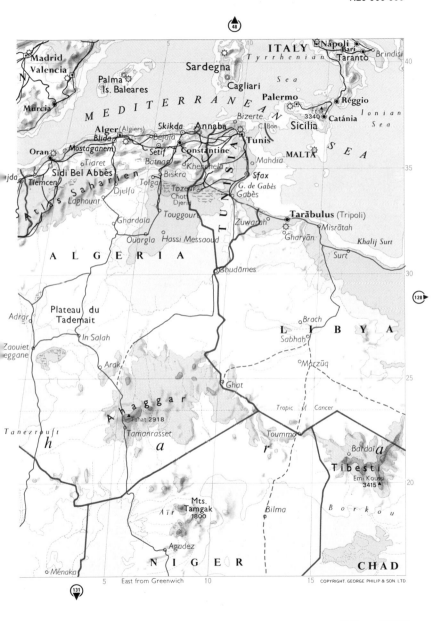

48

Madrid
Valencia
N
Murcia

Palma
Is. Baleares

Sardegna

ITALY
Tyrrhenian

Napoli
Bari
Taranto
Brindisi

40

Cagliari

Sea

Palermo

Réggio

M E D I T E R R A N E A N

Bizerte
Etna
3340
Catánia

Ionian
Sea

Oran
Mostaganem
Alger (Algiers)
Blida
Bejaia
Skikda
Annaba
C. Bon

Sicilia

Tunis

S E A

Sidi Bel Abbès
jda
Tlemcen

Setif
Batna
Constantine

Tiaret
Khenchela

MALTA

35

A t l a s
S a h a r i e n
Laghouat
Djelfa
Biskra
Tolga
Tozeur
Chott
Djerid

Mahdia

Sfax

Ghardaïa
Touggour

G. de Gabès
Gabès

T U N I S I A

Zuwarah

Tarābulus (Tripoli)

Ouargla
Hassi Messaoud

Gharyān
Misrātah

Khalij Surt

A L G E R I A

Ghudāmes

Surt

30

128

Plateau du
Tademaït

Adrar

Brach

L I B Y A

In Salah

Sabhah

Zaouiet
eggane

Arak

Marzūq

25

Ghat

A h a g g a r

Tanezrouft
h

Tahat 2918
Tamanrasset

a

Tropic of Cancer

Toummo

r

Bardaï
a

Tibesti
Emi Koussi
3415

20

Mts.
Tamgak
1800
Aïr

Bilma

B o r k o u

Agadez

Ménaka

N I G E R

CHAD

131

Map 127

Africa: North East

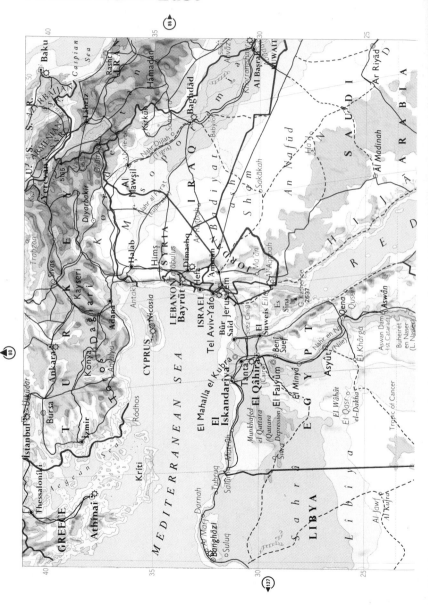

Map 128

128

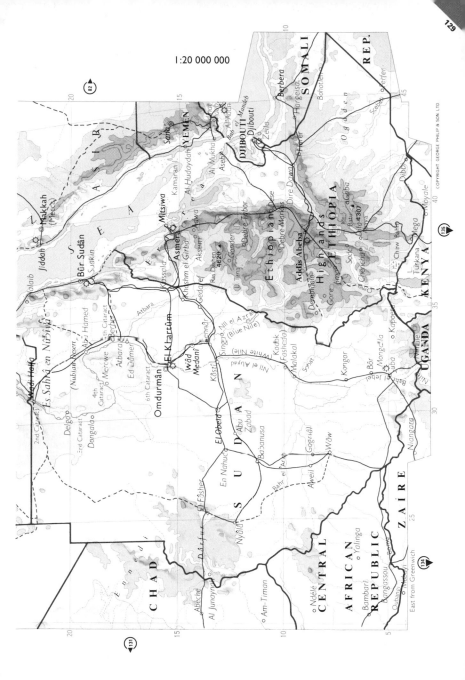

1:20 000 000

82

20

15

10

45

COPYRIGHT GEORGE PHILIP & SON LTD

SOMALI REP.

Berbera

Bohotleh

O g a d e n

Zeila

Djibouti

Berbera

Horgeisa

Scebeli

Gerlen

Mänäab

Bab APADEN

DJIBOUTI

Dire Dawa

Hirer

Harer

Djibbb

40

Moyale

YEMEN

San'a

Al-Hudaydah

Al Mukha

Kamaran

Aswa

Erer

Dibbr

135

Makkah (Mecca)

Jiddah

Bûr Sûdân

Suakin

Mitsiwa

Asmera

Debre Tabor

Debre Markos

Debre Birhan

Addis Abeba

Nega

Chew Bahir

Kenya

R E D   S E A

A S I R

E r i t r e a

Kassala

Khashm el Girba

Aksem

Aswa

Gonder

Tana

Ras Dashen 4620

E t h i o p i a n   H i g h l a n d s

ETHIOPIA

Sodo

Goba

Mt. 4307

L. Chelega

L. Turkana

Dese

Debre

Gore

Imi

Dembidolo

Gambela

35

Golalb

Holalb

Wadi Halfa

Es Sahtá en Nûbiya

Delgo

Dongola

Dongola

2nd Cataract

3rd Cataract

4th Cataract

(Nubian Desert)

Abu Hamed

Merowe

5th Cataract

Atbara

Berber

6th Cataract

Ed Damer

Atbara

Gedaref

Sennâr

Singa

Gedaref

Nil el Azra (Blue Nile)

Nil el Abyad (White Nile)

Kôdôk

Fashoda

Sobat

Malakal

Kongor

Bôr

Mongalla

Juba

Nimule

UGANDA

30

Omdurmân

El Khartûm

Wâd Medani

Kôstî

El Obeid

Abu Zabad

Bodanusa

En Nahud

Gogrial

Wâw

Bahr el Arab

Aweil

Bahr el Jebel

Niangara

ZAIRE

25

Nyala

D a r f u r

El Fasher

S U D A N

Am-Timan

131

Al Junoyno

Abeche

C H A D

Ennedi

Ndélé

Yalinga

Bambari

Bangassou

Ouban

CENTRAL AFRICAN REPUBLIC

134

East from Greenwich

5

10

15

20

Map 129

Africa: West

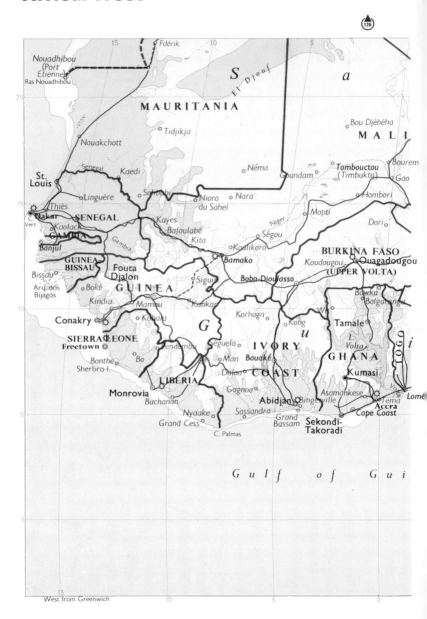

Map 130

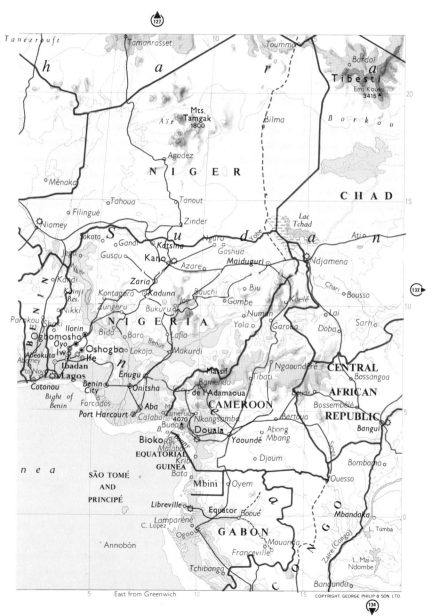

1:20 000 000

Tanezrouft Tamanrasset   Toummo   Bardaï
h   a   r   Tibesti
                                Emi Koussi
                                3415
                        Bilma   Borkou
            Mts.
            Tamgak
            1800
        Aïr
        Agadez

N I G E R   CHAD
°Ménaka
        °Tahoua   Tanout   Atio n
°Filingué   Zinder   Lac
°Niamey   Tchad
        Sokoto S   u   d   a
            °Gandi °Katsina Nguru Yobe   Ndjamena
        °Gusau Kano   Gashua Maiduguri   Chari °Bousso
                Azare
        Zaria   Biu   Koélé
        °Kontagora Kaduna Bauchi   Lai   Sarh
°Kandi °Zungeru Bukuru   Gombe Numan   Garoua Doba
°Kinji   Yola
Res.   N I G E R I A
°Nikki   Baro Lafia
B Parakou °Iloin Bida Benue Makurdi
E °Ogbomosho Oyo Lokoja   Ngaoundéré CENTRAL
N Abeokuta Iwo Oshogbo   Massif   °Bossangoa
I °Ife   Tibati   AFRICAN
N Lagos Enugu   Bamenda de l'Adamaoua Bébori
Cotonou Benin °Onitsha   Bossembélé REPUBLIC
Bight of City   CAMEROON
Benin Forcados °Aba   Nkongsamba Bertoua Bangui
Port Harcourt Calabar 4070 Ahong
        Buea Douala Yaoundé Mbang
        Bioko
        Malabo   Djoum   Bomboma°
        EQUATORIAL Kribi
n e a   GUINEA Bata   Ouesso
        SÃO TOMÉ Mbini °Oyem
        AND
        PRINCIPE
        Libreville Equator Booué C o n g o
        Lamparené °Ogoou GABON Mbandaka
        C. López   L. Tumba
°Annobón   °Mouanda
                Franceville   L. Mai-
            Tchibanga   Ndombe
                        Bandundu°

Map 131

Africa: East

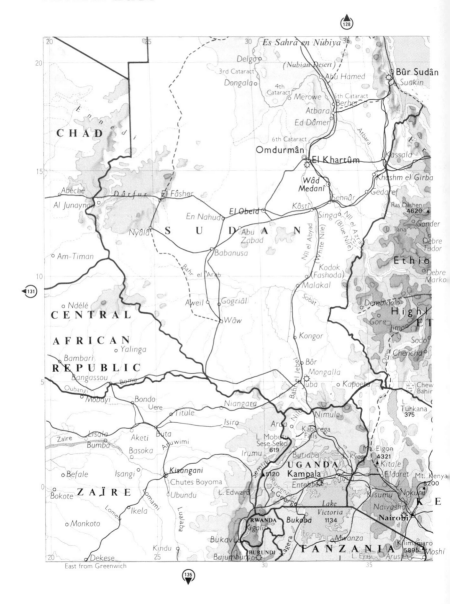

128

20　25　30　Es Sahra en Nûbiya

Delgo

(Nubian Desert)

3rd Cataract　Abu Hamed　Bûr Sudân

20　Dongala　4th　Suakin

Cataract　Merowe　6th Cataract

Atbara　Berber

Ed Dâmer

C H A D　Atbara

6th Cataract

Omdurmân　Kassala

El Khartûm

15　Wâd　Khashm el Girba

Abéché　Dârfur　El Fâsher　Medanî　Gedaref

Al Junaynah　Sennâr　Ras Dashen

En Nahud　El Obeid　Kôsti　4620

Singa　Gonder

Nyâlâ　S U D A N　L. Tana

Abu　Debre

Zabad　Tabor

Am-Timan　Babanusa　E t h i o

Kodok　Debre

Bahr el Arab　(Fashoda)　Marko

Aweil　Gogriâl　Malakal　Dembidolo　High

131　Sobat　Gore　ET

Ndélé　Wâw　Jimma

Sodo

C E N T R A L　Kongor　Chencha

A F R I C A N　Bôr

Yalinga　Mongalla

Bambari　Juba　Kapoeta　Chew

R E P U B L I C　Bahr el Jebel　Bahir

Bangassou　Bomu　L.

Oubangi　Turkana

Mobayi　Bondo　Niangara　Nimule　375

Uere　Titule　Isiro　Arua　Kabarega

Zaïre　Lisala　Aketi　Buta　Falls　Mt. Elgon

Bumba　Basoka　Aruwimi　Irumu　L. Mobutu　4321

Sese-Seko　Butiaba　Kyoga　Kitale

Befale　Isangi　Kisangani　619　Eldoret　Mt. Kenya

Bokote　Z A Ï R E　Chutes Boyoma　5120　U G A N D A　5200

Monkoto　Lomami　Ubundu　L. Edward　Kampala　Kisumu　Nakuru

Ikela　Lualaba　Entebbe　Naivasha　K E

Lake　Nairobi

R W A N D A　Victoria

Dekese　Kindu　Bukavu　Kigali　Bukoba　1134　Mwanza　Kilimanjaro

20　25　BURUNDI　Kagera　T A N Z A N I A　5895　Moshi

Bujumbura　L. Eyasi　Arusha

East from Greenwich　30　35

135

Map 132

1:20 000 000

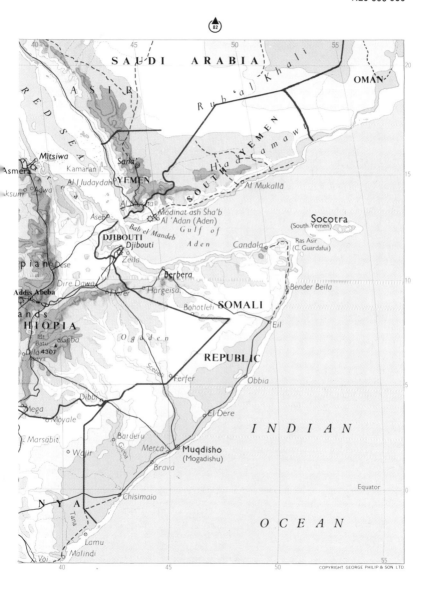

Map 133

Africa: Central

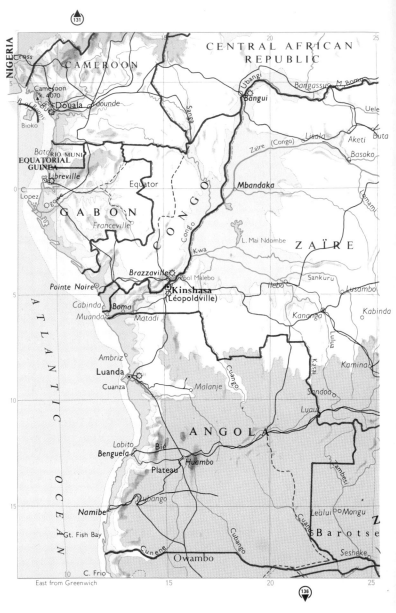

NIGERIA

CAMEROON

CENTRAL AFRICAN REPUBLIC

Cross

5

Cameroon Pk. 4070

Douala

Yaounde

Sanga

Ubangi

Bangui

Bangassus M. Boma

Uele

Bioko

Bata

RIO MUNI

EQUATORIAL GUINEA

Libreville

C. Lopez

GABON

Equator

Franceville

0

Ogove

CONGO

Congo

Kwa

Zaïre (Congo)

Lisala

Aketi

Buta

Basoko

Mbandaka

L. Mai Ndombe

ZAÏRE

Lomami

Brazzaville

Pool Malebo

Pointe Noire

Kinshasa (Léopoldville)

Itebo

Sankuru

Lusambo

Cabinda

Boma

Muanda

Matadi

Kananga

Lulua

Kabinda

Kasai

5

ATLANTIC

OCEAN

Ambriz

Luanda

Cuanza

Cuango

Malanje

Kamina

Sandoa

Lyau

10

ANGOLA

Lobito

Benguela

Bié

Huambo

Plateau

Zambesi

Lealui

Mongu

Z

Namibe

Lubango

Cuando

Barotse

Gt. Fish Bay

Cubango

Seshe ke

C. Frio

Cunene

Owambo

Map 134

1:20 000 000

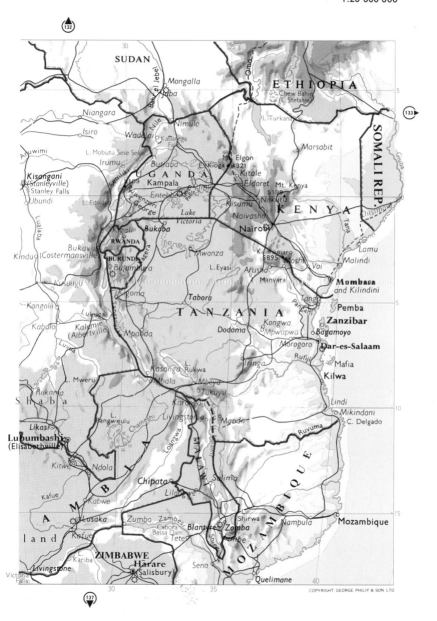

SUDAN

Mongalla
Bahr el Jebel
Juba
Nimule
Niangara
Isiro
Wadelai
Nile
KaBanega Falls
L. Mobutu Sese Seko
Irumu
Buraba
L. Kioga
Mt. Elgon 4321
Kitale
UGANDA
Kampala
Entebbe
5109
L. Edward
George
Lake Victoria
Kisumu
Nakuru
Eldoret
Mt. Kenya 5199
Kisangani
(Stanleyville)
Stanley Falls
Ubundi
Ruwenzori
Aruwimi
Lualaba
Kigali
Bukoba
RWANDA
Bukavu
(Costermansville)
Kindu
BURUNDI
Bujumbura
Kagera
Kongolo
Nyunzu
Kabalo
Kalemie
(Albertville)
Luvua
Luhuga
Mpanda
Kigoma
Tabora
Mwanza
L. Eyasi
Manyara
Arusha
Moshi
Kilimanjaro 5895
Voi
ETHIOPIA
Chew Bahir
(L. Stefanie)
L. Turkana
Marsabit
Giuba
SOMALI REP.
KENYA
Naivasha
Nairobi
Lamu
Malindi
Tana
Mombasa
and Kilindini
Pemba
Zanzibar

TANZANIA
Dodoma
Kongwa
Mpwapwa
Morogoro
Bagamoyo
Dar-es-Salaam
Pangani
Tanga
Mafia
Kilwa
Rufiji
Iringa
L. Rukwa
Kasanga
Mbala
L. Mweru
Bukama
Shaba
Likasi
Lubumbashi
(Elisabethville)
Kitwe
Ndola
Kafue
Kabwe
Lusaka
Mbeya
Tukuyu
Karonga
Livingstone
L. Bangweulu
Chambeshi
Mbanda
C. Delgado
Mikindani
Lindi
Ruvuma
MOZAMBIQUE
Chipata
Lilongwe
Salima
Zumbo
Zambezi
Cabora Bassa Dam
Tete
Blantyre
Zomba
Shirwa
Limbe
Nampula
Mozambique
Quelimane
Sena
ZIMBABWE
Harare
(Salisbury)
L. Kariba
Livingstone
Victoria Falls
land
Kafue
M A L A W I
L. Malawi
Lukuga
Loangwa

COPYRIGHT GEORGE PHILIP & SON LTD

Map 135

Africa: South

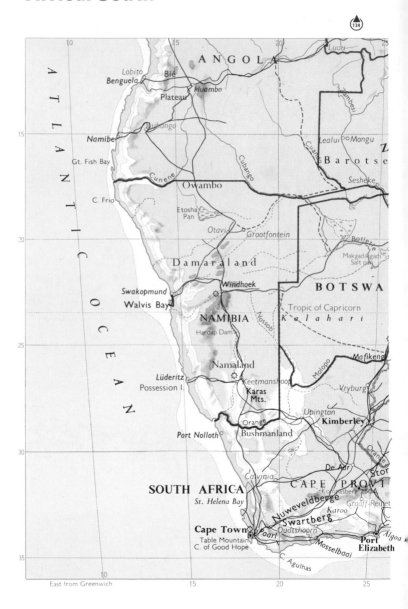

A N G O L A

Lobito
Benguela
Bié

Huambo

Plateau

Cubango

Namibe

Lealui   Mongu

Gt. Fish Bay

B a r o t s e

Cunene

Sesheke

C. Frio

Owambo

Etosha
Pan

Otavi   Grootfontein

Botlet

Makgadikgadi
Salt pan

D a m a r a l a n d

A T L A N T I C   O C E A N

Swakopmund
Walvis Bay

Windhoek

B O T S W A

Tropic of Capricorn

NAMIBIA

K a l a h a r i

Hardap Dam

Nossob

Namaland

Lüderitz
Possession I.

Keetmanshoop

Karas
Mts.

Molopo

Mafikeng

Vryburg

Upington

Kimberley

Orange

Port Nolloth

Bushmanland

Orange

De Aar

Stor

Calvinia

CAPE PROV

SOUTH AFRICA

Kompasberg 2504

Graaff-Reinet

St. Helena Bay

Nuweveldberge

Karoo

Swartberg

Cape Town

Oudtshoorn

Paarl

Algoa

Table Mountain
C. of Good Hope

Mosselbaai

Port
Elizabeth

C. Agulhas

East from Greenwich

Map 136

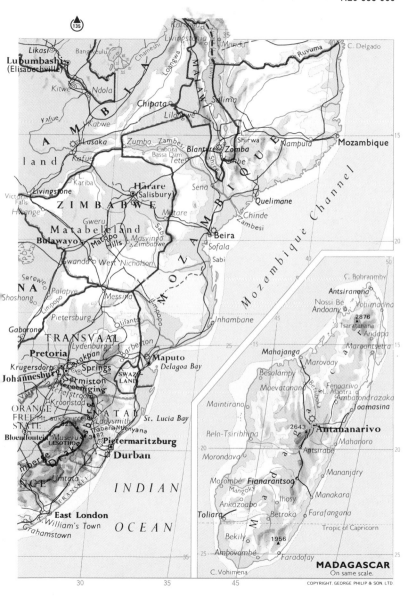

1:20 000 000

135

Likasi
Lubumbashi
(Elisabethville)
Bangweulu
Chameshi
Kitwe
Ndola
Karonga
Livingstonia
Mandu
Ruvuma
C. Delgado
Kafue
Kabwe
Chipata
Lilongwe
Salima
Z A M B I A
M A L A W I
Lusaka
Zumbu
Zambesi
Zambesi
Cabora
Bassa Dam
Blantyre
Tete
Shirwa
Zomba
Nampula
Mozambique
land
Kafue
Shire
Victoria
Falls
Livingstone
Kariba
L.
Kariba
Harare
Salisbury
Sena
Chinde
Zambesi
Quelimane
Hwange
Z I M B A B W E
Gweru
Mutare
Matabeleland
Masvingo
Z. Zimbabwe
Beira
Sofala
M O Z A M B I Q U E   C h a n n e l
Bulawayo
Matopo
Hills
Gwanda
West Nicholson
Sabi
Serowe
Palapye
Limpopo
Messina
Inhambane
C. Bobraomby
Shoshong
N A
Gaborone
Pietersburg
Olifants
Limpopo
Antsiranana
Nossi Be
Andoany
Votimadina
T R A N S V A A L
Barberton
Lydenburg
Krakpan
Mahajanga
2876
Tsaratanana
Andapa
Maroantsetra
Pretoria
Springs
Maputo
Delagoa Bay
Marovoay
Johannesburg
Germiston
Vereeniging
SWAZI-
LAND
Besalampy
Maevatanana
Fenoarivo
L. Alaotra
Ambatondrazaka
Toamasina
Chelstroom
Kroonstad
Maintirano
ORANGE
FREE
STATE
Mt. aux Sources
Ladysmith
St. Lucia Bay
2643
Antananarivo
Bloemfontein
Maseru
LESOTHO
Pietermaritzburg
Belo-Tsiribihina
Antsirabe
Mahanoro
N A T A L
Durban
Morondava
Mananjary
Umtata
I N D I A N
Mofombé
Fianarantsoa
Mangoky
Ihosy
Manakara
East London
William's Town
O C E A N
Ankazoabo
Betroka
Farafangana
Grahamstown
Toliara
Bekily
1956
Tropic of Capricorn
Ambovombe
Faradofay
C. Vohimena

MADAGASCAR
On same scale.

COPYRIGHT. GEORGE PHILIP & SON. LTD

Map 137

North America: Physical

1:60 000 000

ASIA

ARCTIC OCEAN

Greenland

Petermann's Pk. 2940

Denmark Str.

Wrangel I.

C. Dezhnev
Pt. Barrow
Bering Str.
C. Prince of Wales
St. Lawrence I.
Yukon

Beaufort Sea

Parry Is.
Sverdrup Is.
Axel Heiberg Land
Queen Elizabeth Is.
Ellesmere I.

M'Clure Str.
N.Mag. Pole
Viscount Melville Sd.
Devon I.
Lancaster Sound

Banks I.

Baffin Bay

Davis Strait

Mackenzie

Victoria I.

Baffin Island

Mt. McKinley 6194

Alaska

Arctic Circle
Gt. Bear L.
Mackenzie

Tundra

Fox Basin

Southampton

Cumberland Sd.

C. Chidley
C. Farewell

Kodiak I.
Mt. Logan 6050
St. Elias Mts.
Mt. St. Elias 5489

Coast Range

Chesterfield Inlet

Hudson Strait

Ungava Peninsula

Labrador

Hamilton Inlet

Gt. Slave L.

Hudson

Bay

Queen Charlotte Is.
Mt. Waddington 4041
Vancouver I.

Peace
Athabasca
Robson Pk. 3954
Yellowhead P.
Kicking Horse P.
Fraser

Rocky

Great

Plains

Nelson

L. Winnipeg

James Bay

Laurentian Plateau

Belle Isle Str.
Newfoundland

Athabasca L.
Saskatchewan

Columbia
Rainier 4392
Cascade Ra.
Crowsnest P.
Missouri

Mountains

L. Superior

Ottawa
St. Lawrence

G. of St. Lawrence

Cobot Str.
C. Breton I.
Nova Scotia

Mt. Shasta 4317
C. Mendocino
Snake
Gt. Salt L.

Black Hills 2207

L. Huron

Niagara Falls
L. Ontario

C. Sable

Coast Ra.
Sa. Nevada
Great Basin
Death Valley
Mt. Whitney 4418
Colorado

Gannett Pk. 4202
Long's Pk. 4345
Mt. Elbert 4399
Blanca Pk. 4364

Platte

L. Michigan

L. Erie

Appalachian Mts.

Allegheny Mts.

C. Cod

Mississippi

Ohio

Cumberland Plat.

Blue Ridge

Chesapeake B.
C. Hatteras

Colorado Plat.
Rio Grande

Llano Estacado

Ozark Plateau

Arkansas
Tennessee
Red

Mississippi

ATLANTIC OCEAN

Lower California

G. of California

Sierra Madre

Mississippi Delta

Florida

Gulf of Mexico

Rio Grande

Bahama Is.

Tropic of Cancer

Cuba
Florida Str.
Greater Antilles

Hispaniola
P. Rico

San Lucas
C. San Lucas

Mexican Plateau

Gulf of Campêche

Yucatan Strait

Yucatan

Jamaica

Revilla Gigedo
Santiago
Popocatepetl 5452
Citlaltepetl 5700

G. of Honduras

Caribbean Sea

PACIFIC OCEAN

Isthmus of Tehuantepec

Central America

Vol. Fuego 3754

L. Nicaragua

SOUTH AMERICA

West from Greenwich

COPYRIGHT. GEORGE PHILIP & SON. LTD.

Map 138

North America: Political

1:60 000 000

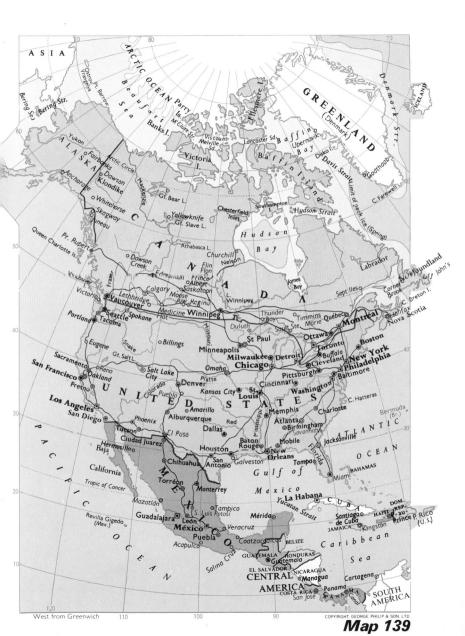

West from Greenwich

COPYRIGHT. GEORGE PHILIP & SON. LTD

Map 139

Canada: South East

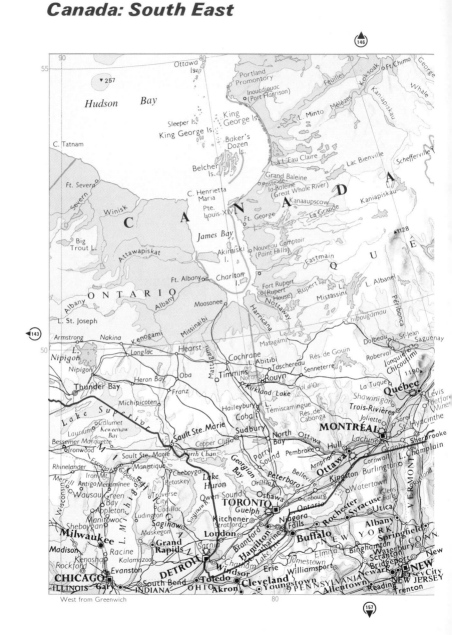

West from Greenwich

Map 140

1:15 000 000

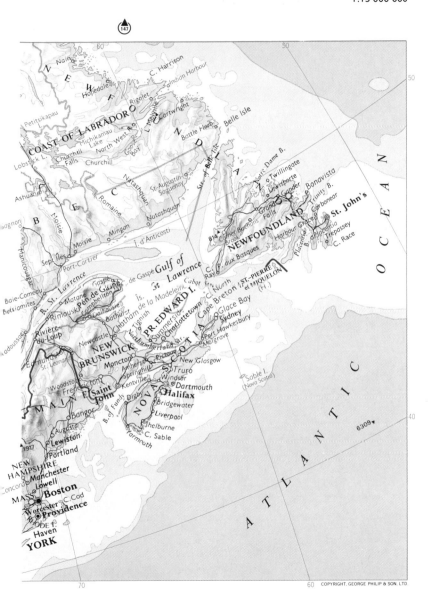

147

N E W F O U N D L A N D

Nain

Hopedale

C. Harrison

Indian Harbour

Petitsikapau

COAST OF LABRADOR

Michikamau Lake

North West R.

Churchill Falls

Churchill

Rigolet

Lewisville

Cartwright

Battle Harbour

Belle Isle

Lobstick L.

Ashuanipi

Romaine

R. Natashquan

St-Augustin Saguenay

Str. of Belle Isle

Notre Dame B.

Twillingate

Lewisporte

Bonavista

St. John's

Gagnon

Moisie

Moisie

Mingan

Notashquan

Brook

Corner Buchans

Grand

Gander

Trinity B.

Harbour Grace

Carbonear

B

Sept Îles

Port-Cartier

Î. d'Anticosti

814

NEWFOUNDLAND

Placentia

B. of Placentia

Trepassey

C. Race

Baie-Comeau

Betsiamites

R. St. Lawrence

de Gaspé

Gulf of St. Lawrence

dux Basques

C. Ray

Cabot Str.

ST-PIERRE

et MIQUELON

(Fr.)

O C E A N

Manicouagan

Matane

Pen. de Gaspé

Rimouski

Campbellton

Îs. de la Madeleine

Chatham

C. North

Cape Breton I.

A

T

L

A

N

T

I

C

Rivière-du-Loup

Dalhousie

Bathurst

Tignish

PR. EDWARD I.

Summerside

Charlottetown

Glace Bay

Sydney

Port Hawkesbury

Mulgrave

Edmundston

St. Léonard

Newcastle

NEW

BRUNSWICK

Moncton

Northumberland Str.

Pictou

N O V A   S C O T I A

New Glasgow

Sable I.

(Nova Scotia)

Woodstock

Fredericton

Springhill

Amherst

Truro

Windsor

M A I N E

Saint John

Kentville

Digby

Dartmouth

Halifax

6309

Bangor

B. of Fundy

Bridgewater

Liverpool

Augusta

Shelburne

C. Sable

Yarmouth

1917

Lewiston

NEW HAMPSHIRE

Portland

Concord

Manchester

Lowell

MASS.

Boston

Worcester

C. Cod

Providence

R. ODE I.

Haven

YORK

70

60

50

50

40

40

Map 141

141

Canada: South West and Alaska

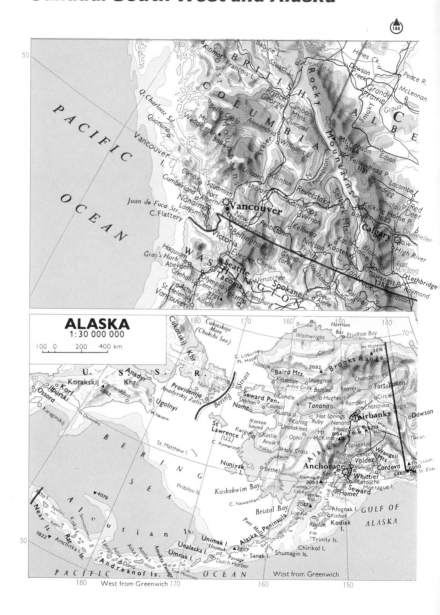

Map 142

1:15 000 000

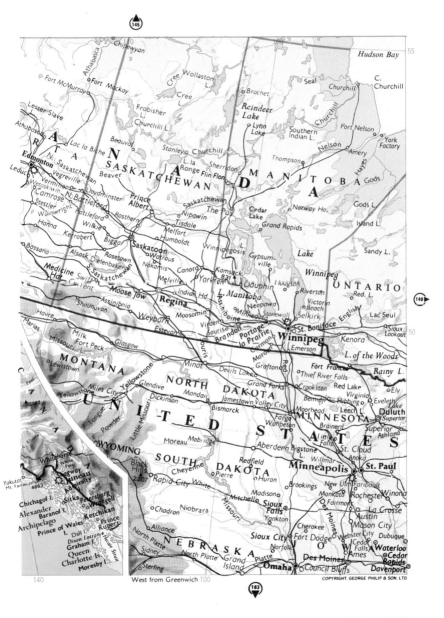

Map 143

West from Greenwich 100

Canada: North West

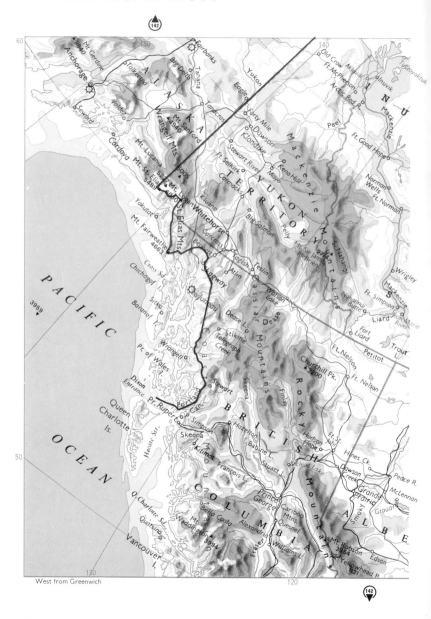

West from Greenwich

Map 144

1:15 000 000

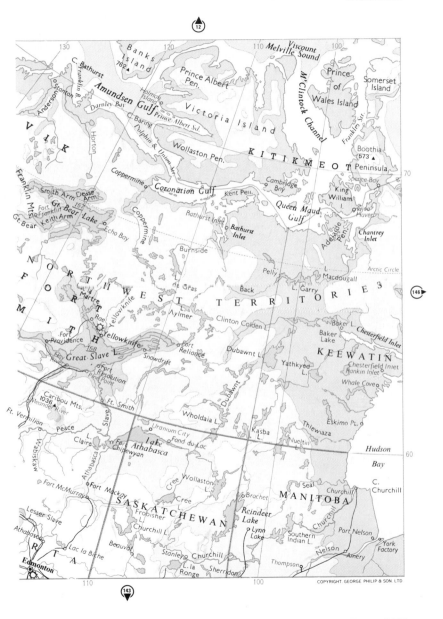

Map 145

Canada: North East

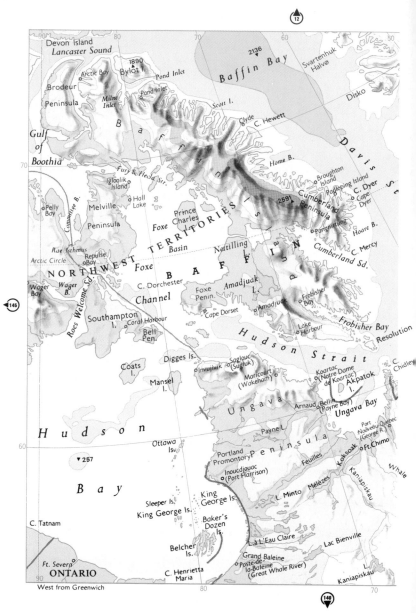

Map 146

1:15 000 000

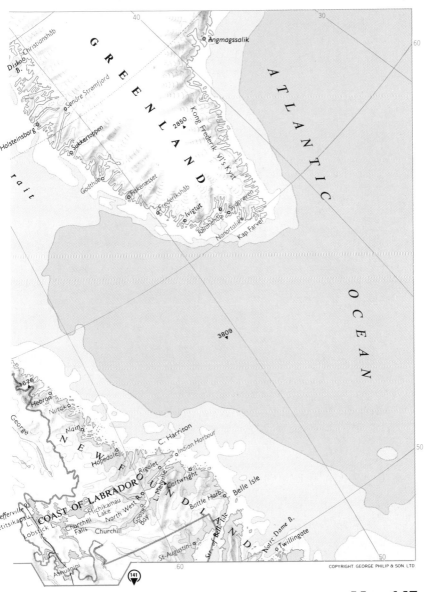

Map 147

Canada: Saint Lawrence Estuary

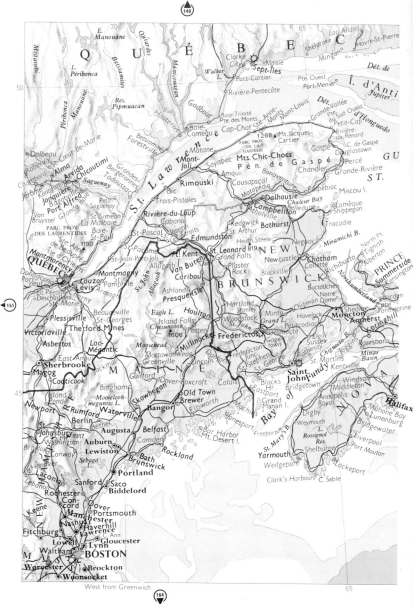

Map 148

West from Greenwich

1:7 000 000

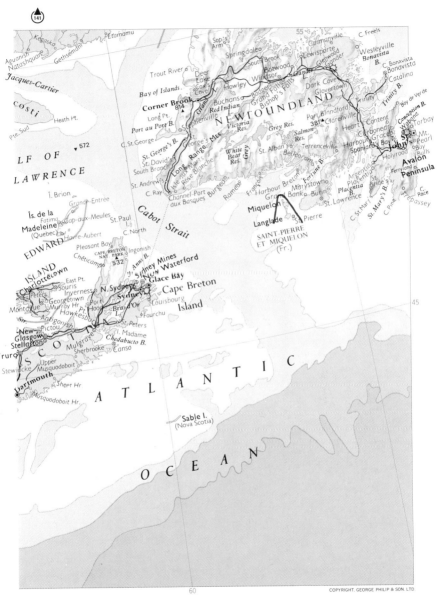

C. Freels
Kogaska
Etamamu
Sop's Arm
Cottaraville
Westeyville
Bonavista B.
Springdale
Aguanish
Natashquan
Gethsemani
South Brook
Botwood
Lewisporte
Glenwood
Gander
C. Bonavista
Bonavista
Trout River
Deer Lake
Howley
Windsor
Grand Falls
Bishop's Falls
Dark Cove
Catalina
Jacques-Cartier
Bay of Islands
Cove
Buchans
Gambo
Glovertown
Trinity
Trinity B.
Boy of Verde
Corner Brook
814
Grand
Red Indian
NEWFOUNDLAND
Port Blandford
Clarenville
381
Conception B.
costi
Heath Pt.
Stephenville
Victoria Res.
Grey Res.
Heart's Content
Carbonear
Harbour Grace
Sydney
Torbay
Pte.-Sud
572
Port au Port B.
C. St.George
St. George's B.
George's Range Mts.
White Bear Res.
Grey
St. Alban's
Salmon Res.
Belleoram
Terrenceville
Spaniard's Bay
Holyrood
St. John's
Mt. Pearl
LF OF
St. David's
South Branch
St. Andrews
Isle aux Morts
Rose Blanche
Harbour Breton
Fortune B.
Argentia
Placentia
B.
Bay Bulls
LAWRENCE
Î. Brion
Grande-Entrée
C. Ray
Channel-Port aux Basques
Burgeo
Ramea
Fromsse
Grand Banks
Marystown
Burin
St. Lawrence
Placentia
Ferryland
Avalon
Peninsula
C. Race
Îs. de la Madeleine (Quebec)
Fatima
Cap-aux-Meules
Havre-Aubert
St. Paul I.
Miquelon
St. Pierre
C. St. Mar's B.
St. Mary's B.
C. Pine
Trepassey
EDWARD
Pleasant Bay
Langlade
C. North
SAINT-PIERRE ET MIQUELON (Fr.)
ISLAND
CAPE BRETON NAT. PARK
532
Ingonish
Chéticamp
Charlottetown
St. Ann's B.
Sydney Mines
New Waterford
Glace Bay
Cape Breton
East Pt.
Souris
Inverness
N. Sydney
Sydney
Georgetown
Port Hood
Bras d'Or L.
Louisbourg
Island
Montague
Murray Hr.
Pictou
Fourchu
Peters
St. Peters
New Glasgow
Stellarton
Antigonish
SCOTIA
Î. Madame
Chedabucto B.
Canso
ruro
Mulgrave
Sherbrooke
Stewiacke
Upper Musquodoboit
ATLANTIC
Dartmouth
Sheet Hr.
Musquodoboit Hr.
Sable I. (Nova Scotia)
OCEAN
45
60

Canada: The Great Lakes

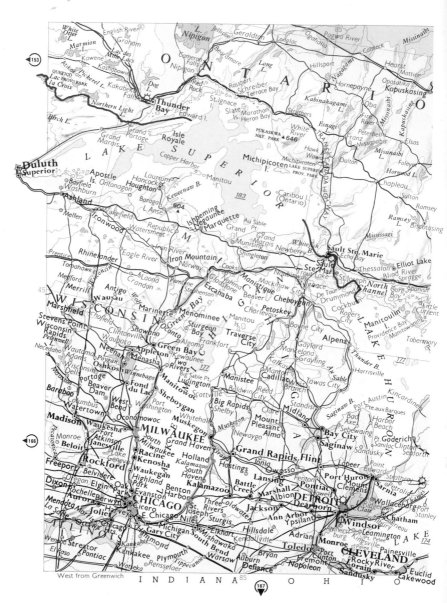

Map 150

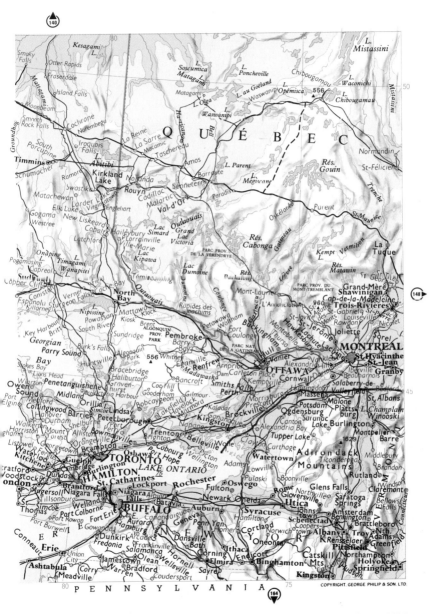

1:7 000 000

Map 151

Canada: Southern Saskatchewan and Manitoba

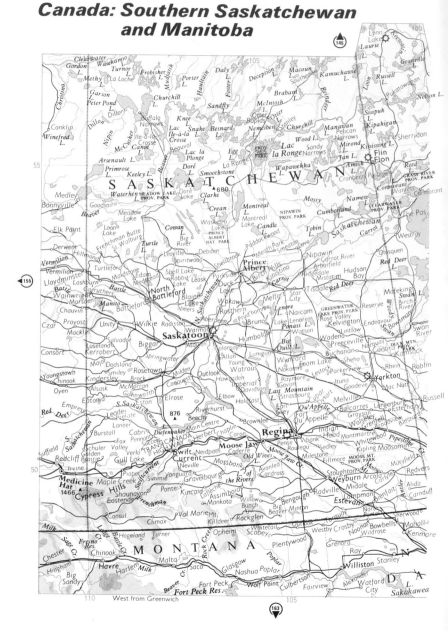

Map 152

152

1:7 000 000

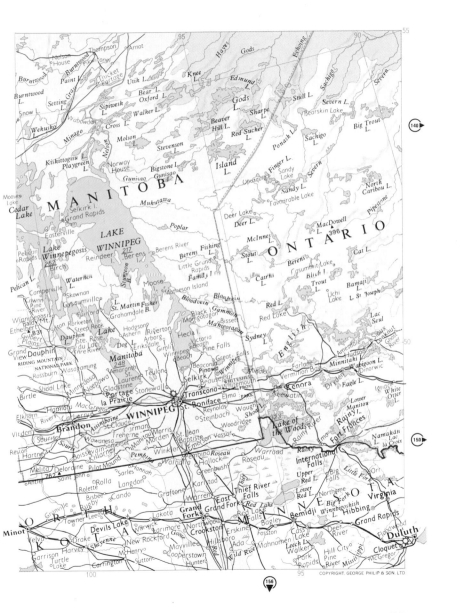

COPYRIGHT. GEORGE PHILIP & SON. LTD

Map 153

Canada: Southern British Columbia and Alberta

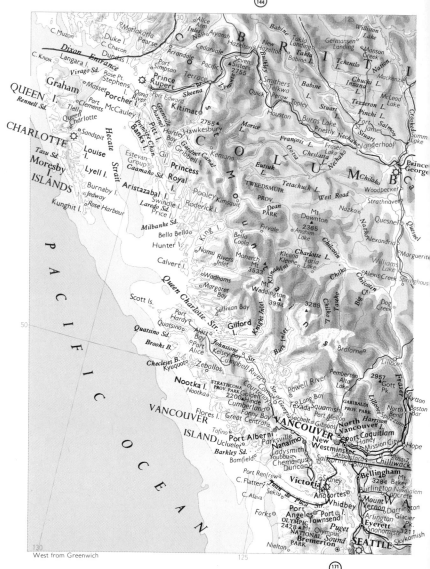

Map 154

1:7 000 000

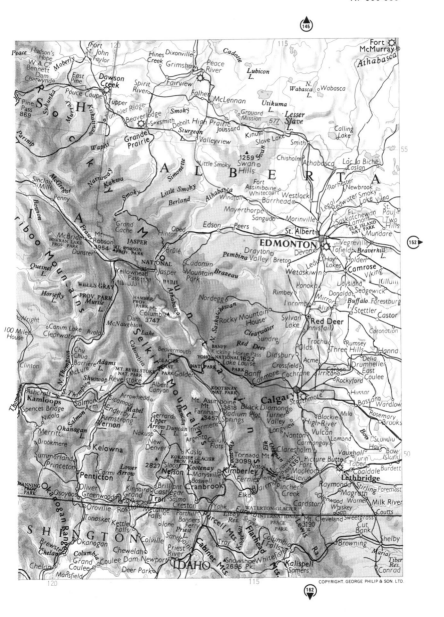

Map 155

U.S.A.: North East

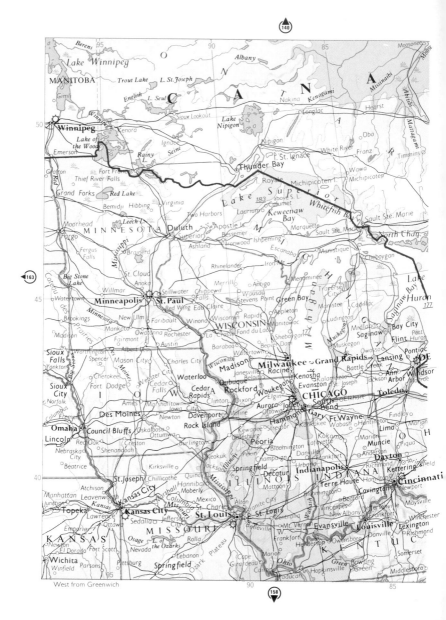

Map 156

1:12 000 000

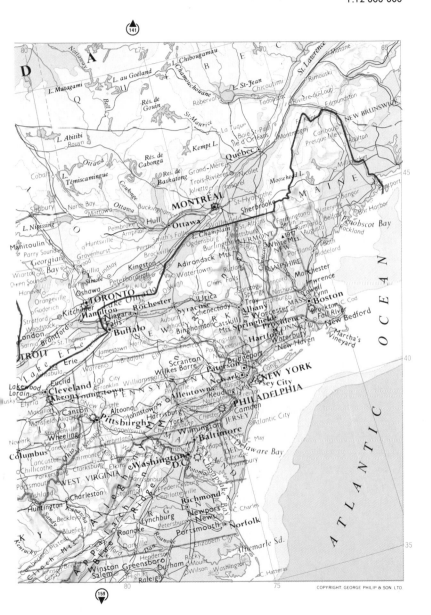

D A

Nottaway
L. au Goéland
L. Chibougamau
B F C
St-Jean
Chicoutimi
Rés. de
Gouin
Roberval
Rimouski
St. Lawrence
Matane

L. Matagami

Bell

Rés. de
Gouin
St-Maurice
Tadoussac
Rivière-du-Loup
Edmundston
NEW BRUNSWICK

L. Abitibi
Bouyn
La Tuque
Baie St-Paul
Île d'Orléans
Montmagny
Caribou
Presque Isle
Houlton

Ottawa
Rés. de
Cabonga
Kempt L.
Québec
45

Cobalt
L.
Témiscamingue
Coulonge
Rés. de
Baskatong
Grand-Mère
Trois-Rivières
Nicolet
Sorel
Moosehead L.
M A I N E
Millm
eport

Sudbury
North Bay
Marrows
Ottawa
Buckingham
MONTREAL
St-Hyacinthe
Sherbrooke
Bangor
Bar Harbor

L. Nipissing
Pembroke
Hull
Ottawa
Arnprior
Smith's Falls
Perth
St. Albans
Pittsford
VERMONT
Berlin
Rumford
Augusta
Waterv
Belfast
Penobscot Bay
Rockland

Manitoulin
Huntsville
L. Champlain
Ogdensburg
Burlington
White Mts.
NEW
HAMPSHIRE
Portland
Bath
Biddeford

Parry Sound
Gravenhurst
wood
Adirondack Mts.
Watertown
Barre
Concord
Manchester
O C E A N

Georgian
Bay
Orillia
Lindsay
Kingston
Rutland
Laconia
Nashua
Lowell
Lawrence
Lynn

Wiarton
Owen Sound
Simcoe
Peterborough
Oswego
Rome
Utica
Saratoga
Springs
Troy
Fitchburg
MASS.
Boston
C. Cod

Hanover
Orangeville
Oshawa
TORONTO
Lake Ontario
Rochester
Syracuse
Auburn
Schenectady
Albany
Worcester
Brockton
Fall River

Goderich
Stratford
Kitchener
Hamilton
Niagara
Falls
Y O R K
Binghamton
Catskill
Mts.
Springfield
Providence
New Bedford

Woodstock
London
Brantford
St. Thomas
Buffalo
N E W
Ithaca
Poughkeepsie
Hartford
CONN.
Waterbury
New Haven
Martha's
Vineyard

Sarnia
Erie
Jamestown
Hornell
Kingston
Bridgeport
Long
ROIT
Lake Erie
Ashtabula
Bradford
Scranton
Wilkes Barre
Paterson
Yonkers
Island
40

Lakewood
Euclid
Cleveland
Warren
Oil City
Franklin
Williamsport
Newark
Jersey City
NEW YORK

Lorain
Elyria
Akron
Youngstown
P E N N S Y L V A N I A
Allentown
Reading
Trenton
Philadelphia

Massillon
Canton
New Castle
Johnstown
Altoona
Harrisburg
Lancaster
York
Chester
Camden
JERSEY
Atlantic City

Columbus
Zanesville
Pittsburgh
Connellsville
Chambersburg
Wilmington
Baltimore
May

Lancaster
Ohio
Fairmont
Cumberland
M D
Annapolis
Delaware Bay

Chillicothe
Clarksburg
Elkins
Washington
D.C.
Cambridge

Portsmouth
WEST VIRGINIA
Harrisonburg
Fredericksburg
Salisbury
Chesapeake

Ashland
Charleston
Staunton
Charlottesville
Richmond
C. Charles

Huntington
Beckley
Roanoke
Lynchburg
Newport
News
Portsmouth
Norfolk

K Y
Bluefield
Roanoke
Danville
Elizabeth City
Albemarle Sd.

Winston
Salem
Greensboro
Durham
Wilson
Washington
C. Hatteras

High Pt.
Raleigh
80
75

Map 157

U.S.A.: South East

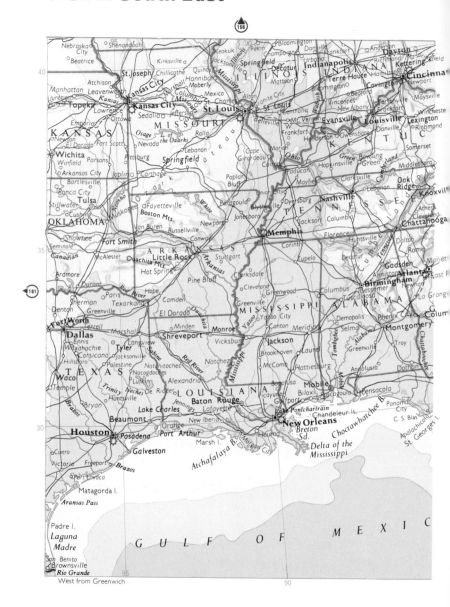

Map 158

1:12 000 000

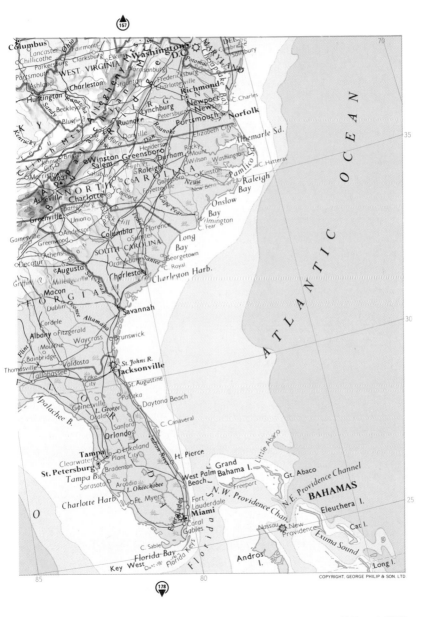

Map 159

U.S.A.: South West and Hawaii

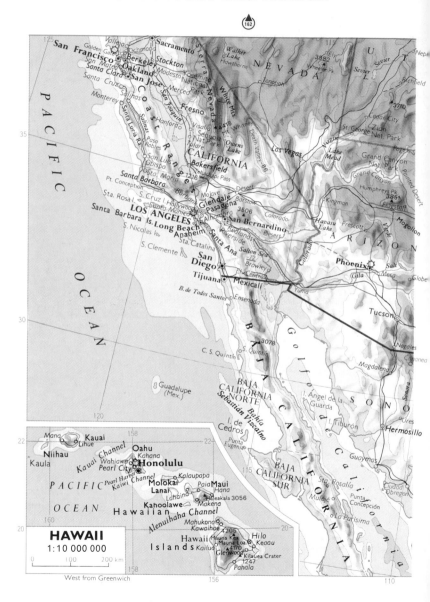

162

HAWAII
1:10 000 000

0   100   200 km

West from Greenwich

Map 160

1:12 000 000

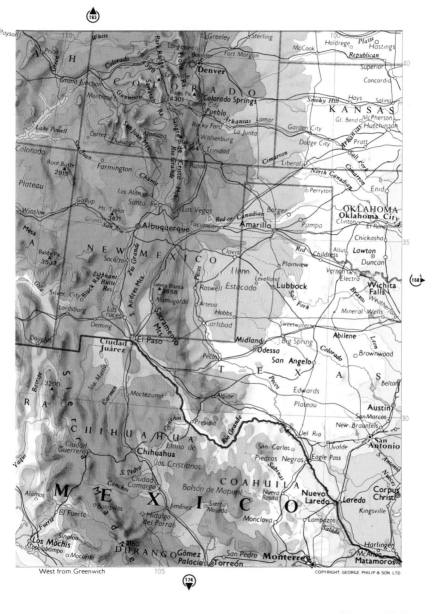

COPYRIGHT. GEORGE PHILIP & SON. LTD

Map 161

U.S.A.: North West

142

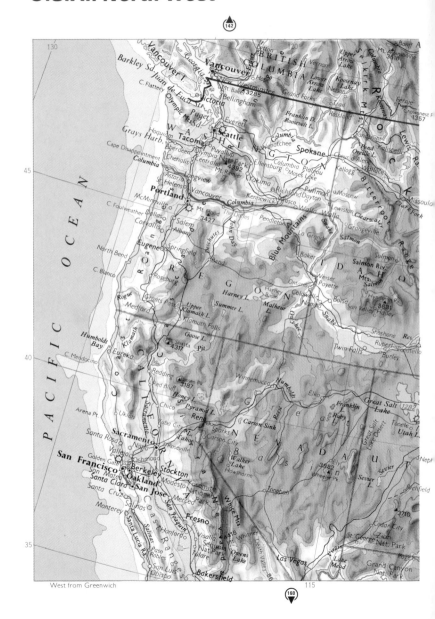

West from Greenwich

180

Map 162

1:12 000 000

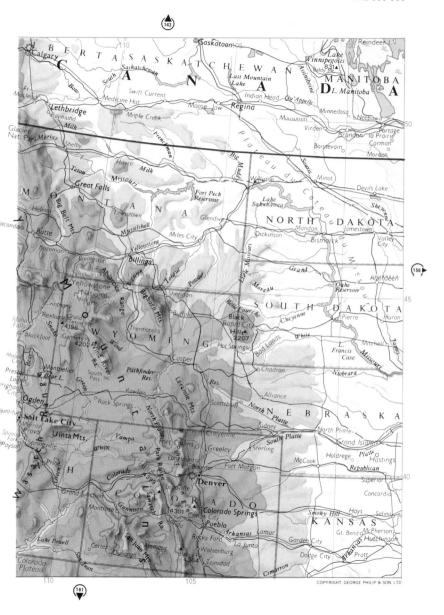

Map 163

U.S.A.:

Boston, New York, Washington

1:6 000 000

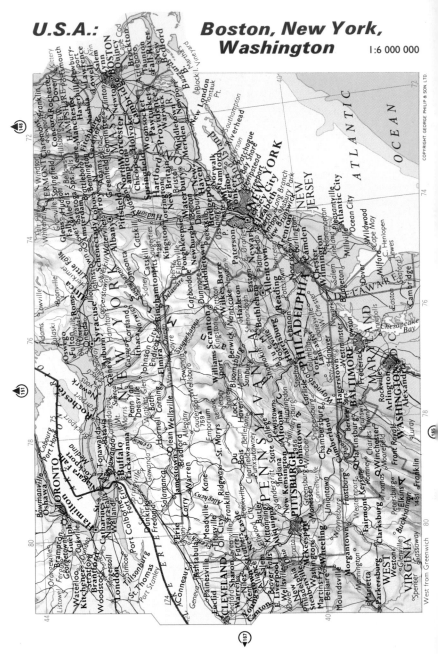

West from Greenwich

Map 164

U.S.A.: *Washington, Atlanta*

1:6 000 000

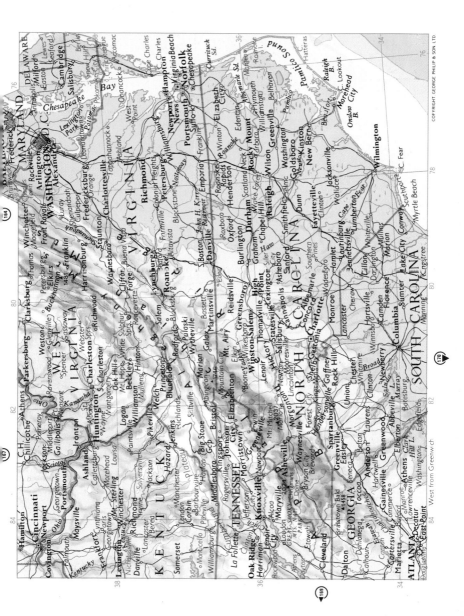

COPYRIGHT GEORGE PHILIP & SON LTD

West from Greenwich

Map 165

U.S.A.: Upper Mississippi

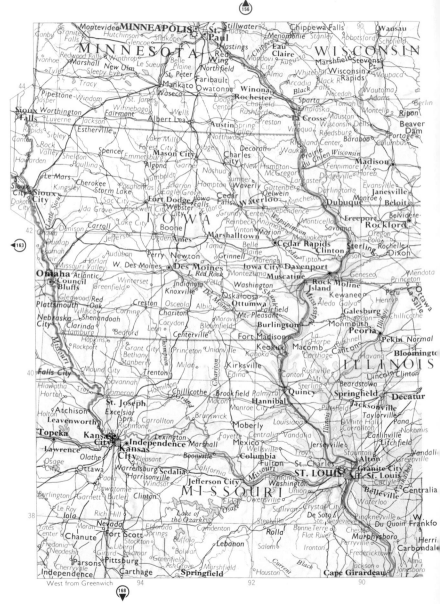

Map 166

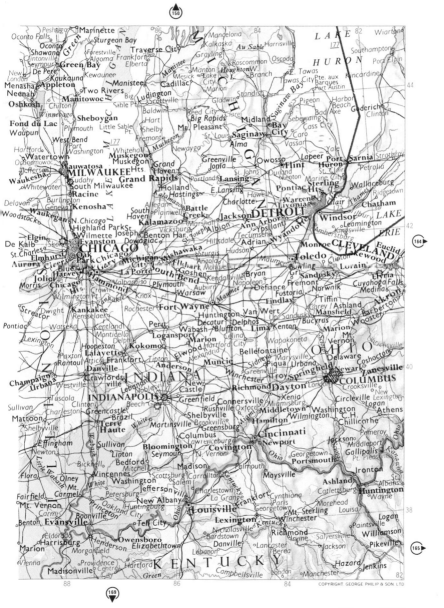

1:6 000 000

Map 167

U.S.A.: Lower Mississippi and Gulf Coast

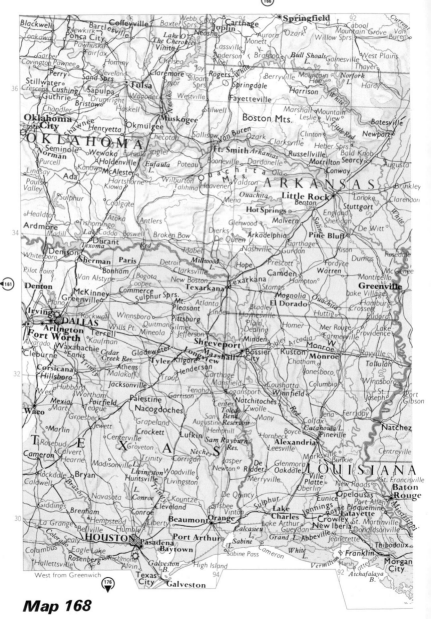

West from Greenwich

Map 168

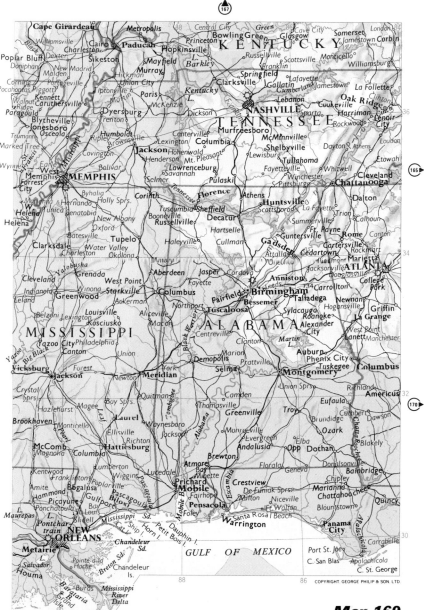

1:6 000 000

GULF OF MEXICO

COPYRIGHT GEORGE PHILIP & SON LTD

Map 169

U.S.A.: *Florida*

1:6 000 000

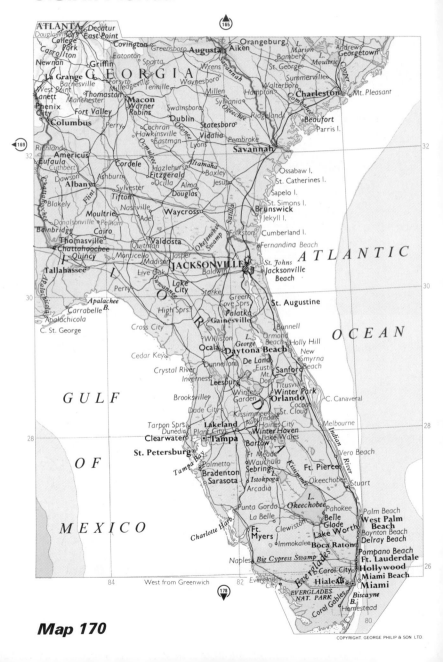

Map 170

U.S.A.: *Columbia Basin*

1:6 000 000

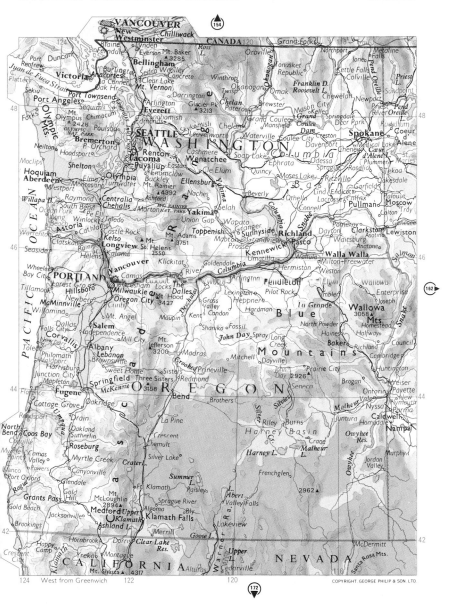

COPYRIGHT. GEORGE PHILIP & SON LTD.

Map 171

U.S.A.: California

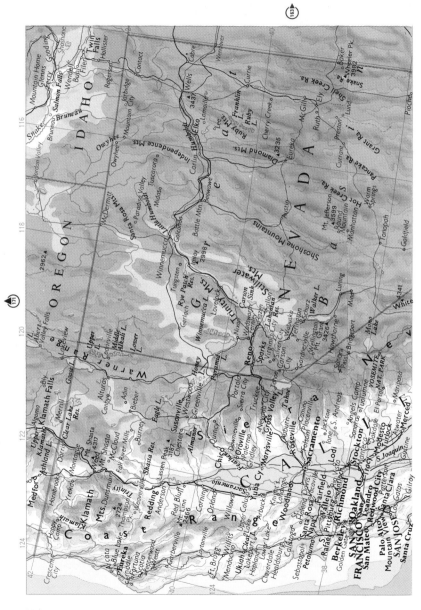

Map 172

1:6 000 000

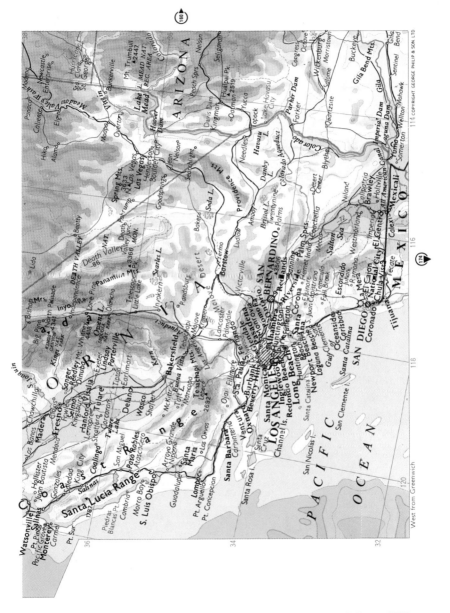

Map 173

Mexico: West

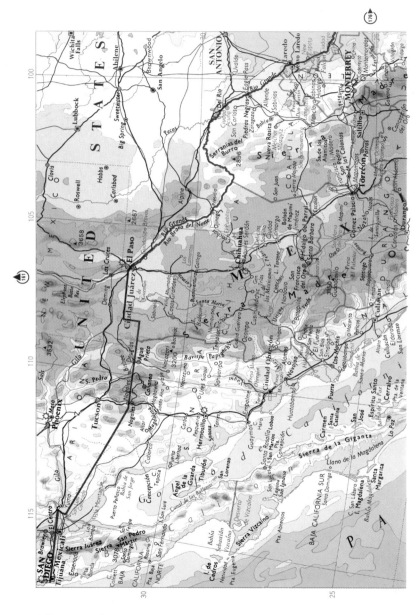

Map 174

1:12 000 000

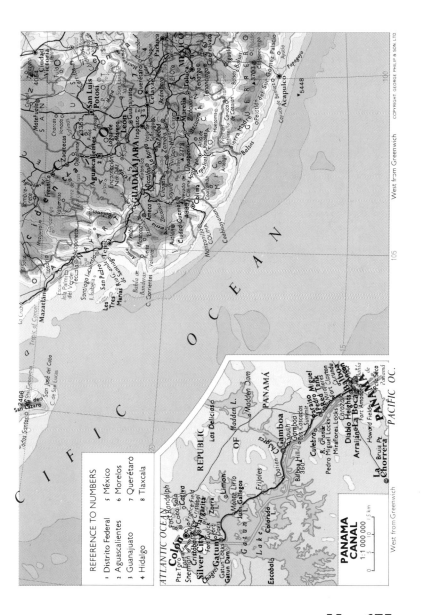

West from Greenwich

COPYRIGHT GEORGE PHILIP & SON LTD

REFERENCE TO NUMBERS

1 Distrito Federal 5 México
2 Aguascalientes   6 Morelos
3 Guanajuato   7 Querétaro
4 Hidalgo   8 Tlaxcala

PANAMA
CANAL
1:1 000 000
0 5   5 km

West from Greenwich

Map 175

Mexico: East

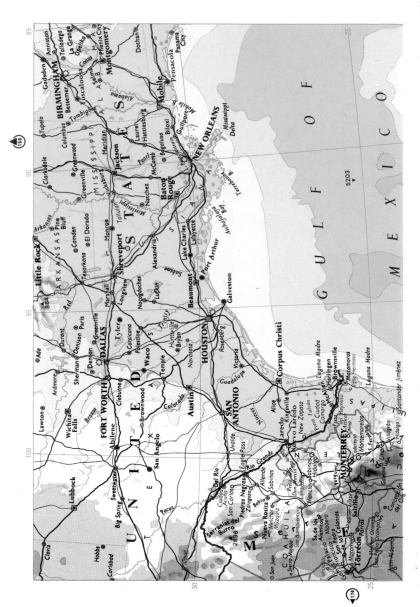

Map 176

1:12 000 000

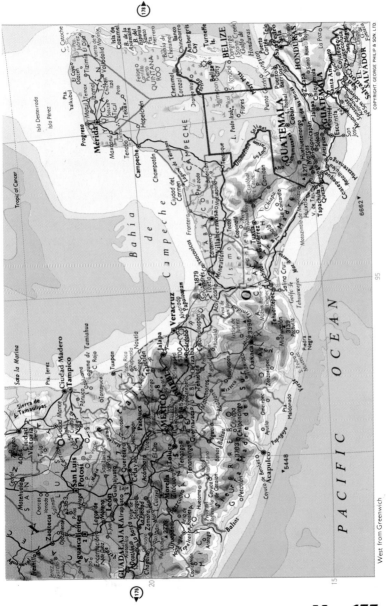

West from Greenwich

COPYRIGHT GEORGE PHILIP & SON. LTD.

Map 177

Caribbean: West

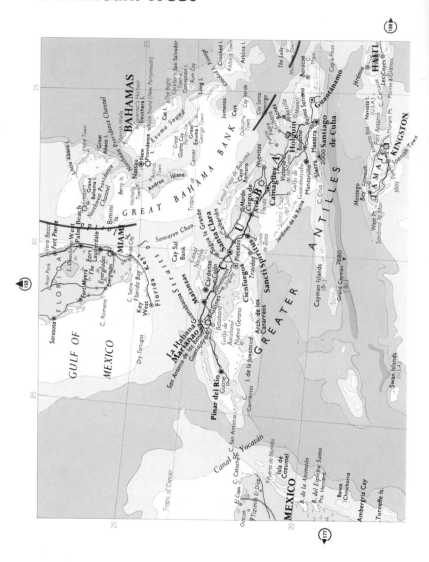

Map 178

1:12 000 000

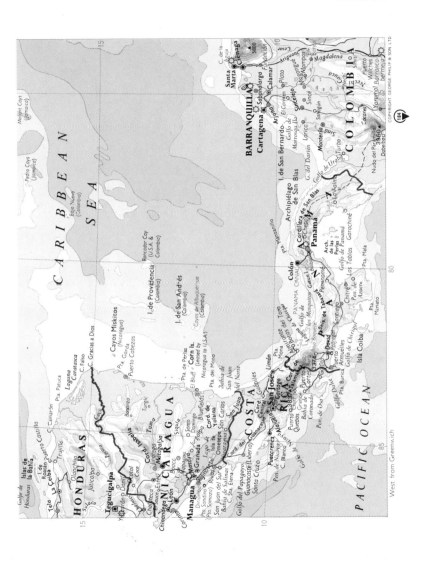

Map 179

Caribbean: East

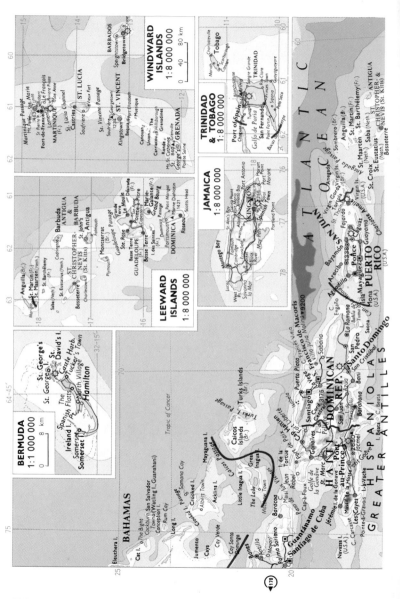

BERMUDA
1:1 000 000
0   8 km

St. George's
St. George's
St. David's I.
The
Castle Harb.
Ireland I.
Spanish Flatts
Tucker's Town
Somerset I.
North Village
Somerset
Hamilton

LEEWARD ISLANDS
1:8 000 000

Anguilla (Br.)
St. Martin (Fr.)
St. Maarten (Neth.)
Marigot
Saba (Neth.)
St. Eustatius (Neth.)
ST. CHRISTOPHER-NEVIS (St. Kitts)
Basseterre
Charlestown
Codrington
Barbuda
ANTIGUA & BARBUDA
Antigua
St. John's
Montserrat
Plymouth
Falmouth
GUADELOUPE (Fr.)
Basse Terre
Basse Terre
Grande Terre
Pointe-à-Pitre
Marie Galante (Fr.)
Grand Bourg
DOMINICA
Portsmouth
Morne Diablotin 1421
Roseau
Scotts Head
Ste. Rose
La Soufrière
Capesterre
Dominica Passage
Guadeloupe Passage
St. Louis
Désirade (Fr.)
Le Moule
Mont Morget

WINDWARD ISLANDS
1:8 000 000
0   40   80 km

BARBADOS
Speightstown
Bridgetown
St. Marie
Ste. Marie
MARTINIQUE
Mt. Pelée
St. Pierre
Fort-de-France
Lamentin
Le Lorrain
Le François
Le Robert
Le Marin
Ste. Anne
Rivière Pilote
St. Lucia Channel
ST. LUCIA
Castries
Soufrière
Vieux Fort
St. Vincent Passage
ST. VINCENT
Kingstown
Bequia
Port Elizabeth
Mustique
Bequia Channel
Canouan
Carriacou
Union I.
Ronde I.
St. George's
Pointe Saline
GRENADA
Mt. St. Catherine 840

TRINIDAD & TOBAGO
1:8 000 000

Tobago
Charlotteville
Scarborough
Plymouth
Roxborough
Moruga
TRINIDAD
Port of Spain
Arima
Sangre Grande
Guanoguayare
Tunapuna
San Fernando
Princes Town
Point Fortin
Siparia
Rio Claro
Galeota Point
Punta de Icacos
Gulf of Paria
Golfo de Paria
Bocas del Dragón

JAMAICA
1:8 000 000

Montego Bay
Falmouth
Lucea
Savanna-la-Mar
Negril
West Pt.
Spanish Town
KINGSTON
Portland Point
Portland Bight
May Pen
Mandeville
Ocho Rios
Port Maria
Port Antonio
Morant Bay
St. Ann's Bay
Morant
Port Morant
Old Harbour

ATLANTIC OCEAN

ATLANTIC

Anegada
Virgin Gorda
Virgin Is. (Br.)
Tortola
St. Thomas (Neth.)
St. John (U.S.A.)
St. Croix (U.S.A.)
Virgin Islands (U.S.A.)
Sombrero (Br.)
Anguilla (Br.)
St. Martin (Fr.)
St. Maarten (Neth.)
St. Barthélemy (Fr.)
Saba (Neth.)
St. Eustatius (Neth.)
ST. CHRISTOPHER-NEVIS (St. Kitts)
Basseterre
ANTIGUA
Bassa Seca
PUERTO RICO (U.S.A.)
San Juan
Bayamón
Arecibo
Aguadilla
Mayagüez
Ponce
Guayama
Fajardo
Caguas
Humacao
El Yunque 1338
Isla de Mona
Mona Passage

HISPANIOLA
DOMINICAN REP.
Santo Domingo
San Cristóbal
San Pedro
La Romana
Higüey
Hato Mayor
Seibo
El Seibo
Bani
Azua
Barahona
Neiba
Elías Piña
San Juan
Bonao
La Vega
Santiago
Puerto Plata
Monte Cristi
Dajabón
San Francisco de Macorís
Cordillera Central 3175
Pico Duarte 3175
Francisco Vieo
Villa Julia
Molina 9200
C. Engaño
Sabana
Saona
C. Beata
Pedernales
I. Beata

HAITI
Port-au-Prince
Cap-Haïtien
Gonaïves
St. Marc
Jacmel
Jérémie
Les Cayes
Môle-St.-Nicolas
Golfe de la Gonâve
Île de la Gonâve
I. de la Tortue (Fr.)
Massif de la Hotte
Pointe-à-Gravois
C. Carcasse
Navassa I. (U.S.A.)
Les Coyes
Île-à-Vache
I. Tiburon

GREATER ANTILLES

BAHAMAS
Eleuthera I.
Cat I.
The Bight
Cockburn Town
San Salvador (Watling I., Guanahani)
Conception I.
Long I.
Rum Cay
Crooked I.
Acklins I.
Albert Town
Long Cay
Samana Cay
Mayaguana I.
Caicos Islands (Br.)
Turks Islands (Br.)
Grand Turk
Matthew Town
Little Inagua I.
Great Inagua I.
The Lakes
Crooked I. Passage
Mayaguana Passage
Caicos Passage
Turks I. Passage
Jumento Cays
Cay Verde
Cay Santo Domingo

GUANTÁNAMO
Santiago de Cuba
Guantánamo
Bayamo
Antilla
Mayarí
Palma Soriano
Baracoa
Bordcoa

Tropic of Cancer

178

1:12 000 000

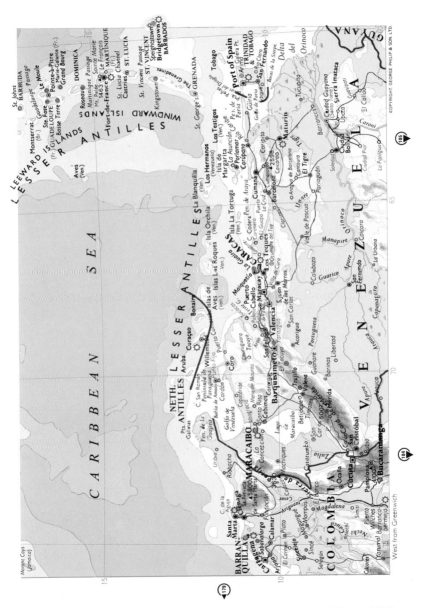

COPYRIGHT GEORGE PHILIP & SON LTD.

Map 181

South America: Physical

1:50 000 000

Curaçao (Neth.)

Trinidad

G. of
Darien

▲ 5800

Cord. de Mérida

Orinoco

Llanos

Kaieteur Falls

Sa. Pacaraima

Roraima
▲ 2810

Demerara

Courantyne

Surinam

G u i a n a

Sa. de
Tumucumaque

Amazon

Marajó I.

Pará

Equator

Casiquiare

Orinoco

Essequibo

Cotopaxi
▲ 5897

Chimborazo
▲ 6267

Putumayo

Japurá

Negro

Pta. Pariñas

Marañón

Ucayali

Amazon

S e l v a s

Purus

Madeira

S. Antônio
Falls

Aripuana

Tapajós

Xingu

Tocantins

Parnaíba

C. de São Roque

C. Branco

▲ 6768

Guaporé

São Francisco

Plateau of
Mato Grosso

Brazilian Highlands

L. Titicaca

Illampu Ancohuma
▲ 6550

Bolivian Plateau

Pilcomayo

Sa. da
Mantiqueira
▲ 2890

C. Frio

Tropic of Capricorn

8050

Juramiu Desert

Gran Chaco

Paraguay

Paraná

Sa. do Mar

Iguaçu
Falls

Ojos del Solado
▲ 6863

Pampas

Uruguay

Entre Rios

Lagoa
dos Patos

Aconcagua
▲ 6960

Juan
Fernández

Colorado

Rio de la Plata

Pta. Mogotes

A T L A N T I C

Negro

Chiloé

G. of San Matías

Valdés Pen.

Chubut

Chonos
Arch.

G. of San Jorge

O C E A N

6212
▼

P A C I F I C   O C E A N

A n d e s

P a t a g o n i a

▲ 4058

West from Greenwich

Magellan's Str.

Falkland Is.

Tierra del Fuego

C. Froward

Staten I.

C. Horn

COPYRIGHT GEORGE PHILIP & SON LTD

Map 182

South America: 1:50 000 000
Political

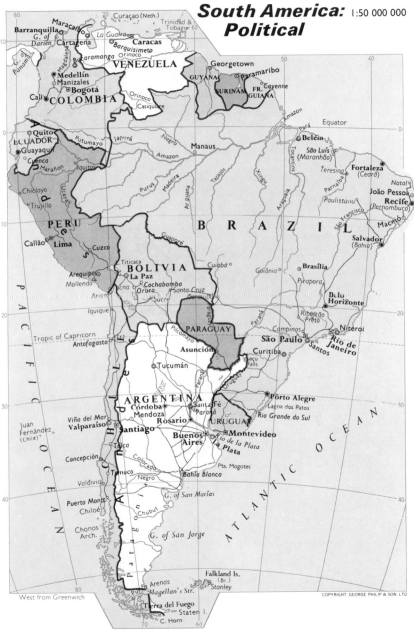

80
Barranquilla
Maracaibo
Curaçao (Neth.)
70
Trinidad & Tobago
60
G. of
Darién
La Guaira
Cartagena
10
Barquisimeto
Caracas
Bucaramanga
Orinoco
VENEZUELA
Georgetown
50
40
Medellín
GUYANA
Paramaribo
Manizales
SURINAM
FR.
Cayenne
Cali
Bogotá
SURINAM
GUIANA
COLOMBIA
Casiquiare
Amazon
Pará
Equator
0
Quito
Putumayo
Japurá
Negro
Manaus
Belém
0
ECUADOR
São Luís
(Maranhão)
Guayaquil
Amazon
Tocantins
Cuenca
Marañón
Iquitos
Teresina
Fortaleza
(Ceará)
Chiclayo
Ucayali
Purus
Madeira
Tapajós
Xingu
Natal
Trujillo
Parnaíba
João Pessoa
PERU
Araguaia
Paulistana
Recife
(Pernambuco)
Maceió
10
B   R   A   Z   I   L
10
Callao
Lima
Cuzco
Guaporé
São Francisco
Salvador
(Bahia)
Titicaca
Cuiabá
BOLIVIA
Arequipa
La Paz
Goiânia
Brasília
Mollendo
Cochabamba
Pirapora
Arica
Oruro
Santa Cruz
B lo
Sucre
Horizonte
Iquique
Ribeirão
Preto
20
Tropic of Capricorn
Pilcomayo
PARAGUAY
Paraná
Campinas
Niteroi
20
Antofagasta
Asunción
São Paulo
Santos
Rio de
Janeiro
Iguacu
Falls
Curitiba
Tucumán
Paraná
ARGENTINA
Uruguay
Pôrto Alegre
Córdoba
Santa Fé
Lagoa dos Patos
30
Viña del Mar
Mendoza
Paraná
Rio Grande do Sul
30
Valparaíso
Rosario
URUGUAY
Juan
Fernández
(Chile)
Santiago
Buenos
Montevideo
Talca
Aires
Rio de la Plata
La Plata
Concepción
Colorado
Pta. Mogotes
Temuco
Bahía Blanca
Valdivia
Negro
40
Puerto Montt
G. of San Matías
40
Chiloé
Chubut
Chonos
Arch.
G. of San Jorge
80
West from Greenwich
Arenas
Falkland Is.
(Br.)
Stanley
Magellan's Str.
70
60
P   A   C   I   F   I   C   O   C   E   A   N

A   T   L   A   N   T   I   C   O   C   E   A   N

Tierra del Fuego
Staten I.
C. Horn

COPYRIGHT GEORGE PHILIP & SON LTD

Map 183

South America: North West

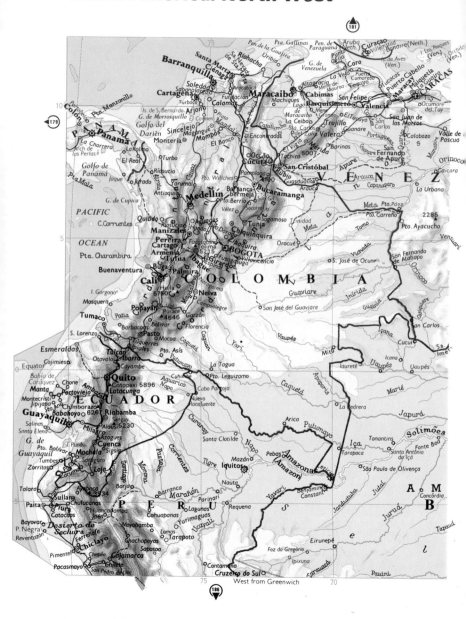

Map 184

1:16 000 000

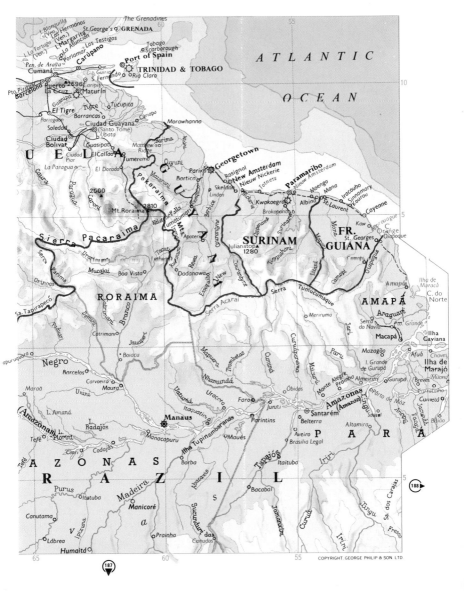

The Grenadines
I. Blanquilla
(Ven.) Los Hermanos
(Ven.) I. Margarita St.George's GRENADA
I. La Tortuga (Ven.) La Asunción
(Ven.) Porlamar Los Testigos
Pen. de Araya Tobago
Scarborough
Cumaná Carúpano Port of Spain
Pto. Píritu Barcelona S. Fernando TRINIDAD & TOBAGO
La Cruz 2696 Caripito Rio Claro
El Tigre Maturín
Soledad Barrancas Tigre Tucupita
Ciudad Guayana Caripo
Ciudad (Santo Tomé) Morawhanna
Bolívar Ubata
Ciudad Guasipati
Piar El Callao Matthews
La Paragua El Dorado Ridge
2500 Bartica Georgetown
Mt.Roraima 2810 Parika Rosignol
New Amsterdam
Nieuw Nickerie
Kaieteur Falls Linden Skeldon Totness Paramaribo
Nieuw Amsterdam
SIERRA Pacaraima Mts. Apoterí Moengo Mana
Sierra Pacaraima Julianatop Albina St. Laurent Iracoubo
1280 Sinnamary
VENEZUELA Cayenne
Caura Paragua Caroní FR. Kaw Cayenne
Orinoco GUYANA SURINAM GUIANA Orange C.
Mucajai Boa Vista Dadanawa St. Georges
RORAIMA Serra Acaraí Serra Tumucumaque AMAPÁ
Sa. Tapirapecó Serra Meruma Araguari
Parima do Navio Pta. Grande
Catrimani Branco Jatapú Macapá
Jauaperi Ilha
Caviana
Negro Mapuera Trombetas Mazagão Afuá
Barcelos Catumá I. Grande Gurupá Ilha de
Carvoeiro Moura de Gurupá Almeirim Gurupá Marajó
Maraã Uatumã Nhamundá Óbidos Monte Alegre Prainho Breves
Unini Uraçará Faro Santarém Porto de Móz Curralinho
Amanã Itaquatiara Juruti Amazonas Cametá
L. Badajós Parintins Belterra (Amazon)
Tefé Florinú Manaus Altamira
Coari Manacapuru Maués Aveiro PARÁ
Codajás Ilha Tupinambaranas Brasília Legal
AMAZONAS Borba Parintins
BRAZIL Tapajós Itaituba Iriri
Purus Itatuba Madeira Tapajós
Manicoré Bacabal
Canutama Aripuanã Jamanxim
Lábrea Humaitá Prainha Sucunduri das
Canudas Curuá Sa. dos Carajás
Xingu
Fresco

Map 185

South America: West

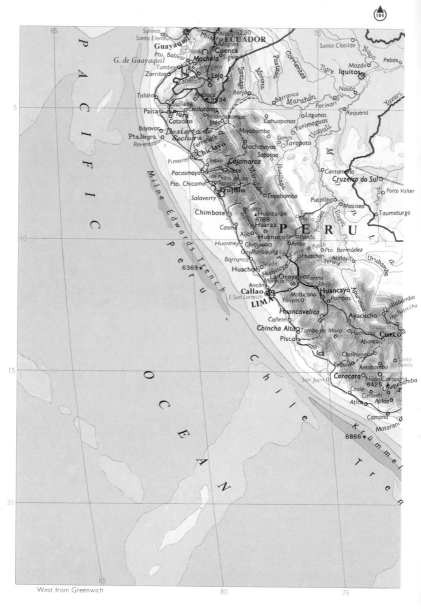

West from Greenwich

Map 186

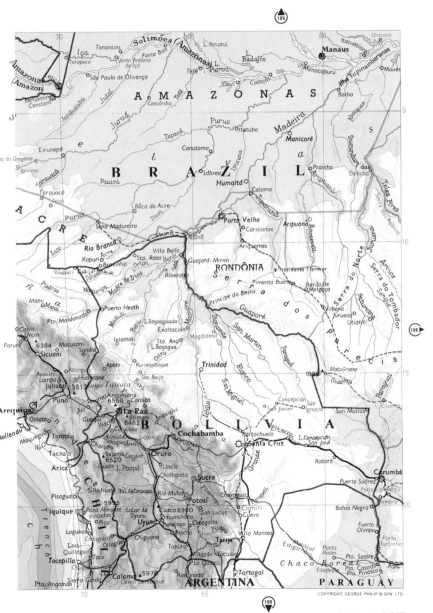

1:16 000 000

Map 187

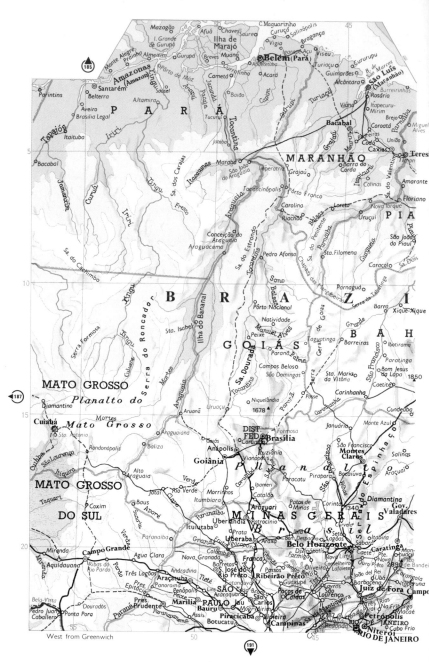

Map 188

West from Greenwich

South America: East

1:16 000 000

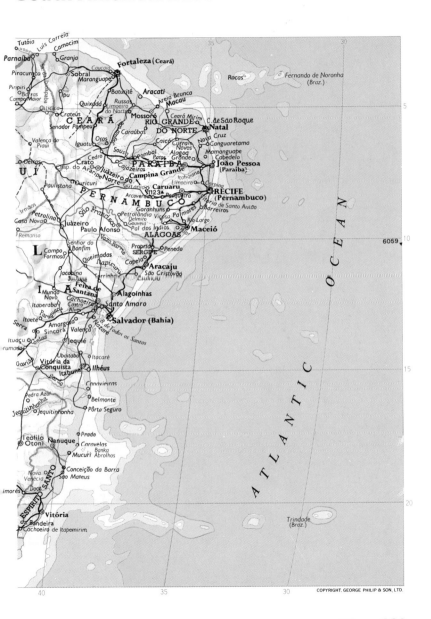

Tutóia · Luís Correia · Camocim
Parnaíba · Granja · Caucaia · Fortaleza (Ceará)
Piracuruca · Sobral · Maranguape
Piripiri · Ipu · Baturité · Aracati
Barras · Campo Maior · Quixadá · Russas · Macau
Oiticica · Limoeiro do Norte
Crateús · Mossoró · Ceará Mirim · C. de São Roque
Senador Pompeu · CEARÁ · RIO GRANDE · Natal
Caraúbas · DO NORTE
Valença do Piauí · Iguatu · Orós · Caicó · Currais Novos · Cruz
Souza · Canguaretama
Oeiras · Cedro · Pombal · Patos · Alagoa Grande · Mamanguape · Cabedelo
U I · Crato · Juazeiro · Chap. do Araripe · Norte · Cajazeiros · PARAÍBA · João Pessoa (Paraíba)
Paulistana · Ouricuri · Campina Grande · Itabaiana
Limoeiro · Surping
Sertania · Caruaru · RECIFE (Pernambuco)
Irmãos · PERNAMBUCO · Arcoverde · 1123 · Pesqueira · Vitória de Santo Antão
Petrolina · Petrolândia · Garanhuns · Viçosa · Palmares · Barreiros
Casa Nova · Juàzeiro · São Francisco · Delmiro · Gouveia · Rio Largo
Remanso · Paulo Afonso · Pal dos Índios · Maceió
L · Senhor do Bonfim · Vaza-Barris · ALAGOAS · Propriá · Penedo
Campo Formoso · Queimadas · SERGIPE
Itapicuru · Capela
Jacobina · Jaguaripe · Esplinciu · Aracaju
Juacuíba · São Cristóvão
I · A · Santana · Alagoinhas
Munda Novo · Feira de
Itaberaba · Cachoeira · Castro Alves · Santo Amaro
Paraguaçu · Valença
Itaeté · Amargosa · Sincorá · B. de Todos os Santos · Salvador (Bahia)
Serra · Contas · Nazaré
Ituaçu · Jequié
rumado · Gavião · Ubaitaba · Itacaré
Vitória da Conquista · Ilhéus
Itabuna
Pardo · Canavieiras
Pedra Azul · Belmonte
Jequitinhonha · Jequitinhonha · Pôrto Seguro
Teófilo Otoni · Nanuque · Prado
Banka · Caravelas
Mucuri · Abrolhos
Nova Venécia · Conceição da Barra · São Mateus
imorés · Doce · ESPÍRITO SANTO
Vitória · Bandeira
Cachoeira de Itapemirim

Rocas
Fernando de Noronha (Braz.)

A T L A N T I C   O C E A N

6059

Trindade (Braz.)

35   30   5   10   15   20   40   35   30

Map 189

South America: Central

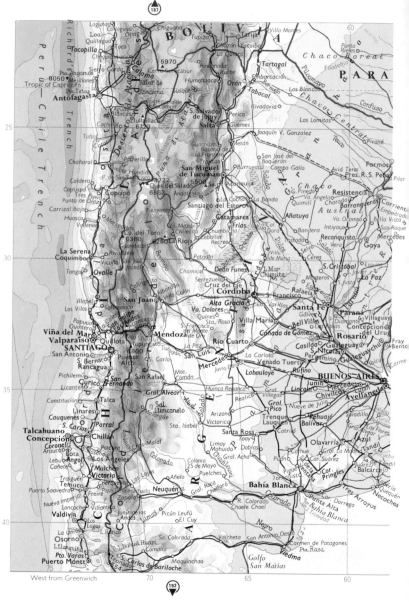

Map 190

1:16 000 000

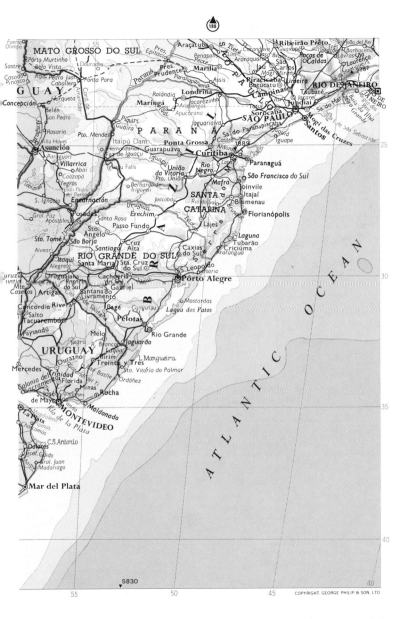

Map 191

South America: South

1:16 000 000

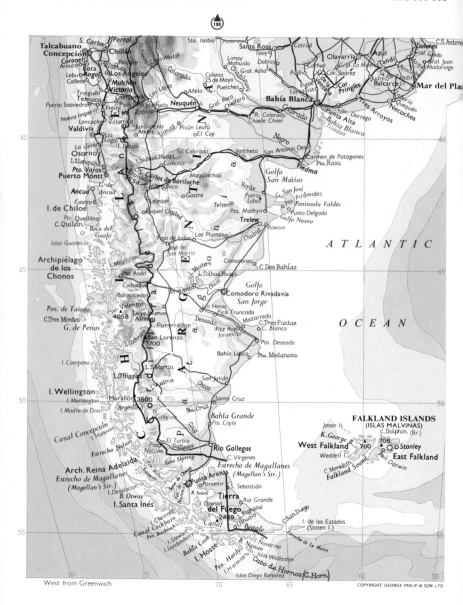

190

ATLANTIC

OCEAN

FALKLAND ISLANDS
(ISLAS MALVINAS)

Jason Is.   C. Dolphin (Br.)
K. George   700 705
West Falkland   O Stanley
Weddell I.   **East Falkland**
          San Carlos
          Darwin
C. Meredith
Falkland Sound

I. de los Estados
(Staten I.)

West from Greenwich

Map 192

Index

Introduction to Index

The number printed in bold type against each entry indicates the map page where the feature can be found. This is followed by its geographical coordinates. The first coordinate indicates latitude, i.e. distance north or south of the Equator. The second coordinate indicates longitude, i.e. distance east or west of the meridian of Greenwich in England (shown as 0° longitude). Both latitude and longitude are measured in degrees and minutes (with 60 minutes in a degree), and appear on the map as horizontal and vertical gridlines respectively. Thus the entry for Paris in France reads.

Paris, France........39 48 50N 2 20 E

This entry indicates that Paris is on page **39,** at latitude 48 degrees 50 minutes north (approximately five-sixths of the distance between horizontal gridlines 48 and 49 , marked on either side of the page) and at longitude 2 degrees 20 minutes east (approximately one-third of the distance between vertical gridlines 2 and 3, marked at top and bottom of the page). Paris can be found where lines extended from these two points cross on the page. The geographical coordinates are sometimes only approximate but are close enough for the place to be located. Rivers have been indexed to their mouth or confluence.

An open square □ signifies that the name refers to an administrative subdivision of a country while a solid square ■ follows the name of a country. An arrow ⤳ follows the name of a river.

The alphabetical order of names composed of two or more words is governed primarily by the first word and then by the second. This rule applies even if the second word is a description or its abbreviation, R., L., I. for example.

> North Walsham
> Northallerton
> Northampton
> Northern Circars
> Northumberland Is.
> Northumberland Str.

Names composed of a proper name (Gibraltar) and a description (Strait of) are positioned alphabetically by the proper name. This is the case where the definite article follows a proper name (Mans, Le). If the same word occurs in the name of a town and a geographical feature, the town name is listed first followed by the name or names of the geographical features.

Names beginning with M', Mc are all indexed as if they were spelled Mac. All names beginning St. are alphabetised under Saint, but Sankt, Sint, Santa and San are all spelt in full and are alphabetised accordingly.

If the same place name occurs twice or more times in the index and all are in the same country, each is followed by the name of the administrative subdivision in which it is located. The names are placed in the alphabetical order of the subdivisions. If the same place name occurs twice or more in the index and the places are in different countries they will be followed by their country names, the latter governing the alphabetical order. In a mixture of these situations the primary order is fixed by the alphabetical sequence of the countries and the secondary order by that of the country subdivisions.

Abbreviations used

A.S.S.R. – *Autonomous Soviet Socialist Republic*
Ala. – *Alabama*
Arch. – *Archipelago*
Ark. – *Arkansas*
Austral. – *Australia*
B. – *Baie, Bahia, Bay, Boca, Bucht, Bugt*
B.C. – *British Columbia*
Bangla. – *Bangladesh*
Br. – *British*
C. – *Cabo, Cap, Cape, Coast, Costa*
C. Rica – *Costa Rica*
Calif. – *California*
Cap. Terr. – *Capital Territory*
Cat. – *Cataract*
Cent. – *Central*
Chan. – *Channel*
Colo. – *Colorado*
Conn. – *Connecticut*
Cord. – *Cordillera*
D.C. – *District of Columbia*
Del. – *Delaware*
Dét. – *Détroit*
Dom. Rep. – *Dominican Republic*
Domin. – *Dominica*
E. – *East, Eastern*
Est. – *Estrecho*
Falk. Is. – *Falkland Is.*
Fla. – *Florida*
Fr. Gui. – *French Guiana*
G. – *Golfe, Golfo, Gulf, Guba, Gebel*
Ga. – *Georgia*
Gt. – *Great*
Guat. – *Guatemala*
Hants. – *Hampshire*
Hd. – *Head*
Hond. – *Honduras*
Hts. – *Heights*
I.(s) – *Ile, Ilha, Insel, Isla, Island(s)*
I. of W. – *Isle of Wight*
Ill. – *Illinois*
Ind. – *Indiana*
Ind. Oc. – *Indian Ocean*
J. – *Jabal, Jazira*
K. – *Kap. Kapp*
Kans. – *Kansas*

Ky. – *Kentucky*
L. – *Lac, Lacul, Lago, Lagoa, Lake, Limni, Loch, Lough*
La. – *Louisiana*
Lag. – *Laguna*
Lancs. – *Lancashire*
Man. – *Manitoba*
Mass. – *Massachusetts*
Md. – *Maryland*
Mich. – *Michigan*
Minn. – *Minnesota*
Miss. – *Mississippi*
Mo. – *Missouri*
Mont. – *Montana*
Mt.(s) – *Mont, Monta, Monti, Muntii, Montaña, Mount, Mountain(s)*
N. – *North, Northern*
N.B. – *New Brunswick*
N.C. – *North Carolina*
N. Dak. – *North Dakota*
N.H. – *New Hampshire*
N.J. – *New Jersey*
N. Mex. – *New Mexico*
N.S.W. – *New South Wales*
N.W.T. – *North West Territories*
N.Y. – *New York*
N.Z. – *New Zealand*
Nebr. – *Nebraska*
Neth. – *Netherlands*
Nev. – *Nevada*
Nfld. – *Newfoundland*
Nic. – *Nicaragua*
Okla. – *Oklahoma*
Ont. – *Ontario*
Oreg. – *Oregon*
Os. – *Ostrov*
Oz. – *Ozero*
P. – *Pass, Passo, Pasul, Pulau*
P.E.I. – *Prince Edward Island*
Pa. – *Pennsylvania*
Pac. Oc. – *Pacific Ocean*
Papua N.G. – *Papua New Guinea*
Pen. – *Peninsula*
Pk. – *Peak*
Plat. – *Plateau*
P-ov. – *Poluostrov*
Pt. – *Point*
Pta. – *Ponta, Punta*
Queens. – *Queensland*

R. – *Rio, River, Rivière*
R.I. – *Rhode Island*
R.S.F.S.R. – *Russian Soviet Federative Socialist Republic*
Ra.(s) – *Range(s)*
Raj. – *Rajasthan*
Rep. – *Republic*
Res. – *Reserve, Reservoir*
S. – *South, Southern, Sea, Sur*
S.C. – *South Carolina*
S.S.R. – *Soviet Socialist Republic*
S. Africa – *South Africa*
S. Dak. – *South Dakota*
Sa. – *Serra, Sierra*
Salop. – *Shropshire*
Sard. – *Sardinia*
Sask. – *Saskatchewan*
Sd. – *Sound*
Sev. – *Severnaya*
Si. Arabia – *Saudi Arabia*
St. – *Saint*
Sta. – *Santa*
Ste. – *Sainte*
Str. – *Strait, Stretto*
Switz. – *Switzerland*
Tas. – *Tasmania*
Tenn. – *Tennessee*
Terr. – *Territory*
Tex. – *Texas*
Tipp. – *Tipperary*
Trin. & Tob. – *Trinidad and Tobago*
U.K. – *United Kingdom*
U.S.A. – *United States of America*
U.S.S.R. – *Union of Soviet Socialist Republics*
Ut. P. – *Uttar Pradesh*
Va. – *Virginia*
Vic. – *Victoria*
Vol. – *Volcano*
Vt. – *Vermont*
Wash. – *Washington*
W. – *West, Western, Wadi*
W. Va. – *West Virginia*
Wis. – *Wisconsin*
Worcs. – *Worcestershire*
Yorks. – *Yorkshire*

Name								Name						
Aachen	42	50	47N	6	4 E			Adélie, Terre	15	68	0S	140	0 E
Aalborg = Ålborg	61	57	2N	9	54 E			Aden = Al 'Adan	83	12	45N	45	0 E
Aalsmeer	40	52	17N	4	43 E			Aden, G. of	133	13	0N	50	0 E
Aalst	42	50	56N	4	2 E			Adige →	47	45	9N	12	20 E
Aalten	41	51	56N	6	35 E			Adirondack Mts.	151	44	0N	74	15W
Aarhus = Århus	61	56	8N	10	11 E			Admiralty Is.	115	2	0S	147	0 E
Aba	131	5	10N	7	19 E			Adoni	90	15	33N	77	18W
Ābādān	84	30	22N	48	20 E			Adrian	167	41	55N	84	0W
Ābādeh	85	31	8N	52	40 E			Adriatic Sea	52	43	0N	16	0 E
Abadla	126	31	2N	2	45W			Adwa	132	14	15N	38	52 E
Abai	191	25	58S	55	54W			Adzhar A.S.S.R. □	70	42	0N	42	0 E
Abakan	74	53	40N	91	10 E			Ægean Sea	55	37	0N	25	0 E
Abancay	186	13	35S	72	55W			Æolian Is. = Eólie, I.	49	38	30N	14	50 E
Abariringa I.	122	2	50S	171	40W			Aerht'ai Shan	100	46	40N	92	45 E
Abashiri	103	44	0N	144	15 E			Afars & Issas, Terr. of =					
Abashiri-Wan	103	44	0N	144	30 E			Djibouti ■	133	12	0N	43	0 E
Abaya, L.	133	6	30N	37	50 E			Afghanistan ■	87	33	0N	65	0 E
Abbay = Nîl el Azraq →	129	15	38N	32	31 E			Afuá	188	0	15S	50	20W
Abbeville, France	38	50	6N	1	49 E			Afyonkarahisar	80	38	45N	30	33 E
Abbeville, U.S.A.	165	34	12N	82	21W			Agadir	126	30	28N	9	35W
Abéché	129	13	50N	20	35 E			Agano →	103	37	57N	139	8 E
Abeokuta	131	7	3N	3	19 E			Agartala	93	23	50N	91	23 E
Aberaeron	26	52	15N	4	16W			Agen	36	44	12N	0	38 E
Aberayron = Aberaeron	26	52	15N	4	16W			Ageo	107	35	58N	139	36 E
Aberdare	27	51	43N	3	27W			Aghil Pass	89	36	15N	76	35 E
Aberdeen, U.K.	33	57	9N	2	6W			Agra	89	27	17N	77	58 E
Aberdeen, S. Dak., U.S.A.	163	45	30N	98	30W			Ağri Daği	81	39	50N	44	15 E
Aberdeen, Wash., U.S.A.	171	47	0N	123	50W			Agua Clara	188	20	25S	52	45W
Aberdovey	26	52	33N	4	3W			Agua Prieta	174	31	18N	109	34W
Aberfeldy	33	56	37N	3	50W			Aguadas	184	5	40N	75	38W
Abergavenny	26	51	49N	3	1W			Aguadilla	180	18	27N	67	10W
Aberystwyth	26	52	25N	4	6W			Aguas Blancas	190	24	15S	69	55W
Abha	82	18	0N	42	34 E			Aguascalientes	175	21	53N	102	18W
Abidjan	130	5	26N	3	58W			Aguascalientes □	175	22	0N	102	30W
Abilene	161	32	22N	99	40W			Agulhas, Kaap	136	34	52S	20	0 E
Abington	25	55	30N	3	42W			Ahaggar	127	23	0N	6	30 E
Abkhaz A.S.S.R. □	70	43	0N	41	0 E			Ahaura →	123	42	21S	171	34 E
Abohar	89	30	10N	74	10 E			Ahmadabad	91	23	0N	72	40 E
Aboméy	131	7	10N	2	5 E			Ahmadnagar	91	19	7N	74	46 E
Abong-Mbang	131	4	0N	13	8 E			Ahmedabad = Ahmadabad	91	23	0N	72	40 E
Abrud	56	46	19N	23	5 E			Ahmednagar = Ahmadnagar	91	19	7N	74	46 E
Abruzzi □	47	42	15N	14	0 E			Ahvāz	84	31	20N	48	40 E
Absaroka Ra.	163	44	40N	110	0W			Ahvenanmaa = Åland	66	60	15N	20	0 E
Abū al Khaşīb	84	30	25N	48	0 E			Ahwar	83	13	30N	46	40 E
Abū 'Alī	84	27	20N	49	27 E			Aigle, L'	39	48	46N	0	38 E
Abū 'Arīsh	82	16	58N	45	20 E			Aigues-Mortes	37	43	35N	4	12 E
Abu Dhabi = Abū Ẓaby	85	24	28N	54	22 E			Aiken	170	33	34N	81	50W
Abu Hamed	129	19	32N	33	13 E			Ailsa Craig	30	55	15N	5	7W
Abū Ẓāby	85	24	28N	54	22 E			Aimorés	189	19	30S	41	4W
Abunã	187	9	40S	65	20W			Aïn Ben Tili	126	25	59N	9	27W
Abunã →	187	9	41S	65	20W			Aioi	109	34	48N	134	28 E
Abut Hd.	123	43	7S	170	15 E			Aïr	127	18	30N	8	0 E
Acámbaro	177	20	2N	100	44W			Airdrie	31	55	53N	3	57W
Acaponeta	175	22	30N	105	22W			Aire →	29	53	42N	0	55W
Acapulco	177	16	51N	99	56W			Airlie Beach	121	20	16S	148	43 E
Acatlán	177	18	10N	98	3W			Aisne →	37	49	26N	2	50 E
Acayucan	177	17	57N	94	55W			Aix-en-Provence	37	43	32N	5	27 E
Accra	130	5	35N	0	6W			Aix-la-Chapelle = Aachen	42	50	47N	6	4 E
Accrington	28	53	46N	2	22W			Aix-les-Bains	37	45	41N	5	53 E
Achill I.	34	53	58N	10	5W			Aizuwakamatsu	105	37	30N	139	56 E
Achinsk	74	56	20N	90	20 E			Ajaccio	36	41	55N	8	40 E
Aconcagua, Cerro	190	32	39S	70	0W			Ajanta Ra.	91	20	28N	75	50 E
Aconquija, Mt.	190	27	0S	66	0W			Ajmer	91	26	28N	74	37 E
Açores, Is. dos = Azores	126	38	44N	29	0W			Akaishi-Dake	107	35	27N	138	9 E
Acre = 'Akko	80	32	55N	35	4 E			Akaishi-Sammyaku	107	35	25N	138	10 E
Acre □	187	9	1S	71	0W			Akashi	109	34	45N	135	0 E
Ad Dawhah	85	25	15N	51	35 E			Akershus fylke □	60	60	0N	11	10 E
Ada	168	34	50N	96	45W			Akhelóös →	54	38	36N	21	14 E
Adamaoua, Massif de l'	131	7	20N	12	20 E			Akhisar	80	38	56N	27	48 E
Adamawa Highlands =								Aki	109	33	30N	133	54 E
Adamaoua, Massif de l'	131	7	20N	12	20 E			Aki-Nada	109	34	5N	132	40 E
Adaminaby	117	36	0S	148	45 E			Akita	103	39	45N	140	7 E
Adams, Mt.	171	46	10N	121	28W			'Akko	80	32	55N	35	4 E
Adam's Bridge	90	9	15N	79	40 E			Aklavik	144	68	12N	135	0W
Adana	80	37	0N	35	16 E			Akō	109	34	45N	134	24 E
Adapazarı	80	40	48N	30	25 E			Akola	91	20	42N	77	2 E
Adare, C.	15	71	0S	171	0 E			Akranes	64	64	19N	21	58W
Addis Ababa = Addis Abeba	133	9	2N	38	42 E			Akron	167	41	7N	81	31W
Addis Abeba	133	9	2N	38	42 E			Aksaray	80	38	25N	34	2 E
Adelaide	119	34	52S	138	30 E			Aksarka	69	66	31N	67	50 E
Adelaide Pen.	145	68	15N	97	30W			Akşehir	80	38	18N	31	30 E

Place	Ref	Lat	Long
Aksum	132	14 5N	38 40 E
Aktyubinsk	70	50 17N	57 10 E
Akune	108	32 1N	130 12 E
Akureyri	64	65 40N	18 6W
Al 'Adan	83	12 45N	45 0 E
Al Amādīyah	81	37 5N	43 30 E
Al Amārah	84	31 55N	47 15 E
Al 'Aqabah	80	29 31N	35 0 E
Al Baṣrah	84	30 30N	47 50 E
Al Ḥadīthah	81	31 28N	37 8 E
Al Ḥāmad	80	31 30N	39 30 E
Al Ḥasakah	81	36 35N	40 45 E
Al Ḥawrah	83	13 50N	47 35 E
Al Ḥayy	84	32 5N	46 5 E
Al Ḥillah, Iraq	84	32 30N	44 25 E
Al Ḥillah, Si. Arabia	83	23 35N	46 50 E
Al Hindīyah	84	32 30N	44 10 E
Al Ḥudaydah	82	14 50N	43 0 E
Al Ḥūfuf	84	25 25N	49 45 E
Al Jāfūrah	84	25 0N	50 15 E
Al Jawf, Libya	128	24 10N	23 24 E
Al Jawf, Si. Arabia	82	29 55N	39 40 E
Al Jazirah	81	33 30N	44 0 E
Al Khalīl	80	31 32N	35 6 E
Al Kūt	84	32 30N	46 0 E
Al Kuwayt	84	29 30N	47 30 F
Al Lādhiqīyah	80	35 30N	35 45 E
Al Lidām	82	20 33N	44 45 E
Al Luḥayyah	82	15 45N	42 40 E
Al Madīnah	82	24 35N	39 52 E
Al Manāmāh	85	26 10N	50 30 E
Al Marj	128	32 25N	20 30 E
Al Mawṣil	81	36 15N	43 5 E
Al Mubarraz	84	25 30N	49 40 E
Al Muḥarraq	85	26 15N	50 40 E
Al Mukallā	83	14 33N	49 2 E
Al Qaṭīf	84	26 35N	50 0 E
Al Quds = Jerusalem	80	31 47N	35 10 E
Al Qunfudhah	82	19 3N	41 4 E
Al Qurnah	84	31 1N	47 25 E
Al 'Ubaylah	83	21 59N	50 57 E
Al 'Uthmānīyah	84	25 5N	49 22 E
Al Wajh	82	26 10N	36 30 E
Alabama □	169	33 0N	87 0W
Alabama →	169	31 8N	87 57W
Alagoas □	189	9 0S	36 0W
Alagoinhas	189	12 7S	38 20W
Alajuela	179	10 2N	84 8W
Alamogordo	161	32 59N	106 0W
Alamos	174	27 1N	108 56W
Alamosa	163	37 30N	106 0W
Åland	66	60 15N	20 0 E
Alaska □	142	65 0N	150 0W
Alaska, G. of	142	58 0N	145 0W
Alaska Pen.	142	56 0N	160 0W
Alaska Range	142	62 50N	151 0W
Alba Iulia	56	46 8N	23 39 F
Albacete	51	39 0N	1 50W
Albania ■	52	41 0N	20 0 E
Albany, Australia	120	35 1S	117 58 E
Albany, Ga., U.S.A.	170	31 40N	84 10W
Albany, N.Y., U.S.A.	164	42 35N	73 47W
Albany, Oreg., U.S.A.	171	44 41N	123 0W
Albany →	140	52 17N	81 31W
Albemarle	165	35 27N	80 15W
Albemarle Sd.	165	36 0N	76 30W
Albert	38	50 0N	2 38 E
Albert, L. = Mobutu Sese Seko, L.	132	1 30N	31 0 E
Albert Lea	166	43 32N	93 20W
Alberta □	155	54 40N	115 0W
Albertville = Kalemie	135	5 55S	29 9 E
Albi	37	43 56N	2 9 E
Albion	167	42 15N	84 45W
Ålborg	61	57 2N	9 54 E
Alborz, Reshteh-ye Kūhhā-ye	86	36 0N	52 0 E
Albuquerque	161	35 5N	106 47W
Alburquerque	50	39 15N	6 59W
Albury	117	36 3S	146 56 E
Alcántara	188	2 20S	44 30W
Alcázar de San Juan	50	39 24N	3 12W
Alcira	51	39 9N	0 30W
Aldan →	75	63 28N	129 35 E
Aldeburgh	25	52 9N	1 35 E
Alderney	36	49 42N	2 12W
Aldershot	25	51 15N	0 43W
Alençon	39	48 27N	0 4 E
Aleppo = Ḥalab	80	36 10N	37 15 E
Alès	37	44 9N	4 5 E
Alessándria	46	44 54N	8 37 E
Ålesund	65	62 28N	6 12 E
Aleutian Is.	142	52 0N	175 0W
Alexander Arch.	143	57 0N	135 0W
Alexander City	169	32 58N	85 57W
Alexandra, Australia	117	37 8S	145 40 E
Alexandra, N.Z.	123	45 14S	169 25 E
Alexandretta = İskenderun	80	36 32N	36 10 E
Alexandria = El Iskandarîya	128	31 0N	30 0 E
Alexandria, La., U.S.A.	168	31 20N	92 30W
Alexandria, Va., U.S.A.	164	38 47N	77 1W
Alexandrina, L.	119	35 25S	139 10 E
Alexandroúpolis	55	40 50N	25 54 E
Alexis Creek	154	52 10N	123 20W
Alfreton	29	53 6N	1 22W
Algarve	50	36 58N	8 20W
Alger	127	36 42N	3 8 E
Algeria ■	127	35 10N	3 11 E
Algiers = Alger	127	36 42N	3 8 E
Algoa B.	136	33 50S	25 45 E
Alhambra	173	34 2N	118 10W
Alicante	51	38 23N	0 30W
Alice Springs	114	23 40S	133 50 E
Aligarh	89	27 55N	78 10 E
Alipur Duar	92	26 30N	89 35 E
Aliquippa	164	40 38N	80 18W
Alkmaar	40	52 37N	4 45 E
Allahabad	92	25 25N	81 58 E
Alleghery Mts.	100	00 0N	00 0W
Allen, Bog of	35	53 15N	7 0W
Allende	174	28 20N	100 51W
Allentown	164	40 36N	75 30W
Alleppey	90	9 30N	76 28 E
Aller →	42	52 57N	9 10 E
Allier →	37	46 57N	3 4 E
Alloa	31	56 7N	3 49W
Alma, Canada	148	48 35N	71 40W
Alma, U.S.A.	167	43 25N	84 40W
Alma Ata	71	43 15N	76 57 E
Almada	50	38 40N	9 9W
Almelo	41	52 22N	6 42 E
Almería	51	36 52N	2 27W
Almirante	179	9 10N	82 30W
Alor	113	8 15S	124 30 E
Alor Setar	96	6 7N	100 22 E
Alpena	150	45 6N	83 24W
Alphen	40	51 29N	4 58 E
Alpine	161	30 25N	103 35W
Alps	16	47 0N	8 0 E
Alsace	37	48 15N	7 25 E
Alsask	152	51 21N	109 59W
Alston	28	54 48N	2 26W
Alta Gracia	190	31 40S	64 30W
Altagracia	184	10 45N	71 30W
Altai = Aerht'ai Shan	100	46 40N	92 45 E
Altamaha →	170	31 19N	81 17W
Altamira	188	3 12S	52 10W
Alto Adige = Trentino-Alto Adige □	47	46 30N	11 0 E
Alton	166	38 55N	90 5W
Altona	43	53 32N	9 56 E
Altoona	164	40 32N	78 24W
Altun Shan	100	38 30N	88 0 E
Alvarado	177	18 46N	95 46W
Älvsborgs län □	60	58 30N	12 30 E
Alwar	89	27 38N	76 34 E
Alxa Zuoqi	98	38 50N	105 40 E
Am-Timan	129	11 0N	20 10 E
Amadjuak	146	64 0N	72 39W
Amadjuak L.	146	65 0N	71 8W
Amagasaki	106	34 42N	135 20 E
Amagi	108	33 25N	130 39 E
Amakusa-Nada	108	32 35N	130 5 E

Amaïner	**91** 21 5N 75 5 E
Amapá	**185** 2 5N 50 50W
Amapá □	**185** 1 40N 52 0W
Amarillo	**161** 35 14N 101 46W
Amasya	**80** 40 40N 35 50 E
Amatitlán	**177** 14 29N 90 38W
Amazon = Amazonas ↝	**185** 0 5S 50 0W
Amazonas □	**185** 4 0S 62 0W
Amazonas ↝	**185** 0 5S 50 0W
Ambala	**89** 30 23N 76 56 E
Ambato	**184** 1 5S 78 42W
Ambikapur	**92** 23 15N 83 15 E
Ambleside	**28** 54 26N 2 58W
Ambo	**186** 10 5S 76 10W
Ambon	**113** 3 35S 128 20 E
Amboyna I.	**112** 7 50N 112 50 E
Amderma	**69** 69 45N 61 30 E
Ameca	**175** 20 33N 104 2W
Ameca, R. ↝	**175** 20 41N 105 18W
Ameland	**41** 53 27N 5 45 E
American Highland	**14** 73 0S 75 0 E
American Samoa ■	**123** 14 20S 170 40W
Americus	**170** 32 0N 84 10W
Amersfoort	**40** 52 9N 5 23 E
Amery	**143** 56 34N 94 3W
Ames	**166** 42 0N 93 40W
Amga ↝	**75** 62 38N 134 32 E
Amgu	**75** 45 45N 137 15 E
Amgun ↝	**75** 52 56N 139 38 E
Amherst	**148** 45 48N 64 8W
Amherstburg	**150** 42 6N 83 6W
Amiens	**38** 49 54N 2 16 E
Amlwch	**26** 53 24N 4 21W
'Ammān	**80** 31 57N 35 52 E
Amorgós	**55** 36 50N 25 57 E
Amos	**151** 48 35N 78 5W
Amoy = Xiamen	**99** 24 25N 118 4 E
Amravati	**91** 20 55N 77 45 E
Amreli	**91** 21 35N 71 17 E
Amritsar	**89** 31 35N 74 57 E
Amsterdam, Neth.	**40** 52 23N 4 54 E
Amsterdam, U.S.A.	**164** 42 58N 74 10W
Amudarya ↝	**70** 43 40N 59 0 E
Amundsen Gulf	**145** 71 0N 124 0W
Amundsen Sea	**15** 72 0S 115 0W
Amur ↝	**75** 52 56N 141 10 E
An Nafūd	**82** 28 15N 41 0 E
An Najaf	**84** 32 3N 44 15 E
An Nāşirīyah	**84** 31 0N 46 15 E
An Nhon	**95** 13 55N 109 7 E
An Nu'ayrīyah	**84** 27 30N 48 30 E
An Uaimh	**34** 53 39N 6 40W
Anabar ↝	**72** 73 8N 113 36 E
Anaconda	**163** 46 7N 113 0W
Anacortes	**171** 48 30N 122 40W
Anadolu	**80** 38 0N 30 0 E
Anadyr ↝	**73** 64 55N 176 5 E
Anadyrskiy Zaliv	**73** 64 0N 180 0 E
Anaheim	**173** 33 50N 118 0W
Anambas Is.	**111** 3 20N 106 30 E
Anamur	**80** 36 8N 32 58 E
Anan	**109** 33 54N 134 40 E
Anápolis	**188** 16 15S 48 50W
Anārak	**85** 33 25N 53 40 E
Anatolia = Anadolu	**80** 38 0N 30 0 E
Añatuya	**190** 28 20S 62 50W
Anchorage	**142** 61 10N 149 50W
Ancohuma, Nevada	**187** 16 0S 68 50W
Ancona	**47** 43 37N 13 30 E
Ancud	**192** 42 0S 73 50W
Ancud, G. de	**192** 42 0S 73 0W
Åndalsnes	**65** 62 35N 7 43 E
Andalucía □	**50** 37 35N 5 0W
Andalusia	**169** 31 19N 86 30W
Andalusia □ = Andalucía □	**50** 37 35N 5 0W
Andaman Is.	**94** 12 30N 92 30 E
Andaman Sea	**94** 13 0N 96 0 E
Andaman Str.	**94** 12 15N 92 20 E
Andelys, Les	**39** 49 15N 1 25 E
Anderson, Ind., U.S.A.	**167** 40 5N 85 40W
Anderson, S.C., U.S.A.	**165** 34 32N 82 40W
Andes, Cord. de los	**182** 20 0S 68 0W
Andhra Pradesh □	**91** 16 0N 79 0 E
Andikíthira	**55** 35 52N 23 15 E
Andizhan	**71** 41 10N 72 0 E
Andorra ■	**36** 42 30N 1 30 E
Andover	**24** 51 13N 1 29W
Andreanof Is.	**142** 52 0N 178 0W
Andrewilla	**118** 26 31S 139 17 E
Ándria	**49** 41 13N 16 17 E
Andropov	**68** 58 5N 38 50 E
Ándros	**55** 37 50N 24 57 E
Andros I.	**178** 24 30N 78 0W
Angara ↝	**74** 58 30N 97 0 E
Angarsk	**74** 52 30N 104 0 E
Angaston	**119** 34 30S 139 8 E
Ånge	**66** 62 31N 15 35 E
Ängelholm	**61** 56 15N 12 58 E
Angels Camp	**172** 38 8N 120 30W
Ångerman ↝	**66** 64 0N 17 20 E
Angers	**36** 47 30N 0 35W
Angkor	**95** 13 22N 103 50 E
Anglesey	**26** 53 17N 4 20W
Angmagssalik	**147** 65 40N 37 20W
Angol	**190** 37 56S 72 45W
Angola ■	**134** 12 0S 18 0 E
Angoulême	**36** 45 39N 0 10 E
Angoumois	**36** 45 50N 0 25 E
Anguilla	**180** 18 14N 63 5W
Angus, Braes of	**33** 56 51N 3 10W
Anhui □	**99** 32 0N 117 0 E
Anhwei □ = Anhui □	**99** 32 0N 117 0 E
Anin	**94** 15 36N 97 50 E
Anjō	**106** 34 57N 137 5 E
Anjou	**36** 47 20N 0 15W
Anju	**98** 39 36N 125 40 E
Ankang	**99** 32 40N 109 1 E
Ankara	**80** 40 0N 32 54 E
Ann Arbor	**167** 42 17N 83 45W
Annaba	**127** 36 50N 7 46 E
Annam = Trung-Phan	**95** 16 0N 108 0 E
Annamitique, Chaîne	**95** 17 0N 106 0 E
Annan	**31** 55 0N 3 17W
Annapolis	**164** 39 0N 76 30W
Annecy	**37** 45 55N 6 8 E
Anniston	**169** 33 45N 85 50W
Annobón	**131** 1 25S 5 36 E
Annonay	**37** 45 15N 4 40 E
Annotto Bay	**180** 18 17N 77 3W
Anqing	**99** 30 30N 117 3 E
Anse, L'	**150** 46 47N 88 28W
Anshan	**98** 41 3N 122 58 E
Anshun	**99** 26 18N 105 57 E
Anstruther	**31** 56 14N 2 40W
Antabamba	**186** 14 40S 73 0W
Antakya	**80** 36 14N 36 10 E
Antalya	**80** 36 52N 30 45 E
Antalya Körfezi	**80** 36 15N 31 30 E
Antananarivo	**137** 18 55S 47 31 E
Antarctic Pen.	**14** 67 0S 60 0W
Antarctica	**14** 90 0S 0 0 E
Anti Atlas	**126** 30 0N 8 30W
Antibes	**37** 43 34N 7 6 E
Anticosti, Î. d'.	**148** 49 30N 63 0W
Antigo	**150** 45 8N 89 5W
Antigua, Guat.	**177** 14 34N 90 41W
Antigua, W. Indies	**180** 17 0N 61 50W
Antigua and Barbuda ■	**180** 17 20N 61 48W
Antilla	**178** 20 40N 75 50W
Antioch	**172** 38 7N 121 45W
Antioquia	**184** 6 40N 75 55W
Antipodes Is.	**11** 49 45S 178 40 E
Antofagasta	**190** 23 50S 70 30W
Antrim	**34** 54 43N 6 13W
Antrim, Mts. of	**34** 54 57N 6 8W
Antsiranana	**137** 12 25S 49 20 E
Antwerp = Antwerpen	**42** 51 13N 4 25 E
Antwerpen	**42** 51 13N 4 25 E
Anvers = Antwerpen	**42** 51 13N 4 25 E
Anvik	**142** 62 37N 160 20W
Anxious B.	**119** 33 24S 134 45 E
Anyang	**98** 36 5N 114 21 E

Anzhero-Sudzhensk	71	56 10N	86	0 E
Ánzio	46	41 28N	12	37 E
Aoga-Shima	105	32 28N	139	46 E
Aomori	103	40 45N	140	45 E
Apalachee B.	170	30 0N	84	0W
Apalachicola	170	29 40N	85	0W
Apalachicola ~►	170	29 40N	85	0W
Aparri	112	18 22N	121	38 E
Apatzingan	175	19 5N	102	21W
Apeldoorn	41	52 13N	5	57 E
Apennines	16	44 20N	10	20 E
Apizaco	177	19 25N	98	9W
Aplao	186	16 0S	72	40W
Apolo	187	14 30S	68	30W
Apostle Is.	150	47 0N	90	30W
Apostolos Andreas, C.	80	35 42N	34	35 E
Appalachian Mts.	138	38 0N	80	0W
Appingedam	41	53 19N	6	51 E
Appleby	28	54 35N	2	29W
Appleton	167	44 17N	88	25W
Apulia = Púglia □	49	41 0N	16	30 E
Apure ~►	184	7 37N	66	25W
Aqabah = Al 'Aqabah	80	29 31N	35	0 E
Aquidauana	188	20 30S	55	50W
Áquila, L'	47	42 21N	13	24 E
Aquiles Serdán	174	28 36N	105	53W
Ar Riyāḍ	83	24 41N	46	42 E
Ar Ruṭbah	81	33 0N	40	15 E
Ara	92	25 35N	84	32 E
Arab, Bahr el ~►	129	9 50N	29	0 E
Arab, Shatt al	84	30 0N	48	31 E
Arabia	76	25 0N	45	0 E
Arabian Gulf = Gulf, The	85	27 0N	50	0 E
Arabian Sea	76	16 0N	65	0 E
Aracaju	189	10 55S	37	4W
Aracati	189	4 30S	37	44W
Araguba	190	01 19C	60	20W
Arad	56	46 10N	21	20 E
Arafura Sea	113	9 0S	135	0 E
Aragón □	51	41 25N	1	0W
Araguacema	188	8 50S	49	20W
Araguaia ~►	188	5 21S	48	41W
Araguari	188	18 38S	48	11W
Arāk	84	34 0N	49	40 E
Arakan Coast	93	19 0N	94	0 E
Arakan Yoma	93	20 0N	94	40 E
Araks = Aras, Rūd-e ~►	81	39 10N	47	10 E
Aral Sea = Aralskoye More...	70	44 30N	60	0 E
Aralsk	70	46 50N	61	20 E
Aralskoye More	70	44 30N	60	0 E
Aran I.	34	55 0N	8	30W
Aran Is.	35	53 5N	9	42W
Aranjuez	50	40 1N	3	40W
Aransas Pass	158	27 55N	97	9W
Arao	108	32 59N	130	25 E
Araraquara	188	21 50S	48	0W
Ararat	119	37 16S	143	0 E
Ararat, Mt. = Aĝri Daĝi	81	39 50N	44	15 E
Aras, Rūd-e ~►	81	39 10N	47	10 E
Araya, Pen. de	185	10 40N	64	0W
Arbīl	81	36 15N	44	5 E
Arbroath	31	56 34N	2	35W
Arcachon	36	44 40N	1	10W
Arcadia	170	27 20N	81	50W
Archangel = Arkhangelsk	69	64 40N	41	0 E
Arcot	90	12 53N	79	20 E
Arctic Bay	146	73 1N	85	7W
Arctic Ocean	12	78 0N	160	0W
Arctic Red River	144	67 15N	134	0W
Ardabīl	81	38 15N	48	18 E
Ardennes	42	50 0N	5	10 E
Ardgour	32	56 45N	5	25W
Ardlethan	117	34 22S	146	53 E
Ardmore	168	34 10N	97	5W
Ardnacrusha	35	52 43N	8	38W
Ardnamurchan, Pt. of	32	56 44N	6	14W
Ards Pen.	34	54 30N	5	25W
Arecibo	180	18 29N	66	42W
Arequipa	187	16 20S	71	30W
Arezzo	46	43 28N	11	50 E
Argentan	39	48 45N	0	1W
Argentário, Mte.	46	42 23N	11	11 E
Argentina ■	190	35 0S	66	0W
Argentino, L.	192	50 10S	73	0W
Árgos	54	37 40N	22	43 E
Argostólion	54	38 12N	20	33 E
Argun ~►	74	53 20N	121	28 E
Århus	61	56 8N	10	11 E
Arica, Chile	187	18 32S	70	20W
Arica, Colombia	184	2 0S	71	50W
Arida	106	34 5N	135	8 E
Arima	180	10 38N	61	17W
Ario de Rosales	175	19 12N	101	43W
Aripuanã	187	9 25S	60	30W
Aripuanã ~►	187	5 7S	60	25W
Ariquemes	187	9 55S	63	6W
Arisaig	32	56 55N	5	50W
Aristazabal I.	154	52 40N	129	10W
Arizona □	160	34 20N	111	30W
Arjona	184	10 14N	75	22W
Arkadelphia	168	34 5N	93	0W
Arkansas □	168	35 0N	92	30W
Arkansas ~►	168	33 48N	91	4W
Arkansas City	158	37 4N	97	3W
Arkhangelsk	69	64 40N	41	0 E
Arklow	35	52 48N	6	10W
Arkticheskiy, Mys	72	81 10N	95	0 E
Arles	37	43 41N	4	40 E
Arlington	164	30 52N	77	5W
Armagh	34	54 22N	6	40W
Armavir	70	45 2N	41	7 E
Armenia	184	4 35N	75	45W
Armenia S.S.R. □	70	40 0N	41	0 E
Armentières	38	50 40N	2	50 E
Armidale	116	30 30S	151	40 E
Armstrong	155	50 25N	119	10W
Arnaouti, C.	80	35 6N	32	17 E
Arnaud ~►	146	50 50N	69	46W
Arnhem	41	51 58N	5	55 E
Arnhem, C.	115	12 20S	137	30 E
Arnhem Land	114	13 10S	134	30 E
Arnprior	151	45 26N	76	21W
Arran	30	55 34N	5	12W
Arras	38	50 17N	2	46 E
Arriaga	177	16 14N	93	54W
Árta	54	39 8N	21	2 E
Artigas	191	30 20S	56	30W
Artois	38	50 20N	2	30 E
Aru, Kepulauan	113	6 0S	134	30 E
Arua	132	3 1N	30	58 E
Aruanã	188	14 54S	51	10W
Aruba	181	12 30N	70	0W
Arusha	135	3 20S	36	40 E
Arvida	148	48 25N	71	14W
Arys	71	42 26N	68	48 E
'As Saffānīyah	84	28 5N	48	50 E
As Samāwah	84	31 15N	45	15 E
As Sulaymānīyah	83	24 9N	47	18 E
As Şumaymānīyah	81	35 35N	45	29 E
As Suwaydā'	80	32 40N	36	30 E
As Şuwayraḥ	84	32 55N	45	0 E
Asahi	107	35 43N	140	39 E
Asahi-Gawa ~►	109	34 36N	133	58 E
Asahigawa	103	43 46N	142	22 E
Asama-Yama	107	36 24N	138	31 E
Asamankese	130	5 50N	0	40W
Asansol	92	23 40N	87	1 E
Asbestos	148	45 47N	71	58W
Ascensión I.	125	8 0S	14	15W
Áscoli Piceno	47	42 51N	13	34 E
Aseb	133	13 0N	42	40 E
Ash Shām, Bādiyat	80	32 0N	40	0 E
Ash Shāmīyah	84	31 55N	44	35 E
Ash Shāriqah	85	25 23N	55	26 E
Ash Shaṭrah	84	31 30N	46	10 E
Ashburton	123	43 53S	171	48 E
Ashby-de-la-Zouch	28	52 45N	1	29W
Ashcroft	155	50 40N	121	20W
Asheboro	165	35 43N	79	46W
Asheville	165	35 39N	82	30W
Ashford, Australia	116	29 15S	151	3 E
Ashford, U.K.	25	51 8N	0	53 E

Ashikaga	**107**	36 28N	139	29 E
Ashizuri-Zaki	**109**	32 44N	133	0 E
Ashkhabad	**70**	38 0N	57	50 E
Ashland, Kans., U.S.A.	**156**	37 13N	99	43W
Ashland, Ky., U.S.A.	**165**	38 25N	82	40W
Ashland, Oreg., U.S.A.	**171**	42 10N	122	38W
Ashland, Wis., U.S.A.	**150**	46 40N	90	52W
Ashq'elon	**80**	31 42N	34	35 E
Ashtabula	**164**	41 52N	80	50W
Ashton-under-Lyne	**28**	53 30N	2	8W
Ashuanipi, L.	**147**	52 45N	66	15W
Asinara I.	**48**	41 5N	8	15 E
'Asīr □	**82**	18 40N	42	30 E
Asir, Ras	**133**	11 55N	51	10 E
Asmara = Asmera	**132**	15 19N	38	55 E
Asmera	**132**	15 19N	38	55 E
Aso	**108**	33 0N	131	5 E
Aso-Zan	**108**	32 53N	131	6 E
Aspiring, Mt.	**123**	44 23S	168	46 E
Assam □	**93**	26 0N	93	0 E
Assen	**41**	53 0N	6	35 E
Assiniboia	**152**	49 40N	105	59W
Assiniboine ➤	**153**	49 53N	97	8W
Assisi	**46**	43 4N	12	36 E
Asti	**46**	44 54N	8	11 E
Astipálaia	**55**	36 32N	26	22 E
Astoria	**171**	46 16N	123	50W
Astrakhan	**70**	46 25N	48	5 E
Asturias □	**50**	43 15N	6	0W
Asunción	**191**	25 10S	57	30W
Aswân	**128**	24 4N	32	57 E
Asyût	**128**	27 11N	31	4 E
At Ţafīlah	**80**	30 45N	35	30 E
At Ta'if	**82**	21 5N	40	27 E
Atacama, Desierto de	**190**	24 0S	69	20W
Atacama, Salar de	**190**	23 30S	68	20W
Atalaya	**186**	10 45S	73	50W
Atami	**107**	35 5N	139	4 E
Atbara	**129**	17 42N	33	59 E
'Atbara ➤	**129**	17 40N	33	56 E
Atchafalaya B.	**168**	29 30N	91	20W
Atchison	**166**	39 40N	95	10W
Athabasca	**155**	54 45N	113	20W
Athabasca ➤	**145**	58 40N	110	50W
Athabasca, L.	**145**	59 15N	109	15W
Athenry	**35**	53 18N	8	45W
Athens = Athínai	**55**	37 58N	23	46 E
Athens, Ala., U.S.A.	**169**	34 49N	86	58W
Athens, Ga., U.S.A.	**165**	33 56N	83	24W
Athens, Ohio, U.S.A.	**167**	39 25N	82	6W
Athens, Tenn., U.S.A.	**169**	35 45N	84	38W
Athens, Tex., U.S.A.	**168**	32 11N	95	48W
Atherton	**121**	17 17S	145	30 E
Athínai	**55**	37 58N	23	46 E
Athlone	**34**	53 26N	7	57W
Atholl, Forest of	**33**	56 51N	3	50W
Áthos	**55**	40 9N	24	22 E
Athy	**35**	53 0N	7	0W
Atico	**186**	16 14S	73	40W
Atlanta	**170**	33 50N	84	24W
Atlantic	**166**	41 25N	95	0W
Atlantic City	**164**	39 25N	74	25W
Atlantic Ocean	**9**	0 0	20	0W
Atlas Mts. = Haut Atlas	**126**	32 30N	5	0W
Atmore	**169**	31 2N	87	30W
Atsugi	**107**	35 25N	139	21 E
Atsumi	**106**	34 35N	137	4 E
Atsumi-Wan	**106**	34 44N	137	13 E
Attawapiskat ➤	**140**	52 57N	82	18W
Attleboro	**164**	41 56N	71	18W
Aubagne	**37**	43 17N	5	37 E
Aube ➤	**37**	48 34N	3	43 E
Aubenas	**37**	44 37N	4	24 E
Auburn, Ala., U.S.A.	**169**	32 37N	85	30W
Auburn, N.Y., U.S.A.	**164**	42 57N	76	39W
Auckland	**122**	36 52S	174	46 E
Auckland Is.	**15**	50 40S	166	5 E
Aude ➤	**37**	43 13N	3	14 E
Augsburg	**43**	48 22N	10	54 E
Augusta, Ga., U.S.A.	**170**	33 29N	81	59W
Augusta, Maine, U.S.A.	**148**	44 20N	69	46W

Aunis	**36**	46 5N	0	50W
Aurangabad	**91**	19 50N	75	23 E
Aurillac	**37**	44 55N	2	26 E
Aurora	**167**	41 42N	88	12W
Aust-Agder fylke □	**60**	58 55N	7	40 E
Austin, Minn., U.S.A.	**166**	43 37N	92	59W
Austin, Tex., U.S.A.	**161**	30 20N	97	45W
Austral Is. = Tubuai Is.	**123**	25 0S	150	0W
Australia ■	**114**	23 0S	135	0 E
Australian Alps	**117**	36 30S	148	30 E
Australian Cap. Terr. □	**117**	35 30S	149	0 E
Austria ■	**45**	47 0N	14	0 E
Autlán	**175**	19 40N	104	30W
Auvergne	**37**	45 20N	3	15 E
Auxerre	**39**	47 48N	3	32 E
Avalon Pen.	**149**	47 30N	53	20W
Aveiro	**185**	3 10S	55	5W
Avellaneda	**190**	34 50S	58	10W
Aves, I. de	**181**	15 45N	63	55W
Avesnes-sur-Helpe	**38**	50 8N	3	55 E
Aveyron ➤	**36**	44 7N	1	5 E
Aviemore	**33**	57 11N	3	50W
Avignon	**37**	43 57N	4	50 E
Ávila	**50**	40 39N	4	43W
Avon □	**27**	51 30N	2	40W
Avon ➤, Avon, U.K.	**24**	51 30N	2	43W
Avon ➤, Hants., U.K.	**24**	50 44N	1	45W
Avonmouth	**27**	51 30N	2	42W
Avranches	**36**	48 40N	1	20W
Awaji-Shima	**109**	34 30N	134	50 E
Aweil	**129**	8 42N	27	20 E
Axel Heiberg I.	**12**	80 0N	90	0W
Axminster	**27**	50 47N	3	1W
Ayabe	**106**	35 20N	135	20 E
Ayacucho	**186**	13 0S	74	0W
Aylos Evstrátios	**55**	39 34N	24	58 E
Ayon, Ostrov	**73**	69 50N	169	0 E
Ayr, Australia	**121**	19 35S	147	25 E
Ayr, U.K.	**31**	55 28N	4	37W
Ayre, Pt. of	**28**	54 27N	4	21W
Aytos	**53**	42 42N	27	16 E
Ayutla	**177**	16 58N	99	17W
Az Zahrān	**84**	26 10N	50	7 E
Az Zubayr	**84**	30 20N	47	50 E
Azamgarh	**92**	26 5N	83	13 E
Azbine = Aïr	**127**	18 30N	8	0 E
Azerbaijan S.S.R. □	**70**	40 20N	48	0 E
Azores	**126**	38 44N	29	0W
Azov Sea = Azovskoye More	**68**	46 0N	36	30 E
Azovskoye More	**68**	46 0N	36	30 E
Azúa de Compostela	**180**	18 25N	70	44W
Azuero, Pen. de	**179**	7 30N	80	30W
Azul	**190**	36 42S	59	43W

Ba Ngoi = Cam Lam	**95**	11 54N	109	10 E
Baarn	**40**	52 12N	5	17 E
Bāb el Māndeb	**133**	12 35N	43	25 E
Babahoyo	**184**	1 40S	79	30W
Babinda	**121**	17 20S	145	56 E
Babine L.	**154**	54 48N	126	0W
Bābol	**86**	36 40N	52	50 E
Babuyan Is.	**112**	19 10N	121	40 E
Babylon	**84**	32 40N	44	30 E
Bac Ninh	**95**	21 13N	106	4 E
Bac Phan	**95**	22 0N	105	0 E
Bac Quang	**95**	22 30N	104	48 E
Bacabal	**188**	4 15S	44	45W
Bacău	**57**	46 35N	26	55 E
Back ➤	**145**	65 10N	104	0W
Bacolod	**112**	10 40N	122	57 E
Bad Lands	**163**	43 40N	102	10W
Badajoz	**50**	38 50N	6	59W
Badakhshān □	**87**	36 30N	71	0 E
Badalona	**51**	41 26N	2	15 E
Badanah	**82**	30 58N	41	30 E
Baden-Baden	**42**	48 45N	8	15 E
Baden-Württemberg □	**42**	48 40N	9	0 E
Bādghīsāt □	**87**	35 0N	63	0 E
Badin	**88**	24 38N	68	54 E

Name	Pg	Lat°	Lat′	NS	Long°	Long′	EW
Baffin □	146	70	0N		80	0W	
Baffin B.	13	72	0N		64	0W	
Baffin I.	146	68	0N		75	0W	
Bafra	80	41	34N		35	54 E	
Bäft	85	29	15N		56	38 E	
Bagé	191	31	20S		54	15W	
Baghdād	84	33	20N		44	30 E	
Baghlān	87	36	12N		69	0 E	
Baghlān □	87	36	0N		68	30 E	
Bahamas ■	178	24	0N		75	0W	
Baharampur	92	24	2N		88	27 E	
Bahawalpur	89	29	24N		71	40 E	
Bahía = Salvador	189	13	0S		38	30W	
Bahía □	189	12	0S		42	0W	
Bahía Blanca	190	38	35S		62	13W	
Bahr el Jebel →	129	7	30N		30	30 E	
Dahraich	92	27	38N		81	37 E	
Bahrain ■	85	26	0N		50	35 E	
Baia Mare	56	47	40N		23	35 E	
Baie Comeau	148	49	12N		68	10W	
Baie-St-Paul	148	47	28N		70	32W	
Ba'ijī	81	35	0N		43	30 E	
Baikal, L. = Baykal, Oz.	74	53	0N		108	0 E	
Baile Atha Cliath = Dublin	35	53	20N		6	18W	
Bailleul	38	50	44N		2	41 E	
Bainbridge	170	30	53N		84	34W	
Baird Mts.	142	67	10N		160	15W	
Bairnsdale	117	37	48S		147	36 E	
Baiyin	98	36	45N		104	14 E	
Baja	59	46	12N		18	59 E	
Baja California	174	31	10N		115	12W	
Baja California Norte □	174	30	0N		115	0W	
Baja California Sur □	174	25	50N		111	50W	
Bajimba, Mt.	116	29	17S		152	6 E	
Baker	171	44	50N		117	55W	
Baker I.	122	0	10N		176	35W	
Baker Lake	145	64	20N		96	3W	
Bakersfield	173	35	25N		119	0W	
Bākhtarān	84	34	23N		47	0 E	
Bakony Forest = Bakony Hegység	59	47	10N		17	30 E	
Bakony Hegység	59	47	10N		17	30 E	
Baku	70	40	25N		49	45 E	
Bala	26	52	54N		3	36W	
Balabac, Str.	112	7	53N		117	5 E	
Balabakk	80	34	0N		36	10 E	
Balaghat	91	21	49N		80	12 E	
Balaghat Ra.	91	18	50N		76	30 E	
Balaklava	119	34	7S		138	22 E	
Balakovo	68	52	4N		47	55 E	
Balaton	59	46	50N		17	40 E	
Balboa	179	9	0N		79	30W	
Balbriggan	34	53	35N		6	10W	
Balcarce	190	38	0S		58	10W	
Balclutha	123	46	15S		169	45 E	
Baldy Peak	161	33	50N		109	30W	
Baleares, Islas	51	39	30N		3	0 E	
Balearic Is. = Baleares, Islas	51	39	30N		3	0 E	
Bali	111	8	20S		115	0 E	
Balikesir	80	39	35N		27	58 E	
Balikpapan	111	1	10S		116	55 E	
Balkan Mts. = Stara Planina	53	43	15N		23	0 E	
Balkan Pen.	17	42	0N		22	0 E	
Balkh □	87	36	30N		67	0 E	
Balkhash	71	46	50N		74	50 E	
Balkhash, Ozero	71	46	0N		74	50 E	
Ballachulish	32	56	40N		5	10W	
Ballarat	117	37	33S		143	50 E	
Ballard, L.	120	29	20S		120	10 E	
Ballater	33	57	2N		3	2W	
Ballina, Australia	116	28	50S		153	31 E	
Ballina, Mayo, Ireland	34	54	7N		9	10W	
Ballina, Tipp., Ireland	35	52	49N		8	27W	
Ballinasloe	35	53	20N		8	12W	
Ballinrobe	34	53	36N		9	13W	
Ballycastle	34	55	12N		6	15W	
Ballymena	34	54	53N		6	18W	
Ballymoney	34	55	5N		6	30W	
Ballyshannon	34	54	30N		8	10W	
Balmaceda	192	46	0S		71	50W	
Balmoral	33	57	3N		3	13W	
Balrampur	92	27	30N		82	20 E	
Balranald	117	34	38S		143	33 E	
Balsas, R. →	177	17	55N		102	10W	
Baltic Sea	16	56	0N		20	0 E	
Baltimore	164	39	18N		76	37W	
Baluchistan □	88	27	30N		65	0 E	
Bamako	130	12	34N		7	55W	
Bambari	129	5	40N		20	35 E	
Bamberg	43	49	54N		10	53 E	
Bāmīān □	87	35	0N		67	0 E	
Ban Aranyaprathet	95	13	41N		102	30 E	
Ban Don = Surat Thani	96	9	6N		99	20 E	
Ban Houei Sai	95	20	22N		100	32 E	
Ban Khe Bo	95	19	10N		104	39 E	
Ban Khun Yuam	94	18	49N		97	57 E	
Ban Nong Pling	94	15	40N		100	10 E	
Ban Phai	95	16	4N		102	44 E	
Banaras = Varanasi	92	25	22N		83	0 E	
Banbridge	34	54	21N		6	17W	
Banbury	25	52	4N		1	21W	
Bancroft	151	45	3N		77	51W	
Banda	91	25	30N		80	26 E	
Banda, Kepulauan	113	4	37S		129	50 E	
Banda Aceh	111	5	35N		95	20 E	
Banda Banda, Mt.	116	31	10S		152	28 E	
Banda Sea	113	6	0S		130	0 E	
Bandar = Machilipatnam	92	16	12N		81	8 E	
Bandar 'Abbās	85	27	15N		56	15 E	
Bandar-e Anzalī	81	37	30N		49	30 E	
Bandar-e Khomeyni	84	30	30N		49	5 E	
Bandar-e Lengeh	85	26	35N		54	58 E	
Bandar-e Nakhīlū	85	26	58N		53	30 E	
Bandar-e Torkeman	86	37	0N		54	10 E	
Bandar Seri Begawan	112	4	52N		115	0 E	
Bandeira, Pico da	188	20	26S		41	47W	
Bandirma	80	40	20N		28	0 E	
Bandon	35	51	44N		8	45W	
Bandung	111	6	54S		107	36 E	
Banes	178	21	0N		75	42W	
Banff, Canada	155	51	10N		115	34W	
Banff, U.K.	33	57	40N		2	32W	
Bangalore	90	12	59N		77	40 E	
Bangassou	129	4	55N		23	7 E	
Banggai	113	1	40S		123	30 E	
Banghāzī	128	32	11N		20	3 E	
Bangka, Selat	111	2	30S		105	30 E	
Bangkok	94	13	45N		100	35 E	
Bangladesh ■	92	24	0N		90	0 E	
Bangor, N. Ireland, U.K.	34	54	40N		5	40W	
Bangor, Wales, U.K.	26	53	13N		4	9W	
Bangor, U.S.A.	148	44	48N		68	42W	
Bangui	131	4	23N		18	35 E	
Bangweulu, L.	135	11	0S		30	0 E	
Bani	180	18	16N		70	22W	
Banja Luka	52	44	49N		17	11 E	
Banjarmasin	111	3	20S		114	35 E	
Banjul	130	13	28N		16	40W	
Bankipore	92	25	35N		85	10 E	
Banks I., B.C., Canada	154	53	20N		130	0W	
Banks I., N.W.T., Canada	145	73	15N		121	30W	
Banks Pen.	123	43	45S		173	15 E	
Banks Str.	119	40	40S		148	10 E	
Bann →	34	54	30N		6	31W	
Banning	173	33	58N		116	52W	
Bannockburn	31	56	5N		3	55W	
Bannu	89	33	0N		70	18 E	
Bantry	35	51	40N		9	28W	
Baoding	98	38	50N		115	28 E	
Baoji	99	34	20N		107	5 E	
Baotou	98	40	32N		110	2 E	
Ba'qūbah	81	33	45N		44	50 E	
Bar	52	42	8N		19	8 E	
Bar Harbor	148	44	15N		68	20W	
Baraboo	166	43	28N		89	46W	
Baracoa	178	20	20N		74	30W	
Barahona	180	18	13N		71	7W	
Barail Range	93	25	15N		93	20 E	
Baramula	89	34	15N		74	20 E	
Baran	91	25	9N		76	40 E	
Baranof I.	143	57	0N		135	10W	
Baranovichi	68	53	10N		26	0 E	

Place	Page	Lat	Dir	Long	Dir
Barbacoas	**184**	1 45N	78	0W
Barbados ■	**180**	13 0N	59	30W
Barbuda I.	**180**	17 30N	61	40W
Barca, La	**175**	20 17N	102	34W
Barcaldine	**121**	23 43S	145	6 E
Barcelona, Spain	**51**	41 21N	2	10 E
Barcelona, Venezuela	**185**	10 10N	64	40W
Barcelos	**185**	1 0S	63	0W
Barddhaman	**92**	23 14N	87	39 E
Bardera	**133**	2 20N	42	27 E
Bardsey I.	**26**	52 46N	4	47W
Bareilly	**89**	28 22N	79	27 E
Barentin	**38**	49 33N	0	58 E
Barents Sea	**13**	73 0N	39	0 E
Bargara	**121**	24 50S	152	25 E
Bari	**49**	41 6N	16	52 E
Bari Doab	**89**	30 20N	73	0 E
Barīm	**82**	12 39N	43	25 E
Barinas	**184**	8 36N	70	15W
Barisal	**92**	22 45N	90	20 E
Barito ↠	**111**	4 0S	114	50 E
Barlee, L.	**120**	29 15S	119	30 E
Barletta	**49**	41 20N	16	17 E
Barmer	**91**	25 45N	71	20 E
Barmera	**119**	34 15S	140	28 E
Barmouth	**26**	52 44N	4	3W
Barnard Castle	**28**	54 33N	1	55W
Barnaul	**71**	53 20N	83	40 E
Barneveld	**41**	52 7N	5	36 E
Barnsley	**28**	53 33N	1	29W
Barnstaple	**27**	51 5N	4	3W
Baro	**131**	8 35N	6	18 E
Baroda = Vadodara	**91**	22 20N	73	10 E
Barpeta	**93**	26 20N	91	10 E
Barquisimeto	**184**	10 4N	69	19W
Barra	**32**	57 0N	7	30W
Barra Hd.	**32**	56 47N	7	40W
Barraba	**116**	30 21S	150	35 E
Barranca	**186**	10 45S	77	50W
Barrancabermeja	**184**	7 0N	73	50W
Barrancas	**185**	8 55N	62	5W
Barranqueras	**190**	27 30S	59	0W
Barranquilla	**184**	11 0N	74	50W
Barre	**151**	44 15N	72	30W
Barreiros	**188**	8 49S	35	12W
Barrhead	**155**	54 10N	114	24W
Barrie	**151**	44 24N	79	40W
Barrier Ra.	**118**	31 0S	141	30 E
Barrington Tops	**116**	32 6S	151	28 E
Barrow ↠	**35**	52 10N	6	57W
Barrow, Pt.	**138**	71 22N	156	30W
Barrow-in-Furness	**28**	54 8N	3	15W
Barry	**27**	51 23N	3	19W
Barry's Bay	**151**	45 29N	77	41W
Barsi	**91**	18 10N	75	50 E
Barstow	**173**	34 58N	117	2W
Bartica	**185**	6 25N	58	40W
Bartow	**170**	27 53N	81	49W
Basel	**44**	47 35N	7	35 E
Bashi Channel	**99**	21 15N	122	0 E
Bashkir A.S.S.R. □	**69**	54 0N	57	0 E
Basilan	**112**	6 35N	122	0 E
Basildon	**25**	51 34N	0	29 E
Basilicata □	**49**	40 30N	16	0 E
Basim = Washim	**91**	20 3N	77	0 E
Basle = Basel	**44**	47 35N	7	35 E
Basoka	**134**	1 16N	23	40 E
Basque Provinces = Vascongadas	**50**	42 50N	2	45W
Basra = Al Başrah	**84**	30 30N	47	50 E
Bass Rock	**31**	56 5N	2	40W
Bass Str.	**117**	39 15S	146	30 E
Bassano	**155**	50 48N	112	20W
Basse-Terre	**180**	16 0N	61	40W
Bassein	**93**	16 45N	94	30 E
Basseterre	**180**	17 17N	62	43W
Basti	**92**	26 52N	82	55 E
Bastia	**36**	42 40N	9	30 E
Batabanó	**178**	22 40N	82	20W
Batamay	**74**	63 30N	129	15 E
Batan Is.	**112**	20 25N	121	59 E
Batang	**101**	30 1N	99	0 E
Batavia	**164**	43 0N	78	10W
Batemans Bay	**117**	35 44S	150	11 E
Batesville	**168**	35 48N	91	40W
Bath, U.K.	**27**	51 22N	2	22W
Bath, Maine, U.S.A.	**148**	43 50N	69	49W
Bath, N.Y., U.S.A.	**164**	42 20N	77	17W
Bathurst = Banjul	**130**	13 28N	16	40W
Bathurst, Australia	**117**	33 25S	149	31 E
Bathurst, Canada	**148**	47 37N	65	43W
Bathurst, C.	**145**	70 34N	128	0W
Bathurst Inlet	**145**	66 50N	108	1W
Batlow	**117**	35 31S	148	9 E
Batman	**81**	37 55N	41	5 E
Batna	**127**	35 34N	6	15 E
Baton Rouge	**168**	30 30N	91	5W
Batopilas	**174**	27 1N	107	44W
Battambang	**95**	13 7N	103	12 E
Batticaloa	**90**	7 43N	81	45 E
Battle	**25**	50 55N	0	30 E
Battle Creek	**167**	42 20N	85	6W
Battle Harbour	**147**	52 16N	55	35W
Battleford	**152**	52 45N	108	15W
Batu Gajah	**96**	4 28N	101	3 E
Batu Is.	**111**	0 30S	98	25 E
Batumi	**70**	41 30N	41	30 E
Bauchi	**131**	10 22N	9	48 E
Bauru	**188**	22 10S	49	0W
Bavaria = Bayern □	**43**	49 7N	11	30 E
Bawdwin	**93**	23 5N	97	20 E
Bawean	**111**	5 46S	112	35 E
Bawku	**130**	11 3N	0	19W
Bay City	**167**	43 35N	83	51W
Bay Shore	**164**	40 44N	73	15W
Bayamo	**178**	20 20N	76	40W
Bayamón	**180**	18 24N	66	10W
Bayan Har Shan	**101**	34 0N	98	0 E
Bayan Hot = Alxa Zuoqi	**98**	38 50N	105	40 E
Bayern □	**43**	49 7N	11	30 E
Bayeux	**36**	49 17N	0	42W
Bayfield	**150**	43 34N	81	42W
Baykal, Oz.	**74**	53 0N	108	0 E
Baykonur	**71**	47 48N	65	50 E
Bayonne	**36**	43 30N	1	28W
Bayreuth	**43**	49 56N	11	35 E
Bayrūt	**80**	33 53N	35	31 E
Baytown	**168**	29 42N	94	57W
Beachy Head	**25**	50 44N	0	16 E
Beagle, Canal	**192**	55 0S	68	30W
Béarn	**36**	43 8N	0	36W
Beauce, Plaine de la	**37**	48 10N	1	45 E
Beaudesert	**116**	27 59S	153	0 E
Beaufort	**170**	32 25N	80	40W
Beaufort Sea	**12**	72 0N	140	0W
Beaugency	**39**	47 47N	1	38 E
Beauharnois	**151**	45 20N	73	52W
Beauly	**33**	57 29N	4	27W
Beaumaris	**26**	53 16N	4	7W
Beaumont	**168**	30 5N	94	8W
Beaumont-sur-Oise	**39**	49 9N	2	17 E
Beauséjour	**153**	50 5N	96	35W
Beauvais	**38**	49 25N	2	8 E
Beauval	**152**	55 9N	107	37W
Beaver	**142**	66 20N	147	30W
Beaver ↠	**152**	55 26N	107	45W
Beaver Falls	**164**	40 44N	80	20W
Beaverlodge	**155**	55 11N	119	29W
Beawar	**91**	26 3N	74	18 E
Bečej	**52**	45 36N	20	3 E
Béchar	**127**	31 38N	2	18W
Beckley	**165**	37 50N	81	8W
Bedford, U.K.	**25**	52 8N	0	29W
Bedford, U.S.A.	**167**	38 50N	86	30W
Bedford □	**25**	52 4N	0	28W
Beenleigh	**116**	27 43S	153	10 E
Be'er Sheva'	**80**	31 15N	34	48 E
Beersheba = Be'er Sheva'	**80**	31 15N	34	48 E
Beeston	**29**	52 55N	1	11W
Bega	**117**	36 41S	149	51 E
Behbehān	**84**	30 30N	50	15 E
Beibei	**99**	29 47N	106	22 E

Name	Pg	Lat		Long	
Beihai	99	21 28N	109	6 E
Beijing	98	39 55N	116	20 E
Beira	137	19 50S	34	52 E
Beira-Alta	50	40 35N	7	35W
Beira-Baixa	50	40 2N	7	30W
Beira-Litoral	50	40 5N	8	30W
Beirut = Bayrūt	80	33 53N	35	31 E
Bejaia	127	36 42N	5	2 E
Békéscsaba	59	46 40N	21	5 E
Bela	92	25 50N	82	0 E
Bela Crkva	52	44 55N	21	27 E
Belaya Tserkov	68	49 45N	30	10 E
Belcher Is.	140	56 15N	78	45W
Belém	188	1 20S	48	30W
Belfast, U.K.	34	54 35N	5	56W
Belfast, U.S.A.	148	44 30N	69	0W
Belfort	37	47 38N	6	50 E
Belgaum	91	15 55N	74	35 E
Belgium ■	42	50 30N	5	0 E
Belgorod	68	50 35N	36	35 E
Belgrade = Beograd	52	44 50N	20	37 E
Belitung	111	3 10S	107	50 E
Belize ■	177	17 0N	88	30W
Belize City	177	17 25N	88	0W
Bell Peninsula	146	63 50N	82	0W
Bell Ville	190	32 40S	62	40W
Bella Coola	154	52 25N	126	40W
Bellaire	164	40 1N	80	46W
Bellary	90	15 10N	76	56 E
Belle Fourche ~→	163	44 25N	102	19W
Belle Glade	170	26 43N	80	38W
Belle Isle	147	51 57N	55	25W
Belle Isle, Str. of	141	51 30N	56	30W
Bellefontaine	167	40 20N	83	45W
Belleville, Canada	151	44 10N	77	23W
Belleville, U.S.A.	166	38 30N	90	0W
Bellevue	155	49 35N	114	22W
Bellin	146	60 0N	70	0W
Bellingham	171	48 45N	122	27W
Bellingshausen Sea	14	66 0S	80	0W
Belmont	117	33 4S	151	42 E
Belmopan	177	17 18N	88	30W
Belo Horizonte	188	19 55S	43	56W
Belogorsk	75	51 0N	128	20 E
Beloit	166	42 35N	89	0W
Belomorsk	68	64 35N	34	30 E
Belovo	71	54 30N	86	0 E
Beloye More	69	66 30N	38	0 E
Beloye Ozero	68	45 15N	46	50 E
Belper	28	53 2N	1	29W
Belukha	71	49 50N	86	50 E
Belyy, Ostrov	69	73 30N	71	0 E
Bemidji	156	47 30N	94	50W
Ben Lomond, N.S.W., Australia	116	30 1S	151	40 E
Ben Lomond, Tas., Australia	119	41 38S	147	42 E
Ben Macdhui	33	57 4N	3	40W
Ben More, Central, U.K.	32	56 23N	4	31W
Ben More, Strathclyde, U.K.	30	56 26N	6	2W
Ben More Assynt	32	58 7N	4	51W
Ben Nevis	32	56 48N	5	0W
Benalla	117	36 30S	146	0 E
Benares = Varanasi	92	25 22N	83	0 E
Benbecula	32	57 26N	7	21W
Benbonyathe, Mt.	118	30 25S	139	11 E
Bencubbin	120	30 48S	117	52 E
Bend	171	44 2N	121	15W
Bendemeer	116	30 53S	151	8 E
Bender Beila	133	9 30N	50	48 E
Bendigo	117	36 40S	144	15 E
Benevento	49	41 7N	14	45 E
Bengal, Bay of	92	15 0N	90	0 E
Bengbu	99	32 58N	117	20 E
Benghazi = Banghāzī	128	32 11N	20	3 E
Benguela	134	12 37S	13	25 E
Beni ~→	187	10 23S	65	24W
Beni Suef	128	29 5N	31	6 E
Benidorm	51	38 33N	0	9W
Benin ■	131	10 0N	2	0 E
Benin, Bight of	131	5 0N	3	0 E
Benin City	131	6 20N	5	31 E
Benjamin Constant	187	4 40S	70	15W
Bennett	144	59 56N	134	53W
Bennettsville	165	34 38N	79	39W
Benton	168	34 30N	92	35W
Benue ~→	131	7 48N	6	46 E
Benxi	98	41 20N	123	48 E
Beograd	52	44 50N	20	37 E
Beppu	108	33 15N	131	30 E
Berau, Teluk	113	2 30S	132	30 E
Berber	129	18 0N	34	0 E
Berbera	133	10 30N	45	2 E
Berck-sur-Mer	38	50 25N	1	36 E
Berezniki	69	59 24N	56	46 E
Bérgamo	46	45 42N	9	40 E
Bergen, Neth.	40	52 40N	4	43 E
Bergen, Norway	60	60 23N	5	20 E
Bergen-op-Zoom	40	51 30N	4	18 E
Bergerac	36	44 51N	0	30 E
Berhala, Selat	111	1 0S	104	15 E
Berhampore = Baharampur	92	24 2N	88	27 E
Berhampur	92	19 15N	84	54 E
Bering Sea	142	58 0N	167	0 E
Bering Str.	142	66 0N	170	0W
Berkeley	172	37 52N	122	20W
Berkshire □	25	51 30N	1	20W
Berkshire Downs	24	51 30N	1	30W
Berlin, Germany	43	52 32N	13	24 E
Berlin, U.S.A.	148	44 29N	71	10W
Bermuda ■	180	32 45N	65	0W
Bern	44	46 57N	7	28 E
Bernay	39	49 5N	0	35 E
Berne = Bern	44	46 57N·	7	28 E
Berri	119	34 14S	140	35 E
Berry	37	47 0N	2	0 E
Bertoua	131	4 30N	13	45 E
Berwick-upon-Tweed	31	55 47N	2	0W
Berwyn Mts.	26	52 54N	3	26W
Besançon	37	47 15N	6	0 E
Bessemer, Ala., U.S.A.	169	33 25N	86	57W
Bessemer, Mich., U.S.A.	158	46 27N	90	0W
Bethel	142	60 50N	161	50W
Bethlehem	164	40 39N	75	24W
Béthune	38	50 30N	2	38 E
Betsiboka ~→	137	16 3S	46	36 E
Beverley	29	53 52N	0	26W
Beverly Hills	173	34 4N	118	29W
Beverwijk	40	52 28N	4	38 E
Bexhill	24	50 51N	0	29 E
Beyneu	70	45 10N	55	3 E
Beyşehir Gölü	80	37 40N	31	45 E
Béziers	37	43 20N	3	12 E
Bezwada = Vijayawada	92	16 31N	80	39 E
Bhadravati	90	13 49N	75	40 E
Bhagalpur	92	25 10N	87	0 E
Bhakra Dam	89	31 30N	76	45 E
Bhandara	91	21 5N	79	42 E
Bhanrer Ra.	91	23 40N	79	45 E
Bharat = India ■	78	20 0N	78	0 E
Bharatpur	89	27 15N	77	30 E
Bharuch	91	21 47N	73	0 E
Bhatpara	92	22 50N	88	25 E
Bhaunagar = Bhavnagar	91	21 45N	72	10 E
Bhavnagar	91	21 45N	72	10 E
Bhilwara	91	25 25N	74	38 E
Bhima ~→	91	16 25N	77	17 E
Bhiwandi	91	19 20N	73	0 E
Bhiwani	89	28 50N	76	9 E
Bhopal	91	23 20N	77	30 E
Bhubaneshwar	92	20 15N	85	50 E
Bhusaval	91	21 3N	75	46 E
Bhutan ■	92	27 25N	90	30 E
Biafra, B. of = Bonny, Bight of	131	3 30N	9	20 E
Biała Podlaska	58	52 4N	23	6 E
Białystok	58	53 10N	23	10 E
Biarritz	36	43 29N	1	33W
Bibai	103	43 19N	141	52 E
Bicester	25	51 53N	1	9W
Biche, L. la	155	54 50N	112	3W
Bidar	91	17 55N	77	35 E
Biddeford	148	43 30N	70	28W

Bideford **27** 51 1N 4 13W
Bié, Planalto de . . . . **136** 12 0S 16 0 E
Bieber **172** 41 4N 121 6W
Biel . . . . **44** 47 8N 7 14 E
Bielé Karpaty . . . . **59** 49 5N 18 0 E
Bielefeld . . . . **42** 52 2N 8 31 E
Bielsko-Biała . . . . **59** 49 50N 19 2 E
Bien Hoa . . . . **95** 10 57N 106 49 E
Bienne = Biel . . . . **44** 47 8N 7 14 E
Bienville, L. **146** 55 5N 72 40W
Big Belt Mts. **163** 46 50N 111 30W
Big Cypress Swamp **170** 26 12N 81 10W
Big Horn Mts. = Bighorn Mts. . . **163** 44 30N 107 30W
Big Rapids **167** 43 42N 85 27W
Big Sioux ⤳ **156** 42 30N 96 25W
Big Spring **161** 32 10N 101 25W
Big Stone Gap **165** 36 52N 82 45W
Big Trout L. **153** 53 40N 90 0W
Biggar, Canada **152** 52 4N 108 0W
Biggar, U.K. **31** 55 38N 3 31W
Bighorn ⤳ **163** 46 9N 107 28W
Bighorn Mts. **163** 44 30N 107 30W
Bihar . . . . **92** 25 5N 85 40 E
Bihar □ . . . . **92** 25 0N 86 0 E
Bijagós, Arquipélago dos **130** 11 15N 16 10W
Bijapur . . . . **91** 16 50N 75 55 E
Bijeljina . . . . **52** 44 46N 19 17 E
Bikaner . . . . **89** 28 2N 73 18 E
Bikin . . . . **75** 46 50N 134 20 E
Bilaspur . . . . **92** 22 2N 82 15 E
Bilauk Taungdan . . . . **94** 13 0N 99 0 E
Bilbao **50** 43 16N 2 56W
Billingham **29** 54 36N 1 18W
Billings **163** 45 43N 108 29W
Billiton Is. = Belitung . . . . **111** 3 10S 107 50 E
Bilma . . . . **127** 18 50N 13 30 E
Biloela . . . . **121** 24 24S 150 31 E
Biloxi **169** 30 24N 88 53W
Bina-Etawah . . . . **91** 24 13N 78 14 E
Bīnālūd, Kūh-e . . . . **86** 36 30N 58 30 E
Bindi Bindi . . . . **120** 30 37S 116 22 E
Bingara . . . . **116** 29 52S 150 36 E
Bingerville **130** 5 18N 3 49W
Bingham **148** 45 5N 69 50W
Binghamton **164** 42 9N 75 54W
Binh Dinh = An Nhon . . . . **95** 13 55N 109 7 E
Binnaway . . . . **116** 31 28S 149 24 E
Binzert = Bizerte . . . . **127** 37 15N 9 50 E
Bioko . . . . **131** 3 30N 8 40 E
Bir Mogreïn **126** 25 10N 11 25W
Birchip . . . . **119** 35 56S 142 55 E
Bird I. = Aves, I. de **181** 15 45N 63 55W
Birdum . . . . **114** 15 39S 133 13 E
Birkenhead **28** 53 24N 3 1W
Birmingham, U.K. **24** 52 30N 1 55W
Birmingham, U.S.A. **169** 33 31N 86 50W
Birobidzhan . . . . **75** 48 50N 132 50 E
Birr **35** 53 7N 7 55W
Bisai . . . . **106** 35 16N 136 44 E
Biscay, B. of **36** 45 0N 2 0W
Biscostasing **150** 47 18N 82 9W
Bishop Auckland **28** 54 40N 1 40W
Bishop's Stortford . . . . **25** 51 52N 0 11 E
Bismarck **163** 46 49N 100 49W
Bismarck Arch. . . . . **115** 2 30S 150 0 E
Bissagos = Bijagós,
  Arquipélago dos **130** 11 15N 16 10W
Bissau **130** 11 45N 15 45W
Bitola . . . . **52** 41 5N 21 10 E
Bitolj = Bitola . . . . **52** 41 5N 21 10 E
Bitterroot Range **162** 46 0N 114 20W
Biu . . . . **131** 10 40N 12 3 E
Biwa-Ko . . . . **106** 35 15N 136 10 E
Biysk . . . . **71** 52 40N 85 0 E
Bizen . . . . **109** 34 43N 134 8 E
Bizerte . . . . **127** 37 15N 9 50 E
Bjørnøya . . . . **13** 74 30N 19 0 E
Black ⤳ = Da ⤳ . . . . **95** 21 15N 105 20 E
Black Diamond **155** 50 45N 114 14W
Black Forest = Schwarzwald . **42** 48 0N 8 0 E
Black Hills **163** 44 0N 103 50W

Black Mts. **26** 51 52N 3 5W
Black Sea . . . . **17** 43 30N 35 0 E
Blackall . . . . **121** 24 25S 145 45 E
Blackburn **28** 53 44N 2 30W
Blackpool **28** 53 48N 3 3W
Blackwater . . . . **121** 23 35S 148 53 E
Blackwater ⤳, Meath,
  Ireland **34** 53 46N 7 0W
Blackwater ⤳, Munster,
  Ireland **35** 51 55N 7 50W
Blackwater ⤳, U.K. **34** 54 31N 6 35W
Blackwell **168** 36 55N 97 20W
Blaenau Ffestiniog **26** 53 0N 3 57W
Blagoveshchensk . . . . **75** 50 20N 127 30 E
Blair Atholl **33** 56 46N 3 50W
Blairmore **155** 49 40N 114 25W
Blanc, Mont . . . . **37** 45 48N 6 50 E
Blanca Peak **163** 37 35N 105 29W
Blanche L. . . . . **118** 29 15S 139 40 E
Blanco, C. **171** 42 50N 124 40W
Blandford Forum **24** 50 52N 2 10W
Blantyre . . . . **137** 15 45S 35 0 E
Blarney **35** 51 57N 8 35W
Blaydon **28** 54 56N 1 47W
Blayney . . . . **117** 33 32S 149 14 E
Blekinge län □ . . . . **61** 56 20N 15 20 E
Blenheim . . . . **123** 41 38S 173 57 E
Bletchley **25** 51 59N 0 44W
Blida . . . . **127** 36 30N 2 49 E
Blind River **150** 46 10N 82 58W
Blitar . . . . **111** 8 5S 112 11 E
Bloemfontein . . . . **137** 29 6S 26 14 E
Blois . . . . **36** 47 35N 1 20 E
Bloody Foreland **34** 55 10N 8 18W
Bloomington, Ill., U.S.A. **166** 40 27N 89 0W
Bloomington, Ind., U.S.A. . . . **167** 39 10N 86 30W
Bloomsburg **164** 41 0N 76 30W
Blue Mts., Oreg., U.S.A. **171** 45 15N 119 0W
Blue Mts., Pa., U.S.A. **164** 40 30N 76 30W
Blue Nile = Nîl el Azraq ⤳ . . **129** 15 38N 32 31 E
Blue Ridge Mts. **165** 36 30N 80 15W
Bluefield **165** 37 18N 81 14W
Bluefields **179** 12 20N 83 50W
Bluestack, mt. **34** 54 46N 8 5W
Bluff . . . . **123** 46 37S 168 20 E
Blumenau **191** 27 0S 49 0W
Blyth **28** 55 8N 1 32W
Bo **130** 7 55N 11 50W
Bo Hai . . . . **98** 39 0N 120 0 E
Boa Vista **185** 2 48N 60 30W
Boaco **179** 12 29N 85 35W
Bobadah . . . . **116** 32 19S 146 41 E
Bobcaygeon **151** 44 33N 78 33W
Bobo-Dioulasso **130** 11 8N 4 13W
Bobraomby, Tanjon' i . . . . . . **137** 12 40S 49 10 E
Bobruysk . . . . **68** 53 10N 29 15 E
Bôca do Acre **187** 8 50S 67 27W
Boca Raton **170** 26 21N 80 5W
Bocas del Toro **179** 9 15N 82 20W
Bocholt . . . . **42** 51 50N 6 35 E
Bochum . . . . **42** 51 28N 7 12 E
Boden . . . . **67** 65 50N 21 42 E
Bodensee . . . . **44** 47 35N 9 25 E
Bodhan . . . . **91** 18 40N 77 44 E
Bodmin **27** 50 28N 4 44W
Bodmin Moor **27** 50 33N 4 36W
Bodø . . . . **64** 67 17N 14 24 E
Bogalusa **169** 30 50N 89 55W
Boggabilla . . . . **116** 28 36S 150 24 E
Boggabri . . . . **116** 30 45S 150 0 E
Boggeragh Mts. **35** 52 2N 8 55W
Bognor Regis **25** 50 47N 0 40W
Bogong, Mt. . . . . **117** 36 47S 147 17 E
Bogor . . . . **111** 6 36S 106 48 E
Bogota **184** 4 34N 74 0W
Boguchany . . . . **74** 58 40N 97 30 E
Bohain . . . . **38** 49 59N 3 28 E
Bohemian Forest =
  Böhmerwald . . . . **43** 49 30N 12 40 E
Böhmerwald . . . . **43** 49 30N 12 40 E
Bohol . . . . **112** 9 50N 124 10 E

Bohol Sea	112	9 0N	124	0 E
Bohotleh	133	8 20N	46	25 E
Boise	162	43 43N	116	9W
Boissevain	153	49 15N	100	5W
Boké	130	10 56N	14	17W
Bolan Pass	88	29 50N	67	20 E
Bolaños, R. →	175	21 12N	104	5W
Bolbec	38	49 30N	0	30 E
Bolgatanga	130	10 44N	0	53W
Bolívar	190	36 15S	60	53W
Bolivia ■	187	17 6S	64	0W
Bolinäs	60	61 21N	16	24 E
Bollon	116	28 2S	147	29 E
Bologna	47	44 30N	11	20 E
Boloven, Cao Nguyen	95	15 10N	106	30 E
Bolsena, L. di	46	42 35N	11	55 E
Bolhovik, Ootrov	72	78 30N	102	0 C
Bolshoi Kavkas	70	42 50N	44	0 E
Bolshoy Begichev, Ostrov	72	74 20N	112	30 E
Bolsward	41	53 3N	5	32 E
Bolton	28	53 35N	2	26W
Bolzano	47	46 30N	11	20 E
Boma	134	5 50S	13	4 E
Bombala	117	36 56S	149	15 E
Bombay	91	18 55N	72	50 E
Bomu →	129	4 40N	23	30 E
Bon, C.	127	37 1N	11	2 E
Bonaire	181	12 10N	68	15W
Bonavista	149	48 40N	53	5W
Bonifacio, Bouches de	48	41 12N	9	15 E
Bonn	42	50 43N	7	6 E
Bonneval	39	48 11N	1	24 E
Bonnie Rock	120	30 29S	118	22 E
Bonny, Bight of	131	3 30N	9	20 E
Bonnyville	152	54 20N	110	45W
Bonthe	130	7 30N	12	33W
Boonah	116	27 58S	152	41 E
Boone	166	42 5N	93	53W
Boonville	167	38 3N	87	13W
Boorowa	117	34 28S	148	44 E
Boothia, Gulf of	146	71 0N	90	0W
Boothia Pen.	145	71 0N	94	0W
Bootle	28	53 28N	3	1W
Bôr	129	6 10N	31	40 E
Borås	60	57 43N	12	56 E
Borãzjãn	85	29 22N	51	10 E
Bordeaux	36	44 50N	0	36W
Borders □	31	55 35N	2	50W
Bordertown	119	36 19S	140	45 E
Bordj Omar Driss	127	28 10N	6	40 E
Borger	161	35 40N	101	20W
Borja	186	4 20S	77	40W
Borlänge	60	60 29N	15	26 E
Borneo	111	1 0N	115	0 E
Bornholm	61	55 10N	15	0 E
Borujerd	84	33 55N	48	50 E
Borzya	74	50 24N	116	31 E
Boscastle	27	50 42N	4	42W
Boshan	98	36 28N	117	49 E
Bosna →	52	45 4N	18	29 E
Bosna i Hercegovina □	52	44 0N	18	0 E
Bosnia = Bosna i				
Hercegovina □	52	44 0N	18	0 E
Bōsō-Hantō	107	35 20N	140	20 E
Bosporus = Karadeniz				
Boğazı	80	41 10N	29	10 E
Bossangoa	131	6 35N	17	30 E
Bossembélé	131	5 25N	17	40 E
Bossier City	168	32 28N	93	48W
Bosten Hu	100	41 55N	87	40 E
Boston, U.K.	29	52 59N	0	2W
Boston, U.S.A.	164	42 20N	71	0W
Bothnia, G. of	67	63 0N	20	0 E
Botletle →	136	20 10S	23	15 E
Botoşani	57	47 42N	26	41 E
Botswana ■	136	22 0S	24	0 E
Botucatu	188	22 55S	48	30W
Bou Djébéha	126	18 25N	2	45W
Bouaké	130	7 40N	5	2W
Bougie = Bejaia	127	36 42N	5	2 E
Boulogne-sur-Mer	38	50 42N	1	36 E
Bourbonnais	37	46 28N	3	0 E
Bourem	130	17 0N	0	24W
Bourg-en-Bresse	37	46 13N	5	12 E
Bourges	37	47 9N	2	25 E
Bourgogne	37	47 0N	4	30 E
Bourke	116	30 8S	145	55 E
Bournemouth	24	50 43N	1	53W
Bousso	131	10 34N	16	52 E
Bouvet I. = Bouvetøya	14	54 26S	3	24 E
Bouvetøya	14	54 26S	3	24 E
Bowen	121	20 0S	148	16 E
Bowland, Forest of	28	54 0N	2	30W
Bowling Green, Ky., U.S.A.	169	37 0N	86	25W
Bowling Green, Ohio, U.S.A.	167	41 22N	83	40W
Bowling Green, C.	121	19 19S	147	25 E
Bowmanville	151	43 55N	78	41W
Dowral	117	34 28S	150	27 E
Boyle	34	53 58N	8	19W
Boyne →	34	53 43N	6	15W
Boyne City	150	45 13N	85	1W
Boyup Brook	120	33 50S	116	23 E
Bozeman	163	45 40N	111	0W
Bozen = Bolzano	47	46 30N	11	20 E
Brač	52	43 20N	16	40 E
Bracciano, L. di	46	42 8N	12	11 E
Bracebridge	151	45 2N	79	19W
Bräcke	66	62 45N	15	26 E
Brad	56	46 10N	22	50 E
Bradenton	170	27 25N	82	35W
Bradford, U.K.	28	53 47N	1	45W
Bradford, U.S.A.	164	41 58N	78	41W
Braemar	33	57 2N	3	20W
Braga	50	41 35N	8	25W
Bragança, Brazil	188	1 0S	47	2W
Bragança, Portugal	50	41 48N	6	50W
Brahmanbaria	93	23 58N	91	15 E
Brahmani →	92	20 39N	86	46 E
Brahmaputra →	93	24 2N	90	59 E
Braidwood	117	35 27S	149	49 E
Brăila	57	45 19N	27	59 E
Brainerd	156	46 20N	94	10W
Braintree	25	51 53N	0	34 E
Brampton	151	43 45N	79	45W
Branco →	185	1 20S	61	50W
Branco, Cabo	182	7 9S	34	47W
Brandenburg	43	52 24N	12	33 E
Brandon	153	49 50N	99	57W
Brantford	151	43 10N	80	15W
Brasil, Planalto	188	18 0S	46	30W
Brasília	188	15 47S	47	55 E
Braşov	57	45 38N	25	35 E
Brassey, Banjaran	111	5 0N	117	15 E
Brasstown Bald, Mt.	165	34 54N	83	45W
Bratislava	59	48 10N	17	7 E
Bratsk	74	56 10N	101	30 E
Brattleboro	164	42 53N	72	37W
Braunschweig	43	52 17N	10	28 E
Drava	133	1 20N	44	8 E
Bravo del Norte →	174	25 57N	97	9W
Brawley	173	32 58N	115	30W
Bray	35	53 12N	6	6W
Brazil	167	39 32N	87	8W
Brazil ■	188	10 0S	50	0W
Brazilian Highlands = Brasil,				
Planalto	188	18 0S	46	30W
Brazos →	168	28 53N	95	23W
Brazzaville	134	4 9S	15	12 E
Brčko	52	44 54N	18	46 E
Breadalbane	31	56 30N	4	15W
Bream Bay	122	35 56S	174	28 E
Brecon	26	51 57N	3	23W
Brecon Beacons	26	51 53N	3	27W
Breda	40	51 35N	4	45 E
Breiðafjörður	64	65 15N	23	15W
Bremen	42	53 4N	8	47 E
Bremerhaven	42	53 34N	8	35 E
Bremerton	171	47 30N	122	38W
Brenham	168	30 5N	96	27W
Brentwood	25	51 37N	0	19 E
Bréscia	46	45 33N	10	13 E
Breslau = Wrocław	58	51 5N	17	5 E

Name						
Brest, France	**36**	48	24N	4	31W
Brest, U.S.S.R.	**68**	52	10N	23	40 E
Bretagne	**36**	48	0N	3	0W
Bretçu	**57**	46	7N	26	18 E
Breton Sd.	**169**	29	40N	89	12W
Brett, C.	**122**	35	10S	174	20 E
Brewer	**148**	44	43N	68	50W
Brewster	**171**	48	10N	119	51W
Brewton	**169**	31	9N	87	2W
Brezhnev	**68**	55	42N	52	19 E
Briançon	**37**	44	54N	6	39 E
Bridgend	**27**	51	30N	3	35W
Bridgeport	**164**	41	12N	73	12W
Bridgeton	**164**	39	29N	75	10W
Bridgetown, Australia	**120**	33	58S	116	7 E
Bridgetown, Barbados	**180**	13	0N	59	30W
Bridgnorth	**24**	52	33N	2	25W
Bridgwater	**27**	51	7N	3	0W
Bridlington	**29**	54	6N	0	11W
Bridport	**27**	50	43N	2	45W
Brigham City	**163**	41	30N	112	1W
Bright	**117**	36	42S	146	56 E
Brighton, Australia	**119**	42	42S	147	16 E
Brighton, U.K.	**25**	50	50N	0	9W
Brindisi	**49**	40	39N	17	55 E
Brisbane	**116**	27	25S	153	2 E
Bristol, U.K.	**27**	51	26N	2	35W
Bristol, Conn., U.S.A.	**164**	41	44N	72	57W
Bristol, Tenn., U.S.A.	**165**	36	36N	82	11W
Bristol B.	**142**	58	0N	160	0W
Bristol Channel	**27**	51	18N	4	30W
Bristow	**168**	35	55N	96	28W
British Columbia □	**154**	55	0N	125	15W
British Guiana = Guyana ■	**185**	5	0N	59	0W
British Honduras = Belize ■	**177**	17	0N	88	30W
British Isles	**18**	55	0N	4	0W
Brittany = Bretagne	**36**	48	0N	3	0W
Brive-la-Gaillarde	**36**	45	10N	1	32 E
Brlik	**71**	44	0N	74	5 E
Brno	**59**	49	10N	16	35 E
Broach = Bharuch	**91**	21	47N	73	0 E
Broad Law	**31**	55	30N	3	22W
Broad Sd.	**121**	22	0S	149	45 E
Broads, The	**29**	52	45N	1	30 E
Brochet	**145**	57	53N	101	40W
Brockton	**164**	42	8N	71	2W
Brockville	**151**	44	35N	75	41W
Brod	**52**	41	35N	21	17 E
Brodeur Pen.	**146**	72	30N	88	10W
Broken Hill = Kabwe	**135**	14	30S	28	29 E
Broken Hill	**118**	31	58S	141	29 E
Bromley	**25**	51	20N	0	5 E
Brookhaven	**169**	31	40N	90	25W
Brooks	**155**	50	35N	111	55W
Brooks Ra.	**142**	68	40N	147	0W
Brosna ⟶	**35**	53	8N	8	0W
Brough	**28**	54	32N	2	19W
Broughty Ferry	**31**	56	29N	2	50W
Brouwershaven	**40**	51	45N	3	55 E
Brownsville	**158**	25	56N	97	25W
Brownwood	**161**	31	45N	99	0W
Bruay-en-Artois	**38**	50	29N	2	33 E
Bruce, Mt.	**114**	22	37S	118	8 E
Bruce Rock	**120**	31	52S	118	8 E
Bruck an der Leitha	**45**	48	1N	16	47 E
Bruges = Brugge	**42**	51	13N	3	13 E
Brugge	**42**	51	13N	3	13 E
Brunei = Bandar Seri Begawan	**112**	4	52N	115	0 E
Brunei ■	**111**	4	50N	115	0 E
Bruno	**152**	52	20N	105	30W
Brunswick = Braunschweig	**43**	52	17N	10	28 E
Brunswick, Ga., U.S.A.	**170**	31	10N	81	30W
Brunswick, Maine, U.S.A.	**148**	43	53N	69	50W
Bruny I.	**119**	43	20S	147	15 E
Brussel	**42**	50	51N	4	21 E
Bruthen	**117**	37	42S	147	50 E
Bruton	**27**	51	6N	2	28W
Bryan, Ohio, U.S.A.	**167**	41	30N	84	30W
Bryan, Tex., U.S.A.	**168**	30	40N	96	27W
Bryan, Mt.	**119**	33	30S	139	0 E
Bryansk	**68**	53	13N	34	25 E
Brzeg	**58**	50	52N	17	30 E
Bucaramanga	**184**	7	0N	73	0W
Buchan	**33**	57	32N	2	8W
Buchan Ness	**33**	57	29N	1	48W
Buchanan	**130**	5	57N	10	2W
Buchans	**149**	48	50N	56	52W
Bucharest = Bucureşti	**57**	44	27N	26	10 E
Buckhannon	**165**	39	2N	80	10W
Buckhaven	**31**	56	10N	3	2W
Buckingham, Canada	**151**	45	37N	75	24W
Buckingham, U.K.	**25**	52	0N	0	59W
Buckingham □	**25**	51	50N	0	55W
Buckleboo	**118**	32	54S	136	12 E
Bucureşti	**57**	44	27N	26	10 E
Bucyrus	**167**	40	48N	83	0W
Budalin	**93**	22	20N	95	10 E
Budapest	**59**	47	29N	19	5 E
Budaun	**89**	28	5N	79	10 E
Bude	**27**	50	49N	4	33W
Budgewoi Lake	**117**	33	13S	151	34 E
Buenaventura, Colombia	**184**	3	53N	77	4W
Buenaventura, Mexico	**174**	29	51N	107	29W
Buenos Aires	**190**	34	30S	58	20W
Buffalo	**164**	42	55N	78	50W
Bug ⟶	**58**	52	31N	21	5 E
Buga	**184**	4	0N	76	15W
Bugun Shara	**100**	49	0N	104	0 E
Builth Wells	**26**	52	10N	3	26W
Buir Nur	**98**	47	50N	117	42 E
Bujumbura	**135**	3	16S	29	18 E
Bukachacha	**74**	52	55N	116	50 E
Bukavu	**23**	2	20S	28	52 E
Bukhara	**70**	39	48N	64	25 E
Bukit Mertajam	**96**	5	22N	100	28 E
Bukittinggi	**111**	0	20S	100	20 E
Bukoba	**135**	1	20S	31	49 E
Bukuru	**131**	9	42N	8	48 E
Bulahdelah	**117**	32	23S	152	13 E
Bulandshahr	**89**	28	28N	77	51 E
Bulawayo	**137**	20	7S	28	32 E
Bulgaria ■	**53**	42	35N	25	30 E
Bull Shoals L.	**168**	36	40N	93	5W
Bully-les-Mines	**38**	50	27N	2	44 E
Bulsar = Valsad	**91**	20	40N	72	58 E
Bulun	**72**	70	37N	127	30 E
Bunbury	**120**	33	20S	115	35 E
Buncrana	**34**	55	8N	7	28W
Bundaberg	**116**	24	54S	152	22 E
Bundi	**91**	25	30N	75	35 E
Bundoran	**34**	54	24N	8	17W
Bungo-Suidō	**109**	33	0N	132	15 E
Buorkhaya, Mys	**72**	71	50N	132	40 E
Bûr Sa'îd	**128**	31	16N	32	18 E
Bûr Sûdân	**129**	19	32N	37	9 E
Buraymī, Al Wāhāt al	**83**	24	10N	55	43 E
Burbank	**173**	34	9N	118	23W
Burdur	**80**	37	45N	30	22 E
Burdwan = Barddhaman	**92**	23	14N	87	39 E
Burgas	**53**	42	33N	27	29 E
Burgenland □	**45**	47	20N	16	20 E
Burgos	**50**	42	21N	3	41W
Burgundy = Bourgogne	**37**	47	0N	4	30 E
Burin	**149**	47	1N	55	14W
Burkina Faso ■	**130**	12	0N	1	0W
Burlington, Canada	**151**	43	18N	79	45W
Burlington, Iowa, U.S.A.	**166**	40	50N	91	5W
Burlington, N.C., U.S.A.	**165**	36	7N	79	27W
Burlington, N.J., U.S.A.	**164**	40	5N	74	50W
Burlington, Vt., U.S.A.	**151**	44	27N	73	14W
Burma ■	**93**	21	0N	96	30 E
Burnie	**119**	41	4S	145	56 E
Burnley	**28**	53	47N	2	15W
Burns	**171**	43	40N	119	4W
Burns Lake	**154**	54	20N	125	45W
Burra	**119**	33	40S	138	55 E
Bursa	**80**	40	15N	29	5 E
Burton-upon-Trent	**28**	52	48N	1	39W
Buru	**113**	3	30S	126	30 E
Burundi ■	**135**	3	15S	30	0 E
Bury	**28**	53	36N	2	19W

Bury St. Edmunds ... 25 52 15N 0 42 E
Buryat A.S.S.R. □ ... 74 53 0N 110 0 E
Buskerud fylke □ ... 60 60 13N 9 0 E
Busselton ... 120 33 42S 115 15 E
Bussum ... 40 52 16N 5 10 E
Bute ... 30 55 48N 5 2W
Butiaba ... 132 1 50N 31 20 E
Butler ... 164 40 52N 79 52W
Butte ... 163 46 0N 112 31W
Butterworth ... 96 5 24N 100 23 E
Butuan ... 112 8 57N 125 33 E
Butung ... 113 5 0S 122 45 E
Buxton ... 28 53 16N 1 54W
Buyaga ... 74 59 50N 127 0 E
Buzău ... 57 45 10N 26 50 E
Buzen ... 108 33 35N 131 5 E
Duzzards Day ... 164 41 45N 70 38W
Bydgoszcz ... 58 53 10N 18 0 E
Byelorussian S.S.R. □ ... 68 53 30N 27 0 E
Bylot I. ... 146 73 13N 78 34W
Byrd Land ... 15 79 30S 125 0W
Byron Bay ... 116 28 43S 153 37 E
Byrranga, Gory ... 72 75 0N 100 0 E
Bytom ... 58 50 25N 18 54 E

Cabimas ... 184 10 23N 71 25W
Cabinda ... 134 5 33S 12 11 E
Cabinda □ ... 134 5 0S 12 30 E
Cabo Pantoja ... 184 1 0S 75 10W
Cabonga, Réservoir ... 151 47 20N 76 40W
Caboolture ... 116 27 5S 152 58 E
Cabora Bassa Dam ... 137 15 20S 32 50 E
Caborca ... 174 30 40N 112 10W
Cabot Strait ... 149 47 15N 59 40W
Cabrera, I. ... 51 39 8N 2 57 E
Cabri ... 152 50 35N 108 25W
Cačak ... 52 43 54N 20 20 E
Cáceres ... 50 39 26N 6 23W
Cache Bay ... 151 46 22N 80 0W
Cachoeira ... 189 12 30S 39 0W
Cachoeira de Itapemirim ... 189 20 51S 41 7W
Cachoeira do Sul ... 191 30 3S 52 53W
Cader Idris ... 26 52 43N 3 56W
Cadibarrawirracanna, L. ... 118 28 52S 135 27 E
Cadillac, Canada ... 151 48 14N 78 23W
Cadillac, U.S.A. ... 167 44 16N 85 25W
Cádiz ... 50 36 30N 6 20W
Cádiz, G. de ... 50 36 40N 7 0W
Caen ... 36 49 10N 0 22W
Caernarfon ... 26 53 8N 4 17W
Caernarfon B. ... 26 53 4N 4 40W
Caernarvon = Caernarfon ... 26 53 8N 4 17W
Caerphilly ... 27 51 34N 3 13W
Cagayan de Oro ... 112 8 30N 124 40 E
Cágliari ... 48 39 15N 9 6 E
Caguas ... 180 18 14N 66 4W
Caha Mts. ... 35 51 45N 9 40W
Caher ... 35 52 23N 7 56W
Cahors ... 36 44 27N 1 27 E
Cahuapanas ... 186 5 15S 77 0W
Caibarién ... 178 22 30N 79 30W
Caicos Is. ... 180 21 40N 71 40W
Cairngorm Mts. ... 33 57 6N 3 42W
Cairns ... 121 16 57S 145 45 E
Cairo = El Qâhira ... 128 30 1N 31 14 E
Cairo ... 169 37 0N 89 10W
Cajamarca ... 186 7 5S 78 28W
Calabar ... 131 4 57N 8 20 E
Calabozo ... 184 9 0N 67 28W
Calábria □ ... 49 39 24N 16 30 E
Calais, France ... 38 50 57N 1 56 E
Calais, U.S.A. ... 148 45 11N 67 20W
Calama, Brazil ... 187 8 0S 62 50W
Calama, Chile ... 190 22 30S 68 55W
Calamar ... 184 10 15N 74 55W
Calamian Group ... 112 11 50N 119 55 E
Calca ... 187 13 22S 72 0W
Calcutta ... 92 22 36N 88 24 E
Caldwell ... 171 43 45N 116 42W

Calgary ... 155 51 0N 114 10W
Cali ... 184 3 25N 76 35W
Calicut ... 90 11 15N 75 43 E
California □ ... 172 37 25N 120 0W
California, Golfo de ... 174 28 0N 112 0W
Callander ... 31 56 15N 4 14W
Callao ... 186 12 0S 77 0W
Caloundra ... 116 26 45S 153 10 E
Caltanissetta ... 49 37 30N 14 3 E
Cam Lam ... 95 11 54N 109 10 E
Cam Ranh ... 95 11 54N 109 12 E
Camagüey ... 178 21 20N 78 0W
Camanár ... 186 16 30S 72 50W
Camargue ... 37 43 34N 4 34 E
Camarones ... 192 44 50S 65 40W
Cambay = Khambhat ... 91 22 23N 72 33 E
Camboja ■ ... 95 12 15N 105 0 E
Camborne ... 27 50 13N 5 18W
Cambrai ... 38 50 11N 3 14 E
Cambrian Mts. ... 26 52 25N 3 52W
Cambridge, Canada ... 151 43 23N 80 15W
Cambridge, N.Z. ... 122 37 54S 175 29 E
Cambridge, U.K. ... 25 52 13N 0 8 E
Cambridge, Mass., U.S.A. ... 164 42 20N 71 8W
Cambridge, Md., U.S.A. ... 164 38 33N 76 2W
Cambridge, Ohio, U.S.A. ... 167 40 1N 81 35W
Cambridge Bay ... 145 69 10N 105 0W
Cambridge Gulf ... 114 14 55S 128 15 E
Cambridgeshire □ ... 25 52 12N 0 7 E
Camden, Ark., U.S.A. ... 168 33 40N 92 50W
Camden, N.J., U.S.A. ... 164 39 57N 75 7W
Camden, S.C., U.S.A. ... 165 34 17N 80 34W
Cameroon ■ ... 131 6 0N 12 30 E
Cameroun, Mt. ... 131 4 13N 9 10 E
Cametá ... 188 2 12S 49 30W
Camiri ... 187 20 3S 63 31W
Camocim ... 189 2 55S 40 50W
Campagna ... 46 40 40N 15 5 E
Campania □ ... 49 40 50N 14 45 E
Campbell I. ... 15 52 30S 169 0 E
Campbell River ... 154 50 5N 125 20W
Campbellton ... 148 47 57N 66 43W
Campbelltown, Australia ... 117 34 4S 150 49 E
Campbeltown, U.K. ... 30 57 34N 4 2W
Campeche ... 177 19 51N 90 32W
Campeche ... 177 19 0N 90 30W
Campeche, B. de ... 177 20 0N 94 0W
Camperdown ... 119 38 14S 143 9 E
Camperville ... 153 51 59N 100 9W
Campina Grande ... 189 7 20S 35 47W
Campinas ... 188 22 50S 47 0W
Campo Grande ... 188 20 25S 54 40W
Campos ... 188 21 50S 41 20W
Camrose ... 155 53 0N 112 50W
Can Tho ... 95 10 2N 105 46 E
Canada ■ ... 139 60 0N 100 0W
Cañada de Gómez ... 190 32 40S 61 30W
Canadian ► ... 150 05 27N 95 3W
Çanakkale Boğazi ... 80 40 0N 26 0 E
Cananea ... 174 30 57N 110 18W
Canarias, Islas ... 126 28 30N 16 0W
Canary Is. = Canarias, Islas ... 126 28 30N 16 0W
Canaveral, C. ... 170 28 28N 80 31W
Canberra ... 117 35 15S 149 8 E
Candala ... 133 11 30N 49 58 E
Candia = Iráklion ... 55 35 20N 25 12 E
Canea = Khaniá ... 55 35 30N 24 4 E
Çankiri ... 80 40 40N 33 37 E
Canmore ... 155 51 7N 115 18W
Canna ... 32 57 3N 6 33W
Cannanore ... 90 11 53N 75 27 E
Cannes ... 37 43 32N 7 0 E
Cannock ... 28 52 42N 2 2W
Canora ... 152 51 40N 102 30W
Canowindra ... 117 33 35S 148 38 E
Canso ... 149 45 20N 61 0W
Cantabrian Mts. =
Cantábrica, Cordillera ... 50 43 0N 5 10W
Cantábrica, Cordillera ... 50 43 0N 5 10W
Canterbury ... 25 51 17N 1 5 E
Canterbury □ ... 123 43 45S 171 19 E

Canterbury Bight	**123**	44 16S	171	55 E
Canterbury Plains	**123**	43 55S	171	22 E
Canton = Guangzhou	**99**	23 5N	113	10 E
Canton, Ill., U.S.A.	**166**	40 32N	90	0W
Canton, Miss., U.S.A.	**169**	32 40N	90	1W
Canton, Ohio, U.S.A.	**167**	40 47N	81	22W
Canutama	**185**	6 30S	64	20W
Cap-Chat	**148**	49 6N	66	40W
Cap-de-la-Madeleine	**151**	46 22N	72	31W
Cap-Haïtien	**180**	19 40N	72	20W
Cape Barren I.	**119**	40 25S	148	15 E
Cape Breton I.	**149**	46 0N	60	30W
Cape Coast	**130**	5 5N	1	15W
Cape Dorset	**146**	64 14N	76	32W
Cape Fear ⟶	**165**	34 30N	78	25W
Cape Girardeau	**169**	37 20N	89	30W
Cape May	**164**	39 1N	74	53W
Cape Montague	**149**	46 5N	62	25W
Cape Province □	**136**	32 0S	23	0 E
Cape Town	**136**	33 55S	18	22 E
Cape Verde Is. ■	**9**	17 10N	25	20W
Cape York Peninsula	**115**	12 0S	142	30 E
Caquetá ⟶	**184**	1 15S	69	15W
Caracal	**57**	44 8N	24	22 E
Caracas	**184**	10 30N	66	55W
Caratinga	**188**	19 50S	42	10W
Carberry	**153**	49 50N	99	25W
Carbonara, C.	**48**	39 8N	9	30 E
Carbondale	**166**	37 45N	89	10W
Carbonear	**149**	47 42N	53	13W
Carcassonne	**37**	43 13N	2	20 E
Carcross	**144**	60 13N	134	45W
Cárdenas, Cuba	**178**	23 0N	81	30W
Cárdenas, Mexico	**177**	21 0N	99	40W
Cardiff	**27**	51 28N	3	11W
Cardigan	**26**	52 6N	4	41W
Cardigan B.	**26**	52 30N	4	30W
Cardston	**155**	49 15N	113	20W
Cardwell	**121**	18 14S	146	2 E
Caribbean Sea	**181**	15 0N	75	0W
Cariboo Mts.	**155**	53 0N	121	0W
Caribou	**148**	46 55N	68	0W
Caribou Mts.	**145**	59 12N	115	40W
Carinhanha	**188**	14 15S	44	46W
Carinthia = Kärnten □	**45**	46 52N	13	30 E
Carlisle, U.K.	**28**	54 54N	2	55W
Carlisle, U.S.A.	**164**	40 12N	77	10W
Carlow	**35**	52 50N	6	58W
Carlow □	**35**	52 43N	6	50W
Carlsbad, Calif., U.S.A.	**173**	33 11N	117	25W
Carlsbad, N. Mex., U.S.A.	**161**	32 20N	104	14W
Carlyle	**152**	49 40N	102	20W
Carmacks	**144**	62 5N	136	16W
Carman	**153**	49 30N	98	0W
Carmarthen	**26**	51 52N	4	20W
Carmarthen B.	**27**	51 40N	4	30W
Carnarvon	**120**	24 51S	113	42 E
Carnegie, L.	**114**	26 5S	122	30 E
Carniche, Alpi	**47**	46 36N	13	0 E
Carnsore Pt.	**35**	52 10N	6	20W
Caroline Is.	**122**	8 0N	150	0 E
Caroona	**116**	31 24S	150	26 E
Carpathians, Mts.	**17**	49 50N	21	0 E
Carpaţii Meridionali	**57**	45 30N	25	0 E
Carpentaria, G. of	**115**	14 0S	139	0 E
Carrara	**46**	44 5N	10	7 E
Carrick-on-Shannon	**34**	53 57N	8	7W
Carrick-on-Suir	**35**	52 22N	7	30W
Carrickfergus	**34**	54 43N	5	50W
Carrickmacross	**34**	54 0N	6	43W
Carroll	**166**	42 2N	94	55W
Carrollton	**170**	33 36N	85	5W
Carse of Gowrie	**31**	56 30N	3	10W
Carson City	**172**	39 12N	119	46W
Carstairs	**31**	55 42N	3	41W
Cartagena, Colombia	**184**	10 25N	75	33W
Cartagena, Spain	**51**	37 38N	0	59W
Cartago, Colombia	**184**	4 45N	75	55W
Cartago, C. Rica	**179**	9 50N	85	52W
Cartersville	**169**	34 11N	84	48W
Carthage	**168**	37 10N	94	20W
Cartwright	**147**	53 41N	56	58W
Caruaru	**189**	8 15S	35	55W
Carúpano	**185**	10 39N	63	15W
Caruthersville	**169**	36 10N	89	40W
Carvin	**38**	50 30N	2	57 E
Casablanca	**126**	33 36N	7	36W
Casas Grandes	**174**	30 22N	107	57W
Cascade Ra.	**171**	47 0N	121	30W
Casilda	**190**	33 10S	61	10W
Casino	**116**	28 52S	153	3 E
Casiquiare ⟶	**184**	2 1N	67	7W
Casma	**186**	9 30S	78	20W
Casper	**163**	42 52N	106	20W
Caspian Sea	**70**	43 0N	50	0 E
Cassiar Mts.	**144**	59 30N	130	30W
Castellón de la Plana	**51**	39 58N	0	3W
Castelsarrasin	**36**	44 2N	1	7 E
Casterton	**119**	37 30S	141	30 E
Castilla La Nueva	**50**	39 45N	3	20W
Castilla La Vieja	**50**	41 55N	4	0W
Castle Douglas	**31**	54 57N	3	57W
Castlebar	**34**	53 52N	9	17W
Castleblaney	**34**	54 7N	6	44W
Castlegar	**155**	49 20N	117	40W
Castlemaine	**117**	37 2S	144	12 E
Castlereagh	**34**	53 47N	8	30W
Castletown	**28**	58 35N	3	22W
Castletown Bearhaven	**35**	51 40N	9	54W
Castor	**155**	52 15N	111	50W
Castres	**37**	43 37N	2	13 E
Castricum	**40**	52 33N	4	40 E
Castries	**180**	14 0N	60	50W
Castro	**192**	42 30S	73	50W
Cat I.	**178**	24 30N	75	30W
Catacáos	**186**	5 20S	80	45W
Catalonia = Cataluña □	**51**	41 40N	1	15 E
Cataluña □	**51**	41 40N	1	15 E
Catamarca	**190**	28 30S	65	50W
Catanduanes	**112**	13 50N	124	20 E
Catánia	**49**	37 31N	15	4 E
Catanzaro	**49**	38 54N	16	38 E
Catoche, C.	**177**	21 35N	87	5W
Catskill Mts.	**164**	42 15N	74	15W
Cauca ⟶	**184**	8 54N	74	28W
Caucasus Mts. = Bolshoi Kavkas	**70**	42 50N	44	0 E
Caudry	**38**	50 7N	3	22 E
Cauquenes	**190**	36 0S	72	22W
Cavaillon	**37**	43 50N	5	2 E
Cavan	**34**	54 0N	7	22W
Cawnpore = Kanpur	**91**	26 28N	80	20 E
Caxias	**188**	4 55S	43	20W
Caxias do Sul	**191**	29 10S	51	10W
Cayenne	**185**	5 0N	52	18W
Cayes, Les	**180**	18 15N	73	46W
Cayman Is.	**178**	19 40N	80	30W
Ceanannus Mor	**34**	53 42N	6	53W
Ceará = Fortaleza	**189**	3 45S	38	35W
Ceará □	**189**	5 0S	40	0W
Cebu	**112**	10 18N	123	54 E
Cedar ⟶	**166**	41 17N	91	21W
Cedar City	**162**	37 41N	113	3W
Cedar Falls	**166**	42 39N	92	29W
Cedar L.	**152**	53 10N	100	0W
Cedar Rapids	**166**	42 0N	91	38W
Cedartown	**169**	34 1N	85	15W
Ceduna	**118**	32 7S	133	46 E
Cegléd	**59**	47 11N	19	47 E
Ceiba, La	**179**	15 40N	86	50W
Celaya	**177**	20 31N	100	37W
Celebes = Sulawesi □	**113**	2 0S	120	0 E
Celebes Sea	**113**	3 0N	123	0 E
Center	**168**	31 50N	94	10W
Centerville	**166**	40 45N	92	57W
Central □	**31**	56 10N	4	30W
Central, Cordillera	**184**	5 0N	75	0W
Central African Republic ■	**129**	7 0N	20	0 E
Central Auckland □	**122**	37 30S	175	30 E
Central Makran Range	**88**	26 30N	64	15 E
Central Russian Uplands	**17**	54 0N	36	0 E
Central Siberian Plateau	**77**	65 0N	105	0 E

Centralia ... 166 38 32N 89 5W
Cephalonia = Kefallinía ... 54 38 20N 20 30 E
Ceram = Seram ... 113 3 10S 129 0 E
Ceram Sea = Seram Sea ... 113 2 30S 128 30 E
Cerignola ... 49 41 17N 15 53 E
Cerigo = Kíthira ... 55 36 9N 23 0 E
Cerritos ... 177 22 26N 100 17W
Cesena ... 47 44 9N 12 14 E
Ceskomoravská Vrchovina ... 59 49 30N 15 40 E
Ceský Těšín ... 59 49 45N 18 39 E
Cessnock ... 117 32 50S 151 21 E
Cetinje ... 52 42 23N 18 59 E
Ceuta ... 126 35 52N 5 18W
Cévennes ... 37 44 10N 3 50 E
Ceylon = Sri Lanka ■ ... 90 7 30N 80 50 E
Chachapoyas ... 186 6 15S 77 50W
Chachoengsao ... 95 13 42N 101 5 E
Chad ■ ... 131 15 0N 17 15 E
Chad, L. = Tchad, L. ... 131 13 30N 14 30 E
Chadron ... 163 42 50N 103 0W
Chagos Arch. ... 76 6 0S 72 0 E
Chāh Bahār ... 85 25 20N 60 40 E
Chakradharpur ... 92 22 45N 85 40 E
Chala ... 186 15 48S 74 20W
Chalcis = Khalkís ... 55 38 27N 23 42 E
Chalhuanca ... 186 14 15S 73 15W
Chalisgaon ... 91 20 30N 75 10 E
Challapata ... 187 18 53S 66 50W
Chalon-sur-Saône ... 37 46 48N 4 50 E
Châlons-sur-Marne ... 37 48 58N 4 20 E
Chambal —► ... 91 26 29N 79 15 E
Chambersburg ... 164 39 53N 77 41W
Chambéry ... 37 45 34N 5 55 E
Chamonix ... 37 45 55N 6 51 E
Champagne ... 37 49 0N 4 40 E
Champaign ... 167 40 8N 88 14W
Champlain, L. ... 151 44 30N 73 20W
Chañaral ... 190 26 23S 70 40W
Chandigarh ... 89 30 43N 76 47 E
Chandler ... 118 27 0S 133 19 E
Chang Jiang —► ... 99 31 48N 121 10 E
Changchiak'ou =
Zhangjiakou ... 98 40 48N 114 55 E
Ch'angchou = Changzhou ... 99 31 47N 119 58 E
Changchun ... 98 43 57N 125 17 E
Changde ... 99 29 4N 111 35 E
Changhai = Shanghai ... 99 31 15N 121 26 E
Changsha ... 99 28 12N 113 0 E
Changzhi ... 98 36 10N 113 6 E
Changzhou ... 99 31 47N 119 58 E
Channel Is. ... 36 49 30N 2 40W
Channel-Port aux Basques ... 149 47 30N 59 9W
Chanthaburi ... 95 12 38N 102 12 E
Chantilly ... 39 49 12N 2 29 E
Chanute ... 166 37 45N 95 25W
Chao Phraya —► ... 94 13 32N 100 36 E
Ch'aoan ... 99 23 41N 116 33 E
Chapala, L. de ... 175 20 15N 103 0W
Chapayevsk ... 68 53 0N 49 40 E
Chapel Hill ... 185 35 53N 79 3W
Chapleau ... 150 47 50N 83 24W
Charagua ... 187 19 45S 63 10W
Charaña ... 187 17 30S 69 25W
Chard ... 27 50 52N 2 59W
Chardzhou ... 70 39 6N 63 34 E
Chari —► ... 131 12 58N 14 31 E
Chārīkār ... 87 35 0N 69 10 E
Charleroi ... 42 50 24N 4 27 E
Charles, C. ... 165 37 10N 75 59W
Charles City ... 166 43 2N 92 41W
Charleston, S.C., U.S.A. ... 170 32 47N 79 56W
Charleston, W. Va., U.S.A. ... 165 38 24N 81 36W
Charleville = Rath Luirc ... 35 52 21N 8 40W
Charleville ... 116 26 24S 146 15 E
Charleville-Mézières ... 37 49 44N 4 40 E
Charlotte, Mich., U.S.A. ... 167 42 36N 84 48W
Charlotte, N.C., U.S.A. ... 165 35 16N 80 46W
Charlotte Amalie ... 180 18 22N 64 56W
Charlotte Harbor ... 170 26 58N 82 4W
Charlottenburg ... 43 52 31N 13 15 E
Charlottesville ... 165 38 1N 78 30W

Charlottetown ... 149 46 14N 63 8W
Charlton, Australia ... 117 36 16S 143 24 E
Charlton, U.S.A. ... 166 40 59N 93 20W
Charters Towers ... 121 20 5S 146 13 E
Chartres ... 39 48 29N 1 30 E
Chascomús ... 191 35 30S 58 0W
Château-du-Loir ... 39 47 40N 0 25 E
Château-Thierry ... 39 49 3N 3 20 E
Châteaubriant ... 36 47 43N 1 23W
Châteaudun ... 39 48 3N 1 20 E
Châteauroux ... 37 46 50N 1 40 E
Châtellerault ... 36 46 50N 0 30 E
Chatham, N.B., Canada ... 148 47 2N 65 28W
Chatham, Ont., Canada ... 141 42 24N 82 11W
Chatham, U.K. ... 25 51 22N 0 32 E
Chatta-Hantō ... 106 34 45N 136 55 E
Chattahoochee —► ... 170 30 43N 84 51W
Chattanooga ... 169 35 2N 85 17W
Chaumont ... 37 48 7N 5 8 E
Chauny ... 38 49 37N 3 12 E
Cheboksary ... 68 56 8N 47 12 E
Cheboygan ... 150 45 38N 84 29W
Checheno-Ingush A.S.S.R. □ ... 70 43 30N 45 29 E
Chegdomyn ... 75 51 7N 133 1 E
Chegga ... 126 25 27N 5 40W
Chehalis ... 171 46 44N 122 59W
Cheju Do ... 99 33 29N 126 34 E
Chokiang = Zhejiang □ ... 99 29 0N 120 0 F
Chelforó ... 190 39 0S 66 33W
Chelkar Tengiz, Solonchak ... 70 48 0N 62 30 E
Chelm ... 58 51 8N 23 30 E
Chelmża ... 58 53 10N 18 39 E
Cheltenham ... 24 51 55N 2 5W
Chelyabinsk ... 71 55 10N 61 24 E
Chemainus ... 154 48 55N 123 42W
Chemnitz = Karl-Marx-Stadt . 43 50 50N 12 55 E
Chemult ... 171 43 14N 121 47W
Chen, Gora ... 73 65 16N 141 50 E
Chencha ... 132 6 15N 37 32 E
Chenchiang = Zhenjiang ... 99 32 11N 119 26 E
Chengchou = Zhengzhou ... 99 34 45N 113 34 E
Chengde ... 98 40 59N 117 58 E
Chengdu ... 99 30 38N 104 2 E
Ch'engtu = Chengdu ... 99 30 38N 104 2 E
Cheo Reo ... 95 13 25N 108 28 E
Chepstow ... 27 51 38N 2 40W
Cher —► ... 36 47 21N 0 29 E
Cherbourg ... 36 49 39N 1 40W
Cheremkhovo ... 74 53 8N 103 1 E
Cherepovets ... 68 59 5N 37 55 E
Cherkassy ... 68 49 27N 32 4 E
Chernigov ... 68 51 28N 31 20 E
Chernovtsy ... 68 48 15N 25 52 E
Chernoye ... 72 70 30N 89 10 E
Cherokee ... 166 42 40N 95 30W
Cherrapunji ... 93 25 17N 91 47 E
Cherskiy ... 73 68 45N 161 18 E
Cherskogo Khrebet ... 73 65 0N 143 0 E
Cherwell —► ... 25 51 46N 1 18W
Chesapeake ... 165 36 43N 76 15W
Chesapeake Bay ... 165 38 0N 76 12W
Cheshire □ ... 28 53 14N 2 30W
Cheshskaya Guba ... 69 67 20N 47 0 E
Chester, U.K. ... 28 53 12N 2 53W
Chester, Pa., U.S.A. ... 164 39 54N 75 20W
Chester, S.C., U.S.A. ... 165 34 44N 81 13W
Chesterfield ... 28 53 14N 1 26W
Chesterfield Inlet ... 145 63 30N 90 45W
Chetumal ... 177 18 30N 88 18W
Cheviot, The ... 31 55 29N 2 8W
Cheviot Hills ... 31 55 20N 2 30W
Chew Bahir ... 132 4 40N 36 50 E
Cheyenne ... 163 41 9N 104 49W
Cheyenne —► ... 163 44 40N 101 15W
Chhapra ... 92 25 48N 84 44 E
Chiamussu = Jiamusi ... 98 46 40N 130 26 E
Chiang Mai ... 94 18 47N 98 59 E
Chiapa —► ... 177 16 42N 93 0W
Chiapas □ ... 177 16 30N 92 30W
Chiba ... 107 35 30N 140 7 E
Chibougamau ... 151 49 56N 74 24W

Chicago **167** 41 53N 87 40W
Chicago Heights.......... **167** 41 29N 87 37W
Chichagof I.............. **143** 58 0N 136 0W
Chichester **25** 50 50N   0 47W
Chichibu .... **107** 36 5N 139 10 E
Ch'ich'ihaerh = Qiqihar...... **98** 47 26N 124 0 E
Chiclayo **186** 6 42S 79 50W
Chico **172** 39 45N 121 54W
Chicopee **164** 42 6N 72 37W
Chicoutimi **148** 48 28N 71 5W
Chidambaram............. **90** 11 20N 79 45 E
Chidley C. **146** 60 23N 64 26W
Chigasaki............... **107** 35 19N 139 24 E
Chihli, G. of = Bo Hai....... **98** 39 0N 120 0 E
Chihuahua **174** 28 38N 106 5W
Chihuahua □............. **174** 28 30N 106 0W
Chikugo .... **108** 33 14N 130 28 E
Chilapa................. **177** 17 40N 99 11W
Childress **161** 34 30N 100 15W
Chile ■................. **190** 35 0S 72 0W
Chilin = Jilin .... **98** 43 44N 126 30 E
Chilka L................ **92** 19 40N 85 25 E
Chillán **190** 36 40S 72 10W
Chillicothe, Mo., U.S.A. **166** 39 45N 93 30W
Chillicothe, Ohio, U.S.A. **167** 39 20N 82 58W
Chilliwack **154** 49 10N 121 54W
Chiloé, I. de **192** 42 30S 73 50W
Chilpancingo **177** 17 30N 99 30W
Chiltern Hills **25** 51 44N   0 42W
Chimborazo.............. **184** 1 29S 78 55W
Chimbote **186** 9 0S 78 35W
Chimkent .... **71** 42 18N 69 36 E
Chin □ .... **93** 22 0N 93 0 E
China ■ .... **79** 30 0N 110 0 E
Chinan = Jinan........... **98** 36 38N 117 1 E
Chinandega **179** 12 35N 87 12W
Chincha Alta **186** 13 25S 76 7W
Chinchilla .... **116** 26 45S 150 38 E
Chinchou = Jinzhou ...... **98** 41 5N 121 3 E
Chindwin ～ .... **93** 21 26N 95 15 E
Ch'ingtao = Qingdao ..... **98** 36 5N 120 20 E
Chinju .... **98** 35 12N 128 2 E
Chinnampo .... **98** 38 52N 125 10 E
Chino .... **107** 35 59N 138 9 E
Chinon .... **36** 47 10N   0 15 E
Chippenham **24** 51 27N   2 7W
Chippewa Falls.......... **166** 44 55N 91 22W
Chiquián **186** 10 10S 77 0W
Chiquimula **177** 14 51N 89 37W
Chiquinquira **184** 5 37N 73 50W
Chirala .... **90** 15 50N 80 26 E
Chirchik .... **71** 41 29N 69 35 E
Chita .... **74** 52 0N 113 35 E
Chitral................. **89** 35 50N 71 56 E
Chitré **179** 7 59N 80 27W
Chittagong.............. **93** 22 19N 91 48 E
Chittagong □ .... **93** 24 5N 91 0 E
Chivilcoy **190** 34 55S 60 0W
Chkalov = Orenburg ..... **70** 51 45N 55 6 E
Chōfu .... **107** 35 39N 139 33 E
Choix **174** 26 43N 108 17W
Chojnice................ **58** 53 42N 17 32 E
Cholet.................. **36** 47 4N   0 52W
Choluteca **179** 13 20N 87 14W
Chon Buri............... **95** 13 21N 101 1 E
Chongjin .... **98** 41 47N 129 50 E
Chŏngju .... **98** 36 39N 127 27 E
Chongqing .... **99** 29 35N 106 25 E
Chŏnju .... **98** 35 50N 127 4 E
Chonos, Arch. de los **192** 45 0S 75 0W
Chorley................. **28** 53 39N   2 39W
Chorzów................. **58** 50 18N 18 57 E
Chōshi .... **107** 35 45N 140 51 E
Christchurch, N.Z. .... **123** 43 33S 172 47 E
Christchurch, U.K. **24** 50 44N   1 33W
Christianshåb **147** 68 50N 51 18W
Christmas I. = Kiritimati **123** 1 58N 157 27W
Christmas I. .... **111** 10 30S 105 40 E
Ch'uanchou = Quanzhou .... **99** 24 55N 118 34 E
Chūbu □ .... **106** 36 45N 137 30 E
Chubut ～ **192** 43 20S 65 5W

Chūgoku □ .... **109** 35 0N 133 0 E
Chūgoku-Sanchi.......... **109** 35 0N 133 0 E
Chukotskiy Khrebet .... **73** 68 0N 175 0 E
Chukotskoye More **73** 68 0N 175 0W
Chula Vista **173** 32 39N 117 8W
Chulman .... **74** 56 52N 124 52 E
Chulucanas **186** 5 8S 80 10W
Chumikan .... **75** 54 40N 135 10 E
Chumphon .... **94** 10 35N 99 14 E
Chunchŏn .... **98** 37 58N 127 44 E
Chungking = Chongqing ... **99** 29 35N 106 25 E
Chuquibamba............. **186** 15 47S 72 44W
Chur .... **44** 46 52N   9 32 E
Churchill ～, Man., Canada . **143** 58 47N 94 12W
Churchill ～, Nfld., Canada . **147** 53 19N 60 10W
Churchill, C............ **143** 58 46N 93 12W
Churchill Falls **147** 53 36N 64 19W
Churchill Pk. **144** 58 10N 125 10W
Churu .... **89** 28 20N 74 50 E
Chuvash A.S.S.R.□ .... **68** 55 30N 47 0 E
Chuxiong .... **101** 25 2N 101 28 E
Cicero.................. **167** 41 48N 87 48W
Ciego de Avila......... **178** 21 50N 78 50W
Ciénaga **184** 11 1N 74 15W
Cienfuegos **178** 22 10N 80 30W
Cimarron ～ **161** 36 10N 96 17W
Cincinnati.............. **167** 39 10N 84 26W
Cinto, Mt. .... **36** 42 24N   8 54 E
Ciotat, La .... **37** 43 12N   5 36 E
Circle **142** 65 50N 144 10W
Circleville **167** 39 35N 82 57W
Cirebon .... **111** 6 45S 108 32 E
Cirencester **24** 51 43N   1 59W
Citlaltépetl, Volcán **177** 19 1N 97 16W
Ciudad Acuña............ **174** 29 20N 100 58W
Ciudad Bolívar **185** 8 5N 63 36W
Ciudad Camargo, Chihuahua,
  Mexico **174** 27 40N 105 10W
Ciudad Camargo,
  Tamaulipas, Mexico....... **176** 26 19N 98 50W
Ciudad de Valles **177** 21 59N 99 1W
Ciudad del Carmen **177** 18 38N 91 50W
Ciudad Guayana **185** 8 0N 62 30W
Ciudad Guzmán **175** 19 41N 103 29W
Ciudad Juárez **174** 31 44N 106 29W
Ciudad Madero........... **177** 22 16N 97 50W
Ciudad Mante **177** 22 44N 98 57W
Ciudad Obregón **174** 27 29N 109 56W
Ciudad Real **50** 38 59N   3 55W
Ciudad Rodrigo **50** 40 35N   6 32W
Ciudad Trujillo = Santo
  Domingo **180** 18 30N 64 54W
Ciudad Victoria **177** 23 44N 99 8W
Civril .... **80** 38 20N 29 43 E
Cizre .... **81** 37 19N 42 10 E
Clare .... **119** 33 50S 138 37 E
Clare □................. **35** 52 20N   9 0W
Clare ～ **35** 53 22N   9 5W
Clare I. **34** 53 48N 10 0W
Claremont **164** 43 23N 72 20W
Claremore **168** 36 40N 95 37W
Claremorris **34** 53 45N   9 0W
Claresholm **155** 50 0N 113 33W
Clark Fork ～ **162** 48 9N 116 15W
Clarksburg **164** 39 18N 80 21W
Clarksdale **169** 34 12N 90 33W
Clarkston **171** 46 28N 117 2W
Clarksville **169** 36 32N 87 20W
Clear, C. **20** 51 26N   9 30W
Clearwater, Canada...... **155** 51 38N 120 2W
Clearwater, U.S.A....... **170** 27 58N 82 45W
Cleburne **168** 32 18N 97 25W
Clee Hills **24** 52 26N   2 35W
Cleethorpes............. **29** 53 33N   0 2W
Cleeve Hill **24** 51 54N   2 0W
Clermont, Australia........ **121** 22 49S 147 39 E
Clermont, France .... **39** 49 23N   2 24 E
Clermont-Ferrand .... **37** 45 46N   3 4 E
Clevedon **27** 51 26N   2 52W
Cleveland, Miss., U.S.A. **169** 33 43N 90 43W
Cleveland, Ohio, U.S.A...... **167** 41 28N 81 43W

Name	Map	Lat	Long
Cleveland, Tenn., U.S.A.	169	35 9N	84 52W
Cleveland, Tex., U.S.A.	169	30 18N	95 0W
Cleveland □	29	54 35N	1 8E
Cleveleys	28	53 52N	3 3W
Clew B.	34	53 54N	9 50W
Clifton Beach	121	16 46S	145 39E
Clifton Forge	165	37 49N	79 51W
Clinton, Canada	150	43 37N	81 32W
Clinton, Iowa, U.S.A.	166	41 50N	90 12W
Clinton, Mass., U.S.A.	164	42 26N	71 40W
Clinton, Mo., U.S.A.	166	38 20N	93 46W
Clinton, Okla., U.S.A.	161	35 30N	99 0W
Clinton, S.C., U.S.A.	165	34 30N	81 54W
Clinton Colden L.	145	63 58N	107 27W
Clonakilty	35	51 37N	8 53W
Cloncurry	115	20 40S	140 28E
Clones	34	54 10N	7 13W
Clonmel	35	52 22N	7 42W
Clovis	161	34 20N	103 10W
Cluj-Napoca	56	46 47N	23 38E
Clunes	117	37 20S	143 45E
Clwyd □	26	53 5N	3 20W
Clyde →	31	55 56N	4 29W
Clyde, Firth of	30	55 20N	5 0W
Clydebank	31	55 54N	4 25W
Coahuila □	174	27 20N	102 0W
Coaldale	155	49 45N	112 35W
Coalinga	173	36 10N	120 21W
Coalville	29	52 43N	1 21W
Coast Mts.	144	55 0N	129 0W
Coast Ranges	173	41 0N	123 0W
Coatbridge	31	55 52N	4 2W
Coatepeque	177	14 46N	91 55W
Coats I.	146	62 30N	83 0W
Coats Land	14	77 0S	25 0W
Coatzacoalcos	177	18 9N	94 25W
Cobalt	161	47 25N	79 42W
Cobán	177	15 30N	90 21W
Cobar	116	31 27S	145 48E
Cóbh	35	51 50N	8 18W
Cobham	118	30 18S	142 7E
Cobourg	151	43 58N	78 10W
Cobram	117	35 54S	145 40E
Cocanada = Kakinada	92	16 57N	82 11E
Cochabamba	187	17 26S	66 10W
Cochin China = Nam-Phan	95	10 30N	106 0E
Cochran	170	32 25N	83 23W
Cochrane	151	49 0N	81 0W
Cockburn, Canal	192	54 30S	72 0W
Coco →	179	15 0N	83 8W
Coco Chan.	94	13 50N	93 25E
Cocos Is.	111	12 10S	96 55E
Cod, C.	164	42 8N	70 10W
Codajás	185	3 55S	62 0W
Codó	185	4 30S	43 55W
Cœur d'Alene	171	47 45N	116 51W
Coffs Harbour	116	30 16S	153 5E
Cohoes	164	42 47N	73 42W
Cohuna	117	35 45S	144 15E
Coiba, I.	179	7 30N	81 40W
Coihaique	192	45 30S	71 45W
Coimbatore	90	11 2N	76 59E
Coimbra	50	40 15N	8 27W
Cojimies	184	0 20N	80 0W
Cojutepequé	177	13 41N	88 54W
Colac	117	38 21S	143 35E
Colchester	25	51 54N	0 55E
Coldstream	31	55 39N	2 14W
Coleman	155	49 40N	114 30W
Coleraine, Australia	119	37 36S	141 40E
Coleraine, U.K.	34	55 8N	6 40W
Colima	175	19 14N	103 43W
Colima □	175	19 10N	104 0W
Coll	30	56 40N	6 35W
College Park	170	33 42N	84 27W
Collie	120	33 22S	116 8E
Collingwood	151	44 29N	80 13W
Collinsville	121	20 30S	147 56E
Collooney	34	54 11N	8 28W
Colmar	37	48 5N	7 20E
Colne	28	53 51N	2 11W
Cologne = Köln	42	50 56N	6 58E
Colomb-Béchar = Béchar	127	31 38N	2 18W
Colômbia	188	20 10S	48 40W
Colombia ■	184	3 45N	73 0W
Colombo	90	6 56N	79 58E
Colón, Cuba	178	22 42N	80 54W
Colón, Panama	179	9 20N	79 54W
Colonia	191	34 25S	57 50W
Colonsay	30	56 4N	6 12W
Colorado □	163	37 40N	106 0W
Colorado →, Argentina	190	39 50S	62 8W
Colorado →, Calif., U.S.A.	173	34 45N	114 40W
Colorado →, Tex., U.S.A.	161	28 36N	95 58W
Colorado Desert	160	34 20N	116 0W
Colorado Plateau	161	36 40N	110 30W
Colorado Springs	163	38 55N	104 50W
Columbia, Miss., U.S.A.	169	31 16N	89 50W
Columbia, Mo., U.S.A.	166	38 58N	92 20W
Columbia, S.C., U.S.A.	165	34 0N	81 0W
Columbia, Tenn., U.S.A.	169	35 40N	87 0W
Columbia →	171	46 15N	124 5W
Columbia Basin	171	47 30N	118 30W
Columbretes, Is.	51	39 50N	0 50E
Columbus, Ga., U.S.A.	170	32 30N	84 58W
Columbus, Ind., U.S.A.	187	39 14N	85 55W
Columbus, Miss., U.S.A.	169	33 30N	88 26W
Columbus, Ohio, U.S.A.	167	39 57N	83 1W
Colwyn Bay	26	53 17N	3 44W
Comeragh Mts.	35	52 17N	7 35W
Comilla	93	23 28N	91 10E
Comitán	177	16 18N	92 9W
Committee B.	146	68 30N	86 30W
Communism Pk. = Kommunizma, Pik.	71	39 0N	72 2E
Como	46	45 48N	9 5E
Como, L. di	46	46 5N	9 17E
Comodoro Rivadavia	192	45 50S	67 40W
Comorin, C.	90	8 3N	77 40E
Comoro Is. ■	125	12 10S	44 15E
Comox	154	49 42N	124 55W
Compiègne	38	49 24N	2 50E
Côn Dao	95	8 45N	106 45E
Conakry	130	9 29N	13 49W
Conceição da Barra	189	18 35S	39 45W
Concepción, Argentina	191	27 20S	65 35W
Concepción, Chile	190	36 50S	73 0W
Concepción, Est. de	192	50 30S	74 55W
Concepción del Oro	174	24 38N	101 25W
Concepción del Uruguay	190	32 35S	58 20W
Conchos, R. →	174	29 35N	104 25W
Concord, Calif., U.S.A	172	37 59N	122 2W
Concord, N.C., U.S.A.	165	35 28N	80 35W
Concord, N.H., U.S.A.	164	43 12N	71 30W
Concordia, Argentina	190	31 20S	58 2W
Concordia, U.S.A.	161	39 35N	97 40W
Condamine	155	26 56S	150 9E
Condé	38	50 26N	3 34E
Condobolin	117	33 4S	147 6E
Congleton	28	53 10N	2 12W
Congo = Zaïre →	134	6 4S	12 24E
Congo (Kinshasa) ■ = Zaïre ■	134	3 0S	23 0E
Congo ■	134	1 0S	16 0E
Congo Basin	124	0 10S	24 30E
Conjeeveram = Kanchipuram	90	12 52N	79 45E
Connacht	34	53 23N	8 40W
Conneaut	164	41 55N	80 32W
Connecticut □	164	41 40N	72 40W
Connecticut →	157	41 17N	72 21W
Connemara	34	53 29N	9 45W
Connors Ra.	121	21 40S	149 10E
Consett	28	54 52N	1 50W
Constance = Konstanz	44	47 39N	9 10E
Constance, L. = Bodensee	44	47 35N	9 25E
Constanța	57	44 14N	28 38E
Constantine	127	36 25N	6 42E
Contamana	186	7 19S	74 55W
Conway = Conwy	26	53 17N	3 50W
Conway = Conwy →	26	53 18N	3 50W
Conway, N.H., U.S.A.	148	43 58N	71 8W
Conway, S.C., U.S.A.	165	33 49N	79 2W

Conwy	**26**	53 17N	3	50W
Conwy ~►	**26**	53 18N	3	50W
Cook, Mt.	**123**	43 36S	170	9 E
Cook Inlet	**142**	59 0N	151	0W
Cook Is.	**123**	17 0S	160	0W
Cook Strait	**123**	41 15S	174	29 E
Cookeville	**169**	36 12N	85	30W
Cookstown	**34**	54 40N	6	43W
Coolah	**116**	31 48S	149	41 E
Coolamon	**117**	34 46S	147	8 E
Coolangatta	**116**	28 11S	153	29 E
Coolgardie	**120**	30 55S	121	8 E
Cooma	**117**	36 12S	149	8 E
Coonabarabran	**116**	31 14S	149	18 E
Coonamble	**116**	30 56S	148	27 E
Cooper Cr. ~►	**118**	12 7S	132	41 E
Coorong, The	**119**	35 50S	139	20 E
Coorow	**120**	29 53S	116	2 E
Coos Bay	**171**	43 26N	124	7W
Cootamundra	**117**	34 36S	148	1 E
Copenhagen = København ..	**61**	55 41N	12	34 E
Copiapó	**190**	27 30S	70	20W
Copper Center	**142**	62 10N	145	25W
Coppermine	**145**	67 50N	115	5W
Coppermine ~►	**145**	67 49N	116	4W
Coquilhatville = Mbandaka .	**134**	0 1N	18	18 E
Coquimbo	**190**	30 0S	71	20W
Coracora	**186**	15 5S	73	45W
Coral Gables	**170**	25 45N	80	16W
Coral Harbour	**146**	64 8N	83	10W
Coral Sea	**121**	15 0S	150	0 E
Corbeil-Essonnes	**39**	48 36N	2	26 E
Corbin	**165**	37 0N	84	3W
Corby	**25**	52 29N	0	41W
Cordele	**170**	31 55N	83	49W
Córdoba, Argentina	**190**	31 20S	64	10W
Córdoba, Mexico	**177**	18 53N	96	56W
Córdoba, Spain	**50**	37 50N	4	50W
Córdoba, Sierra de	**190**	31 10S	64	25W
Cordova	**142**	60 36N	145	45W
Corfu = Kérkira	**54**	39 38N	19	50 E
Corinth = Kórinthos	**54**	37 56N	22	55 E
Corinth	**169**	34 54N	88	30W
Corinth, G. of = Korinthiakós Kólpos	**54**	38 16N	22	30 E
Corinto, Brazil	**188**	18 20S	44	30W
Corinto, Nic.	**179**	12 30N	87	10W
Cork	**35**	51 54N	8	30W
Cork □	**35**	51 50N	8	50W
Corlu	**80**	41 11N	27	49 E
Corn Is. = Maíz, Islas del	**179**	12 15N	83	4W
Corner Brook	**140**	48 57N	57	58W
Cornwall	**151**	45 2N	74	44W
Cornwall □	**27**	50 26N	4	40W
Coro	**184**	11 25N	69	41W
Coroatá	**188**	4 8S	44	0W
Corocoro	**187**	17 15S	68	28W
Coroico	**187**	16 0S	67	50W
Coromandel Coast	**90**	12 30N	81	0 E
Corona	**173**	33 49N	117	36W
Coronado	**173**	32 45N	117	9W
Coronation Gulf	**145**	68 25N	110	0W
Coronel	**190**	37 0S	73	10W
Coronel Pringles	**190**	38 0S	61	30W
Corowa	**117**	35 58S	146	21 E
Corozal	**177**	9 19N	75	18W
Corpus Christi	**161**	27 50N	97	28W
Corrib, L.	**34**	53 5N	9	10W
Corrientes	**190**	27 30S	58	45W
Corrientes, C., Colombia .	**184**	5 30N	77	34W
Corrientes, C., Cuba	**178**	21 43N	84	30W
Corrientes, C., Mexico	**175**	20 25N	105	42W
Corrigin	**120**	32 20S	117	53 E
Corse	**36**	42 0N	9	0 E
Corsica = Corse	**36**	42 0N	9	0 E
Corsicana	**168**	32 5N	96	30W
Cortez	**163**	37 24N	108	35W
Cortland	**164**	42 35N	76	11W
Corum	**80**	40 30N	34	57 E
Corumbá	**187**	19 0S	57	30W
Coruña, La	**50**	43 20N	8	25W
Corunna = Coruña, La	**50**	43 20N	8	25W
Corvallis	**171**	44 36N	123	15W
Cosamaloapan	**177**	18 23N	95	50W
Cosenza	**49**	39 17N	16	14 E
Coshocton	**167**	40 17N	81	51W
Costa Blanca	**51**	38 25N	0	10W
Costa Brava	**51**	41 30N	3	0 E
Costa del Sol	**50**	36 30N	4	30W
Costa Dorada	**51**	40 45N	1	15 E
Costa Rica ■	**179**	10 0N	84	0W
Cotagaita	**187**	20 45S	65	40W
Côte d'Or	**37**	47 10N	4	50 E
Coteau des Prairies	**156**	44 30N	97	0W
Cotonou	**131**	6 20N	2	25 E
Cotopaxi, Vol.	**184**	0 40S	78	30W
Cotswold Hills	**24**	51 42N	2	10W
Cottbus	**43**	51 44N	14	20 E
Coulommiers	**39**	48 50N	3	3 E
Council	**142**	64 55N	163	45W
Council Bluffs	**166**	41 20N	95	50W
Courantyne ~►	**185**	5 55N	57	5W
Courtrai = Kortrijk	**42**	50 50N	3	17 E
Coventry	**24**	52 25N	1	31W
Covington, Ga., U.S.A.	**170**	33 36N	83	50W
Covington, Ky., U.S.A.	**167**	39 5N	84	30W
Cowdenbeath	**31**	56 7N	3	20W
Cowes	**25**	50 45N	1	18W
Cowra	**117**	33 49S	148	42 E
Coxim	**188**	18 30S	54	55W
Cracow = Kraków	**58**	50 4N	19	57 E
Craigavon = Lurgan	**34**	54 28N	6	20W
Craiova	**57**	44 21N	23	48 E
Cranbrook, Australia	**120**	34 18S	117	33 E
Cranbrook, Canada	**155**	49 30N	115	46W
Crateús	**189**	5 10S	40	39W
Crato	**189**	7 10S	39	25W
Crawfordsville	**167**	40 2N	86	51W
Crawley	**24**	51 7N	0	10W
Creil	**39**	49 15N	2	34 E
Cremona	**46**	45 8N	10	2 E
Crépy-en-Valois	**39**	49 14N	2	54 E
Cres	**52**	44 58N	14	25 E
Crescent City	**172**	41 45N	124	12W
Creston, Canada	**155**	49 10N	116	31W
Creston, U.S.A.	**166**	41 0N	94	20W
Crestview	**169**	30 45N	86	35W
Crete = Kríti	**55**	35 15N	25	0 E
Creuse ~►	**36**	47 0N	0	34 E
Creusot, Le	**37**	46 50N	4	24 E
Crewe	**28**	53 6N	2	28W
Criciúma	**191**	28 40S	49	23W
Crieff	**31**	56 22N	3	50W
Crimea = Krymskiy P-ov.	**68**	45 0N	34	0 E
Crişul Alb ~►	**56**	46 42N	21	17 E
Crişul Negru ~►	**56**	46 38N	22	26 E
Crna Gora	**52**	42 10N	21	30 E
Crna Gora □	**52**	42 40N	19	20 E
Croatia = Hrvatska □	**52**	45 20N	18	0 E
Crockett	**168**	31 20N	95	30W
Cromarty	**33**	57 40N	4	2W
Cromer	**29**	52 56N	1	18 E
Crooked I.	**180**	22 50N	74	10W
Crookwell	**117**	34 28S	149	24 E
Cross Fell	**28**	54 44N	2	29W
Cross L.	**153**	54 45N	97	30W
Crosse, La	**166**	43 48N	91	13W
Crowley	**168**	30 15N	92	20W
Crowsnest Pass	**155**	49 40N	114	40W
Cruz, C.	**178**	19 50N	77	50W
Cruz Alta	**191**	28 45S	53	40W
Cruz del Eje	**190**	30 45S	64	50W
Cruzeiro do Sul	**186**	7 35S	72	35W
Crystal Brook	**119**	33 21S	138	12 E
Cu Lao Hon	**95**	10 54N	108	18 E
Cuando ~►	**134**	14 0S	19	30 E
Cuanza ~►	**134**	9 2S	13	30 E
Cuba ■	**178**	22 0N	79	0W
Cubango ~►	**134**	18 50S	22	25 E
Cucuí	**184**	1 12N	66	50W
Cúcuta	**184**	7 54N	72	31W
Cuddalore	**90**	11 46N	79	45 E

Cuddapah . . . . **90** 14 30N 78 47 E
Cue . . . . **120** 27 25S 117 54 E
Cuenca, Ecuador **184** 2 50S 79 9W
Cuenca, Spain **51** 40 5N 2 10W
Cuenca, Serranía de **51** 39 55N 1 50W
Cuernavaca **177** 18 55N 99 15W
Cuevo **187** 20 15S 63 30W
Cuiabá **188** 15 30S 56 0W
Cuillin Hills **32** 57 14N 6 15W
Cuitzeo, L. de **175** 19 55N 101 5W
Culcairn . . . . **117** 35 41S 147 3 E
Culiacán **174** 24 48N 107 24W
Cullarin Range . . . . **117** 34 30S 149 30 E
Culloden Moor **33** 57 29N 4 7W
Culverden . . . . **123** 42 47S 172 49 E
Cumaná **185** 10 30N 64 5W
Cumberland **164** 39 40N 78 43W
Cumberland → **169** 36 15N 87 0W
Cumberland Is. . . . . **121** 20 35S 149 10 E
Cumberland Pen. **146** 67 0N 64 0W
Cumberland Plat. **169** 36 0N 84 30W
Cumberland Sd. **146** 65 30N 66 0W
Cumbria □ **28** 54 35N 2 55W
Cumbrian Mts. **28** 54 30N 3 0W
Cumbum . . . . **90** 15 40N 79 10 E
Cummins . . . . **119** 34 16S 135 43 E
Cumnock **31** 55 27N 4 18W
Cunene → . . . . **134** 17 20S 11 50 E
Cunnamulla . . . . **116** 28 2S 145 38 E
Curaçao **181** 12 10N 69 0W
Curaray → **184** 2 20S 74 5W
Curiapo **185** 8 33N 61 5W
Curicó **190** 34 55S 71 20W
Curitiba **191** 25 20S 49 10W
Curtis Group . . . . **117** 39 30S 146 37 E
Curuá → **188** 5 23S 54 22W
Curuçá **188** 0 43S 47 50W
Curuzú Cuatiá **191** 29 50S 58 5W
Cushing **168** 35 59N 96 46W
Cusihuiriáchic **174** 28 14N 106 50W
Cuthbert **170** 31 47N 84 47W
Cuttack . . . . **92** 20 25N 85 57 E
Cuxhaven . . . . **42** 53 51N 8 41 E
Cuyahoga Falls **167** 41 8N 81 30W
Cuzco, Bolivia **187** 20 0S 66 50W
Cuzco, Peru **186** 13 32S 72 0W
Cwmbran **27** 51 39N 3 0W
Cypress Hills **152** 49 40N 109 30W
Cyprus ■ . . . . **80** 35 0N 33 0 E
Cyrenaica . . . . **124** 27 0N 23 0 E
Czechoslovakia ■ . . . . . **59** 49 0N 17 0 E
Czeremcha . . . . **58** 52 31N 23 21 E
Częstochowa . . . . **58** 50 49N 19 7 E

Da → . . . . **95** 21 15N 105 20 E
Da Hinggan Ling . . . . . . **98** 48 0N 121 0 E
Da Nang . . . . **95** 16 4N 108 13 E
Da Yunhe → . . . . **99** 34 25N 120 5 E
Daba Shan . . . . **99** 32 0N 109 0 E
Dacca = Dhaka . . . . **92** 23 43N 90 26 E
Dacca □ = Dhaka □ . . . . **93** 24 25N 90 25 E
Dadanawa **185** 2 50N 59 30W
Dadra and Nagar Haveli □ . . **91** 20 5N 73 0 E
Daghestan A.S.S.R. □ . . . **70** 42 30N 47 0 E
Dahomey = Benin ■ . . . **131** 10 0N 2 0 E
Dai-Sen . . . . **109** 35 22N 133 32 E
Daiō-Misaki . . . . **106** 34 15N 136 45 E
Daisetsu-Zan . . . . **103** 43 30N 142 57 E
Daito . . . . **109** 35 19N 132 58 E
Dajarra . . . . **115** 21 42S 139 30 E
Dakar **130** 14 34N 17 29W
Dakhla **126** 23 50N 15 53W
Dakhla, El Wâhât el- . . . **128** 25 30N 28 50 E
Ðakovica . . . . **52** 42 22N 20 26 E
Dalandzadgad . . . . **98** 43 27N 104 30 E
Dalbeattie **31** 54 55N 3 50W
Dalby . . . . **116** 27 10S 151 17 E
Dalhousie **148** 48 5N 66 26W
Dali . . . . **99** 25 40N 100 10 E

Dalian . . . . **98** 38 50N 121 40 E
Daliang Shan . . . . **99** 28 0N 102 45 E
Dallas, Oreg., U.S.A. . . **171** 45 0N 123 15W
Dallas, Tex., U.S.A. . . . **168** 32 50N 96 50W
Dalmacija □ . . . . **52** 43 20N 17 0 E
Dalmatia = Dalmacija □ . . **52** 43 20N 17 0 E
Daloa **130** 7 0N 6 30W
Dalton **169** 34 47N 84 58W
Daly Waters . . . . **114** 16 15S 133 24 E
Daman . . . . **91** 20 25N 72 57 E
Damaraland . . . . **136** 21 0S 17 0 E
Damascus = Dimashq . . **80** 33 30N 36 18 E
Damāvand . . . . **86** 35 47N 52 0 E
Damāvand, Qolleh-ye . . **86** 35 56N 52 10 E
Dampier . . . . **114** 20 41S 116 42 E
Dampier Arch. . . . . **114** 20 38S 116 32 E
Danbury **164** 41 23N 73 29W
Dandenong . . . . **117** 38 0S 145 15 E
Dandong . . . . **98** 40 10N 124 20 E
Dangriga **177** 17 0N 88 13W
Dannevirke . . . . **122** 40 12S 176 8 E
Dansville **164** 42 32N 77 41W
Danville, Ill., U.S.A. . . . **167** 40 10N 87 40W
Danville, Ky., U.S.A. . . **167** 37 40N 84 45W
Danville, Va., U.S.A. . . **165** 36 40N 79 20W
Danzig = Gdańsk . . . . . **58** 54 22N 18 40 E
Dar es Salaam . . . . . . **135** 6 50S 39 12 E
Darbhanga . . . . **92** 26 15N 85 55 E
Dardanelles = Çanakkale
   Boğazı . . . . **80** 40 0N 26 0 E
Dârfûr . . . . **129** 13 40N 24 0 E
Dargan Ata . . . . **70** 40 29N 62 10 E
Dargaville . . . . **122** 35 57S 173 52 E
Darién, G. del **184** 9 0N 77 0W
Darjeeling = Darjiling . . **92** 27 3N 88 18 E
Darjiling . . . . **92** 27 3N 88 18 E
Darling → . . . . **119** 34 4S 141 54 E
Darling Downs . . . . . . **116** 27 30S 150 30 E
Darling Ra. . . . . **120** 32 30S 116 0 E
Darlington **28** 54 33N 1 33W
Darmstadt . . . . **42** 49 51N 8 40 E
Darnley, C. . . . . **14** 68 0S 69 0 E
Dart → **27** 50 24N 3 36W
Dartmoor **27** 50 36N 4 0W
Dartmouth, Canada . . . **149** 44 40N 63 30W
Dartmouth, U.K. **27** 50 21N 3 35W
Darwin . . . . **114** 12 25S 130 51 E
Dasht-e Kavīr . . . . **86** 34 30N 55 0 E
Dasht-e Lūt . . . . **85** 31 30N 58 0 E
Dasht-e Mārgow . . . . . **87** 30 40N 62 30 E
Datia . . . . **91** 25 39N 78 27 E
Datong . . . . **98** 40 6N 113 18 E
Daugavpils . . . . **68** 55 53N 26 32 E
Dauphin **153** 51 9N 100 5W
Dauphiné . . . . **37** 45 15N 5 25 E
Davangere . . . . **90** 14 25N 75 55 E
Davao . . . . **112** 7 0N 125 40 E
Davenport **166** 41 30N 90 40W
Daventry **24** 52 16N 1 10W
David **179** 8 30N 82 30W
Davis Sea . . . . **15** 66 0S 92 0 E
Davis Str. **146** 65 0N 58 0W
Davos . . . . **44** 46 48N 9 49 E
Dawson **144** 64 10N 139 30W
Dawson Creek **155** 55 45N 120 15W
Dawson Range . . . . . . **121** 24 30S 149 48 E
Daylesford . . . . **117** 37 21S 144 9 E
Dayr az Zawr . . . . **81** 35 20N 40 5 E
Dayton, Ohio, U.S.A. . . **167** 39 45N 84 10W
Dayton, Wash., U.S.A. . **171** 46 20N 118 10W
Daytona Beach **170** 29 14N 81 0W
De Aar . . . . **136** 30 39S 24 0 E
De Land **170** 29 1N 81 19W
De Ridder **168** 30 48N 93 15W
De Soto **166** 38 7N 90 33W
Deakin . . . . **114** 30 46S 128 0 E
Deal . . . . **25** 51 13N 1 25 E
Dean, Forest of **24** 51 50N 2 35W
Deán Funes **190** 30 20S 64 20W
Dease → **144** 59 56N 128 32W
Dease Lake **144** 58 25N 130 6W

Name		Lat		Long	
Death Valley	173	36 19N	116	52W
Deauville	38	49 23N	0	2 E
Debar	52	41 31N	20	30 E
Debre Markos	132	10 20N	37	40 E
Debre Tabor	132	11 50N	38	26 E
Debrecen	59	47 33N	21	42 E
Decatur, Ala., U.S.A.	169	34 35N	87	0W
Decatur, Ga., U.S.A.	170	33 47N	84	17W
Decatur, Ill., U.S.A.	166	39 50N	89	0W
Deccan	76	18 0N	79	0 E
Dedéagach = Alexandroúpolis	55	40 50N	25	54 E
Dee ⟶, Scotland, U.K.	33	57 4N	2	7W
Dee ⟶, Wales, U.K.	26	53 15N	3	7W
Deepwater	116	29 25S	151	51 E
Deer Lake	149	49 11N	57	27W
Defiance	167	41 20N	84	20W
Deh Bīd	85	30 39N	53	11 E
Dehra Dun	89	30 20N	78	4 E
Dej	56	47 10N	23	52 E
Del Rio	161	29 23N	100	50W
Delano	173	35 48N	119	13W
Delaware □	164	39 0N	75	40W
Delaware ⟶	164	39 20N	75	25W
Delaware B.	157	38 50N	75	0W
Delft	40	52 1N	4	22 E
Delfzijl	41	53 20N	6	55 E
Delgado, C.	137	10 45S	40	40 E
Delgo	129	20 6N	30	40 E
Delhi	89	28 38N	77	17 E
Delice ⟶	80	39 45N	34	15 E
Delicias	174	28 13N	105	28W
Delong, Ostrova	72	76 40N	149	20 E
Deloraine	119	41 30S	146	40 E
Delray Beach	170	26 27N	80	4W
Demanda, Sierra de la	50	42 15N	3	0W
Dembidolo	132	8 34N	34	50 E
Deming	161	32 10N	107	50W
Demopolis	169	32 30N	87	48W
Den Burg	40	53 3N	4	47 E
Den Haag = 's-Gravenhage	40	52 7N	4	17 E
Den Helder	40	52 57N	4	45 E
Den Oever	40	52 56N	5	2 E
Denain	38	50 20N	3	22 E
Denbigh	26	53 12N	3	26W
Denham	120	25 56S	113	31 E
Deniliquin	117	35 30S	144	58 E
Denison	168	33 50N	96	40W
Denizli	80	37 42N	29	2 E
Denmark	120	34 59S	117	25 E
Denmark ■	61	55 30N	9	0 E
Denmark Str.	13	66 0N	30	0W
Denton	168	33 12N	97	10W
D'Entrecasteaux Is.	115	9 0S	151	0 E
Denver	163	39 45N	105	0W
Deolali	91	19 58N	73	50 E
Deoria	92	26 31N	83	48 E
Deosai Mts.	89	35 40N	75	0 E
Dera Ghazi Khan	89	30 5N	70	43 E
Dera Ismail Khan	89	31 50N	70	50 E
Derby	28	52 55N	1	28W
Derby □	28	52 55N	1	28W
Derg, L.	35	53 0N	8	20W
Derry = Londonderry	34	55 0N	7	20W
Derryveagh Mts.	34	55 0N	8	40W
Derwent ⟶, Cumbria, U.K.	28	54 42N	3	22W
Derwent ⟶, Derby, U.K.	29	52 53N	1	17W
Derwent ⟶, N. Yorks., U.K.	29	53 45N	0	57W
Derwent Water, L.	28	54 35N	3	9W
Des Moines	166	41 35N	93	37W
Des Moines ⟶	166	40 23N	91	25W
Deschutes ⟶	171	45 30N	121	0W
Dese	133	11 5N	39	40 E
Despeñaperros, Paso	50	38 24N	3	30W
Dessau	43	51 49N	12	15 E
Dessye = Dese	133	11 5N	39	40 E
Desvrès	38	50 40N	1	48 E
Detroit	167	42 23N	83	5W
Deurne	41	51 27N	5	49 E
Deutsche Bucht	42	54 10N	7	51 E
Devakottai	90	9 55N	78	45 E
Deventer	41	52 15N	6	10 E
Devizes	24	51 21N	2	0W
Devon I.	13	75 10N	85	0W
Devonport, Australia	119	41 10S	146	22 E
Devonport, N.Z.	122	36 49S	174	49 E
Devonport, U.K.	27	50 23N	4	11W
Devonshire □	27	50 50N	3	40W
Dewsbury	28	53 42N	1	38W
Dezfūl	84	32 20N	48	30 E
Dezhneva, Mys	73	66 5N	169	40W
Dhahran = Az Zahrān	84	26 10N	50	7 E
Dhaka	92	23 43N	90	26 E
Dhaka □	93	24 25N	90	25 E
Dhamar	83	14 30N	44	20 E
Dhar	91	22 35N	75	26 E
Dharmapuri	90	12 10N	78	10 E
Dharwad	90	15 22N	75	15 E
Dhidhimótikhon	55	41 22N	26	29 E
Dhikti	55	35 8N	25	22 E
Dhodhekánisos	55	36 35N	27	0 E
Dhuburi	92	26 2N	89	59 E
Dhule	91	20 58N	74	50 E
Di Linh, Cao Nguyen	95	11 30N	108	0 E
Diamantina	188	18 17S	43	40W
Diamantina ⟶	115	26 45S	139	10 E
Diamantino	188	14 30S	56	30W
Dibrugarh	93	27 29N	94	55 E
Dickinson	163	46 50N	102	48W
Didsbury	155	51 35N	114	10W
Diefenbaker L.	152	51 0N	106	55W
Dieppe	38	49 54N	1	4 E
Dieren	41	52 3N	6	6 E
Digby	148	44 38N	65	50W
Digne	37	44 5N	6	12 E
Dijlah, Nahr ⟶	81	31 0N	47	25 E
Dijon	37	47 20N	5	0 E
Dila	133	6 21N	38	22 E
Dillon	165	34 26N	79	20W
Dimashq	80	33 30N	36	18 E
Dimboola	119	36 28S	142	7 E
Dîmbovita ⟶	57	44 14N	26	13 E
Dimitrovgrad	53	42 5N	25	35 E
Dimitrovo = Pernik	53	42 35N	23	2 E
Dinan	36	48 28N	2	2W
Dinara Planina	52	44 0N	16	30 E
Dinaric Alps = Dinara Planina	52	44 0N	16	30 E
Dindigul	90	10 25N	78	0 E
Dingle	35	52 9N	10	17W
Dingle B.	35	52 3N	10	20W
Dingwall	33	57 36N	4	26W
Dinuba	173	36 31N	119	22W
Dire Dawa	133	9 35N	41	45 E
Diriamba	179	11 51N	86	19W
Dirranbandi	116	28 33S	148	17 E
Disappointment L.	114	23 20S	122	40 E
Discovery B.	119	38 10S	140	40 E
Disko	146	69 45N	53	30W
Diss	25	52 23N	1	6 E
District of Columbia □	164	38 55N	77	0W
Diu	91	20 45N	70	58 E
Dives-sur-Mer	39	49 18N	0	8W
Dixon	166	41 50N	89	30W
Dixon Entrance	154	54 30N	132	0W
Diyarbakir	81	37 55N	40	18 E
Djakarta = Jakarta	111	6 9S	106	49 E
Djelfa	130	34 40N	3	15 E
Djerid, Chott	127	33 42N	8	30 E
Djibouti	133	11 30N	43	5 E
Djibouti ■	133	12 0N	43	0 E
Djoum	131	2 41N	12	35 E
Dmitriya Lapteva, Proliv	72	73 0N	140	0 E
Dnepr ⟶	68	46 30N	32	18 E
Dnepropetrovsk	68	48 30N	35	0 E
Dnestr ⟶	68	46 18N	30	17 E
Dnestrovski = Belgorod	68	50 35N	36	35 E
Dnieper = Dnepr ⟶	68	46 30N	32	18 E
Dniester = Dnestr ⟶	68	46 18N	30	17 E
Dobruja	57	44 30N	28	15 E
Dodecanese = Dhodhekánisos	55	36 35N	27	0 E
Dodge City	161	37 42N	100	0W

Name	Page	Lat °	′	N/S	Long °	′	E/W
Dodoma	135	6	8	S	35	45	E
Doesburg	41	52	1	N	6	9	E
Doetinchem	41	51	59	N	6	18	E
Dogger Bank	124	54	50	N	2	0	E
Doi Luang	95	18	30	N	101	0	E
Dojran	54	41	10	N	22	45	E
Dokkum	41	53	20	N	5	59	E
Dolbeau	148	48	53	N	72	18	W
Dole	37	47	7	N	5	31	E
Dolgellau	26	52	44	N	3	53	W
Dolgelley = Dolgellau	26	52	44	N	3	53	W
Dolomites = Dolomiti	47	46	30	N	11	40	E
Dolomiti	47	46	30	N	11	40	E
Dolores	191	36	20	S	57	40	W
Dolphin and Union Str.	145	69	5	N	114	45	W
Domel I. = Letsôk-aw Kyun	94	11	30	N	98	25	E
Dominica ■	180	15	20	N	61	20	W
Dominican Rep. ■	180	19	0	N	70	30	W
Don →, U.K.	33	57	14	N	2	5	W
Don →, U.S.S.R.	68	47	4	N	39	18	E
Donaghadee	34	54	38	N	5	32	W
Donau →	42	48	10	N	17	0	E
Doncaster	29	53	31	N	1	9	W
Dondra Head	90	5	55	N	80	40	E
Donegal	34	54	39	N	8	8	W
Donegal □	34	54	53	N	8	0	W
Donegal B.	34	54	30	N	8	35	W
Donetsk	68	48	0	N	37	45	E
Dongara	120	29	14	S	114	57	E
Dongen	40	51	38	N	4	56	E
Dongting Hu	99	29	18	N	112	45	E
Donnelly's Crossing	122	35	42	S	173	38	E
Donnybrook	120	33	34	S	115	48	E
Doon →	31	55	26	N	4	41	W
Dorada, La.	184	5	30	N	74	40	W
Dorchester	27	50	42	N	2	28	W
Dordrecht, O.	116	66	27	N	77	27	W
Dordogne □	36	45	5	N	0	40	E
Dordrecht	40	51	48	N	4	39	E
Dornoch	33	57	52	N	4	0	W
Dorrigo	116	30	20	S	152	44	E
Dorris	172	41	59	N	121	58	W
Dorset □	27	50	48	N	2	25	W
Dortmund	42	51	32	N	7	28	E
Dothan	169	31	10	N	85	25	W
Douai	38	50	21	N	3	4	E
Douala	131	4	0	N	9	45	E
Douarnenez	36	48	6	N	4	21	W
Douglas, U.K.	28	54	9	N	4	29	W
Douglas, U.S.A.	170	31	32	N	82	52	W
Doullona	38	50	10	N	2	20	E
Dounreay	33	58	34	N	3	44	W
Dourados	188	22	9	S	54	50	W
Douro →	50	41	8	N	8	40	W
Douro Litoral □	50	41	10	N	8	20	W
Dove →	28	52	51	N	1	36	W
Dover, U.K.	25	51	7	N	1	19	E
Dover, Del., U.S.A.	164	39	10	N	75	31	W
Dover, N.H., U.S.A.	164	43	12	N	70	51	W
Dover, Str. of	38	51	0	N	1	30	E
Dovey →	26	52	32	N	4	0	W
Downham Market	25	52	36	N	0	22	E
Downpatrick	34	54	20	N	5	43	W
Drachten	41	53	7	N	6	5	E
Dragoman, Prokhod	53	43	0	N	22	53	E
Draguignan	37	43	30	N	6	27	E
Drakensberg	137	31	0	S	28	0	E
Dráma	55	41	9	N	24	10	E
Drammen	60	59	42	N	10	12	E
Drau = Drava →	59	45	33	N	18	55	E
Drava →	59	45	33	N	18	55	E
Drayton Valley	155	53	12	N	114	58	W
Drenthe □	41	52	52	N	6	40	E
Dresden	43	51	2	N	13	45	E
Dreux	39	48	44	N	1	23	E
Driffield	29	54	0	N	0	25	W
Drin i zi →	52	41	37	N	20	28	E
Drina →	52	44	53	N	19	21	E
Drogheda	34	53	45	N	6	20	W
Droitwich	24	52	16	N	2	10	W
Dronne →	36	45	2	N	0	9	W
Dronning Maud Land	14	72	30	S	12	0	E
Drumheller	155	51	25	N	112	40	W
Drummond Ra.	121	23	45	S	147	10	E
Drummondville	151	45	55	N	72	25	W
Dryden	153	49	47	N	92	50	W
Du Bois	164	41	8	N	78	46	W
Du Quoin	166	38	0	N	89	10	W
Dubai = Dubayy	85	25	18	N	55	20	E
Dubawnt →	145	64	33	N	100	6	W
Dubawnt, L.	143	63	4	N	101	42	W
Dubayy	85	25	18	N	55	20	E
Dubbo	116	32	11	S	148	35	E
Dublin, Ireland	35	53	20	N	6	18	W
Dublin, U.S.A.	170	32	30	N	82	34	W
Dublin □	34	53	24	N	6	20	W
Dubrovnik	52	42	39	N	18	6	E
Dubuque	166	42	30	N	90	41	W
Dudley	24	52	30	N	2	5	W
Dugi Otok	52	44	0	N	15	0	E
Duisburg	42	51	27	N	6	42	E
Duluth	150	46	48	N	92	10	W
Dumbarton	31	55	58	N	4	35	W
Dumfries	31	55	4	N	3	37	W
Dumfries & Galloway □	31	55	0	N	4	0	W
Dun Laoghaire	35	53	17	N	6	9	W
Dunârea →	57	45	30	N	8	15	E
Dunaújváros	59	47	0	N	18	57	E
Dunbar	31	56	0	N	2	32	W
Dunblane	31	56	10	N	3	58	W
Duncan, Canada	154	48	45	N	123	40	W
Duncan, U.S.A.	161	34	25	N	98	0	W
Duncan Pass.	94	11	0	N	92	30	E
Dundalk	34	54	1	N	6	25	W
Dundas, Canada	151	43	17	N	79	59	W
Dundas, Greenland	13	77	0	N	69	0	W
Dundee	31	56	29	N	3	0	W
Dundrum	34	54	17	N	5	50	W
Dunedin	123	45	50	S	170	33	E
Dunedoo	116	32	0	S	149	25	E
Dunfermline	31	56	5	N	3	28	W
Dungannon	34	54	30	N	6	47	W
Dungarvan	35	52	6	N	7	40	W
Dungeness	25	50	54	N	0	59	E
Dungog	117	32	22	S	151	46	E
Dunhuang	100	40	8	N	94	36	E
Dunkeld	33	56	34	N	3	36	W
Dunkerque	38	51	2	N	2	20	E
Dunkery Beacon	27	51	15	N	3	37	W
Dunkirk = Dunkerque	38	51	2	N	2	20	E
Dunkirk	164	42	30	N	79	18	W
Dúnleary = Dun Laoghaire	35	53	17	N	6	9	W
Dunmore	164	41	27	N	75	38	W
Dunn	165	35	18	N	78	36	W
Dunnet Hd.	33	58	38	N	3	22	W
Duns	31	55	47	N	2	20	W
Dunsmuir	172	41	10	N	122	18	W
Dunstan Mts.	123	44	53	S	169	35	E
Durance →	37	43	55	N	4	45	E
Durango, Mexico	174	24	3	N	104	39	W
Durango, U.S.A.	163	37	16	N	107	50	W
Durango □	174	24	50	N	104	50	W
Durant	168	34	0	N	96	25	W
Durazno	191	33	25	S	56	31	W
Durban	137	29	49	S	31	1	E
Durg	92	21	15	N	81	22	E
Durham, U.K.	28	54	47	N	1	34	W
Durham, U.S.A.	165	36	0	N	78	55	W
Durham □	28	54	42	N	1	45	W
Durmitor	52	43	10	N	19	0	E
Durness	32	58	34	N	4	45	W
D'Urville I.	122	40	50	S	173	55	E
Dushanbe	71	38	33	N	68	48	E
Düsseldorf	42	51	15	N	6	46	E
Duwādimi	82	24	35	N	44	15	E
Duyun	99	26	18	N	107	29	E
Duzce	80	40	50	N	31	10	E
Duzdab = Zāhedān	86	29	30	N	60	50	E
Dvina, Sev. →	69	64	32	N	40	30	E
Dvinsk = Daugavpils	68	55	53	N	26	32	E
Dyer, C.	146	66	40	N	61	0	W
Dyersburg	169	36	2	N	89	20	W

Name					
Dyfed □	26	52	0N	4	30W
Dysart	121	22	32S	148	23 E
Dzamin Üüd	98	43	50N	111	58 E
Dzerzhinsk	68	53	40N	27	1 E
Dzhalal-Abad	71	40	56N	73	0 E
Dzhalinda	75	53	26N	124	0 E
Dzhambul	71	42	54N	71	22 E
Dzhardzhan	72	68	10N	124	10 E
Dzhetygara	71	52	11N	61	12 E
Dzhezkazgan	71	47	44N	67	40 E
Dzhugdzur, Khrebet	75	57	30N	138	0 E
Dzuumod	98	47	45N	106	58 E
Eagle	142	64	44N	141	7W
Eagle Pass	161	28	45N	100	35W
Eagle River	150	45	55N	89	17W
Ealing	25	51	30N	0	19W
Earn →	31	56	20N	3	19W
Easley	165	34	52N	82	35W
East Angus	148	45	30N	71	40W
East Bengal	92	24	0N	90	0 E
East Beskids = Vychodné					
Beskydy	59	49	30N	22	0 E
East C.	122	37	42S	178	35 E
East Chicago	167	41	40N	87	30W
East China Sea	99	30	5N	126	0 E
East Falkland	192	51	30S	58	30W
East Germany ■	43	52	0N	12	0 E
East Indies	77	0	0	120	0 E
East Kilbride	31	55	46N	4	10W
East Liverpool	164	40	39N	80	35W
East London	137	33	0S	27	55 E
East Main = Eastmain	140	52	10N	78	30W
East Pakistan =					
Bangladesh ■	92	24	0N	90	0 E
East Point	170	33	40N	84	28W
East St. Louis	166	38	37N	90	4W
East Schelde → =					
Oosterschelde	40	51	33N	4	0 E
East Siberian Sea	73	73	0N	160	0 E
East Sussex □	25	51	0N	0	20 E
Eastbourne, N.Z.	123	41	19S	174	55 E
Eastbourne, U.K.	25	50	46N	0	18 E
Eastern Ghats	90	14	0N	78	50 E
Eastleigh	25	50	58N	1	21W
Eastmain	140	52	10N	78	30W
Eastmain →	140	52	27N	78	26W
Easton	164	40	41N	75	15W
Eau Claire	166	44	46N	91	30W
Eau Claire, L. à l'	146	56	10N	74	25W
Ebbw Vale	26	51	47N	3	12W
Eboli	49	40	39N	15	2 E
Ebro →	51	40	43N	0	54 E
Echizen-Misaki	106	35	59N	135	57 E
Echo Bay	145	46	29N	84	4W
Echuca	117	36	10S	144	20 E
Ecuador ■	184	2	0S	78	0W
Ed Dâmer	129	17	27N	34	0 E
Edam	40	52	31N	5	3 E
Eddystone	27	50	11N	4	16W
Ede	41	52	4N	5	40 E
Eden	117	37	3S	149	55 E
Eden →	28	54	57N	3	2W
Edenhope	119	37	4S	141	19 E
Edge Hill	24	52	7N	1	28W
Edhessa	54	40	48N	22	5 E
Edinburgh	31	55	57N	3	12W
Edirne	80	41	40N	26	34 E
Edmonton, Australia	121	17	2S	145	46 E
Edmonton, Canada	155	53	30N	113	30W
Edmundston	148	47	23N	68	20W
Edson	155	53	35N	116	28W
Edward, L.	132	0	25S	29	40 E
Edward VII Land	15	80	0S	150	0W
Edwards Plat.	161	30	30N	101	5W
Effingham	167	39	8N	88	30W
Égadi, Ísole	48	37	55N	12	16 E
Eger	59	47	53N	20	27 E
Egmont, Mt.	122	39	17S	174	5 E
Eğridir Gölü	80	37	53N	30	50 E
Egypt ■	128	28	0N	31	0 E
Eifel	42	50	10N	6	45 E
Eigg	32	56	54N	6	10W
Eil	133	8	0N	49	50 E
Eindhoven	41	51	26N	5	30 E
Eirunepé	187	6	35S	69	53W
El Aaiún	126	27	9N	13	12W
El Cajon	173	32	49N	117	0W
El Callao	185	7	18N	61	50W
El Centro	173	32	50N	115	40W
El Cerro	187	17	30S	61	40W
El Dere	133	3	50N	47	8 E
El Djouf	126	20	0N	11	30 E
El Dorado	168	33	10N	92	40W
El Escorial	50	40	35N	4	7W
El Faiyûm	128	29	19N	30	50 E
El Fâsher	129	13	33N	25	26 E
El Ferrol	50	43	29N	8	15W
El Fuerte	174	26	25N	108	39W
El Geteina	129	14	50N	32	27 E
El Iskandarîya	128	31	0N	30	0 E
El Jadida	126	33	11N	8	17W
El Khârga	128	25	30N	30	33 E
El Khartûm	129	15	31N	32	35 E
El Mahalla el Kubra	128	31	0N	31	0 E
El Minyâ	128	28	7N	30	33 E
El Obeid	129	13	8N	30	10 E
El Oro	177	27	15N	103	30W
El Paso	161	31	50N	106	30W
El Progreso	177	15	26N	87	51W
El Qâhira	128	30	1N	31	14 E
El Qasr	128	25	44N	28	42 E
El Salvador ■	177	13	50N	89	0W
El Suweis	128	29	58N	32	31 E
El Tigre	185	8	44N	64	15W
El Turbio	192	51	45S	72	5W
Elat	80	29	30N	34	56 E
Elâzığ	81	38	37N	39	14 E
Elba	46	42	48N	10	15 E
Elbasani	52	41	9N	20	9 E
Elbe →	42	53	50N	9	0 E
Elbert, Mt.	163	39	5N	106	27W
Elberton	165	34	7N	82	51W
Elbeuf	39	49	17N	1	2 E
Elbing = Elblag	58	54	10N	19	25 E
Elblag	58	54	10N	19	25 E
Elbrus	70	43	21N	42	30 E
Elburg	41	52	26N	5	50 E
Elburz Mts. = Alborz,					
Reshteh-ye Kūhhā-ye	86	36	0N	52	0 E
Elche	51	38	15N	0	42W
Eldorado	174	24	20N	107	22W
Eldorado Springs	166	37	54N	93	59W
Eldoret	132	0	30N	35	17 E
Eleanora, Peak	120	32	57S	121	9 E
Electra	161	34	0N	99	0W
Elephant Butte Res.	161	33	45N	107	30W
Eleuthera	178	25	0N	76	20W
Elgin, U.K.	33	57	39N	3	20W
Elgin, Ill., U.S.A.	167	42	0N	88	20W
Elgin, Oreg., U.S.A.	171	45	37N	118	0W
Elgon, Mt.	132	1	10N	34	30 E
Elisabethville = Lubumbashi	135	11	40S	27	28 E
Elizabeth, Australia	119	34	42S	138	41 E
Elizabeth, U.S.A.	164	40	37N	74	12W
Elizabeth City	165	36	18N	76	16W
Elizabethton	165	36	20N	82	13W
Elizabethtown	167	37	40N	85	54W
Elk Point	152	53	54N	110	55W
Elkhart	167	41	42N	85	55W
Elkins	165	38	53N	79	53W
Elko	172	40	50N	115	50W
Ellensburg	171	47	0N	120	30W
Ellery, Mt.	117	37	28S	148	47 E
Ellesmere I.	13	79	30N	80	0W
Ellesmere Port	28	53	17N	2	55W
Ellice Is. = Tuvalu ■	122	8	0S	178	0 E
Elliot Lake	150	46	25N	82	35W
Ellore = Eluru	92	16	48N	81	8 E
Ellsworth Land	14	76	0S	89	0W

Ellsworth Mts. 14 78 30S 85 0W
Elmhurst 167 41 52N 87 58W
Elmira 164 42 8N 76 49W
Elrose 152 51 12N 108 0W
Eluru 92 16 48N 81 8 E
Elvas 50 38 50N 7 10W
Elwood 167 40 20N 85 50W
Ely 172 39 10N 114 50W
Elyria 167 41 22N 82 8W
Emāmrūd 86 36 30N 55 0 E
Emba → 70 46 38N 53 14 E
Emden 42 53 22N 7 12 E
Emerald 121 23 32S 148 10 E
Emilia-Romagna □ 46 44 33N 10 40 E
Emmeloord 41 52 44N 5 46 E
Emmen 41 52 48N 6 57 E
Empalme 174 27 58N 110 51W
Emporia, Kans., U.S.A. 158 38 25N 96 10W
Emporia, Va., U.S.A. 165 36 41N 77 32W
Ems → 42 52 37N 9 26 E
En Nahud 129 12 45N 28 25 E
Ena 106 35 25N 137 25 E
Ena-San 106 35 26N 137 36 E
Encarnación 191 27 15S 55 50W
Encarnación de Díaz 175 21 31N 102 14W
Encontrados 184 9 3N 72 14W
Enderby 155 50 35N 119 10W
Enderby Land 14 66 0S 53 0 E
Endicott 164 42 6N 76 2W
Engaño, C. 180 18 30N 68 20W
Engels 68 51 28N 46 6 E
Enggano 111 5 20S 102 40 E
England □ 21 53 0N 2 0W
English Bazar = Ingraj Bazar 92 24 58N 88 10 E
English Channel 16 50 0N 2 0W
Enid 161 36 26N 97 52W
Enkhuizen 40 52 42N 5 17 E
Ennedi 129 17 15N 22 0 E
Ennis 35 52 51N 8 59W
Enniscorthy 35 52 30N 6 35W
Enniskillen 34 54 20N 7 40W
Enriquillo, L. 180 18 20N 72 5W
Enschede 41 52 13N 6 53 E
Ensenada 174 31 52N 116 37W
Enshū-Nada 106 34 27N 137 38 E
Entebbe 132 0 4N 32 28 E
Enterprise 171 45 30N 117 18W
Entre Ríos □ 190 30 30S 58 30W
Enugu 131 6 20N 7 30 E
Enzan 107 35 42N 138 44 E
Eólie, I. 49 38 30N 14 50 E
Epe 41 52 21N 5 59 E
Épernay 39 49 3N 3 56 E
Ephesus 80 37 50N 27 33 E
Épinal 37 48 10N 6 27 E
Epping 25 51 42N 0 8 E
Equatorial Guinea ■ 134 2 0S 8 0 E
Er Rif 126 35 1N 4 1W
Erāwadī Myit → –
  Irrawaddy → 93 15 50N 95 6 E
Ercha 73 69 45N 147 20 E
Erciyaş Dağı 80 38 30N 35 30 E
Erebus, Mt. 15 77 35S 167 0 E
Erechim 191 27 35S 52 15W
Ereğli 80 41 15N 31 30 E
Erfurt 43 50 58N 11 2 E
Erg Chech 126 50 59N 11 0 E
Erie 164 42 10N 80 7W
Erie, L. 151 42 15N 81 0W
Erímanthos 54 37 57N 21 50 E
Erimo-misaki 103 41 50N 143 15 E
Eritrea □ 132 14 0N 41 0 E
Ermoúpolis = Síros 55 37 28N 24 57 E
Erne, Lough 34 54 26N 7 46W
Erode 90 11 24N 77 45 E
Erramala Hills 90 15 30N 78 15 E
Erris Hd. 34 54 19N 10 0W
Erzgebirge 43 50 25N 13 0 E
Erzincan 81 39 46N 39 30 E
Erzurum 81 39 57N 41 15 E
Es Sînâ' 128 29 0N 34 0 E

Esan-Misaki 103 41 40N 141 10 E
Esashi 103 41 52N 140 7 E
Esbjerg 61 55 29N 8 29 E
Escanaba 150 45 44N 87 5W
Escondido 173 33 9N 117 4W
Escuintla 177 14 20N 90 48W
Eşfahān 85 33 0N 53 0 E
Esh Sham = Dimashq 80 33 30N 36 18 E
Esk → 29 54 27N 0 36W
Eskilstuna 60 59 22N 16 32 E
Eskimo Pt. 145 61 10N 94 15W
Eskişehir 80 39 50N 30 35 E
Eslāmābād-e Gharb 84 34 10N 46 30 E
Esmeraldas 184 1 0N 79 40W
Espanola 151 46 15N 81 46W
Esperanza 114 33 45S 121 55 E
Espinazo, Sierra del =
  Espinhaço, Serra do 188 17 30S 43 30W
Espinhaço, Serra do 188 17 30S 43 30W
Espírito Santo □ 189 20 0S 40 45W
Essaouira 126 31 32N 9 42W
Essen 42 51 28N 6 59 E
Essequibo → 185 6 50N 58 30W
Essex □ 25 51 48N 0 30 E
Estados, I. de los 192 54 40S 64 30W
Estell 179 13 9N 86 22W
Estevan 152 49 10N 102 59W
Estherville 166 43 25N 94 50W
Estonian S.S.R. □ 68 58 30N 25 30 E
Estoril 50 38 42N 9 23W
Estrêla, Serra da 50 40 10N 7 45W
Estremadura 50 39 0N 9 0W
Étampes 39 48 26N 2 10 E
Étaples 38 50 30N 1 39 E
Etawah 91 26 48N 79 6 E
Ethiopia ■ 133 8 0N 40 0 E
Ethiopian Highlands 132 10 0N 37 0 E
Etna 49 37 45N 15 0 E
Etosha Pan 136 18 40S 16 30 E
Etzatlán 175 20 46N 104 5W
Euboea = Évvoia 55 38 30N 24 0 E
Euclid 167 41 32N 81 31W
Eucumbene, L. 117 36 2S 148 40 E
Eufaula 169 35 20N 95 33W
Eugene 171 44 0N 123 8W
Eupen 42 50 37N 6 3 E
Euphrates = Furāt, Nahr
  al → 84 31 0N 47 25 E
Eureka, Calif., U.S.A. 172 40 50N 124 0W
Eureka, Nev., U.S.A. 172 39 32N 116 2W
Euroa 117 36 44S 145 35 E
Europa, Pta. de 50 36 3N 5 21W
Europa Pt. = Europa, Pta. de 50 36 3N 5 21W
Europoort 40 51 57N 4 10 E
Euston 119 34 30S 142 46 E
Eutsuk L. 154 53 20N 126 45W
Evans Head 116 29 7S 153 27 E
Evanston 167 42 0N 87 40W
Evansville 167 38 0N 87 35W
Everard, L. 118 31 30S 135 0 E
Everest, Mt. 92 28 5N 86 58 E
Everett 171 48 0N 122 10W
Everglades 170 26 0N 80 30W
Evesham 24 52 6N 1 57W
Évora 50 38 33N 7 57W
Évreux 39 49 0N 1 8 E
Évvoia 55 38 30N 24 0 E
Excelsior Springs 166 39 20N 94 10W
Exe → 27 50 38N 3 27W
Exeter 27 50 43N 3 31W
Exmoor 27 51 10N 3 59W
Exmouth 27 50 37N 3 26W
Extremadura □ 50 39 30N 6 5W
Eyasi, L. 135 3 30S 35 0 E
Eye Pen. 32 58 13N 6 10W
Eyre, L. 118 29 30S 137 26 E
Eyre Mts. 123 45 25S 168 25 E
Eyre Pen. 119 33 30S 137 17 E

Name	Page	Lat		Lon	
Facatativá	**184**	4	49N	74	22W
Faddeyevskiy, Ostrov	**72**	76	0N	150	0 E
Fair Hd.	**34**	55	14N	6	10W
Fairbanks	**142**	64	50N	147	50W
Fairfield, N.Z.	**123**	45	54 S	170	24 E
Fairfield, Ala., U.S.A.	**169**	33	30N	87	0W
Fairfield, Calif., U.S.A.	**172**	38	14N	122	1W
Fairfield, Tex., U.S.A.	**168**	31	40N	96	0W
Fairmont, Minn., U.S.A.	**166**	43	37N	94	30W
Fairmont, W. Va., U.S.A.	**164**	39	29N	80	10W
Fairview	**155**	56	5N	118	25W
Fairweather, Mt.	**143**	58	55N	137	45W
Faisalabad	**89**	31	30N	73	5 E
Faizabad	**92**	26	45N	82	10 E
Fajardo	**180**	18	20N	65	39W
Fakenham	**29**	52	50N	0	51 E
Falam	**93**	23	0N	93	45 E
Falkirk	**31**	56	0N	3	47W
Falkland Is.	**192**	51	30 S	59	0W
Falköping	**60**	58	12N	13	33 E
Fall River	**164**	41	45N	71	5W
Falls City	**166**	40	0N	95	40W
Falmouth, Jamaica	**180**	18	30N	77	40W
Falmouth, U.K.	**27**	50	9N	5	5W
Famagusta	**80**	35	8N	33	55 E
Farāh	**87**	32	20N	62	7 E
Farāh □	**87**	32	25N	62	10 E
Fareham	**25**	50	52N	1	11W
Farewell, C.	**122**	40	29 S	172	43 E
Farewell C. = Farvel, Kap	**147**	59	48N	43	55W
Fargo	**156**	46	52N	96	40W
Farmington, N.H., U.S.A.	**157**	43	25N	71	3W
Farmington, N. Mex., U.S.A.	**161**	36	45N	108	28W
Farnborough	**25**	51	17N	0	46W
Faro	**50**	37	2N	7	55W
Faroe Is.	**16**	62	0N	7	0W
Fars □	**85**	29	30N	55	0 E
Fársala	**54**	39	17N	22	23 E
Farvel, Kap	**147**	59	48N	43	55W
Fāryāb □	**87**	36	0N	65	0 E
Fatehgarh	**89**	27	25N	79	35 E
Fatehpur, Raj., India	**92**	28	0N	74	40 E
Fatehpur, Ut. P., India	**89**	25	56N	81	13 E
Faxaflói	**64**	64	29N	23	0W
Fayetteville, Ark., U.S.A.	**168**	36	0N	94	5W
Fayetteville, N.C., U.S.A.	**165**	35	0N	78	58W
Fazilka	**89**	30	27N	74	2 E
Fdérik	**126**	22	40N	12	45W
Fear, C.	**165**	33	51N	78	0W
Fécamp	**38**	49	45N	0	22 E
Feilding	**122**	40	13 S	175	35 E
Feira de Santana	**189**	12	15 S	38	57W
Felixstowe	**25**	51	58N	1	22 E
Fengjie	**99**	31	5N	109	36 E
Fens, The	**29**	52	45N	0	2 E
Fenyang	**98**	37	19N	111	46 E
Ferfer	**133**	5	4N	45	9 E
Fergana	**71**	40	23N	71	19 E
Fergus Falls	**156**	46	18N	96	7W
Fermoy	**35**	52	4N	8	18W
Fernando de Noronha	**189**	4	0 S	33	10W
Fernando Póo = Bioko	**131**	3	30N	8	40 E
Fernie	**155**	49	30N	115	5W
Ferrara	**47**	44	50N	11	36 E
Ferté-Bernard, La	**39**	48	10N	0	40 E
Fès	**126**	34	0N	5	0W
Feuilles →~	**146**	58	47N	70	4W
Feyzābād	**87**	37	7N	70	33 E
Fezzan	**124**	27	0N	15	0 E
Fianarantsoa	**137**	21	26 S	47	5 E
Fichtelgebirge	**43**	50	10N	12	0 E
Fife □	**31**	56	13N	3	2W
Fife Ness	**31**	56	17N	2	35W
Fiji ■	**122**	17	20 S	179	0 E
Filey	**29**	54	13N	0	18W
Findlay	**167**	41	0N	83	41W
Finisterre, C.	**50**	42	50N	9	19W
Finland ■	**67**	63	0N	27	0 E
Finland, G. of	**67**	60	0N	26	0 E
Finlay →►	**144**	57	0N	125	10W
Finley	**117**	35	38 S	145	35 E
Firenze	**47**	43	47N	11	15 E
Firozabad	**89**	27	10N	78	25 E
Fishguard	**26**	51	59N	4	59W
Fiskenœsset	**147**	63	5N	50	45W
Fitchburg	**164**	42	35N	71	47W
Fitzgerald	**170**	31	45N	83	16W
Fitzroy →►	**121**	23	32 S	150	52 E
Fiume = Rijeka	**52**	45	20N	14	21 E
Flagstaff	**160**	35	10N	111	40W
Flamborough Hd.	**29**	54	8N	0	4W
Flannan Is.	**32**	58	9N	7	52W
Flattery, C.	**171**	48	21N	124	43W
Flèche, La	**39**	47	42N	0	4W
Fleetwood	**28**	53	55N	3	1W
Flekkefjord	**60**	58	18N	6	39 E
Flensburg	**43**	54	46N	9	28 E
Flers	**36**	48	47N	0	33W
Flin Flon	**152**	54	46N	101	53W
Flinders I.	**117**	40	0 S	148	0 E
Flinders Ranges	**118**	31	30 S	138	30 E
Flinders Reefs	**121**	17	37 S	148	31 E
Flint, U.K.	**26**	53	15N	3	7W
Flint, U.S.A.	**167**	43	5N	83	40W
Flint →~	**170**	30	52N	84	38W
Flodden	**31**	55	37N	2	8W
Flora	**167**	38	40N	88	30W
Florence = Firenze	**47**	43	47N	11	15 E
Florence, Ala., U.S.A.	**169**	34	50N	87	40W
Florence, S.C., U.S.A.	**165**	34	12N	79	44W
Flores, Guat.	**177**	16	59N	89	50W
Flores, Indonesia	**113**	8	35 S	121	0 E
Flores Sea	**113**	6	30 S	124	0 E
Floriano	**188**	6	50 S	43	0W
Florianópolis	**191**	27	30 S	48	30W
Florida	**191**	34	7 S	56	10W
Florida □	**170**	28	30N	82	0W
Florida, Straits of	**159**	25	0N	80	0W
Florida B.	**159**	25	0N	81	20W
Florida Keys	**159**	25	0N	80	40W
Flórina	**54**	40	48N	21	26 E
Flushing = Vlissingen	**40**	51	26N	3	34 E
Fly →~	**115**	8	25 S	143	0 E
Foam Lake	**152**	51	40N	103	32W
Fóggia	**49**	41	28N	15	31 E
Foix	**36**	42	58N	1	38 E
Folda	**64**	64	41N	10	50 E
Folkestone	**25**	51	5N	1	11 E
Follette, La	**169**	36	23N	84	9W
Fond-du-Lac, Canada	**145**	59	19N	107	12W
Fond-du-Lac, U.S.A.	**167**	43	46N	88	26W
Fontainebleau	**39**	48	24N	2	40 E
Fonte Boa	**184**	2	33 S	66	0W
Foochow = Fuzhou	**99**	26	5N	119	16 E
Forbes	**117**	33	22 S	148	0 E
Forestburg	**155**	52	35N	112	1W
Forestville	**148**	48	48N	69	2W
Forfar	**33**	56	40N	2	53W
Forli	**47**	44	14N	12	2 E
Formby Pt.	**28**	53	33N	3	7W
Formentera	**51**	38	43N	1	27 E
Formosa = Taiwan ■	**99**	23	30N	121	0 E
Formosa	**191**	26	15 S	58	10W
Forrest City	**169**	35	0N	90	50W
Fort Albany	**140**	52	15N	81	35W
Fort Augustus	**32**	57	9N	4	40W
Fort Chipewyan	**145**	58	42N	111	8W
Fort Collins	**163**	40	30N	105	4W
Fort-Coulonge	**151**	45	50N	76	45W
Fort-de-France	**180**	14	36N	61	2W
Fort Dodge	**166**	42	29N	94	10W
Fort Frances	**153**	48	36N	93	24W
Fort Franklin	**145**	65	10N	123	30W
Fort George	**140**	53	50N	79	0W
Fort Good-Hope	**144**	66	14N	128	40W
Fort Hertz = Putao	**93**	27	28N	97	30 E
Fort Kent	**148**	47	12N	68	30W
Fort-Lamy = Ndjamena	**131**	12	10N	14	59 E
Fort Lauderdale	**170**	26	10N	80	5W
Fort Liard	**144**	60	14N	123	30W
Fort Mackay	**143**	57	12N	111	41W
Fort Macleod	**155**	49	45N	113	30W

Fort McMurray 155 56 44N 111 7W
Fort McPherson 144 67 30N 134 55W
Fort Madison 166 40 39N 91 20W
Fort Morgan 163 40 10N 103 50W
Fort Myers 170 26 39N 81 51W
Fort Nelson 144 58 50N 122 44W
Fort Nelson ～➤ 144 59 32N 124 0W
Fort Payne 169 34 25N 85 44W
Fort Peck L. 163 47 40N 107 0W
Fort Pierce 170 27 29N 80 19W
Fort Providence 145 61 3N 117 40W
Fort Qu'Appelle 152 50 45N 103 50W
Fort Resolution 145 61 10N 113 40W
Fort Rupert 140 51 30N 78 40W
Fort St. James 154 54 30N 124 10W
Fort St. John 155 56 15N 120 50W
Fort Sandeman . . . . 88 31 20N 69 31 E
Fort Saskatchewan 155 53 40N 113 15W
Fort Scott 166 37 50N 94 40W
Fort Severn 140 56 0N 87 40W
Fort Shevchenko . . . . 70 43 40N 51 20 E
Fort Simpson 144 61 45N 121 15W
Fort Smith, Canada 145 60 0N 111 51W
Fort Smith, U.S.A. 168 35 25N 94 25W
Fort Smith Region □ 145 63 0N 120 0W
Fort Trinquet = Bir Mogrein . . 126 25 10N 11 25W
Fort Valley 170 32 33N 83 52W
Fort Vermilion 145 58 24N 116 0W
Fort Wayne 167 41 5N 85 10W
Fort William 32 56 48N 5 8W
Fort Worth 168 32 45N 97 25W
Fort Yukon 142 66 35N 145 20W
Fortaleza 189 3 45S 38 35W
Forth ～➤ 31 56 9N 4 18W
Forth, Firth of 31 56 5N 2 55W
Fortuna 172 40 38N 124 8W
Foulian . . . . 00 ?? 4N 113 5 E
Foster . . . . 117 38 40S 146 15 E
Fougères 36 48 21N 1 14W
Foula, I. 30 60 10N 2 5W
Foulness I. . . . . 24 51 36N 0 55 E
Fourmies . . . . 38 50 1N 4 2 E
Foúrnoi . . . . 55 37 36N 26 32 E
Fouta Djalon 130 11 20N 12 10W
Foveaux Str. . . . . 123 46 42S 168 10 E
Fowey 27 50 20N 4 39W
Foxe Basin 146 66 0N 77 0W
Foxe Chan. 146 65 0N 80 0W
Foxe Pen. 146 65 0N 76 0W
Foxton . . . . 122 40 29S 175 18 E
Foyle, Lough 34 55 6N 7 8W
Foynes 35 52 37N 9 5W
Franca 188 20 33S 47 30W
France ■ . . . . 37 47 0N 3 0 E
Franche-Comté . . . . 37 46 30N 5 50 E
François 180 14 38N 60 57W
Franeker . . . . 41 53 12N 5 33 E
Frankfort, Ind., U.S.A. 167 40 20N 86 33W
Frankfort, Ky., U.S.A. 165 38 12N 84 52W
Frankfurt am Main . . . . 42 50 7N 8 40 E
Frankfurt an der Oder . . . . 43 52 50N 14 31 E
Fränkische Alb . . . . 43 49 20N 11 30 E
Franklin, La., U.S.A. 168 29 45N 91 30W
Franklin, N.H., U.S.A. 164 43 28N 71 39W
Franklin, W. Va., U.S.A. 165 38 38N 79 21W
Franklin D. Roosevelt L. 162 48 30N 118 16W
Franklin Mts. 145 65 0N 125 0W
Franklin Str. 145 72 0N 96 0W
Frankston . . . . 117 38 8S 145 8 E
Franz 150 48 25N 84 30W
Fraser ～➤ 154 49 7N 123 11W
Fraser, Mt. . . . . 120 25 35S 118 20 E
Fraser I. . . . . 116 25 15S 153 10 E
Fraserburgh 33 57 41N 2 0W
Fray Bentos 190 33 10S 58 15W
Frederick 164 39 25N 77 23W
Fredericksburg 165 38 16N 77 29W
Fredericton 148 45 57N 66 40W
Frederikshavn . . . . 61 57 28N 10 31 E
Fredrikstad . . . . 60 59 13N 10 57 E
Freeport, Bahamas 178 26 30N 78 47W

Freeport, Ill., U.S.A. 166 42 18N 89 40W
Freeport, N.Y., U.S.A. 164 40 39N 73 35W
Freeport, Tex., U.S.A. 158 28 55N 95 22W
Freetown 130 8 30N 13 17W
Freiberg . . . . 42 50 55N 13 20 E
Freibourg = Fribourg . . . . 44 46 49N 7 9 E
Fréjus . . . . 37 43 25N 6 44 E
Fremantle . . . . 120 32 7S 115 47 E
Fremont, Calif., U.S.A. 172 37 32N 122 1W
Fremont, Nebr., U.S.A. 166 41 30N 96 30W
French Guiana ■ 185 4 0N 53 0W
French Pass . . . . 123 40 55S 173 55 E
French Terr. of Afars & Issas
  = Djibouti ■ . . . . 133 12 0N 43 0 E
Fresnillo 175 23 10N 102 53W
Fresno 173 36 47N 119 50W
Fria, C. . . . . 136 18 0S 12 0 E
Frías 190 28 40S 65 5W
Fribourg . . . . 44 46 49N 7 9 E
Friendly, Is. = Tonga ■ 123 19 50S 174 30W
Friesland □ . . . . 41 53 5N 5 50 E
Frio, C. 182 22 50S 41 50W
Friuli-Venezia Giulia □ . . . . . . 47 46 0N 13 0 E
Frobisher B. 146 62 30N 66 0W
Frobisher Bay 146 63 44N 68 31W
Frobisher L. 152 56 20N 108 15W
Frome 27 51 16N 2 17W
Frome, L. . . . . 118 30 45S 139 45 E
Frome Downs . . . . 118 31 13S 139 45 E
Front Range 163 40 0N 105 40W
Front Royal 164 38 55N 78 10W
Frontera 177 18 32N 92 38W
Frostburg 164 39 43N 78 57W
Frunze . . . . 71 42 54N 74 46 E
Frutal 188 20 0S 49 0W
Fuchou = Fuzhou . . . . 99 26 5N 119 16 E
Fuchū, Hiroshima, Japan . . . . 109 34 04N 100 11 C
Fuchū, Tōkyō, Japan . . . . 107 35 40N 139 29 E
Fuerte, R. ～➤ 174 25 54N 109 22W
Fuji . . . . 107 35 9N 138 39 E
Fuji-no-miya . . . . 107 35 10N 138 40 E
Fuji-San . . . . 107 35 22N 138 44 E
Fuji-yoshida . . . . 107 35 30N 138 46 E
Fujian □ . . . . 99 26 0N 118 0 E
Fujieda . . . . 107 34 52N 138 16 E
Fujisawa . . . . 107 35 22N 139 29 E
Fukaya . . . . 107 36 12N 139 12 E
Fukien = Fujian □ . . . . 99 26 0N 118 0 E
Fukuchiyama . . . . 106 35 19N 135 9 E
Fukue-Shima . . . . 104 32 40N 128 45 E
Fukui . . . . 106 36 0N 136 10 C
Fukuoka . . . . 108 33 39N 130 21 E
Fukushima . . . . 103 37 44N 140 28 E
Fukuyama . . . . 109 34 35N 133 20 E
Fulton, Mo., U.S.A. 166 38 50N 91 55W
Fulton, N.Y., U.S.A. 164 43 20N 76 22W
Funabashi . . . . 107 35 45N 140 0 E
Funchal 126 32 38N 16 54W
Fundación 184 10 31N 74 11W
Fundy, B. of 148 45 0N 66 0W
Furāt, Nahr al ～➤ . . . . 84 31 0N 47 25 E
Furneaux Group . . . . 119 40 10S 147 50 E
Furness 28 54 14N 3 8W
Fürth . . . . 43 49 29N 11 0 E
Fury and Hecla Str. 146 69 56N 84 0W
Fushun . . . . 98 41 50N 123 55 E
Fuxin . . . . 98 42 5N 121 48 E
Fuzhou . . . . 99 26 5N 119 16 E
Fylde 28 53 50N 2 58W
Fyn . . . . 61 55 20N 10 30 E
Fyne, L. 30 56 0N 5 20W

Gabès, Golfe de . . . . 127 34 0N 10 30 E
Gabon ■ . . . . 134 0 10S 10 0 E
Gaborone . . . . 137 24 45S 25 57 E
Gachsārān . . . . 85 30 15N 50 45 E
Gadag . . . . 90 15 30N 75 45 E
Gadsden 169 34 1N 86 0W
Gaeta . . . . 49 41 12N 13 35 E

Name	Page	Lat.	Long.
Gaffney	165	35 3N	81 40W
Gagnon	141	51 50N	68 5W
Gainesville, Fla., U.S.A.	170	29 38N	82 20W
Gainesville, Ga., U.S.A.	165	34 17N	83 47W
Gainesville, Tex., U.S.A.	168	33 40N	97 10W
Gainsborough	29	53 23N	0 46W
Gairdner L.	118	31 30S	136 0 E
Galápagos	10	0 0	89 0W
Galas →	96	4 55N	101 57 E
Galashiels	31	55 37N	2 50W
Galaţi	57	45 27N	28 2 E
Galatina	49	40 10N	18 10 E
Galdhøpiggen	60	61 38N	8 18 E
Galesburg	166	40 57N	90 23W
Galicia □	50	42 43N	7 45W
Galilee, L.	121	22 20S	145 50 E
Gallatin	169	36 24N	86 27W
Galle	90	6 5N	80 10 E
Gallinas, Pta.	184	12 28N	71 40W
Gallipoli = Gelibolu	80	40 28N	26 43 E
Gallípoli	49	40 8N	18 0 E
Gällivare	66	67 9N	20 40 E
Galloway	31	55 0N	4 25W
Galloway, Mull of	30	54 38N	4 50W
Gallup	161	35 30N	108 45W
Galty Mts.	35	52 22N	8 10W
Galveston	168	29 15N	94 48W
Galveston B.	168	29 30N	94 50W
Galway	35	53 16N	9 4W
Galway □	34	53 16N	9 3W
Gamagori	106	34 50N	137 14 E
Gambia ■	130	13 25N	16 0W
Gambia →	130	13 28N	16 34W
Gand = Gent	42	51 2N	3 42 E
Gander	149	48 58N	54 35W
Gandhi Sagar	91	24 40N	75 40 E
Gandi	131	12 55N	5 49 E
Ganga →	92	23 20N	90 30 E
Ganges = Ganga →	92	23 20N	90 30 E
Gangtok	92	27 20N	88 37 E
Gannett Pk.	163	43 15N	109 38W
Gansu □	98	36 0N	104 0 E
Ganzhou	99	25 51N	114 56 E
Gao	130	16 15N	0 5W
Gaoxiong	99	22 38N	120 18 E
Garachiné	179	8 0N	78 12W
Garanhuns	189	8 50S	36 30W
Garberville	172	40 11N	123 50W
Garda, L. di	46	45 40N	10 40 E
Garden City	161	38 0N	100 45W
Garden Grove	173	33 47N	117 55W
Gardēz	87	33 37N	69 9 E
Garmsār	86	35 20N	52 25 E
Garonne →	36	45 2N	0 36W
Garoua	131	9 19N	13 21 E
Garrison Res. = Sakakawea, L.	163	47 30N	102 0W
Garry L.	145	65 58N	100 18W
Garvie Mts.	123	45 30S	168 50 E
Garwa = Garoua	131	9 19N	13 21 E
Gary	167	41 35N	87 20W
Garzón	184	2 10N	75 40W
Gascogne	36	43 45N	0 20 E
Gascony = Gascogne	36	43 45N	0 20 E
Gaspé	148	48 52N	64 30W
Gaspé, C. de	148	48 48N	64 7W
Gaspé, Pén. de	148	48 45N	65 40W
Gastonia	165	35 17N	81 10W
Gastre	192	42 20S	69 15W
Gata, C. de	51	36 41N	2 13W
Gateshead	28	54 57N	1 37W
Gauhati	93	26 10N	91 45 E
Gävle	60	60 40N	17 9 E
Gävleborgs län □	60	61 30N	16 15 E
Gawilgarh Hills	91	21 15N	76 45 E
Gawler	119	34 30S	138 42 E
Gawler Ranges	114	32 30S	135 45 E
Gaxun Nur	100	42 22N	100 30 E
Gaya	92	24 47N	85 4 E
Gaylord	150	45 1N	84 41W
Gayndah	116	25 35S	151 32 E
Gaza	80	31 30N	34 28 E
Gaziantep	80	37 6N	37 23 E
Gdańsk	58	54 22N	18 40 E
Gdańska, Zatoka	58	54 30N	19 20 E
Gdynia	58	54 35N	18 33 E
Gedaref	129	14 2N	35 28 E
Geelong	117	38 10S	144 22 E
Gejiu	99	23 20N	103 10 E
Gelderland □	41	52 5N	6 10 E
Geldermalsen	40	51 53N	5 17 E
Geldrop	41	51 25N	5 32 E
Geleen	41	50 57N	5 49 E
Gelibolu	80	40 28N	26 43 E
Gelsenkirchen	42	51 30N	7 5 E
Gemert	41	51 33N	5 41 E
General Alvear	190	35 0S	67 40W
General Pico	190	35 45S	63 50W
Geneva = Genève	44	46 12N	6 9 E
Geneva	164	42 53N	77 0W
Geneva, L. = Léman, Lac	44	46 26N	6 30 E
Genève	44	46 12N	6 9 E
Genk	41	50 58N	5 32 E
Genkai-Nada	108	34 0N	130 0 E
Gennargentu, Mti. del	48	40 0N	9 10 E
Genoa = Génova	46	44 24N	8 56 E
Génova	46	44 24N	8 56 E
Génova, Golfo di	46	44 0N	9 0 E
Gent	42	51 2N	3 42 E
George, L.	132	0 5N	30 10 E
George River = Port Nouveau-Québec	146	58 30N	65 59W
George Town	96	5 25N	100 15 E
Georgetown, Australia	119	18 17S	143 33 E
Georgetown, Canada	151	43 40N	79 56W
Georgetown, Guyana	185	6 50N	58 12W
Georgetown, U.S.A.	170	33 22N	79 15W
Georgia □	170	32 0N	82 0W
Georgian B.	151	45 15N	81 0W
Georgian S.S.R. □	70	42 0N	43 0 E
Gera	43	50 53N	12 11 E
Geraldton, Australia	120	28 48S	114 32 E
Geraldton, Canada	150	49 44N	86 59W
Gereshk	87	31 47N	64 35 E
Germany, East ■	18	52 0N	12 0 E
Germany, West ■	18	52 0N	9 0 E
Germiston	137	26 15S	28 10 E
Gerona	51	41 58N	2 46 E
Ghana ■	130	6 0N	1 0W
Ghat	127	24 59N	10 11 E
Ghawdex = Gozo	49	36 0N	14 13 E
Ghaziabad	89	28 42N	77 26 E
Ghazipur	92	25 38N	83 35 E
Ghaznī	87	33 30N	68 28 E
Ghaznī □	87	32 10N	68 20 E
Ghent = Gent	42	51 2N	3 42 E
Ghowr □	87	34 0N	64 20 E
Ghulam Mohammad Barrage	88	25 30N	68 20 E
Giant's Causeway	34	55 15N	6 30W
Gibara	178	21 9N	76 11W
Gibraltar	50	36 7N	5 22W
Gibraltar, Str. of	50	35 55N	5 40W
Gien	39	47 40N	2 36 E
Gifu	106	35 30N	136 45 E
Gigha	30	55 42N	5 45W
Gijón	50	43 32N	5 42W
Gila →	173	32 43N	114 33W
Gīlān □	81	37 0N	50 0 E
Gilbert Is. = Kiribati ■	122	1 0N	176 0 E
Gilford I.	154	50 40N	126 30W
Gilgandra	116	31 43S	148 39 E
Gilgit	89	35 50N	74 15 E
Gillingham	25	51 23N	0 34 E
Gingin	120	31 22S	115 54 E
Gippsland	117	37 45S	147 15 E
Girardot	184	4 18N	74 48W
Giresun	81	40 55N	38 30 E
Gironde →	36	45 32N	1 7W
Girvan	30	55 15N	4 50W
Gisborne	122	38 39S	178 5 E
Gisors	39	49 15N	1 47 E
Gizhiga	73	62 3N	160 30 E

Gizhiginskaya, Guba .... **73** 61 0N 158 0 E
Giżycko .... **58** 54 2N 21 48 E
Gjoa Haven **145** 68 20N 96 8W
Glace Bay **149** 46 11N 59 58W
Gladstone, Queens., Australia **121** 23 52S 151 16 E
Gladstone, S. Austral.,
  Australia................. **118** 33 15S 138 22 E
Gláma...................... **64** 65 48N 23 0W
Glasgow, U.K. **31** 55 52N 4 14W
Glasgow, U.S.A. **169** 37 2N 85 55W
Glastonbury................ **27** 51 9N 2 42W
Gleiwitz = Gliwice .... **58** 50 22N 18 41 E
Glen Coe **32** 56 40N 5 0W
Glen Innes .... **116** 29 44S 151 44 E
Glen Mor .... **33** 57 12N 4 37 E
Glenburgh .... **120** 25 26S 116 6 E
Glendale **173** 34 7N 118 18W
Glendive **163** 47 7N 104 40W
Glenelg .... **119** 34 58S 138 31 E
Glenns Ferry **172** 43 0N 115 15W
Glenorchy .... **119** 42 49S 147 18 E
Glenrothes............... **31** 56 12N 3 11W
Glens Falls **164** 43 20N 73 40W
Gliwice .... **58** 50 22N 18 41 E
Głogów .... **58** 51 37N 16 5 E
Glossop **28** 53 27N 1 56W
Gloucester............... **24** 51 52N 2 15W
Gloucestershire □ **24** 51 44N 2 10W
Gloversville **164** 43 5N 74 18W
Gniezno .... **58** 52 30N 17 35 E
Go Cong .... **95** 10 22N 106 40 E
Goa .... **91** 15 33N 73 59 E
Goa □................... **90** 15 33N 73 59 E
Goat Fell................ **30** 55 37N 5 11W
Goba .... **133** 7 1N 39 59 E
Gobi.................... **98** 44 0N 111 0 E
Gobō .... **106** 33 53N 135 10 E
Godavari ➝.............. **91** 16 25N 82 18 E
Godbout................. **148** 49 20N 67 38W
Goderich **160** 43 45N 81 41W
Godhra .... **91** 22 49N 73 40 E
Gods L. **153** 54 40N 94 15W
Godthåb................. **147** 64 10N 51 35W
Goeie Hoop, Kaap die ..... **136** 34 24S 18 30 E
Goeree .... **40** 51 50N 4 0 E
Goes................... **40** 51 30N 3 55 E
Gogama **151** 47 35N 81 43W
Goiânia................. **188** 16 43S 49 20W
Goiás □ **188** 12 10S 48 0W
Goirle.................. **40** 51 31N 5 4 E
Gojō .... **106** 34 21N 135 42 E
Gökçeada .... **55** 40 10N 25 50 E
Gold Coast, Australia..... **116** 28 0S 153 25 E
Gold Coast, W. Afr. **124** 4 0N 1 40W
Golden Bay .... **122** 40 40S 172 50 E
Golden Gate **172** 37 54N 122 30W
Golden Hinde **154** 49 40N 125 44W
Golden Vale **35** 52 33N 8 17W
Goldfield **172** 37 45N 117 13W
Goldsboro **165** 35 24N 77 59W
Goldsworthy .... **114** 20 21S 119 30 E
Golfo Aranci .... **48** 41 0N 9 35 E
Gomel.................. **68** 52 28N 31 0 E
Gómez Palacio **174** 25 34N 103 30W
Gonābād .... **86** 34 15N 58 45 E
Gonaïves **180** 19 20N 72 42W
Gonda .... **92** 27 9N 81 58 E
Gonder................. **132** 12 39N 37 30 E
Good Hope, C. of = Goeie
  Hoop, Kaap die......... **136** 34 24S 18 30 E
Goole **29** 53 42N 0 52W
Goondiwindi .... **116** 28 30S 150 21 E
Goose Bay **147** 53 15N 60 20W
Gorakhpur .... **92** 26 47N 83 23 E
Gordonvale .... **121** 17 5S 145 50 E
Gore, Ethiopia .... **132** 8 12N 35 32 E
Gore, N.Z. .... **123** 46 5S 168 58 E
Gorey **35** 52 41N 6 18W
Gorinchem............... **40** 51 50N 4 59 E
Gorki = Gorkiy .... **68** 56 20N 44 0 E

Gorkiy .... **68** 56 20N 44 0 E
Görlitz .... **43** 51 10N 14 59 E
Gorna Oryakhovitsa ...... **53** 43 7N 25 40 E
Gort................... **35** 53 4N 8 50W
Gorzów Wielkopolski ..... **58** 52 43N 15 15 E
Gosford .... **117** 33 23S 151 18 E
Gospič .... **52** 44 35N 15 23 E
Gosport **25** 50 48N 1 8W
Göteborg .... **60** 57 43N 11 59 E
Göteborgs och Bohus län □.. **60** 58 30N 11 30 E
Gotemba .... **107** 35 18N 138 56 E
Gotha .... **43** 50 56N 10 42 E
Gotland .... **60** 57 30N 18 33 E
Gōtsu .... **109** 35 0N 132 14 E
Gottwaldov .... **59** 49 14N 17 40 E
Gouda .... **40** 52 1N 4 42 E
Gouin, Rés. **151** 48 35N 74 40W
Goulburn .... **117** 34 44S 149 44 E
Goundam............... **130** 16 25N 3 45W
Gournay-en-Bray .... **38** 49 29N 1 44 E
Governador Valadares **188** 18 15S 41 57W
Governor's Harbour **178** 25 10N 76 14W
Gower, The **27** 51 35N 4 10W
Goya **190** 29 10S 59 10W
Gozo.................. **49** 36 0N 14 13 E
Graaff-Reinet.......... **136** 32 13S 24 32 E
Gracias a Dios, C. **179** 15 0N 83 10W
Gratton .... **116** 29 38S 152 58 E
Graham **165** 36 5N 79 22W
Graham I............... **154** 53 40N 132 30W
Graham Land **14** 65 0S 64 0W
Grahamstown .... **137** 33 19S 26 31 E
Grain Coast **124** 4 20N 10 0W
Grampian □ **33** 57 0N 3 0W
Grampian Mts. **33** 56 50N 4 0W
Grampians, The .... **119** 37 0S 142 20 E
Gran Chaco **190** 25 0 0 01 0W
Gran Sasso d'Italia ..... **47** 42 25N 13 30 E
Granada, Nic. **179** 11 58N 86 0W
Granada, Spain **50** 37 10N 3 35W
Granby **151** 45 25N 72 45W
Grand Bank **149** 47 6N 55 48W
Grand Bassam **130** 5 10N 3 49W
Grand Canyon **160** 36 3N 112 9W
Grand Cayman **178** 19 20N 81 20W
Grand Cess **130** 4 40N 8 12W
Grand Falls **149** 48 56N 55 40W
Grand Forks, Canada ... **155** 49 0N 118 30W
Grand Forks, U.S.A. **156** 48 0N 97 3W
Grand Island **163** 40 59N 98 25W
Grand Junction **163** 39 0N 108 30W
Grand Mère **151** 46 36N 72 40W
Grand Portage **150** 47 58N 89 41W
Grand Rapids, Canada .. **153** 53 12N 99 19W
Grand Rapids, U.S.A. ... **167** 42 57N 86 40W
Grand St.-Bernard, Col. du .. **44** 45 53N 7 11 E
Grand Teton **163** 43 54N 111 50W
Grand View **153** 51 10N 100 42W
Grande ➝, Bolivia **187** 15 51S 64 39W
Grande ➝, Brazil........ **188** 20 6S 51 4W
Grande, B. **192** 50 30S 68 20W
Grande, La **171** 45 15N 118 0W
Grande, La ➝ **140** 53 50N 79 0W
Grande Baleine, R. de la ➝.. **140** 55 16N 77 47W
Grande de Santiago, R. ➝.. **175** 21 36N 105 26W
Grande Prairie **155** 55 10N 118 50W
Grande-Rivière **148** 48 26N 64 30W
Grange, La **170** 33 4N 85 0W
Grangemouth **31** 56 1N 3 43W
Grangeville **162** 45 57N 116 4W
Granite City **166** 38 45N 90 3W
Grant, Mt. **172** 38 34N 118 48W
Grantham.............. **29** 52 55N 0 39W
Grantown-on-Spey....... **33** 57 19N 3 36W
Grants Pass **171** 42 30N 123 22W
Grass Valley **172** 39 18N 121 0W
Grasse .... **37** 43 38N 6 56 E
Gravelbourg **152** 49 50N 106 35W
Gravelines .... **38** 51 0N 2 10 E
's-Gravenhage .... **40** 52 7N 4 17 E

GRA

Name	Map	Lat		Long	
Gravesend	25	51	25N	0	22 E
Grayling	167	44	40N	84	42W
Graz	45	47	4N	15	27 E
Great Abaco I.	178	26	25N	77	10W
Great Australian Bight	114	33	30S	130	0 E
Great Bahama Bank	178	23	15N	78	0W
Great Barrier I.	122	36	11 S	175	25 E
Great Barrier Reef	121	18	0S	146	50 E
Great Basin	172	40	0N	116	30W
Great Bear L.	145	65	30N	120	0W
Great Britain	16	54	0N	2	15W
Great Divide, The	117	35	0S	149	17 E
Great Dividing Ra.	121	23	0S	146	0 E
Great Exuma I.	178	23	30N	75	50W
Great Falls	163	47	27N	111	12W
Great Inagua I.	180	21	0N	73	20W
Great Indian Desert = Thar Desert	89	28	0N	72	0 E
Great Orme's Head	26	53	20N	3	52W
Great Ouse →	29	52	47N	0	22 E
Great Plains	138	47	0N	105	0W
Great Salt Lake	162	41	0N	112	30W
Great Salt Lake Desert	162	40	20N	113	50W
Great Slave L.	145	61	23N	115	38W
Great Wall	98	38	30N	109	30 E
Great Whernside	28	54	9N	1	59W
Great Yarmouth	29	52	40N	1	45 E
Greater Antilles	181	17	40N	74	0W
Greater Manchester □	28	53	30N	2	15W
Greater Sunda Is.	111	2	30S	110	0 E
Gredos, Sierra de	50	40	20N	5	0W
Greece ■	54	40	0N	23	0 E
Greeley	163	40	30N	104	40W
Green →, Ky., U.S.A.	167	37	54N	87	30W
Green →, Utah, U.S.A.	163	38	11N	109	53W
Green Bay	167	44	30N	88	0W
Greenfield	164	42	38N	72	38W
Greenland □	147	66	0N	45	0W
Greenland Sea	13	73	0N	10	0W
Greenock	30	55	57N	4	46W
Greensboro	165	36	7N	79	46W
Greenville, Ala., U.S.A.	169	31	50N	86	37W
Greenville, Mich., U.S.A.	167	43	12N	85	14W
Greenville, Miss., U.S.A.	168	33	25N	91	0W
Greenville, N.C., U.S.A.	165	35	37N	77	26W
Greenville, S.C., U.S.A.	165	34	54N	82	24W
Greenville, Tenn., U.S.A.	165	36	13N	82	51W
Greenwood, Miss., U.S.A.	169	33	30N	90	4W
Greenwood, S.C., U.S.A.	165	34	13N	82	13W
Grenada	169	33	45N	89	50W
Grenada ■	180	12	10N	61	40W
Grenoble	37	45	12N	5	42 E
Grenville	117	37	46S	143	52 E
Gretna Green	31	55	0N	3	3W
Grey Range	116	27	0S	143	30 E
Grey Res.	149	48	20N	56	30W
Greymouth	123	42	29S	171	13 E
Griffin	170	33	17N	84	14W
Griffith	117	34	18S	146	2 E
Grimsby	29	53	35N	0	5W
Grimshaw	155	56	10N	117	40W
Grinnell	166	41	45N	92	43W
Grodno	68	53	42N	23	52 E
Groningen	41	53	15N	6	35 E
Groningen □	41	53	16N	6	40 E
Grootfontein	136	19	31 S	18	6 E
Groznyy	70	43	20N	45	45 E
Grudziądz	58	53	30N	18	47 E
Grytviken	14	53	50S	37	10W
Gt. Stour = Stour →	25	51	15N	1	20 E
Guadalajara, Mexico	175	20	40N	103	20W
Guadalajara, Spain	50	40	37N	3	12W
Guadalquivir →	50	36	47N	6	22W
Guadalupe = Guadeloupe ■	180	16	20N	61	40W
Guadalupe Bravos	174	31	23N	106	7W
Guadarrama, Sierra de	50	41	0N	4	0W
Guadeloupe ■	180	16	20N	61	40W
Guadiana →	50	37	14N	7	22W
Guadix	50	37	18N	3	11W
Guaíra	191	24	5S	54	10W
Guajará-Mirim	187	10	50S	65	20W
Gualeguay	190	33	10S	59	14W
Gualeguaychú	190	33	3S	59	31W
Guam	10	13	27N	144	45 E
Guanabacoa	178	23	8N	82	18W
Guanacaste, Cordillera del	179	10	40N	85	4W
Guanahani = San Salvador	178	24	0N	74	40W
Guanajay	178	22	56N	82	42W
Guanajuato	177	21	1N	101	15W
Guanajuato □	177	21	0N	101	0W
Guanare	184	8	42N	69	12W
Guangdong □	99	23	0N	113	0 E
Guangxi Zhuangzu Zizhiqu □	99	24	0N	109	0 E
Guangzhou	99	23	5N	113	10 E
Guantánamo	178	20	10N	75	14W
Guaporé →	187	11	55S	65	4W
Guaqui	187	16	41S	68	54W
Guarapuava	191	25	20S	51	30W
Guarda	50	40	32N	7	20W
Guardafui, C. = Asir, Ras	133	11	55N	51	10 E
Guatemala	177	14	40N	90	22W
Guatemala ■	177	15	40N	90	30W
Guaviare →	184	4	3N	67	44W
Guayama	180	17	59N	66	7W
Guayaquil	184	2	15S	79	52W
Guayaquil, G. de	186	3	10S	81	0W
Guaymas	174	27	56N	110	54W
Guddu Barrage	89	28	30N	69	50 E
Gudur	90	14	12N	79	55 E
Guelph	151	43	35N	80	20W
Guernica	50	43	19N	2	40W
Guernsey	36	49	30N	2	35W
Guerrero □	177	17	40N	100	0W
Guilin	99	25	18N	110	15 E
Guimarães	188	2	9S	44	42W
Guinea ■	130	10	20N	10	0W
Guinea, Gulf of	130	3	0N	2	30 E
Guinea-Bissau ■	130	12	0N	15	0W
Güines	178	22	50N	82	0W
Guiyang	99	26	32N	106	40 E
Guizhou □	99	27	0N	107	0 E
Gujarat □	91	23	20N	71	0 E
Gujranwala	89	32	10N	74	12 E
Gujrat	89	32	40N	74	2 E
Gulbarga	91	17	20N	76	50 E
Gulf, The	85	27	0N	50	0 E
Gulfport	169	30	21N	89	3W
Gulgong	116	32	20S	149	49 E
Gull Lake	152	50	10N	108	29W
Gümüsane	81	40	30N	39	30 E
Guna	91	24	40N	77	19 E
Gundagai	117	35	3S	148	6 E
Gunnedah	116	30	59S	150	15 E
Gunningbar Cr. →	116	31	14S	147	6 E
Guntakal	90	15	11N	77	27 E
Guntersville	169	34	18N	86	16W
Guntur	92	16	23N	80	30 E
Gurdaspur	89	32	5N	75	31 E
Gurgaon	89	28	27N	77	1 E
Gurkha	92	28	5N	84	40 E
Gurupi →	188	1	13S	46	6W
Guryev	70	47	5N	52	0 E
Gusau	131	12	12N	6	40 E
Guthrie	168	35	55N	97	30W
Guyana ■	185	5	0N	59	0W
Guyenne	36	44	30N	0	40 E
Guyra	116	30	15S	151	40 E
Gwalior	91	26	12N	78	10 E
Gwent □	27	51	45N	2	55W
Gweru	137	19	28S	29	45 E
Gwynedd □	26	53	0N	4	0W
Gyaring Hu	101	34	50N	97	40 E
Gydanskiy P-ov.	69	70	0N	78	0 E
Gympie	116	26	11S	152	38 E
Gyoda	107	36	10N	139	30 E
Gyöngyös	59	47	48N	20	0 E
Györ	59	47	41N	17	40 E
Gypsumville	153	51	45N	98	40W

Name	Pg	Lat°	Lat′	N/S	Lon°	Lon′	E/W
Ha 'Arava	80	30	50N		35	20	E
Ha Giang	95	22	50N		104	59	E
Haarlem	40	52	23N		4	39	E
Habana, La	178	23	8N		82	22W	
Hachijō-Jima	105	33	5N		139	45	E
Hachinohe	103	40	30N		141	29	E
Hachiōji	107	35	40N		139	20	E
Hadera	80	32	27N		34	55	E
Hadhramaut = Hadramawt	83	15	30N		49	30	E
Hadiya	82	25	30N		36	56	E
Hadramawt	83	15	30N		49	30	E
Hadrians Wall	28	55	0N		2	30W	
Haeju	98	38	3N		125	45	E
Haerhpin = Harbin	98	45	48N		126	40	E
Hafar al Bāṭin	82	28	25N		46	0	E
Hafnarfjörður	64	64	4N		21	57W	
Hatt-Gel	84	31	30N		49	32	E
Hagen	42	51	21N		7	29	E
Hagerstown	164	39	39N		77	46W	
Hagi	108	34	30N		131	22	E
Hags Hd.	35	52	57N		9	30W	
Hague, The = 's-Gravenhage	40	52	7N		4	17	E
Hai'an	99	32	37N		120	27	E
Haifa = Ḥefa	80	32	46N		35	0	E
Haikou	99	20	1N		110	16	E
Ḥā'il	82	27	28N		41	45	E
Hailar	98	49	10N		119	38	E
Hailey	162	43	30N		114	15W	
Haileybury	151	47	30N		79	38W	
Hainan	99	19	0N		110	0	E
Hainan Dao	99	19	0N		109	30	E
Haiphong	95	20	47N		106	41	E
Haiti ■	180	19	0N		72	30W	
Hakken-Zan	106	34	10N		135	54	E
Hakodate	103	41	45N		140	44	E
Ḥalab	80	36	10N		37	15	E
Ḥalaih	129	22	12N		36	30	F
Halberstadt	43	51	53N		11	2	E
Halfmoon Bay	123	46	50S		168	5	E
Halifax, Canada	148	44	38N		63	35W	
Halifax, U.K.	28	53	43N		1	51W	
Halifax B.	121	18	50S		147	0	E
Hallands län □	61	56	50N		12	50	E
Halle	43	51	29N		12	0	E
Halls Creek	114	18	16S		127	38	E
Halmahera	113	0	40N		128	0	E
Halmstad	61	56	41N		12	52	E
Hälsingborg = Helsingborg	61	56	3N		12	42	E
Hamada	109	34	56N		132	4	E
Hamadān	81	34	52N		48	32	E
Hamadān □	81	35	0N		49	0	E
Hamāh	80	35	5N		36	40	E
Hamakita	107	34	45N		137	47	E
Hamamatsu	106	34	45N		137	45	E
Hamar	60	60	48N		11	7	E
Hamburg	43	53	32N		9	59	E
Hämeenlinna	67	61	0N		24	28	E
Hamelin Pool	120	26	22S		114	20	E
Hameln	42	52	7N		9	24	E
Hamhung	98	39	54N		127	30	E
Hamilton, Australia	119	37	45S		142	2	E
Hamilton, Bermuda	180	32	15N		64	45W	
Hamilton, Canada	151	43	15N		79	50W	
Hamilton, N.Z.	122	37	47S		175	19	E
Hamilton, U.K.	31	55	47N		4	2W	
Hamilton, U.S.A.	167	39	20N		84	35W	
Hamm	42	51	40N		7	49	E
Hammerfest	67	70	39N		23	41	E
Hammond, Ind., U.S.A.	167	41	40N		87	30W	
Hammond, La., U.S.A.	169	30	32N		90	30W	
Hampshire □	25	51	3N		1	20W	
Hampshire Downs	25	51	10N		1	10W	
Hampton	165	37	4N		76	18W	
Hanamaki	103	39	23N		141	7	E
Hancock	150	47	10N		88	40W	
Handa	106	34	53N		137	0	E
Handan	98	36	35N		114	28	E
Haney	154	49	12N		122	40W	
Hanford	173	36	23N		119	39W	
Hangayn Nuruu	100	47	30N		100	0	E
Hangchou = Hangzhou	99	30	18N		120	11	E
Hangö	67	59	50N		22	57	E
Hangu	98	39	18N		117	53	E
Hangzhou	99	30	18N		120	11	E
Hanna	155	51	40N		111	54W	
Hannibal	166	39	42N		91	22W	
Hannover	42	52	23N		9	43	E
Hanoi	95	21	5N		105	55	E
Hanover = Hannover	42	52	23N		9	43	E
Hanover, N.H., U.S.A.	148	43	43N		72	17W	
Hanover, Pa., U.S.A.	164	39	46N		76	59W	
Hansi	89	29	10N		75	57	E
Hanyū	107	36	10N		139	32	E
Hanzhong	99	33	10N		107	1	E
Haora	92	22	37N		88	20	E
Haparanda	67	65	52N		24	8	E
Ḥaraḍ, Si. Arabia	83	24	22N		49	0	E
Ḥaraḍ, Yemen	83	16	26N		43	5	E
Harare	137	17	43S		31	2	E
Harbin	98	45	48N		126	40	E
Harbour Breton	149	47	29N		55	50W	
Harbour Grace	149	47	40N		53	22W	
Hardap Dam	136	24	32S		17	50	E
Hardenberg	41	52	34N		6	37	E
Harderwijk	41	52	21N		5	38	E
Hardinxveld	40	51	40N		4	53	E
Hardwar = Haridwar	89	29	58N		78	9	E
Harer	133	9	20N		42	8	E
Harfleur	38	49	30N		0	10	E
Hargeisa	133	9	30N		44	2	E
Hari →	111	1	16S		104	5	E
Haridwar	89	29	58N		78	9	E
Harima-Nada	109	34	30N		134	35	E
Harīrūd →	86	34	20N		62	30	E
Harlech	26	52	52N		4	7W	
Harlingen, Neth.	41	53	11N		5	25	E
Harlingen, U.S.A.	161	26	20N		97	50W	
Harlow	25	51	47N		0	9	E
Harney Basin	171	43	30N		119	0W	
Härnösand	66	62	38N		18	0	E
Harriman	169	36	0N		84	35W	
Harris	32	57	50N		6	55W	
Harris L.	118	31	10S		135	10	E
Harrisburg, Ill., U.S.A.	167	37	42N		88	30W	
Harrisburg, Pa., U.S.A.	164	40	18N		76	52W	
Harrison	168	36	10N		93	4W	
Harrison, C.	147	54	55N		57	55W	
Harrison B.	142	70	25N		151	30W	
Harrisonburg	165	38	28N		78	52W	
Harrogate	28	53	59N		1	32W	
Harrow	25	51	35N		0	15W	
Hartford	164	41	47N		72	41W	
Hartland Pt.	27	51	2N		4	32W	
Hartlepool	29	54	42N		1	11W	
Hartsville	165	34	23N		80	2W	
Harvey, Australia	120	33	5S		115	54	E
Harvey, U.S.A.	167	41	40N		87	40W	
Harwich	25	51	56N		1	18	E
Haryana □	89	29	0N		76	10	E
Hashima	106	35	20N		136	40	E
Hashimoto	106	34	19N		135	37	E
Hastings, N.Z.	122	39	39S		176	52	E
Hastings, U.K.	25	50	51N		0	36	E
Hastings, U.S.A.	163	40	34N		98	22W	
Hastings Ra.	116	31	15S		152	14	E
Hatano	107	35	22N		139	14	E
Hathras	89	27	36N		78	6	E
Hatteras, C.	165	35	10N		75	30W	
Hattiesburg	169	31	20N		89	20W	
Hatvan	59	47	40N		19	45	E
Hau Bon = Cheo Reo	95	13	25N		108	28	E
Hauraki Gulf	122	36	35S		175	5	E
Haut Atlas	126	32	30N		5	0W	
Havana = Habana, La.	178	23	8N		82	22W	
Havant	25	50	51N		0	59W	
Havelock	151	44	26N		77	53W	
Haverfordwest	26	51	48N		4	59W	
Haverhill	164	42	50N		71	2W	
Havre	163	48	34N		109	40W	
Havre, Le	38	49	30N		0	5	E
Hawaii □	160	20	30N		157	0W	
Hawaiian Is.	160	20	30N		156	0W	

Hawea Lake	**123**	44	28S	169	19 E
Hawera	**122**	39	35S	174	19 E
Hawick	**31**	55	25N	2	48W
Hawke B.	**122**	39	25S	177	20 E
Hawke's Bay □	**122**	39	45S	176	35 E
Hawkesbury	**151**	45	37N	74	37W
Hawthorne	**172**	38	31N	118	37W
Hay, Australia	**117**	34	30S	144	51 E
Hay, U.K.	**26**	52	4N	3	9W
Hay River	**145**	60	51N	115	44W
Hayward's Heath	**25**	51	0N	0	5W
Hazard	**165**	37	18N	83	10W
Hazaribag	**92**	23	58N	85	26 E
Hazebrouck	**38**	50	42N	2	31 E
Hazelton	**154**	55	20N	127	42W
Hazleton	**164**	40	58N	76	0W
Healdsburg	**172**	38	33N	122	51W
Healesville	**117**	37	35S	145	30 E
Heanor	**29**	53	1N	1	20W
Hearst	**150**	49	40N	83	41W
Hebei □	**98**	39	0N	116	0 E
Hebel	**116**	28	58S	147	47 E
Hebrides	**16**	57	30N	7	0W
Hebron = Al Khalīl	**80**	31	32N	35	6 E
Hebron	**147**	58	5N	62	30W
Hecate Str.	**154**	53	10N	130	30W
Hechuan	**99**	30	2N	106	12 E
Hedmark fylke □	**60**	61	17N	11	40 E
Heemstede	**40**	52	22N	4	37 E
Heerenveen	**41**	52	57N	5	55 E
Heerlen	**41**	50	55N	6	0 E
Hefa	**80**	32	46N	35	0 E
Hefei	**99**	31	52N	117	18 E
Hegang	**98**	47	20N	130	19 E
Heidelberg	**42**	49	23N	8	41 E
Heilbronn	**42**	49	8N	9	13 E
Heilongjiang □	**98**	48	0N	126	0 E
Heilunkiang = Heilongjiang □	**98**	48	0N	126	0 E
Heinze Is.	**94**	14	25N	97	45 E
Hekimhan	**81**	38	50N	38	0 E
Hekinan	**106**	34	52N	137	0 E
Hekla	**16**	63	56N	19	35W
Helena, Ark., U.S.A.	**169**	34	30N	90	35W
Helena, Mont., U.S.A.	**163**	46	40N	112	0W
Helensburgh	**30**	56	0N	4	44W
Helmand →	**87**	31	12N	61	34 E
Helmond	**41**	51	29N	5	41 E
Helmsdale	**33**	58	7N	3	40W
Helsingborg	**61**	56	3N	12	42 E
Helsinki	**67**	60	15N	25	3 E
Helston	**27**	50	7N	5	17W
Helvellyn	**28**	54	31N	3	1W
Hemel Hempstead	**25**	51	45N	0	28W
Hempstead	**164**	30	5N	96	5W
Henan □	**99**	34	0N	114	0 E
Henderson	**165**	36	20N	78	25W
Hendersonville	**165**	35	21N	82	28W
Hengelo	**41**	52	16N	6	48 E
Hengyang	**99**	26	51N	112	30 E
Hénin-Beaumont	**38**	50	25N	2	58 E
Hennebont	**36**	47	49N	3	19W
Henrietta Maria C.	**140**	55	9N	82	20W
Henty	**117**	35	30S	147	0 E
Henzada	**93**	17	38N	95	26 E
Herāt	**87**	34	20N	62	7 E
Herāt □	**87**	35	0N	62	0 E
Herbert ～►	**121**	18	31S	146	17 E
Herbiers, Les	**36**	46	52N	1	0W
Hercegnovi	**52**	42	30N	18	33 E
Hercegovina = Bosna i Hercegovina □	**52**	44	0N	18	0 E
Hereford	**24**	52	4N	2	42W
Hereford and Worcester □	**24**	52	10N	2	30W
Herford	**42**	52	7N	8	40 E
Hermosillo	**174**	29	4N	110	58W
Heroica = Caborca	**174**	30	40N	112	10W
Heroica Nogales = Nogales	**174**	31	20N	110	56W
Heron Bay	**150**	48	40N	86	25W
Herrin	**166**	37	50N	89	0W
Hertford □	**25**	51	51N	0	5W
's-Hertogenbosch	**40**	51	42N	5	17 E
Hesse = Hessen □	**42**	50	40N	9	20 E
Hessen □	**42**	50	40N	9	20 E
Hewett, C.	**146**	70	16N	67	45W
Hexham	**28**	54	58N	2	7W
Heysham	**28**	54	5N	2	53W
Heywood	**119**	38	8S	141	37 E
Hi-no-Misaki	**109**	35	26N	132	38 E
Hialeach	**170**	25	49N	80	17W
Hibiki-Nada	**108**	34	0N	130	0 E
Hickory	**165**	35	46N	81	17W
Hida-Gawa →	**106**	35	26N	137	3 E
Hida-Sammyaku	**106**	36	30N	137	40 E
Hida-Sanchi	**106**	36	10N	137	0 E
Hidaka	**109**	35	30N	134	44 E
Hidalgo □	**177**	20	30N	99	0W
Hidalgo del Parral	**174**	26	56N	105	40W
Higashi-matsuyama	**107**	36	2	139	25 E
Higashiōsaka	**106**	34	40N	135	37 E
Higasi-Suidō	**108**	34	0N	129	30 E
High Atlas = Haut Atlas	**126**	32	30N	5	0W
High Point	**165**	35	57N	79	58W
High Prairie	**155**	55	30N	116	30W
Highland □	**32**	57	30N	5	0W
Highland Park	**167**	42	10N	87	50W
Ḥijārah, Şaḥrā' al	**84**	30	25N	44	30 E
Hikari	**108**	33	58N	131	58 E
Hikone	**106**	35	15N	136	10 E
Hildesheim	**43**	52	9N	9	55 E
Hillegom	**40**	52	18N	4	35 E
Hillsboro	**171**	45	31N	123	0W
Hillston	**117**	33	30S	145	31 E
Hilo	**160**	19	44N	155	5W
Hilversum	**40**	52	14N	5	10 E
Himachal Pradesh □	**89**	31	30N	77	0 E
Himalaya, Mts.	**101**	29	0N	84	0 E
Hime-Jima	**108**	33	43N	131	40 E
Himeji	**109**	34	50N	134	40 E
Himi	**106**	36	50N	137	0 E
Ḥimş	**80**	34	40N	36	45 E
Hinchinbrook I.	**121**	18	20S	146	15 E
Hinckley	**25**	52	33N	1	21W
Hindmarsh	**119**	34	54S	138	34 E
Hindu Kush	**89**	36	0N	71	0 E
Hindupur	**90**	13	49N	77	32 E
Hines Creek	**155**	56	20N	118	40W
Hingoli	**91**	19	41N	77	15 E
Hinton	**165**	37	40N	80	51W
Hirado	**108**	33	22N	129	33 E
Hirakarta	**106**	34	48N	135	40 E
Hirakud Dam	**92**	21	32N	83	45 E
Hirata	**109**	35	24N	132	49 E
Hiratsuka	**107**	35	19N	139	21 E
Hirosaki	**103**	40	34N	140	28 E
Hiroshima	**109**	34	24N	132	30 E
Hirson	**38**	49	55N	4	4 E
Hispaniola	**180**	19	0N	71	0W
Hita	**108**	33	20N	130	58 E
Hitachi	**107**	36	36N	140	39 E
Hitachiota	**107**	36	30N	140	30 E
Hitchin	**25**	51	57N	0	16W
Hitoyoshi	**108**	32	13N	130	45 E
Hitra	**65**	63	30N	8	45 E
Hiuchi-Nada	**109**	34	5N	133	20 E
Ho Chi Minh City = Thanh Pho Ho Chi Minh	**95**	10	58N	106	40 E
Hoa Binh	**95**	20	50N	105	20 E
Hobart	**119**	42	50S	147	21 E
Hobbs	**161**	32	40N	103	3W
Hodaka-Dake	**106**	36	17N	137	39 E
Hódmezővásárhely	**59**	46	28N	20	22 E
Hoek van Holland	**40**	52	0N	4	7 E
Hofsjökull	**64**	64	49N	18	48W
Hōfu	**108**	34	3N	131	34 E
Hogan Group	**117**	39	13S	147	1 E
Hoh Xil Shan	**101**	35	0N	89	0 E
Hohhot	**98**	40	52N	111	40 E
Hōjō	**109**	33	58N	132	46 E
Hokitika	**123**	42	42S	171	0 E
Hokkaidō □	**103**	43	30N	143	0 E
Holbrook	**117**	35	42S	147	18 E
Holderness	**29**	53	45N	0	5W

Holdrege	163	40 26N	99	22W
Holguín	178	20 50N	76	20W
Holland	167	42 47N	86	7W
Holly Springs	169	34 45N	89	25W
Hollywood, Calif., U.S.A.	173	34 7N	118	25W
Hollywood, Fla., U.S.A.	170	26 0N	80	9W
Holsteinsborg	147	66 40N	53	30W
Holsworthy	27	50 48N	4	21W
Holt	64	63 33N	19	48W
Holy I., Scotland, U.K.	31	55 31N	5	4W
Holy I., Wales, U.K.	26	53 17N	4	37W
Holyhead	26	53 18N	4	38W
Holyoke	164	42 14N	72	37W
Hombori	130	15 20N	1	38W
Home Hill	121	19 43S	147	25 E
Homer	142	59 40N	151	35W
Homs = Ḥimṣ	80	34 40N	36	45 E
Honan = Henan □	99	34 0N	114	0 E
Hondo	108	32 27N	130	12 E
Honduras ■	179	14 40N	86	30W
Honduras, Golfo de	177	16 50N	87	0W
Hong Kong ■	99	22 11N	114	14 E
Hongha →	95	22 0N	104	0 E
Hongshui He →	99	23 48N	109	30 E
Honiton	27	50 48N	3	11W
Honolulu	160	21 19N	157	52W
Honshū	106	36 0N	138	0 E
Hoogeveen	41	52 44N	6	30 E
Hook Hd.	35	52 8N	6	57W
Hook of Holland = Hoek van				
Holland	40	52 0N	4	7 E
Hoorn	40	52 38N	5	4 E
Hope, Canada	154	49 25N	121	25 E
Hope, U.S.A.	168	33 40N	93	36W
Hope Town	178	26 35N	76	57W
Hopedale	147	55 28N	60	13W
Hopei = Hebei □	98	39 0N	116	0 E
Hopelchén	177	19 46N	89	51W
Hopetoun, Vic., Australia	119	35 42S	142	22 E
Hopetoun, W. Austral.,				
Australia	120	33 57S	120	7 E
Hopkinsville	169	36 52N	87	26W
Hoquiam	171	46 50N	123	55W
Hordaland fylke □	60	60 25N	6	15 E
Hormoz	85	27 35N	55	0 E
Hormuz Str.	85	26 30N	56	30 E
Horn, Cape = Hornos, Cabo				
de	192	55 50S	67	30W
Hornavan	66	66 15N	17	30 E
Hornell	164	42 23N	77	41W
Hornos, Cabo de	192	55 50S	67	30W
Hornsby	117	33 42S	151	2 E
Hornsea	29	53 55N	0	10W
Horqin Youyi Qianqi	98	46 5N	122	3 E
Horsens	61	55 52N	9	51 E
Horsham	119	36 44S	142	13 E
Horton →	145	69 56N	126	52W
Hoshiarpur	89	31 30N	75	58 E
Hospet	90	15 15N	76	20 E
Hospitalet de Llobregat	51	41 21N	2	6 E
Hoste, I.	192	55 0S	69	0W
Hot Springs	168	34 30N	93	0W
Houghton	150	47 9N	88	39W
Houghton-le-Spring	28	54 51N	1	28W
Houhora	122	34 49S	173	9 E
Houlton	148	46 5N	67	50W
Houma	169	29 35N	90	44W
Houston, Canada	154	54 25N	126	39W
Houston, U.S.A.	168	29 50N	95	20W
Houtman Abrolhos	120	28 43S	113	48 E
Hovd	100	48 2N	91	37 E
Hove	25	50 50N	0	10W
Howe, C.	117	37 30S	150	0 E
Howrah = Haora	92	22 37N	88	20 E
Hoy I.	33	58 50N	3	15W
Hrádec Králové	58	50 15N	15	50 E
Hrvatska □	52	45 20N	18	0 E
Hsiamen = Xiamen	99	24 25N	118	4 E
Hsian = Xi'an	99	34 15N	109	0 E
Hsinhailien = Lianyungang	99	34 40N	119	11 E
Hsüchou = Xuzhou	99	34 18N	117	10 E
Hua Hin	94	12 34N	99	58 E
Huacho	186	11 10S	77	35W
Huainan	99	32 38N	116	58 E
Huallaga →	186	5 0S	75	30W
Huambo	134	12 42S	15	54 E
Huancane	187	15 10S	69	44W
Huancavelica	186	12 50S	75	5W
Huancayo	186	12 5S	75	12W
Huanchaca	187	20 15S	66	40W
Huang Hai = Yellow Sea	99	35 0N	123	0 E
Huang Ho →	98	37 30N	118	50 E
Huangshi	99	30 10N	115	3 E
Huánuco	186	9 55S	76	15W
Huaraz	186	9 30S	77	32W
Huascarán	186	9 8S	77	36W
Huasco	190	28 30S	71	15W
Huatabampo	174	26 50N	109	38W
Huautla	177	17 51N	100	5W
Hubei □	99	31 0N	112	0 E
Hubli-Dharwad = Dharwad	90	15 22N	75	15 E
Huddersfield	28	53 38N	1	49W
Hudiksvall	66	61 43N	17	10 E
Hudson	164	42 15N	73	46W
Hudson →	164	40 42N	74	2W
Hudson Bay	146	52 51N	102	23W
Hudson Str.	146	62 0N	70	0W
Hudson's Hope	155	56 0N	121	54W
Hue	95	16 30N	107	35 E
Huehuetenango	177	15 20N	91	28W
Huelva	50	37 18N	6	57W
Huesca	51	42 8N	0	25W
Hughenden	121	20 52S	144	10 E
Huila, Nevado del	184	3 0N	76	0W
Huinca Renancó	190	34 51S	64	22W
Huixtla	177	15 9N	92	28W
Huizen	40	52 18N	5	14 E
Hukawng Valley	93	26 30N	96	30 E
Hull, Canada	151	45 25N	75	44W
Hull, U.K.	29	53 45N	0	20W
Hulst	40	51 17N	4	2 E
Hulun Nur	98	49 0N	117	30 E
Humaitá	187	27 2S	58	31W
Humber →	29	53 40N	0	10W
Humberside □	29	53 50N	0	30W
Humboldt, Canada	152	52 15N	105	9W
Humboldt, U.S.A.	169	35 50N	88	55W
Humboldt →	172	40 2N	118	31W
Hume, L.	117	36 0S	147	0 E
Húnaflói	64	65 50N	20	50W
Hunan □	99	27 30N	111	30 E
Hunedoara	56	45 40N	22	50 E
Hungary ■	59	47 20N	19	20 E
Hungary, Plain of	17	47 0N	20	0 E
Hungnam	98	39 49N	127	45 E
Hunsrück	42	49 30N	7	0 E
Hunstanton	29	52 57N	0	30 E
Hunter Ra.	117	32 45S	150	15 E
Huntingdon	25	52 20N	0	11W
Huntington, Ind., U.S.A.	167	40 52N	85	30W
Huntington, W. Va., U.S.A.	165	38 20N	82	30W
Huntington Beach	173	33 40N	118	0W
Huntly	122	37 34S	175	11 E
Huntsville, Canada	151	45 20N	79	14W
Huntsville, Ala., U.S.A.	169	34 45N	86	35W
Huntsville, Tex., U.S.A.	168	30 45N	95	35W
Huonville	119	43 0S	147	5 E
Hupeh □ = Hubei □	99	31 0N	112	0 E
Huron, L.	150	45 0N	83	0W
Hurricane	173	37 10N	113	12W
Húsavík	64	66 3N	17	21W
Hutchinson	161	38 3N	97	59W
Hvar	52	43 11N	16	28 E
Hwang Ho = Huang Ho →	98	37 30N	118	50 E
Hwange	137	18 18S	26	30 E
Hyden	120	32 24S	118	53 E
Hyderabad, India	91	17 22N	78	29 E
Hyderabad, Pakistan	88	25 23N	68	24 E
Hyères	37	43 8N	6	9 E
Hyndman Pk.	162	43 50N	114	10W
Hythe	24	51 4N	1	5 E
Hyūga	108	32 25N	131	35 E

Iaşi	57	47 10N	27 40 E
Ibadan	131	7 22N	3 58 E
Ibagué	184	4 20N	75 20W
Ibara	109	34 36N	133 28 E
Ibaraki	106	34 49N	135 34 E
Ibarra	184	0 21N	78 7W
Iberian Peninsula	16	40 0N	5 0W
Ibiza	51	38 54N	1 26 E
Ibuki-Sanchi	106	35 25N	136 18 E
Ibusuki	108	31 12N	130 40 E
Icá	186	14 0S	75 48W
Iça →	184	2 55S	67 58W
Iceland ■	64	65 0N	19 0W
Icha	73	55 30N	156 0 E
Ich'ang = Yichang	99	30 40N	111 20 E
Ichchapuram	92	19 10N	84 40 E
Ichihara	107	35 28N	140 5 E
Ichikawa	107	35 44N	139 55 E
Ichinomiya	106	35 18N	136 48 E
Ichinoseki	103	38 55N	141 8 E
Idaho □	162	44 10N	114 0W
Idaho Falls	163	43 30N	112 1W
Idhi Óros	55	35 15N	24 45 E
Idhra	55	37 20N	23 28 E
Ierápetra	55	35 0N	25 44 E
Ife	131	7 30N	4 31 E
Igloolik	146	69 20N	81 49W
Iguaçu →	191	25 36S	54 36W
Iguaçu, Cat. del	191	25 41S	54 26W
Iguaçu Falls = Iguaçu, Cat. del	191	25 41S	54 26W
Iguala de la Independencia	177	18 21N	99 32W
Iguassu = Iguaçu →	191	25 36S	54 36W
Iida	107	35 35N	137 50 E
Iisalmi	67	63 32N	27 10 E
Iizuka	108	33 38N	130 42 E
IJmuiden	40	52 28N	4 35 E
IJsselmeer	40	52 45N	5 20 E
IJsselstein	40	52 1N	5 2 E
Ikaría	55	37 35N	26 10 E
Ikeda	109	34 1N	133 48 E
Iki	108	33 45N	129 42 E
Iki-Kaikyō	108	33 40N	129 45 E
Ile-de-France	37	49 0N	2 20 E
Ilebo	134	4 17S	20 55 E
Ilfracombe	27	51 13N	4 8W
Ilhéus	189	14 49S	39 2W
Ili →	71	45 53N	77 10 E
Iliamna L.	142	59 35N	155 30W
Iliodhrómia	55	39 12N	23 50 E
Ilkeston	29	52 59N	1 19W
Illampu = Ancohuma, Nevada	187	16 0S	68 50W
Illinois □	166	40 15N	89 30W
Illinois →	166	38 55N	90 28W
Ilo	187	17 40S	71 20W
Iloilo	112	10 45N	122 33 E
Ilorin	131	8 30N	4 35 E
Imabari	109	34 4N	133 0 E
Imari	108	33 15N	129 52 E
Imatra	67	61 12N	28 48 E
Immingham	29	53 37N	0 12W
Imperial	152	51 21N	105 28W
Imphal	92	24 48N	93 56 E
Imroz = Gökçeada	55	40 10N	25 50 E
Ina	107	35 50N	138 0 E
Iñapari	187	11 0S	69 40W
Inari	67	68 54N	27 5 E
Inarijärvi	67	69 0N	28 0 E
Inazawa	106	35 15N	136 47 E
Inchon	98	37 27N	126 40 E
Indalsälven →	66	62 36N	17 30 E
Independence, Kans., U.S.A.	166	37 10N	95 43W
Independence, Mo., U.S.A.	166	39 3N	94 25W
India ■	78	20 0N	78 0 E
Indian Head	152	50 30N	103 41W
Indiana	164	40 38N	79 9W
Indiana □	167	40 0N	86 0W
Indianapolis	167	39 42N	86 10W
Indigirka →	73	70 48N	148 54 E
Indonesia ■	111	5 0S	115 0 E
Indore	91	22 42N	75 53 E
Indre →	36	47 16N	0 19 E
Indus →	88	24 20N	67 47 E
Indus, Mouth of the	88	24 0N	68 0 E
Inebolu	80	41 55N	33 40 E
Inegöl	80	40 5N	29 31 E
Ingersoll	151	43 4N	80 55W
Ingham	121	18 43S	146 10 E
Ingleborough	28	54 11N	2 23W
Inglewood, N.Z.	122	39 9S	174 14 E
Inglewood, U.S.A.	173	33 58N	118 21W
Ingolstadt	43	48 45N	11 26 E
Ingraj Bazar	92	24 58N	88 10 E
Inhambane	137	23 54S	35 30 E
Ining = Yining	100	43 58N	81 10 E
Inishmore	35	53 8N	9 45W
Inishowen	34	55 14N	7 15W
Inn →	43	48 35N	13 28 E
Innamincka	118	27 44S	140 46 E
Inner Hebrides	32	57 0N	6 30W
Inner Mongolia = Nei Monggol Zizhiqu □	98	42 0N	112 0 E
Innisfail, Australia	121	17 33S	146 5 E
Innisfail, Canada	155	52 0N	113 57W
In'no-shima	109	34 19N	133 10 E
Innsbruck	45	47 16N	11 23 E
Inoucdjouac	146	58 25N	78 15W
Inowrocław	58	52 50N	18 12 E
Inquisivi	187	16 50S	67 10W
Insein	93	16 50N	96 5 E
Interlaken	44	46 41N	7 50 E
Inuvik	144	68 16N	133 40W
Inuvik □	144	70 0N	130 0W
Inuyama	106	35 23N	136 56 E
Inveraray	30	56 13N	5 5W
Invercargill	123	46 24S	168 24 E
Inverell	116	29 45S	151 8 E
Invergordon	33	57 41N	4 10W
Inverness	33	57 29N	4 12W
Investigator Group	119	34 45S	134 20 E
Investigator Str.	119	35 30S	137 0 E
Ioánnina	54	39 42N	20 47 E
Iola	166	38 0N	95 20W
Iona	30	56 20N	6 25W
Ionian Is. = Iónioi Nísoi	54	38 40N	20 0 E
Ionian Sea	54	37 30N	17 30 E
Iónioi Nísoi	54	38 40N	20 0 E
Íos	55	36 41N	25 20 E
Iowa □	166	42 18N	93 30W
Iowa City	166	41 40N	91 35W
Iowa Falls	166	42 30N	93 15W
Ipiales	184	0 50N	77 37W
Ipin = Yibin	99	28 45N	104 32 E
Ípiros □	54	39 30N	20 30 E
Ipoh	96	4 35N	101 5 E
Ipswich, Australia	116	27 35S	152 40 E
Ipswich, U.K.	25	52 4N	1 9 E
Iquique	187	20 19S	70 5W
Iquitos	186	3 45S	73 10W
Iracoubo	185	5 30N	53 10W
Iráklion	55	35 20N	25 12 E
Iran ■	86	33 0N	53 0 E
Iran Ra.	111	2 20N	114 50 E
Irapuato	177	20 41N	101 28W
Iraq ■	81	33 0N	44 0 E
Irbid	80	32 35N	35 48 E
Ireland ■	34	53 0N	8 0W
Irian Jaya □	113	4 0S	137 0 E
Iriri →	188	3 52S	52 37W
Irish Republic ■	20	53 0N	8 0W
Irish Sea	20	54 0N	5 0W
Irkutsk	74	52 18N	104 20 E
Irō-Zaki	107	34 36N	138 51 E
Iron Gate = Portile de Fier	56	44 42N	22 30 E
Iron Knob	118	32 46S	137 8 E
Iron Mountain	150	45 49N	88 4W
Ironbridge	24	52 38N	2 29W
Ironton	167	38 35N	82 40W
Ironwood	150	46 30N	90 10W

Iroquois Falls	151	48 46N	80 41W
Irrawaddy →	93	15 50N	95 6 E
Irtysh →	69	61 4N	68 52 E
Irumu	135	1 32N	29 53 E
Irún	51	43 20N	1 52W
Irvine	31	55 37N	4 40W
Irvinestown	34	54 28N	7 38W
Ísafjörður	64	66 5N	23 9W
Isahaya	108	32 52N	130 2 E
Ischia	49	40 45N	13 51 E
Ise	106	34 25N	136 45 E
Ise-Wan	106	34 43N	136 43 E
Isère →	37	44 59N	4 51 E
Isesaki	107	36 19N	139 12 E
Ishikari-Wan	103	43 25N	141 1 E
Ishinomaki	103	38 32N	141 20 E
Ishioka	107	36 11N	140 16 E
Ishkuman	89	36 30N	73 50 E
Ishpeming	150	46 30N	87 40W
Iskenderun	80	36 32N	36 10 E
Islamabad	89	33 40N	73 10 E
Island L.	153	53 47N	94 25W
Island Pond	148	48 25N	56 23W
Islay	30	55 46N	6 10W
Isle-Adam, L'	39	49 6N	2 14 E
Isle Royale	150	48 0N	88 50W
Isparta	80	37 47N	30 30 E
Israel ■	80	32 0N	34 50 E
Issoire	37	45 32N	3 15 E
Issyk-Kul, Ozero	71	42 25N	77 15 E
Istanbul	80	41 0N	29 0 E
Istra	52	45 10N	14 0 E
Istria = Istra	52	45 10N	14 0 E
Itabuna	189	14 48S	39 16W
Itaituba	185	4 10S	55 50W
Itajaí	181	27 50 0	40 00W
Italy ■	19	42 0N	13 0 E
Itaquatiara	185	2 58S	58 30W
Itaquí	191	29 8S	56 30W
Itchen →	24	50 57N	1 20W
Ithaca = Itháki	54	38 25N	20 40 E
Ithaca	164	42 25N	76 30W
Itháki	54	38 25N	20 40 E
Ito	107	34 58N	139 5 E
Ituaçu	189	13 50S	41 18W
Ituiutaba	188	19 0S	49 25W
Iturup, Ostrov	75	45 0N	148 0 E
Ivano-Frankovsk	68	48 40N	24 40 E
Ivanovo, Byelorussian S.S.R., U.S.S.R.	68	52 7N	25 29 E
Ivanovo, R.S.F.S.R., U.S.S.R.	68	57 5N	41 0 E
Ivigtut	147	61 14N	48 12W
Iviza = Ibiza	51	38 54N	1 26 E
Ivory Coast ■	130	7 30N	5 0W
Iwai-Jima	108	33 47N	131 58 E
Iwaki	105	37 3N	140 55 E
Iwakuni	109	34 15N	132 8 E
Iwami	109	35 32N	134 15 E
Iwamizawa	103	43 12N	141 46 E
Iwanuma	103	38 7N	140 51 E
Iwata	107	34 42N	137 51 E
Iwo	131	7 39N	4 9 E
Ixiamas	187	13 50S	68 5W
Ixtepec	177	16 34N	95 6W
Ixtlán	175	20 11N	102 24W
Ixtlán de Juárez	177	17 23N	96 28W
Iyo	109	33 45N	132 45 E
Iyo-mishima	109	33 58N	133 30 E
Iyo-Nada	109	33 40N	132 20 E
Izamal	177	20 56N	89 1W
Izhevsk = Ustinov	69	56 51N	53 14 E
Izmir	80	38 25N	27 8 E
Izmit	80	40 45N	29 50 E
Izu-Hantō	107	34 45N	139 0 E
Izumi	108	32 5N	130 22 E
Izumi-sano	106	34 23N	135 18 E
Izumiotsu	106	34 30N	135 24 E
Izumo	109	35 20N	132 46 E
Jabalpur	91	23 9N	79 58 E
Jacarèzinho	191	23 5S	50 0W
Jackson, Mich., U.S.A.	167	42 18N	84 25W
Jackson, Miss., U.S.A.	169	32 20N	90 10W
Jackson, Tenn., U.S.A.	169	35 40N	88 50W
Jacksonville, Fla., U.S.A.	170	30 15N	81 38W
Jacksonville, Ill., U.S.A.	166	39 42N	90 15W
Jacksonville, N.C., U.S.A.	165	34 50N	77 29W
Jacksonville, Tex., U.S.A.	168	31 58N	95 19W
Jacmel	180	18 14N	72 32W
Jacobabad	88	28 20N	68 29 E
Jacques Cartier, Dét. de	149	50 0N	63 30W
Jadotville = Likasi	135	10 55S	26 48 E
Jaén, Peru	186	5 25S	78 40W
Jaén, Spain	50	37 44N	3 43W
Jaffa = Tel Aviv-Yafo	80	32 4N	34 48 E
Jaffna	00	9 45N	80 2 E
Jagdalpur	92	19 3N	82 0 E
Jaguariaíva	191	24 10S	49 50W
Jagüey Grande	178	22 35N	81 7W
Jahrom	85	28 30N	53 31 E
Jaipur	91	27 0N	75 50 E
Jakarta	111	6 9S	106 49 E
Jalalabad	87	34 30N	70 29 E
Jalapa, Guat.	177	14 39N	89 59W
Jalapa, Mexico	177	17 43N	92 49W
Jalgaon	91	21 0N	75 42 E
Jalisco □	175	20 20N	103 40W
Jalna	91	19 48N	75 38 E
Jalón →	51	41 47N	1 4W
Jalpaiguri	92	26 32N	88 46 E
Jamaica ■	180	18 10N	77 30W
Jamalpur, Bangla.	92	24 52N	89 56 E
Jamalpur, India	92	25 18N	86 28 E
Jambi	111	1 38S	103 30 E
James →	163	42 52N	97 18W
James B.	140	51 30N	80 0W
Jamestown, Australia	118	33 10S	138 32 E
Jamestown, N. Dak., U.S.A.	163	46 54N	98 42W
Jamestown, N.Y., U.S.A.	164	42 5N	79 18W
Jamkhandi	91	16 30N	75 15 E
Jammu	89	32 43N	74 54 E
Jammu & Kashmir □	89	34 25N	77 0 E
Jamnagar	90	22 30N	70 6 E
Jamshedpur	92	22 44N	86 12 E
Jan Mayen Is.	13	71 0N	9 0W
Janesville	166	42 39N	89 1W
Januária	188	15 25S	44 25W
Jaora	91	23 40N	75 10 E
Japan ■	79	36 0N	136 0 E
Japan, Sea of	102	40 0N	135 0 E
Japurá →	185	3 8S	64 46W
Jargalant = Hovd	100	48 2N	91 37 E
Jargeau	39	47 50N	2 1 E
Jarosław	58	50 2N	22 42 E
Jäsk	85	25 38N	57 45 E
Jasło	59	49 45N	21 30 E
Jasper, Canada	155	52 55N	118 5W
Jasper, U.S.A.	169	33 48N	87 16W
Jassy = Iaşi	57	47 10N	27 40 E
Jataí	188	17 58S	51 48W
Jaú	188	22 10S	48 30W
Jaunpur	92	25 46N	82 44 E
Java, I.	111	7 0S	110 0 E
Java Sea	111	4 35S	107 15 E
Javhlant = Ulyasutay	100	47 56N	97 28 E
Jean Marie River	144	61 32N	120 38W
Jean Rabel	180	19 50N	73 5W
Jedburgh	31	55 28N	2 33W
Jędrzejów	58	50 35N	20 15 E
Jefferson, Mt.	171	44 45N	121 50W
Jefferson City	166	38 34N	92 10W
Jeffersonville	167	38 20N	85 42W
Jelenia Góra	58	50 50N	15 45 E
Jena	43	50 56N	11 33 E
Jenkins	165	37 13N	82 41W
Jennings	168	30 10N	92 45W
Jeparit	119	36 8S	142 1 E
Jequié	189	13 51S	40 5W
Jequitinhonha	189	16 30S	41 0W
Jérémie	180	18 40N	74 10W

Jerez de García Salinas	**175**	22 39N	103	0W
Jerez de la Frontera	**50**	36 41N	6	7W
Jerez de los Caballeros	**50**	38 20N	6	45W
Jericho	**121**	23 38S	146	6 E
Jerilderie	**117**	35 20S	145	41 E
Jerome	**148**	47 37N	82	14W
Jersey, I.	**36**	49 13N	2	7W
Jersey City	**164**	40 41N	74	8W
Jerseyville	**166**	39 5N	90	20W
Jerusalem	**80**	31 47N	35	10 E
Jesselton = Kota Kinabalu	**112**	6 0N	116	4 E
Jhang Maghiana	**89**	31 15N	72	22 E
Jhansi	**91**	25 30N	78	36 E
Jharsuguda	**92**	21 56N	84	5 E
Jhelum —►	**89**	31 20N	72	10 E
Jhunjhunu	**89**	28 10N	75	30 E
Jiamusi	**98**	46 40N	130	26 E
Ji'an	**99**	27 6N	114	59 E
Jiangmen	**99**	22 32N	113	0 E
Jiangsu □	**99**	33 0N	120	0 E
Jiangxi □	**99**	27 30N	116	0 E
Jian'ou	**99**	27 3N	118	17 E
Jiao Xian	**98**	36 18N	120	1 E
Jiaozuo	**99**	35 .16N	113	12 E
Jiaxing	**99**	30 49N	120	45 E
Jiayi	**99**	23 30N	120	24 E
Jibuti = Djibouti ■	**133**	12 0N	43	0 E
Jiddah	**82**	21 29N	39	10 E
Jido	**93**	29 2N	94	58 E
Jihlava	**59**	49 28N	15	35 E
Jilin	**98**	43 44N	126	30 E
Jilong	**99**	25 8N	121	42 E
Jima	**132**	7 40N	36	47 E
Jiménez	**174**	27 8N	104	54W
Jinan	**98**	36 38N	117	1 E
Jingdezhen	**99**	29 20N	117	11 E
Jining, Nei Mongol Zizhiqu, China	**98**	41 5N	113	0 E
Jining, Shandong, China	**99**	35 22N	116	34 E
Jinja	**132**	0 25N	33	12 E
Jinnah Barrage	**89**	32 58N	71	33 E
Jinotega	**179**	13 6N	85	59W
Jinotepe	**179**	11 50N	86	10W
Jinshi	**99**	29 40N	111	50 E
Jinzhou	**98**	41 5N	121	3 E
Jipijapa	**184**	1 0S	80	40W
Jiquilpan de Juárez	**175**	19 59N	102	43W
Jisr ash Shughūr	**80**	35 49N	36	18 E
Jiujiang	**99**	29 42N	115	58 E
Jixi	**98**	45 20N	130	50 E
João Pessoa	**189**	7 10S	34	52W
Jodhpur	**91**	26 23N	73	8 E
Joensuu	**67**	62 37N	29	49 E
Jogjakarta = Yogyakarta	**111**	7 49S	110	22 E
Jōhana	**106**	36 30N	136	57 E
Johannesburg	**137**	26 10S	28	2 E
John o' Groats	**33**	58 39N	3	3W
Johnson City, N.Y., U.S.A.	**164**	42 7N	75	57W
Johnson City, Tenn., U.S.A.	**165**	36 18N	82	21W
Johnston	**31**	51 45N	5	5W
Johnstown, N.Y., U.S.A.	**164**	43 1N	74	20W
Johnstown, Pa., U.S.A.	**164**	40 19N	78	53W
Johor □	**96**	2 5N	103	20 E
Johor Baharu	**96**	1 28N	103	46 E
Joigny	**39**	48 0N	3	20 E
Joinvile	**191**	26 15S	48	55 E
Joliet	**167**	41 30N	88	0W
Joliette	**151**	46 3N	73	24W
Jolo	**112**	6 0N	121	0 E
Jonesboro	**169**	35 50N	90	45W
Jönköping	**60**	57 45N	14	10 E
Jönköpings län □	**61**	57 30N	14	30 E
Jonquière	**148**	48 27N	71	14W
Joplin	**168**	37 0N	94	31W
Jordan ■	**80**	31 0N	36	0 E
Jordan —►	**80**	31 48N	35	32 E
Jorhat	**93**	26 45N	94	12 E
José de San Martín	**192**	44 4S	70	26W
Jowzjān □	**87**	36 10N	66	0 E
Juan de Fuca Str.	**142**	48 15N	124	0W
Juan Fernández, Arch. de	**183**	33 50S	80	0W
Juàzeiro	**189**	9 30S	40	30W
Juàzeiro do Norte	**189**	7 10S	39	18W
Jubbulpore = Jabalpur	**91**	23 9N	79	58 E
Júcar —►	**51**	39 5N	0	10W
Juchitán de Zaragoza	**177**	16 26N	95	1W
Jugoslavia = Yugoslavia ■	**52**	44 0N	20	0 E
Juiz de Fora	**188**	21 43S	43	19W
Juli	**187**	16 10S	69	25W
Juliaca	**187**	15 25S	70	10W
Julianehåb	**147**	60 43N	46	0W
Jullundur	**89**	31 20N	75	40 E
Jumla	**92**	29 15N	82	13 E
Jumna = Yamuna —►	**92**	25 30N	81	53 E
Junagadh	**91**	21 30N	70	30 E
Jundiaí	**191**	24 30S	47	0W
Juneau	**143**	58 20N	134	20W
Junee	**117**	34 53S	147	35 E
Junggar Pendi	**100**	44 30N	86	0 E
Junín	**190**	34 33S	60	57W
Jura, Europe	**37**	46 35N	6	5 E
Jura, U.K.	**30**	56 0N	5	50W
Jurado	**184**	7 7N	77	46W
Juruá —►	**184**	2 37S	65	44W
Juruena	**187**	13 0S	58	10W
Juruena —►	**187**	7 20S	58	3W
Juticalpa	**179**	14 40N	86	12W
Jutland = Jylland	**61**	56 25N	9	30 E
Juventud, I. de la	**178**	21 40N	82	40W
Jylland	**61**	56 25N	9	30 E
Jyväskylä	**67**	62 14N	25	50 E
Kaapstad = Cape Town	**136**	33 55S	18	22 E
Kabala	**130**	9 38N	11	37W
Kabardino-Balkar-A.S.S.R. □.	**70**	43 30N	43	30 E
Kabarega Falls	**132**	2 15N	31	30 E
Kabīr Kūh	**84**	33 0N	47	30 E
Kābul	**87**	34 28N	69	11 E
Kābul □	**87**	34 30N	69	0 E
Kabwe	**135**	14 30S	28	29 E
Kachin □	**93**	26 0N	97	30 E
Kadan Kyun	**94**	12 30N	98	20 E
Kadina	**119**	34 0S	137	43 E
Kaduna	**131**	10 30N	7	21 E
Kaédi	**126**	16 9N	13	28W
Kāf	**80**	31 25N	37	29 E
Kafirévs, Ákra	**55**	38 9N	24	38 E
Kafue —►	**135**	15 30S	26	0 E
Kaga	**106**	36 16N	136	15 E
Kagoshima	**108**	31 35N	130	33 E
Kagoshima-Wan	**108**	31 25N	130	40 E
Kai, Kepulauan	**113**	5 55S	132	45W
Kaieteur Falls	**185**	5 1N	59	10W
Kaifeng	**99**	34 49N	114	30 E
Kaikoura Ra.	**123**	41 59S	173	41 E
Kailua	**160**	19 39N	156	0W
Kaimanawa Mts.	**122**	39 15S	175	56 E
Kainan	**106**	34 9N	135	12 E
Kainji Res.	**131**	10 1N	4	40 E
Kaipara Harbour	**122**	36 25S	174	14 E
Kaiserslautern	**42**	49 30N	7	43 E
Kaitaia	**122**	35 8S	173	17 E
Kajaani	**67**	64 17N	27	46 E
Kajana = Kajaani	**67**	64 17N	27	46 E
Kakabeka Falls	**150**	48 24N	89	37W
Kakamigahara	**106**	35 28N	136	48 E
Kakanui Mts.	**123**	45 10S	170	30 E
Kakegawa	**107**	34 45N	138	1 E
Kakinada	**92**	16 57N	82	11 E
Kakogawa	**109**	34 46N	134	51 E
Kalabáka	**54**	39 42N	21	39 E
Kalahari	**136**	24 0S	21	30 E
Kalamata	**54**	37 3N	22	10 E
Kalamazoo	**167**	42 20N	85	35W
Kalamazoo —►	**167**	42 40N	86	12W
Kalat	**88**	29 8N	66	31 E
Kalaupapa	**160**	21 12N	156	59W
Kalemie	**135**	5 55S	29	9 E
Kalgan = Zhangjiakou	**98**	40 48N	114	55 E
Kalgoorlie-Boulder	**120**	30 40S	121	22 E

Kálimnos	55	37	0N	27	0 E
Kalinin	68	56	55N	35	55 E
Kaliningrad	68	54	42N	20	32 E
Kalispell	162	48	10N	114	22W
Kalisz	58	51	45N	18	8 E
Kalmar	61	56	40N	16	20 E
Kalmar län □	61	57	25N	16	0 E
Kalmyk A.S.S.R. □	70	46	5N	46	1 E
Kalocsa	59	46	32N	19	0 E
Kaluga	68	54	35N	36	10 E
Kama →	68	55	45N	52	0 E
Kamaishi	103	39	16N	141	53 E
Kamakura	107	35	19N	139	33 E
Kamaran	82	15	21N	42	35 E
Kamchatka, P-ov.	73	57	0N	160	0 E
Kamenka	69	53	10N	44	5 E
Kamensk Uralskiy	69	56	25N	62	2 E
Kamenskoye	73	62	45N	165	30 E
Kameoka	106	35	0N	135	35 E
Kameyama	106	34	51N	136	27 E
Kami-koshiki-Jima	108	31	50N	129	52 E
Kamioka	106	36	25N	137	15 E
Kamloops	155	50	40N	120	20W
Kampala	132	0	20N	32	30 E
Kampar	96	4	18N	101	9 E
Kampen	41	52	33N	5	53 E
Kampot	95	10	36N	104	10 E
Kampuchea ─ Cambodia ■	95	12	15N	105	0 E
Kamsack	152	51	34N	101	54W
Kamui-Misaki	103	43	20N	140	21 E
Kamyshin	68	50	10N	45	24 E
Kananga	134	5	55S	22	18 E
Kanawha →	165	38	50N	82	8W
Kanazawa	106	36	30N	136	38 E
Kanchenjunga	92	27	50N	88	10 E
Kanchipuram	90	12	52N	79	45 E
Kandahar ─ Qandahār	87	31	32N	65	30 E
Kandalaksha	69	67	9N	32	30 E
Kandi	131	11	7N	2	55 E
Kandos	117	32	45S	149	58 E
Kandy	90	7	18N	80	43 E
Kangar	97	6	27N	100	12 E
Kangaroo I.	119	35	45S	137	0 E
Kangean Is.	113	6	55S	115	23 E
Kangnŭng	98	37	45N	128	54 E
Kangto	93	27	50N	92	35 E
Kaniapiskau →	146	56	40N	69	30W
Kanin, P-ov.	69	68	0N	45	0 E
Kaniva	119	36	22S	141	18 E
Kankakee	167	41	6N	87	50W
Kankakee →	167	41	23N	88	16W
Kankan	130	10	23N	9	15W
Kanmuri-Yama	109	34	30N	132	4 E
Kannapolis	165	35	32N	80	37W
Kano	131	12	2N	8	30 E
Kan'onji	109	34	7N	133	39 E
Kanoya	108	31	25N	130	50 E
Kanpur	91	26	28N	80	20 E
Kansas □	161	38	40N	98	0W
Kansas →	158	39	7N	94	36W
Kansas City, Kans., U.S.A.	166	39	0N	94	40W
Kansas City, Mo., U.S.A.	166	39	3N	94	30W
Kansk	74	56	20N	95	37 E
Kansu ─ Gansu □	98	36	0N	104	0 E
Kantō □	107	36	15N	139	30 E
Kantō-Sanchi	107	35	59N	138	50 E
Kanuma	107	36	34N	139	42 E
Kaohsiung ─ Gaoxiong	99	22	38N	120	18 E
Kaolack	130	14	5N	16	8W
Kāpīsā □	87	35	0N	69	20 E
Kapoeta	129	4	50N	33	35 E
Kapuas →	111	0	25S	109	20 E
Kapunda	119	34	20S	138	56 E
Kapuskasing	150	49	25N	82	30W
Kaputar, Mt.	116	30	15S	150	10 E
Kara Bogaz Gol, Zaliv	70	41	0N	53	30 E
Kara Kalpak A.S.S.R. □	70	43	0N	60	0 E
Kara Kum ─ Karakum, Peski	70	39	30N	60	0 E
Kara Sea	69	75	0N	70	0 E
Karabük	80	41	12N	32	37 E
Karachi	88	24	53N	67	0 E
Karad	91	17	15N	74	10 E
Karadeniz Boğazı	80	41	10N	29	10 E
Karaganda	71	49	50N	73	10 E
Karaj	86	35	48N	51	0 E
Karakoram Pass	89	35	33N	77	50 E
Karakoram Ra.	89	35	30N	77	0 E
Karakum, Peski	70	39	30N	60	0 E
Karaman	80	37	14N	33	13 E
Karamea Bight	123	41	22S	171	40 E
Karasuk	71	53	44N	78	2 E
Karatau, Khrebet	71	43	30N	69	30 E
Karbalā	84	32	36N	44	3 E
Karelian A.S.S.R. □	68	65	30N	32	30 E
Karen	94	12	49N	92	53 E
Kariba Lake	137	16	40S	28	25 E
Karimata I.	111	1	40S	109	0 E
Karimnagar	91	18	26N	79	10 E
Karimunjawa, Kepulauan	111	5	50S	110	30 E
Kariya	106	34	58N	137	1 E
Karl-Marx-Stadt	43	50	50N	12	55 E
Karlskrona	61	56	10N	15	35 E
Karlsruhe	42	49	3N	8	23 E
Karlstad	60	59	23N	13	30 E
Karnal	89	29	42N	77	2 E
Karnaphuli Res.	93	22	40N	92	20 E
Karnataka □	90	13	15N	77	0 E
Kärnten □	45	46	52N	13	30 E
Kárpathos	55	35	37N	27	10 E
Kars	81	40	40N	43	5 E
Karshi	70	38	53N	65	48 E
Kasai →	134	3	30S	16	10 E
Kasaoka	109	34	30N	133	30 E
Kaseda	108	31	25N	130	19 E
Kāshān	86	34	5N	51	30 E
Kashi	100	39	30N	76	2 E
Kashihara	106	34	27N	135	46 E
Kashima	108	33	7N	130	6 E
Kashima-Nada	107	36	0N	140	45 E
Kashiwa	107	35	52N	139	59 E
Kāshmar	86	35	16N	58	26 E
Kashmir	78	34	0N	76	0 E
Kashun Noerh ─ Gaxun Nur. .	100	42	22N	100	30 E
Kásos	55	35	20N	26	55 E
Kassala	129	16	0N	36	0 E
Kassel	42	51	19N	9	32 E
Kastoría	54	40	30N	21	19 E
Kasugai	106	35	12N	136	59 E
Kasukabe	107	35	58N	139	49 E
Kasumiga-Ura	107	36	0N	140	25 E
Kasur	89	31	5N	74	25 E
Katanning	120	33	40S	117	33 E
Katha	93	24	10N	96	30 E
Katherína, Gebel	128	28	30N	33	57 E
Katherine	114	14	27S	132	20 E
Kathiawar	91	22	20N	71	0 E
Katihar	92	25	34N	87	36 E
Katmandu	92	27	45N	85	20 E
Katoomba	117	33	41S	150	19 E
Katowice	58	50	17N	19	5 E
Katsuta	107	36	25N	140	31 E
Katsuura	107	35	10N	140	20 E
Katsuyama	106	36	3N	136	30 E
Kattegatt	61	57	0N	11	20 E
Katwijk-aan-Zee	40	52	12N	4	24 E
Kauai	160	22	0N	159	30W
Kaukauna	167	44	20N	88	13W
Kaunas	68	54	54N	23	54 E
Kawachi-Nagano	106	34	28N	135	31 E
Kawagoe	107	35	55N	139	29 E
Kawaguchi	107	35	52N	139	45 E
Kawanoe	109	34	1N	133	34 E
Kawarau	122	45	3S	168	45 E
Kawasaki	107	35	35N	139	42 E
Kayah □	93	19	15N	97	15 E
Kayes	130	14	25N	11	30W
Kayseri	80	38	45N	35	30 E
Kazachinskoye	74	56	16N	107	36 E
Kazachye	72	70	52N	135	58 E
Kazakh S.S.R. □	71	50	0N	70	0 E
Kazan	68	55	48N	49	3 E
Kazanlŭk	53	42	38N	25	20 E

Name		Lat	Long
Kāzerūn	85	29 38N	51 40 E
Kazo	107	36 7N	139 36 E
Kéa	55	37 35N	24 22 E
Keaau	160	19 37N	155 3W
Kebnekaise	66	67 53N	18 33 E
Kecskemét	59	46 57N	19 42 E
Kedah □	96	5 50N	100 40 E
Kediri	111	7 51S	112 1 E
Keeling Is. = Cocos Is.	111	12 10S	96 55 E
Keene	164	42 57N	72 17W
Keetmanshoop	136	26 35S	18 8 E
Keewatin	153	49 46N	94 34W
Keewatin □	145	63 20N	95 0W
Kefallinía	54	38 20N	20 30 E
Keflavík	64	64 2N	22 35W
Keighley	28	53 52N	1 54W
Keith, Australia	119	36 6S	140 20 E
Keith, U.K.	33	57 33N	2 58W
Kelang	96	3 2N	101 26 E
Kelantan □	96	5 10N	102 0 E
Kelantan →	96	6 13N	102 14 E
Kellerberrin	120	31 36S	117 38 E
Kellogg	162	47 30N	116 5W
Kells = Ceanannus Mor	34	53 42N	6 53W
Kelowna	155	49 50N	119 25W
Kelso, U.K.	31	55 36N	2 27W
Kelso, U.S.A.	171	46 10N	122 57W
Keluang	96	2 3N	103 18 E
Kelvington	152	52 10N	103 30W
Kemerovo	71	55 20N	86 5 E
Kemi	67	65 44N	24 34 E
Kemi →	67	67 30N	28 30 E
Kempsey	116	31 1S	152 50 E
Kendal	28	54 19N	2 44W
Keng Tung	93	21 0N	99 30 E
Kenitra	126	34 15N	6 40W
Kenmare	35	51 52N	9 35W
Kennewick	171	46 11N	119 2W
Keno Hill	144	63 57N	135 18W
Kenora	153	49 47N	94 29W
Kenosha	167	42 33N	87 48W
Kent	164	41 8N	81 20W
Kent □	25	51 12N	0 40 E
Kent Group	117	39 30S	147 20 E
Kent Pen.	145	68 30N	107 0W
Kentucky □	167	37 20N	85 0W
Kentucky →	167	38 41N	85 11W
Kenya ■	133	1 0N	38 0 E
Kenya, Mt.	132	0 10S	37 18 E
Keokuk	166	40 25N	91 24W
Kepsut	80	39 40N	28 9 E
Kerala □	90	11 0N	76 15 E
Kerang	117	35 40S	143 55 E
Kerch	68	45 20N	36 20 E
Kerki	70	37 50N	65 12 E
Kérkira	54	39 38N	19 50 E
Kerkrade	41	50 53N	6 4 E
Kermadec Is.	122	30 0S	178 15W
Kermān	85	30 15N	57 1 E
Kermān □	85	30 0N	57 0 E
Kermānshāh = Bākhtarān	84	34 23N	47 0 E
Kerrobert	152	52 0N	109 11W
Kerry □	35	52 7N	9 35W
Kerulen →	98	48 48N	117 0 E
Kestenga	68	66 0N	31 50 E
Keswick	28	54 35N	3 9W
Ketchikan	143	55 25N	131 40W
Kettering	156	39 41N	84 10W
Kewanee	166	41 18N	89 55W
Keweenaw B.	150	46 56N	88 23W
Key West	159	24 33N	82 0W
Keyser	164	39 26N	79 0W
Khabarovsk	75	48 30N	135 5 E
Khalkhāl	81	37 37N	48 32 E
Khalkís	55	38 27N	23 42 E
Khalmer Yu	69	67 58N	65 1 E
Khambhat	91	22 23N	72 33 E
Khambhat, G. of	91	20 45N	72 30 E
Khamir	82	16 0N	44 0 E
Khānābād	87	36 45N	69 5 E
Khānaqīn	81	34 23N	45 25 E
Khandwa	91	21 49N	76 22 E
Khanewal	89	30 20N	71 55 E
Khaniá	55	35 30N	24 4 E
Khanka, Ozero	75	45 0N	132 24 E
Kharagpur	92	22 20N	87 25 E
Kharkov	68	49 58N	36 20 E
Khartoum = El Khartûm	129	15 31N	32 35 E
Khashm el Girba	129	14 59N	35 58 E
Khaskovo	53	41 56N	25 30 E
Khatanga	72	72 0N	102 20 E
Khatanga →	72	72 55N	106 0 E
Khenchela	127	35 28N	7 11 E
Kherson	68	46 35N	32 35 E
Kheta →	72	71 54N	102 6 E
Khíos, I.	55	38 20N	26 0 E
Khmer Rep. = Cambodia ■	95	12 15N	105 0 E
Khojak P.	88	30 55N	66 30 E
Kholm	87	36 45N	67 40 E
Khon Kaen	95	16 30N	102 47 E
Khoper →	68	49 30N	42 20 E
Khorāsān □	86	34 0N	58 0 E
Khorat = Nakhon Ratchasima	95	14 59N	102 12 E
Khorat, Cao Nguyen	95	15 30N	102 50 E
Khorog	71	37 30N	71 36 E
Khorramābād	84	33 30N	48 25 E
Khorrāmshahr	84	30 29N	48 15 E
Khulna	92	22 45N	89 34 E
Khulna □	92	22 25N	89 35 E
Khushab	89	32 20N	72 20 E
Khūzestān □	84	31 0N	49 0 E
Khvor	86	33 45N	55 0 E
Khvoy	81	38 35N	45 0 E
Khyber Pass	89	34 10N	71 8 E
Kiama	117	34 40S	150 50 E
Kiangsi = Jiangxi □	99	27 30N	116 0 E
Kiangsu = Jiangsu □	99	33 0N	120 0 E
Kichiga	73	59 50N	163 5 E
Kicking Horse Pass	155	51 28N	116 16W
Kidderminster	24	52 24N	2 13W
Kidnappers, C.	122	39 38S	177 5 E
Kiel	43	54 16N	10 8 E
Kielce	58	50 52N	20 42 E
Kieler Bucht	42	54 30N	10 30 E
Kiev = Kiyev	68	50 30N	30 28 E
Kigali	135	1 59S	30 4 E
Kii-Hantō	106	34 0N	135 45 E
Kii-Sanchi	106	34 20N	136 0 E
Kii-Suidō	109	33 40N	135 0 E
Kikládhes □	55	37 0N	25 0 E
Kikuchi	108	32 59N	130 47 E
Kilcoy	116	26 59S	152 30 E
Kildare □	35	53 10N	6 50W
Kilimanjaro	132	3 7S	37 20 E
Kilis	80	36 50N	37 10 E
Kilkenny	35	52 40N	7 17W
Kilkenny □	35	52 35N	7 15W
Killala B.	34	54 20N	9 12W
Killarney, Canada	153	49 10N	99 40W
Killarney, Ireland	35	52 2N	9 30W
Killary Harbour	34	53 38N	9 52W
Killiecrankie, Pass of	33	56 44N	3 46W
Kilmarnock	31	55 36N	4 30W
Kilmore	117	37 25S	144 53 E
Kilrush	35	52 39N	9 30W
Kimba	118	33 8S	136 23 E
Kimberley, Australia	114	16 20S	127 0 E
Kimberley, Canada	155	49 40N	115 59W
Kimberley, S. Africa	136	28 43S	24 46 E
Kinabalu	112	6 3N	116 14 E
Kincardine	150	44 10N	81 40W
Kindersley	152	51 30N	109 10W
Kindia	130	10 0N	12 52W
King Frederick VI Land = Kong Frederik VI.s Kyst	147	63 0N	43 0W
King George Is.	140	57 20N	80 30W
King I. = Kadan Kyun	94	12 30N	98 20 E
King I., Australia	119	39 50S	144 0 E
King I., Canada	154	52 10N	127 40W
King Sd.	114	16 50S	123 30 E
King William I.	145	69 10N	97 25W
Kingaroy	116	26 32S	151 51 E

Name	Page	Lat	Long
Kingman	173	35 12N	114 2W
King's Lynn	29	52 45N	0 25 E
Kingscote	119	35 40S	137 38 E
Kingsport	165	36 33N	82 36W
Kingston, Canada	151	44 14N	76 30W
Kingston, Jamaica	180	18 0N	76 50W
Kingston, N.Z.	123	45 20S	168 43 E
Kingston, U.S.A.	164	41 55N	74 0W
Kingston South East	119	36 51S	139 55 E
Kingstown	180	13 10N	61 10W
Kingsville	150	42 2N	82 45W
Kingussie	33	57 5N	4 2W
Kinistino	152	52 57N	105 2W
Kinki □	106	33 30N	136 0 E
Kinnairds Hd.	33	57 40N	2 0W
Kinsale, Old Hd. of	35	51 37N	8 32W
Kinshasa	134	4 20S	15 15 E
Kinston	165	35 18N	77 35W
Kintyre	30	55 30N	5 35W
Kintyre, Mull of	30	55 17N	5 55W
Kinu-Gawa →	107	35 36N	139 57 E
Kiparissla	54	37 15N	21 40 E
Kirensk	74	57 50N	107 55 E
Kirgiz S.S.R. □	71	42 0N	75 0 E
Kiribati ■	122	1 0N	176 0 E
Kirikkale	80	39 51N	33 32 E
Kirin = Jilin	98	43 44N	126 30 E
Kiritimati	123	1 58N	157 27W
Kirkcaldy	31	56 7N	3 10W
Kirkcudbright	31	54 50N	4 3W
Kirkee	91	18 34N	73 56 E
Kirkintilloch	31	55 57N	4 10W
Kirkland Lake	151	48 9N	80 2W
Kirksville	166	40 8N	92 35W
Kirkūk	81	35 30N	44 21 E
Kirkwall	33	58 59N	2 59W
Kirov	69	58 35N	49 40 F
Kirovabad	70	40 45N	46 20 E
Kirovograd	68	48 35N	32 20 E
Kirthar Range	88	27 0N	67 0 E
Kiruna	66	67 52N	20 15 E
Kiryū	107	36 24N	139 20 E
Kisangani	135	0 35N	25 15 E
Kisarazu	107	35 23N	139 55 E
Kiselevsk	71	54 5N	86 39 E
Kishangarh	89	27 50N	70 30 E
Kishinev	68	47 0N	28 50 E
Kishiwada	106	34 28N	135 22 E
Kiskunfelégyháza	59	46 42N	19 53 E
Kiso-Gawa →	106	35 20N	136 45 E
Kisumu	132	0 3S	34 45 E
Kita	130	13 5N	9 25W
Kita-Ura	107	36 0N	140 34 E
Kitakami-Gawa →	103	38 25N	141 19 E
Kitakyūshū	108	33 50N	130 50 E
Kitale	132	1 0N	35 0 E
Kitami	103	43 48N	143 54 E
Kitchener	151	43 27N	80 29W
Kithira	55	36 9N	23 0 E
Kithnos	55	37 26N	24 27 E
Kitikmeot □	145	70 0N	110 0W
Kitimat	154	54 3N	128 38W
Kitsuki	108	33 25N	131 37 E
Kittakittaooloo, L.	118	28 3S	138 14 E
Kitwe	135	12 54S	28 13 E
Kiyev	68	50 30N	30 28 E
Klagenfurt	45	46 38N	14 20 E
Klaipeda	68	55 43N	21 10 E
Klamath →	172	41 40N	124 4W
Klamath Falls	171	42 20N	121 50W
Klamath Mts.	172	41 20N	123 0W
Kleena Kleene	154	52 0N	124 59W
Klondike	144	64 0N	139 26W
Kluane L.	144	61 15N	138 40W
Klyuchevsk, mt.	73	55 50N	160 30 E
Knaresborough	28	54 1N	1 29W
Knockmealdown Mts.	35	52 16N	8 0W
Knossos	55	35 16N	25 10 E
Knoxville, Iowa, U.S.A.	166	41 20N	93 5W
Knoxville, Tenn., U.S.A.	165	35 58N	83 57W
Ko Chang	95	12 0N	102 20 E
Ko Kut	95	11 40N	102 32 E
Koartac	146	60 55N	69 40W
Kobarid	52	46 15N	13 30 E
Kobayashi	108	31 56N	130 59 E
Kobdo = Hovd	100	48 2N	91 37 E
Kōbe	106	34 45N	135 10 E
København	61	55 41N	12 34 E
Koblenz	42	50 21N	7 36 E
Kobroor, Kepulauan	113	6 10S	134 30 E
Kočani	53	41 55N	22 25 E
Kōchi	109	33 30N	133 35 E
Kochiu = Gejiu	99	23 20N	103 10 E
Kodaira	107	35 44N	139 29 E
Kodiak I.	142	57 30N	152 45W
Kōfu	107	35 40N	138 30 E
Koga	107	36 11N	139 43 E
Kogota	103	38 33N	141 3 E
Koh-i-Bābā	87	34 30N	67 0 E
Kohat	89	33 40N	71 29 E
Kokand	71	40 30N	70 57 E
Kokchetav	71	53 20N	69 25 E
Koko Kyunzu	94	14 10N	93 25 E
Kokomo	167	40 30N	86 6W
Kokopo	115	4 22S	152 19 E
Kokooak - ►	146	58 30N	68 10W
Kokubu	108	31 44N	130 46 E
Kola Pen. = Kolskiy Poluostrov	69	67 30N	38 0 E
Kolar	90	13 12N	78 15 E
Kolar Gold Fields	90	12 58N	78 16 E
Kolarovgrad	53	43 18N	26 55 E
Kolding	61	55 30N	9 29 E
Kolguyev, Ostrov	69	69 20N	48 30 E
Kolhapur	91	16 43N	74 15 E
Köln	42	50 56N	6 58 E
Kolo	58	52 14N	18 40 E
Kolomna	68	55 8N	38 45 F
Kolskiy Poluostrov	69	67 30N	38 0 E
Kolyma →	73	69 30N	161 0 E
Komagene	107	35 44N	137 58 E
Komaki	106	35 17N	136 55 E
Komandorskiye, Is.	73	55 0N	167 0 E
Komárno	59	47 49N	18 5 E
Komatsu	106	36 25N	136 30 E
Komatsujima	109	34 0N	134 35 E
Komi A.S.S.R. □	69	64 0N	55 0 E
Kommunizma, Pik	71	39 0N	72 2 E
Komoro	107	36 19N	138 26 E
Kompong Cham	95	12 0N	105 30 E
Kompong Chhnang	95	12 20N	104 35 E
Kompong Som	95	10 38N	103 30 E
Komsomolets, Ostrov	72	80 30N	95 0 E
Komsomolsk	75	50 30N	137 0 E
Konarhá □	87	35 30N	71 3 E
Kong	130	8 54N	4 36W
Kong, Koh	95	11 20N	103 0 E
Kong Christian X.s Land	13	74 0N	29 0W
Kong Frederik VI.s Kyst	147	63 0N	43 0W
Kong Frederik VIII s Land	13	78 30N	26 0W
Kongor	129	7 1N	31 27 E
Königsberg = Kaliningrad	68	54 42N	20 32 E
Konin	58	52 12N	18 15 E
Konjic	52	43 42N	17 58 E
Konosha	68	61 0N	40 5 E
Konstanz	44	47 39N	9 10 E
Kontagora	131	10 23N	5 27 E
Konya	80	37 52N	32 35 E
Konya Ovasi	80	38 30N	33 0 E
Koolyanobbing	120	30 48S	119 36 E
Kopaonik Planina	52	43 10N	21 50 E
Kopeysk	71	55 7N	61 37 E
Kopparberg	60	59 52N	15 0 E
Koppeh Dāgh	86	38 0N	58 0 E
Korab	52	41 44N	20 40 E
Korça	52	40 37N	20 50 E
Korčula	52	42 57N	17 8 E
Kordestān □	81	36 0N	47 0 E
Korea Bay	98	39 0N	124 0 E
Korea Strait	104	34 0N	129 30 E
Korhogo	130	9 29N	5 28W
Korinthiakós Kólpos	54	38 16N	22 30 E

Name	Map	Lat °	Lat '	N/S	Long °	Long '	E/W
Kórinthos	**54**	37	56N		22	55	E
Kōriyama	**105**	37	24N		140	23	E
Koroit	**119**	38	18S		142	24	E
Kortrijk	**42**	50	50N		3	17	E
Koryakskiy Khrebet	**73**	61	0N		171	0	E
Kos	**55**	36	50N		27	15	E
Kosciusko	**169**	33	3N		89	34W	
Kosciusko, Mt.	**117**	36	27S		148	16	E
Koshigaya	**107**	35	54N		139	48	E
K'oshih = Kashi	**100**	39	30N		76	2	E
Koshiki-Rettō	**108**	31	45N		129	49	E
Kōshoku	**107**	36	38N		138	6	E
Košice	**59**	48	42N		21	15	E
Kosovska-Mitrovica	**52**	42	54N		20	52	E
Kôstî	**129**	13	8N		32	43	E
Kostroma	**68**	57	50N		40	58	E
Koszalin	**58**	53	50N		16	8	E
Kota	**91**	25	14N		75	49	E
Kota Baharu	**96**	6	7N		102	14	E
Kota Kinabalu	**112**	6	0N		116	4	E
Kotelnich	**68**	58	20N		48	10	E
Kotka	**67**	60	28N		26	58	E
Kotlas	**69**	61	15N		47	0	E
Kotor	**52**	42	25N		18	47	E
Kotuy →	**77**	71	54N		102	6	E
Kotzebue	**142**	66	50N		162	40W	
Kowloon	**99**	22	20N		114	15	E
Kōyama	**108**	31	20N		130	56	E
Koyukuk →	**142**	64	56N		157	30W	
Kozáni	**55**	40	19N		21	47	E
Kozhikode = Calicut	**90**	11	15N		75	43	E
Kōzu-Shima	**107**	34	13N		139	10	E
Kra, Isthmus of = Kra, Kho Khot	**94**	10	15N		99	30	E
Kra, Kho Khot	**94**	10	15N		99	30	E
Kragujevac	**52**	44	2N		20	56	E
Kraków	**58**	50	4N		19	57	E
Kraljevo	**52**	43	44N		20	41	E
Krasnodar	**68**	45	5N		39	0	E
Krasnovodsk	**70**	40	0N		52	52	E
Krasnoyarsk	**74**	56	8N		93	0	E
Krasnyy Kut	**68**	50	50N		47	0	E
Kratie	**95**	12	32N		106	10	E
Kravanh, Chuor Phnum	**95**	12	0N		103	32	E
Krefeld	**42**	51	20N		6	32	E
Kremenchug	**68**	49	5N		33	25	E
Krishna →	**91**	15	57N		80	59	E
Krishnanagar	**92**	23	24N		88	33	E
Kristiansand	**60**	58	9N		8	1	E
Kristianstad	**61**	56	2N		14	9	E
Kristianstads län □	**61**	56	15N		14	0	E
Kristiansund	**65**	63	7N		7	45	E
Kríti	**55**	35	15N		25	0	E
Krivoy Rog	**68**	47	51N		33	20	E
Krk	**52**	45	8N		14	40	E
Kronobergs län □	**61**	56	45N		14	30	E
Kronshtadt	**68**	60	5N		29	45	E
Krotoszyn	**58**	51	42N		17	23	E
Krugersdorp	**137**	26	5S		27	46	E
Krung Thep = Bangkok	**94**	13	45N		100	35	E
Kruševac	**52**	43	35N		21	28	E
Krymskiy P-ov.	**68**	45	0N		34	0	E
Kuala Dungun	**96**	4	45N		103	25	E
Kuala Kangsar	**96**	4	46N		100	56	E
Kuala Lipis	**96**	4	10N		102	3	E
Kuala Lumpur	**96**	3	9N		101	41	E
Kuala Pilah	**96**	2	45N		102	15	E
Kuala Trengganu	**96**	5	20N		103	8	E
Kuangchou = Guangzhou	**99**	23	5N		113	10	E
Kuantan	**96**	3	49N		103	20	E
Kubak	**88**	27	10N		63	10	E
Kuban →	**68**	45	20N		37	30	E
Kubokawa	**109**	33	12N		133	8	E
Kuchinoerabu-Jima	**104**	30	28N		130	11	E
Kucing	**111**	1	33N		110	25	E
Kudamatsu	**108**	34	0N		131	52	E
Kueiyang = Guiyang	**99**	26	32N		106	40	E
Kūh-e-Jebāl Bārez	**85**	29	0N		58	0	E
Kūh-e-Sorkh	**86**	35	30N		58	45	E
Kūhhā-ye-Bashākerd	**85**	26	45N		59	0	E
Kūhhā-ye Sabalān	**81**	38	15N		47	45	E
Kuji	**103**	40	11N		141	46	E
Kuldja = Yining	**100**	43	58N		81	10	E
Kulunda	**71**	52	35N		78	57	E
Kumagaya	**107**	36	9N		139	22	E
Kumamoto	**108**	32	45N		130	45	E
Kumano	**106**	33	54N		136	5	E
Kumano-Nada	**106**	33	47N		136	20	E
Kumasi	**130**	6	41N		1	38W	
Kumon Bum	**93**	26	30N		97	15	E
Kunashir, Ostrov	**75**	44	0N		146	0	E
Kunimi-Dake	**109**	32	33N		131	1	E
Kunlun Shan	**100**	36	0N		86	30	E
Kunming	**101**	25	1N		102	41	E
Kunsan	**98**	35	59N		126	45	E
Kuopio	**67**	62	53N		27	35	E
Kupang	**113**	10	19S		123	39	E
Kurashiki	**109**	34	40N		133	50	E
Kurayoshi	**109**	35	26N		133	50	E
Kure	**109**	34	14N		132	32	E
Kurgan	**71**	55	26N		65	18	E
Kuril Is. = Kurilskiye Ostrova	**75**	45	0N		150	0	E
Kurilskiye Ostrova	**75**	45	0N		150	0	E
Kurnool	**90**	15	45N		78	0	E
Kurobe-Gawe →	**106**	36	55N		137	25	E
Kurri Kurri	**117**	32	50S		151	28	E
Kursk	**68**	51	42N		36	11	E
Kuršumlija	**52**	43	9N		21	19	E
Kurume	**108**	33	15N		130	30	E
Kurunegala	**90**	7	30N		80	23	E
Kusatsu	**106**	34	58N		135	57	E
Kushikino	**108**	31	44N		130	16	E
Kushima	**108**	31	29N		131	14	E
Kushimoto	**106**	33	28N		135	47	E
Kushiro	**103**	43	0N		144	25	E
Kushka	**70**	35	20N		62	18	E
Kushtia	**92**	23	55N		89	5	E
Kuskokwim Bay	**142**	59	50N		162	56W	
Kustanay	**71**	53	10N		63	35	E
Kusu	**108**	33	16N		131	9	E
Kütahya	**80**	39	30N		30	2	E
Kutaisi	**70**	42	19N		42	40	E
Kutaraja = Banda Aceh	**111**	5	35N		95	20	E
Kutno	**58**	52	15N		19	23	E
Kuujjuaq	**146**	58	6N		68	15W	
Kuwait = Al Kuwayt	**84**	29	30N		47	30	E
Kuwait ■	**84**	29	30N		47	30	E
Kuwana	**106**	35	0N		136	43	E
Kuybyshev	**68**	53	8N		50	6	E
Kwakoegron	**185**	5	12N		55	25W	
Kwangju	**98**	35	9N		126	54	E
Kwangsi-Chuang = Guangxi Zhuangzu Zizhiqu □	**99**	24	0N		109	0	E
Kwangtung = Guangdong □	**99**	23	0N		113	0	E
Kweichow = Guizhou □	**99**	27	0N		107	0	E
Kwinana New Town	**120**	32	15S		115	47	E
Kyabram	**117**	36	19S		145	4	E
Kyaukpadaung	**93**	20	52N		95	8	E
Kyle of Lochalsh	**32**	57	17N		5	43W	
Kyneton	**117**	37	10S		144	29	E
Kyō-ga-Saki	**106**	35	45N		135	15	E
Kyoga, L.	**132**	1	35N		33	0	E
Kyogle	**116**	28	40S		153	0	E
Kyōto	**106**	35	0N		135	45	E
Kyrenia	**80**	35	20N		33	20	E
Kyūshū	**108**	33	0N		131	0	E
Kyūshū □	**108**	33	0N		131	0	E
Kyūshū-Sanchi	**108**	32	35N		131	17	E
Kyustendil	**53**	42	16N		22	41	E
Kyzyl	**74**	51	50N		94	30	E
Kyzylkum, Peski	**70**	42	30N		65	0	E
Kzyl-Orda	**71**	44	48N		65	28	E
Labe = Elbe →	**42**	53	50N		9	0	E
Laboulaye	**190**	34	10S		63	30W	
Labrador, Coast of □	**147**	53	20N		61	0W	
Lábrea	**187**	7	15S		64	51W	
Lac la Martre	**145**	63	8N		117	16W	
Laccadive Is. = Lakshadweep Is.	**78**	10	0N		72	30	E

Lachine 151 45 30N 73 40W
Lachute 151 45 39N 74 21W
Lackawanna 164 42 49N 78 50W
Lacombe 155 52 30N 113 44W
Laconia 148 43 32N 71 30W
Ladakh Ra. .... 89 34 0N 78 0 E
Ladoga, L. = Ladozhskoye
  Ozero .... 68 61 15N 30 30 E
Ladozhskoye Ozero........ 68 61 15N 30 30 E
Ladysmith 154 49 0N 123 49W
Lae .... 115 6 40S 147 2 E
Lafayette, Ind., U.S.A. 167 40 25N 86 54W
Lafayette, La., U.S.A........ 168 30 18N 92 0W
Laghmān □ .... 87 34 20N 70 0 E
Laghouat .... 127 33 50N 2 59 E
Lagny .... 39 48 52N 2 40 E
Lagos, Nigeria .... 131 6 25N 3 27 E
Lagos, Portugal 50 37 5N 8 41W
Lagos de Moreno 175 21 21N 101 55W
Laguna 191 28 30S 48 50W
Laguna Beach 173 33 31N 117 52W
Laguna Madre 158 27 0N 97 20W
Lagunas, Chile 187 21 0S 69 45W
Lagunas, Peru............ 186 5 10S 75 35W
Lahore .... 89 31 32N 74 22 E
Lahti .... 67 60 58N 25 40 E
Lahtis = Lahti .... 67 60 58N 25 40 E
Laï....................... 131 9 25N 16 18 E
Laidley .... 116 27 39S 152 20 E
Lairg 33 58 1N 4 24W
Laja, R. de la →→ 177 20 55N 100 46W
Lajes 191 27 48S 50 20W
Lake Cargelligo .... 117 33 15S 146 22 E
Lake Charles 168 30 15N 93 10W
Lake City, Fla., U.S.A. 170 30 10N 82 40W
Lake City, S.C., U.S.A. 165 33 51N 79 44W
Lake Grace .... 120 33 7S 118 28 E
Lake Harbour 146 62 50N 69 50W
Lake Worth 170 26 36N 80 3W
Lakeland 170 28 0N 82 0W
Lakes Entrance........... 117 37 50S 148 0 E
Lakewood 167 41 28N 81 50W
Lakshadweep Is. .... 78 10 0N 72 30 E
Lala Ghat .... 93 24 30N 92 40 E
Lalitpur .... 91 24 42N 78 28 E
Lamar 163 38 9N 102 35W
Lambi Kyun .... 96 10 50N 98 20 E
Lameroo .... 119 35 19S 140 33 E
Lamia .... 54 38 55N 22 26 E
Lammermuir Hills 31 55 50N 2 40W
Lamon Bay .... 112 14 30N 122 20 E
Lampa 187 15 22S 70 22W
Lampang .... 94 18 16N 99 32 E
Lampeter 26 52 6N 4 6W
Lamu .... 133 2 16S 40 55 E
Lanark 31 55 40N 3 48W
Lancang Jiang →→ .... 101 21 40N 101 10 E
Lancashire □ 28 53 40N 2 30W
Lancaster, U.K............ 28 54 3N 2 48W
Lancaster, U.S.A. 164 40 4N 76 19W
Lancaster Sd............. 146 74 13N 84 0W
Lanchow = Lanzhou .... 99 36 1N 103 52 E
Landes, Les 36 44 20N 1 0W
Land's End 27 50 4N 5 43W
Landskrona .... 61 55 53N 12 50 E
Lanett 169 33 0N 85 15W
Langjökull 64 64 39N 20 12W
Langlade 149 46 50N 56 20W
Langøya.................. 64 68 45N 14 50 E
Langres, Plateau de........ 37 47 45N 5 3 E
Languedoc .... 37 43 58N 4 0 E
Lannion 36 48 46N 3 29W
Lansing 167 42 47N 84 40W
Lanzhou .... 99 36 1N 103 52 E
Laois □................... 35 53 0N 7 20W
Laon .... 38 49 33N 3 35 E
Laona 150 45 32N 88 41W
Laos ■ .... 95 17 45N 105 0 E
Lapeer 167 43 3N 83 20W
Lapland = Lappland .... 67 68 7N 24 0 E
Lappland .... 67 68 7N 24 0 E

Laptev Sea .... 72 76 0N 125 0 E
Laramie 163 41 20N 105 38W
Laramie Mts............... 163 42 0N 105 30W
Laredo 161 27 34N 99 29W
Laren .... 40 52 16N 5 14 E
Largs 30 55 48N 4 51W
Lárisa .... 54 39 49N 22 28 E
Larkana .... 88 27 32N 68 18 E
Larnaca .... 80 35 0N 33 35 E
Larne 34 54 52N 5 50W
Laryak .... 69 61 15N 80 0 E
Las Cruces 161 32 18N 106 50W
Las Lajas 190 38 30S 70 25W
Las Palmas 126 28 7N 15 26W
Las Vegas, N. Mex., U.S.A. ... 161 35 35N 105 10W
Las Vegas, Nev., U.S.A. 173 36 10N 115 5W
Lashio.................... 90 22 56N 97 45 E
Latacunga 184 0 50S 78 35W
Latakia = Al Lādhiqīyah .... 80 35 30N 35 45 E
Latium = Lazio □ .... 46 42 10N 12 30 E
Latrobe .... 119 41 14S 146 30 E
Latur .... 91 18 25N 76 40 E
Latvian S.S.R. □ .... 68 56 50N 24 0 E
Lauchhammer .... 43 51 35N 13 48 E
Launceston, Australia ..... 119 41 24S 147 8 F
Launceston, U.K........... 27 50 38N 4 21W
Launglon Bok .... 94 13 50N 97 54 E
Laurel 169 31 41N 89 9W
Laurens 165 34 32N 82 2W
Laurentian Plat........... 138 52 0N 70 0W
Laurinburg 165 34 50N 79 25W
Lausanne .... 44 46 32N 6 38 E
Laut, Pulau .... 111 3 40S 116 10 E
Laut Ketil, Kepulauan ..... 113 4 45S 115 40 E
Lauzon 148 46 48N 71 10W
Laval 36 48 4N 0 48W
Lávrion .... 55 37 40N 24 4 E
Lawrence, Kans., U.S.A. ... 166 39 0N 95 10W
Lawrence, Mass., U.S.A. ... 164 42 40N 71 9W
Lawrenceburg 169 35 12N 87 19W
Lawton 161 34 33N 98 25W
Lazio □................... 46 42 10N 12 30 E
Lea →→ 25 51 30N 0 10W
Leader 152 50 50N 109 30W
Leadhills 31 55 25N 3 47W
Leadville 163 39 17N 106 23W
Leamington, Canada 150 42 3N 82 36W
Leamington, U.K. 24 52 18N 1 32W
Leavenworth 166 39 25N 95 0W
Lebanon, Mo., U.S.A....... 166 37 40N 92 40W
Lebanon, Oreg., U.S.A. 171 44 31N 122 57W
Lebanon, Pa., U.S.A 164 40 20N 76 28W
Lebanon, Tenn., U.S.A. 169 36 15N 86 20W
Lebanon ■ .... 80 34 0N 36 0 E
Lecce .... 49 40 20N 18 10 E
Ledbury 24 52 3N 2 25W
Leduc 155 53 15N 113 30W
Leeds 28 53 48N 1 34W
Leek 28 53 7N 2 2W
Leerdam .... 40 51 54N 5 6 E
Leesburg 170 28 47N 81 52W
Leeton .... 117 34 33S 146 23 E
Leeuwarden .... 41 53 15N 5 48 E
Leeuwin, C. .... 120 34 20S 115 9 E
Leeward Is. 181 16 30N 63 30W
Leghorn = Livorno .... 46 43 32N 10 18 E
Legnica .... 58 51 12N 16 10 E
Leicester 25 52 39N 1 9W
Leicester □ 25 52 40N 1 10W
Leichhardt .... 121 33 53S 151 9 E
Leiden .... 40 52 9N 4 30 E
Leigh Creek South .... 118 30 38S 138 26 E
Leinster .... 120 27 51S 120 36 E
Leinster □ 35 53 0N 7 10W
Leinster, Mt.............. 35 52 38N 6 47W
Leipzig .... 43 51 20N 12 23 E
Leith 31 55 59N 3 10W
Leith Hill 24 51 10N 0 23W
Leitrim □................. 34 54 0N 8 5W
Lek →→ .... 40 51 54N 4 35 E
Leleque 192 42 28S 71 0W

Léman, Lac	**44** 46 26N	6 30 E
Lemmer	**41** 52 51N	5 43 E
Lena →	**72** 72 52N	126 40 E
Leninabad	**71** 40 17N	69 37 E
Leninakan	**70** 40 47N	43 50 E
Leningrad	**68** 59 55N	30 20 E
Leninsk-Kuznetskiy	**71** 54 44N	86 10 E
Leninskoye	**75** 47 56N	132 38 E
Lenoir City	**165** 35 40N	84 20W
Lens, Belgium	**38** 50 33N	3 54 E
Lens, France	**37** 50 26N	2 50 E
Lensk	**74** 60 48N	114 55 E
Leominster, U.K.	**24** 52 15N	2 43W
Leominster, U.S.A.	**164** 42 32N	71 45W
León, Mexico	**177** 21 7N	101 40W
León, Nic.	**179** 12 20N	86 51W
León, Spain	**50** 42 38N	5 34W
León □	**50** 42 40N	5 55W
Leongatha	**117** 38 30S	145 58 E
Léopold II, Lac = Mai-		
Ndombe, L.	**134** 2 0S	18 20 E
Léopoldville = Kinshasa	**134** 4 20S	15 15 E
Lérida	**51** 41 37N	0 39 E
Lerwick	**30** 60 10N	1 10W
Lesbos, I. = Lésvos	**55** 39 10N	26 20 E
Lesotho ■	**137** 29 40S	28 0 E
Lesozavodsk	**75** 45 30N	133 29 E
Lesser Antilles	**181** 15 0N	61 0W
Lesser Slave L.	**155** 55 30N	115 25W
Lésvos	**55** 39 10N	26 20 E
Letchworth	**25** 51 58N	0 13W
Lethbridge	**155** 49 45N	112 45W
Leti, Kepulauan	**113** 8 10S	128 0 E
Leticia	**184** 4 9S	70 0W
Letsôk-aw Kyun	**94** 11 30N	98 25 E
Letterkenny	**34** 54 57N	7 42W
Leuven	**42** 50 52N	4 42 E
Levanger	**65** 63 45N	11 19 E
Levin	**122** 40 37S	175 18 E
Lévis	**148** 46 48N	71 9W
Levkás	**54** 38 40N	20 43 E
Levkôsia = Nicosia	**80** 35 10N	33 25 E
Lewes	**25** 50 53N	0 2 E
Lewis	**32** 58 10N	6 40W
Lewis, Butt of	**32** 58 30N	6 12W
Lewis Ra.	**162** 48 0N	113 15W
Lewisporte	**149** 49 15N	55 3W
Lewiston	**148** 44 3N	70 10 E
Lexington, Ky., U.S.A.	**165** 38 6N	84 30W
Lexington, Mo., U.S.A.	**166** 39 7N	93 55W
Lexington, N.C., U.S.A.	**165** 35 50N	80 13W
Lexington, Oreg., U.S.A.	**171** 45 29N	119 46W
Lexington Park	**165** 38 16N	76 27W
Leyte	**112** 11 0N	125 0 E
Lhasa	**101** 29 50N	91 3 E
Lhazê	**101** 29 5N	87 38 E
Lianyungang	**99** 34 40N	119 11 E
Liaoning □	**98** 41 40N	122 30 E
Liaoyuan	**98** 42 58N	125 2 E
Liard →	**144** 61 51N	121 18W
Libau = Liepaja	**68** 56 30N	21 0 E
Liberec	**58** 50 47N	15 7 E
Liberia ■	**130** 6 30N	9 30W
Lîbïya, Sahrâ'	**128** 27 35N	25 0 E
Libreville	**134** 0 25N	9 26 E
Libya ■	**127** 27 0N	17 0 E
Lichfield	**28** 52 40N	1 50W
Liechtenstein ■	**44** 47 8N	9 35 E
Liège	**42** 50 38N	5 35 E
Liegnitz = Legnica	**58** 51 12N	16 10 E
Lienyünchiangshih =		
Lianyungang	**99** 34 40N	119 11 E
Liepaja	**68** 56 30N	21 0 E
Liévin	**38** 50 24N	2 47 E
Liffey →	**35** 53 21N	6 20W
Lifford	**34** 54 50N	7 30W
Liguria □	**46** 44 30N	9 0 E
Ligurian Sea	**46** 43 20N	9 0 E
Lihou Reefs and Cays	**121** 17 25S	151 40 E
Lihue	**160** 21 59N	159 24W
Likasi	**135** 10 55S	26 48 E
Lille, Belgium	**38** 51 15N	4 50 E
Lille, France	**37** 50 38N	3 3 E
Lille Bœlt	**61** 55 20N	9 45 E
Lillehammer	**60** 61 8N	10 30 E
Lillers	**38** 50 35N	2 28 E
Lillooet	**154** 50 44N	121 57W
Lilongwe	**137** 14 0S	33 48 E
Lima, Peru	**186** 12 0S	77 0W
Lima, U.S.A.	**167** 40 42N	84 5W
Limassol	**80** 34 42N	33 1 E
Limavady	**34** 55 3N	6 58W
Limbe	**137** 15 55S	35 2 E
Limburg □	**41** 51 20N	5 55 E
Limeira	**188** 22 35S	47 28W
Limerick	**35** 52 40N	8 38W
Limerick □	**35** 52 30N	8 50W
Limfjorden	**61** 56 55N	9 0 E
Límnos	**55** 39 50N	25 5 E
Limoges	**36** 45 50N	1 15 E
Limón	**179** 10 0N	83 2W
Limousin	**36** 46 0N	1 0 E
Limpopo →	**137** 25 15S	33 30 E
Linares, Chile	**190** 35 50S	71 40W
Linares, Mexico	**176** 24 50N	99 40W
Linares, Spain	**50** 38 10N	3 40W
Lincoln, Argentina	**190** 34 55S	61 30W
Lincoln, U.K.	**29** 53 14N	0 32W
Lincoln, Ill., U.S.A.	**166** 40 10N	89 20W
Lincoln, Maine, U.S.A.	**148** 45 27N	68 29W
Lincoln, Nebr., U.S.A.	**156** 40 50N	96 42W
Lincoln □	**29** 53 14N	0 32W
Lincoln Sea	**12** 84 0N	55 0W
Lincoln Wolds	**29** 53 20N	0 5W
Lindsay, Canada	**151** 44 22N	78 43W
Lindsay, U.S.A.	**173** 36 14N	119 6W
Línea de la Concepción, La	**50** 36 15N	5 23W
Lingga, Kepulauan	**111** 0 10S	104 30 E
Linguéré	**130** 15 25N	15 5W
Linköping	**60** 58 28N	15 36 E
Linlithgow	**31** 55 58N	3 38W
Linxia	**99** 35 36N	103 10 E
Linz	**45** 48 18N	14 18 E
Lion, G. du	**37** 43 0N	4 0 E
Lípari, Is.	**49** 38 30N	14 50 E
Lipetsk	**68** 52 37N	39 35 E
Lippe →	**42** 51 39N	6 38 E
Lisboa	**50** 38 42N	9 10W
Lisbon = Lisboa	**50** 38 42N	9 10W
Lisburn	**34** 54 30N	6 9W
Lisburne, C.	**142** 68 50N	166 0W
Lisieux	**39** 49 10N	0 12 E
Lismore	**116** 28 44S	153 21 E
Lister, Mt.	**15** 78 0S	162 0 E
Listowel	**35** 52 27N	9 30W
Litchfield	**166** 39 10N	89 40W
Lithgow	**117** 33 25S	150 8 E
Lithuanian S.S.R. □	**68** 55 30N	24 0 E
Little Andaman I.	**94** 10 40N	92 15 E
Little Barrier I.	**122** 36 12S	175 8 E
Little Current	**150** 45 55N	82 0W
Little Falls	**164** 43 3N	74 50W
Little Minch	**32** 57 35N	6 45W
Little Rann	**91** 23 25N	71 25 E
Little Rock	**168** 34 41N	92 10W
Littlehampton	**25** 50 48N	0 32W
Liuzhou	**99** 24 22N	109 22 E
Liverpool, Australia	**117** 33 54S	150 58 E
Liverpool, Canada	**148** 44 5N	64 41W
Liverpool, U.K.	**28** 53 25N	3 0W
Liverpool Plains	**116** 31 15S	150 15 E
Livingston, Guat.	**177** 15 50N	88 50W
Livingston, U.K.	**31** 55 52N	3 33W
Livingston, Mont., U.S.A.	**163** 45 40N	110 40W
Livingston, Tex., U.S.A.	**168** 30 44N	94 54W
Livingstone	**135** 17 46S	25 52 E
Livonia	**167** 42 25N	83 23W
Livorno	**46** 43 32N	10 18 E
Lizard Pt.	**27** 49 57N	5 11W
Ljubljana	**52** 46 4N	14 33 E
Ljusnan →	**66** 61 12N	17 8 E
Llandeilo	**26** 51 53N	4 0W

Name	Pg	Lat	Long
Llandovery	26	51 59N	3 49W
Llandrindod Wells	26	52 15N	3 23W
Llandudno	26	53 19N	3 51W
Llanelli	27	51 41N	4 11W
Llanes	50	43 25N	4 50W
Llangollen	26	52 58N	3 10W
Llanidloes	26	52 28N	3 31W
Llano Estacado	161	34 0N	103 0W
Llanos	184	5 0N	71 35W
Lloydminster	152	53 17N	110 0W
Loc Ninh	95	11 50N	106 34 E
Lochaber	32	56 55N	5 0W
Lochboisdale	32	57 10N	7 20W
Lochem	41	52 9N	6 26 E
Lochgilphead	30	56 2N	5 37W
Lochinver	32	58 9N	5 15W
Lochmaddy	32	57 36N	7 10W
Lochy, L.	32	56 58N	4 55W
Lock Haven	164	41 7N	77 31W
Lockhart	117	35 14S	146 40 E
Lockport	164	43 12N	78 42W
Lodi	172	38 12N	121 16W
Łódź	58	51 45N	19 27 E
Lofoten	64	68 30N	15 0 E
Logan, Utah, U.S.A.	163	41 45N	111 50W
Logan, W. Va., U.S.A.	165	37 51N	81 59W
Logan, Mt	144	60 31N	140 22W
Logansport	167	40 45N	86 21W
Logroño	51	42 28N	2 27W
Loire →	36	47 16N	2 10W
Loja	184	3 59S	79 16W
Lokka	67	67 55N	27 35 E
Lolland	61	54 45N	11 30 E
Lom	53	43 48N	23 12 E
Lomami →	134	0 46N	24 16 E
Lombardia □	46	45 35N	9 45 E
Lombardy = Lombardia □	46	45 35N	9 45 E
Lombok	113	8 45S	116 30 E
Lomé	130	6 9N	1 20 E
Lomond, L.	31	56 8N	4 38W
Lompoc	173	34 41N	120 32W
Łomza	58	53 10N	22 2 E
London, Canada	150	42 59N	81 15W
London, U.K.	25	51 30N	0 5W
Londonderry	34	55 0N	7 20W
Londrina	191	23 18S	51 10W
Long Beach	173	33 46N	118 12W
Long I., Bahamas	178	23 20N	75 10W
Long I., U.S.A.	164	40 50N	73 20W
Long Range Mts.	149	49 30N	57 30W
Long Xuyen	95	10 19N	105 28 E
Longford, Australia	119	41 32S	147 3 E
Longford, Ireland	34	53 43N	7 50W
Longford □	34	53 42N	7 45W
Longlac	150	49 45N	86 25W
Longmont	163	40 10N	105 4W
Longreach	121	23 28S	144 14 E
Longview, Tex., U.S.A.	168	32 30N	94 45W
Longview, Wash., U.S.A.	171	46 9N	122 58W
Looe	27	50 24N	4 25W
Loop Hd.	35	52 34N	9 55W
Lop Nor	100	40 20N	90 10 E
Lopez, C.	134	0 47S	8 40 E
Lorain	167	41 28N	82 55W
Lorca	51	37 41N	1 42W
Lord Howe I.	122	31 33S	159 6 E
Lordsburg	161	32 22N	108 45W
Lorient	36	47 45N	3 23W
Lorn	30	56 26N	5 10W
Lorn, Firth of	30	56 20N	5 40W
Lorraine	37	49 0N	6 0 E
Los Alamos	161	35 57N	106 17W
Los Andes	190	32 50S	70 40W
Los Angeles, Chile	190	37 28S	72 23W
Los Angeles, U.S.A.	173	34 0N	118 10W
Los Angeles Aqueduct	173	35 25N	118 0W
Los Hermanos	181	11 45N	84 25W
Los Mochis	174	25 45N	108 57W
Los Testigos	181	11 23N	63 6W
Lošinj	52	44 30N	14 30 E
Lossiemouth	33	57 43N	3 17W
Lot →	36	44 18N	0 20 E
Lota	190	37 5S	73 10W
Lothian □	31	55 50N	3 0W
Loughborough	29	52 46N	1 11W
Loughrea	35	53 11N	8 33W
Louisbourg	149	45 55N	60 0W
Louise I.	154	52 55N	131 50W
Louisiana □	168	30 50N	92 0W
Louisville, Ky., U.S.A.	167	38 15N	85 45W
Louisville, Miss., U.S.A.	169	33 7N	89 3W
Lourdes	36	43 6N	0 3W
Lourenço-Marques = Maputo	137	25 58S	32 32 E
Louth	29	53 23N	0 0 E
Louth □	34	53 55N	6 30W
Louvain = Leuven	42	50 52N	4 42 E
Louviers	39	49 12N	1 10 E
Lowell	184	42 38N	71 19W
Lower Austria = Niederösterreich □	45	48 25N	15 40 E
Lower California = Baja California	174	31 10N	115 12W
Lower Hutt	123	41 10S	174 55 E
Lower Saxony = Niedersachsen □	42	52 45N	9 0 E
Lowestoft	26	52 29N	1 44 E
Łowicz	58	52 6N	19 55 E
Loxton	119	34 28S	140 31 E
Loyalty Is = Loyauté, Is.	122	21 0S	167 30 E
Loyang = Luoyang	99	34 40N	112 26 E
Loyauté, Is.	122	21 0S	167 30 E
Lualaba →	135	0 26N	25 20 E
Luan Chau	95	21 38N	103 24 E
Luanda	134	8 50S	13 15 E
Luang Prabang	95	19 52N	102 10 E
Luarca	50	43 32N	6 32W
Lubbock	161	33 40N	101 53W
Lübeck	43	53 52N	10 41 E
Lublin	58	51 12N	22 38 E
Lubnān, J.	80	33 50N	35 45 E
Lubumbashi	135	11 40S	27 28 E
Lucca	46	43 50N	10 30 E
Luce Bay	30	54 45N	4 48W
Lučenec	59	48 18N	19 42 E
Lucerne = Luzern	44	47 3N	8 18 E
Lucknow	92	26 50N	81 0 E
Lüda = Dalian	98	38 50N	121 40 E
Lüderitz	136	26 41S	15 8 E
Ludhiana	89	30 57N	75 56 E
Ludington	167	43 58N	86 27W
Ludlow	24	52 23N	2 42W
Ludwigshafen	42	49 27N	8 27 E
Lufkin	168	31 25N	94 40W
Lugano	44	46 0N	8 57 E
Lugansk = Voroshilovgrad	68	48 38N	39 15 E
Lugo	50	43 2N	7 35W
Lugovoye	71	42 55N	72 43 E
Luján	190	34 45S	59 5W
Łuków	58	51 55N	22 23 E
Lule älv →	67	65 35N	22 10 E
Luleå	67	65 35N	22 10 E
Lüleburgaz	80	41 23N	27 22 E
Lulua →	134	6 30S	22 50 E
Luluabourg = Kananga	134	5 55S	22 18 E
Lumberton	165	34 37N	78 59W
Lundy	27	51 10N	4 41W
Lune →	28	54 0N	2 51W
Lüneburg	43	53 15N	10 23 E
Lüneburg Heath = Lüneburger Heide	43	53 0N	10 0 E
Lüneburger Heide	43	53 0N	10 0 E
Lüni →	91	24 41N	71 14 E
Luoyang	99	34 40N	112 26 E
Lurgan	34	54 28N	6 20W
Lusaka	135	15 28S	28 16 E
Luta = Dalian	98	38 50N	121 40 E
Luton	25	51 53N	0 24W
Lutsk	68	50 50N	25 15 E
Luvua →	135	6 50S	27 30 E
Luxembourg	42	49 37N	6 9 E
Luxembourg ■	42	50 0N	6 0 E
Luzern	44	47 3N	8 18 E

Name	Map	Lat		Long	
Luzhou	**99**	28 52N	105	20 E	
Luziânia	**188**	16 20S	48	0W	
Luzon	**112**	16 0N	121	0 E	
Lvov	**68**	49 50N	24	0 E	
Lyakhovskiye, Ostrova	**72**	73 40N	141	0 E	
Lyallpur = Faisalabad	**89**	31 30N	73	5 E	
Lyell I.	**154**	52 40N	131	35W	
Lyell Range	**123**	41 38S	172	20 E	
Lyme Regis	**27**	50 44N	2	57W	
Lymington	**24**	50 46N	1	32W	
Lynchburg	**165**	37 23N	79	10W	
Lynn	**164**	42 28N	70	57W	
Lynn Lake	**152**	56 51N	101	3W	
Lynton	**27**	51 14N	3	50W	
Lyon	**37**	45 46N	4	50 E	
Lyons = Lyon	**37**	45 46N	4	50 E	
Lytham St. Anne's	**28**	53 45N	2	58W	
Lyttelton	**122**	43 35S	172	44 E	
Ma'ān	**80**	30 12N	35	44 E	
Ma'anshan	**99**	31 44N	118	29 E	
Ma'arrat an Nu'mān	**80**	35 43N	36	43 E	
Maas ~►	**40**	51 45N	4	32 E	
Maaseik	**41**	51 6N	5	45 E	
Maastricht	**41**	50 50N	5	40 E	
Mablethorpe	**29**	53 21N	0	14 E	
McAlester	**168**	34 57N	95	46W	
Macao = Macau ■	**99**	22 16N	113	35 E	
Macapá	**185**	0 5N	51	4W	
Macau	**189**	5 0S	36	40W	
Macau ■	**99**	22 16N	113	35 E	
McBride	**155**	53 20N	120	19W	
Macclesfield	**28**	53 16N	2	9W	
McClure Str.	**12**	75 0N	119	0W	
McComb	**169**	31 13N	90	30W	
McCook	**163**	40 15N	100	35W	
McDermitt	**172**	42 0N	117	45W	
Macdonald L.	**114**	23 30S	129	0 E	
Macdonnell Ranges	**114**	23 40S	133	0 E	
McDouall Peak	**118**	29 51S	134	55 E	
Macduff	**33**	57 40N	2	30W	
Macedonia = Makedhonía □	**55**	40 39N	22	0 E	
Maceió	**189**	9 40S	35	41W	
Macfarlane, L.	**118**	32 0S	136	40 E	
Macgillycuddy's Reeks	**35**	52 2N	9	45W	
Machala	**184**	3 20S	79	57W	
Machida	**107**	35 28N	139	23 E	
Machilipatnam	**92**	16 12N	81	8 E	
Machiques	**184**	10 4N	72	34W	
Machynlleth	**26**	52 36N	3	51W	
Mackay	**121**	21 8S	149	11 E	
Mackay, L.	**114**	22 30S	129	0 E	
McKeesport	**164**	40 21N	79	50W	
Mackenzie ~►	**144**	69 10N	134	20W	
Mackenzie Bay	**12**	69 0N	137	30W	
Mackenzie Mts.	**144**	64 0N	130	0W	
McKinley, Mt.	**142**	63 2N	151	0W	
McKinley Sea	**13**	84 0N	10	0W	
McKinney	**168**	33 10N	96	40W	
Macksville	**116**	30 40S	152	56 E	
Maclean	**116**	29 26S	153	16 E	
McLennan	**155**	55 42N	116	50W	
MacLeod Lake	**154**	54 58N	123	0W	
M'Clintock Chan.	**145**	72 0N	102	0W	
McMinnville, Oreg., U.S.A.	**171**	45 16N	123	11W	
McMinnville, Tenn., U.S.A.	**169**	35 43N	85	45W	
McMurdo Sd.	**15**	77 0S	170	0 E	
McMurray = Fort McMurray	**155**	56 44N	111	7W	
McNaughton L.	**155**	52 0N	118	10W	
Macomb	**166**	40 25N	90	40W	
Mâcon, France	**37**	46 19N	4	50 E	
Mâcon, U.S.A.	**170**	32 50N	83	37W	
McPherson	**161**	38 25N	97	40W	
Macpherson Ra.	**116**	28 15S	153	15 E	
Macquarie ~►	**116**	30 5S	147	30 E	
Macquarie Is.	**15**	54 36S	158	55 E	
MacRobertson Land	**14**	71 0S	64	0 E	
Macroom	**35**	51 54N	8	57W	
Madagascar ■	**137**	20 0S	47	0 E	
Madang	**115**	5 12S	145	49 E	
Madaripur	**93**	23 19N	90	15 E	
Made	**40**	51 41N	4	49 E	
Madeira	**126**	32 50N	17	0W	
Madeira ~►	**185**	3 22S	58	45W	
Madeleine, Îs. de la	**149**	47 30N	61	40W	
Madera	**173**	37 0N	120	1W	
Madhya Pradesh □	**91**	21 50N	81	0 E	
Madison, Fla., U.S.A.	**170**	30 29N	83	39W	
Madison, Ind., U.S.A.	**167**	38 42N	85	20W	
Madison, Wis., U.S.A.	**166**	43 5N	89	25W	
Madisonville	**167**	37 20N	87	30W	
Madiun	**111**	7 38S	111	32 E	
Madras = Tamil Nadu □	**90**	11 0N	77	0 E	
Madras, India	**90**	13 8N	80	19 E	
Madras, U.S.A.	**171**	44 40N	121	10W	
Madre, Laguna	**176**	25 0N	97	30W	
Madre de Dios ~►	**187**	10 59S	66	8W	
Madre del Sur, Sa.	**177**	17 0N	100	0W	
Madre Occidental, Sa.	**174**	25 0N	105	0W	
Madre Oriental, Sa.	**177**	22 0N	99	30W	
Madrid	**50**	40 25N	3	45W	
Madura, Selat	**111**	7 30S	113	20 E	
Madurai	**90**	9 55N	78	10 E	
Madurantakam	**90**	12 30N	79	50 E	
Mae Hong Son	**94**	18 54N	98	57 E	
Maebashi	**107**	36 24N	139	4 E	
Maesteg	**27**	51 36N	3	40W	
Maestra, Sierra	**178**	20 15N	77	0W	
Mafeking	**152**	52 40N	101	10W	
Maffra	**117**	37 53S	146	58 E	
Mafia	**135**	7 45S	39	50 E	
Mafikeng	**136**	25 50S	25	38 E	
Mafra	**191**	26 10S	50	0W	
Magadan	**73**	59 38N	150	50 E	
Magallanes, Estrecho de	**192**	52 30S	75	0W	
Magangué	**184**	9 14N	74	45W	
Magdalena, Bolivia	**187**	13 13S	63	57W	
Magdalena, Mexico	**174**	30 38N	110	57W	
Magdalena ~►	**184**	11 6N	74	51W	
Magdeburg	**43**	52 8N	11	36 E	
Magelang	**111**	7 29S	110	13 E	
Magellan's Str. = Magallanes, Estrecho de	**192**	52 30S	75	0W	
Magherafelt	**34**	54 44N	6	37W	
Magnitogorsk	**71**	53 27N	59	4 E	
Magog	**148**	45 18N	72	9W	
Magosa = Famagusta	**80**	35 8N	33	55 E	
Magrath	**155**	49 25N	112	50W	
Mahābād	**81**	36 50N	45	45 E	
Mahajanga □	**137**	17 0S	47	0 E	
Mahakam ~►	**111**	0 35S	117	17 E	
Mahallāt	**86**	33 55N	50	30 E	
Mahanadi ~►	**92**	20 20N	86	25 E	
Maharashtra □	**91**	20 30N	75	30 E	
Mahbubnagar	**91**	16 45N	77	59 E	
Mahia Pen.	**122**	39 9S	177	55 E	
Mahón	**51**	39 53N	4	16 E	
Mahone Bay	**148**	44 30N	64	20W	
Mahukona	**160**	20 11N	155	52W	
Mai-Ndombe, L.	**134**	2 0S	18	20 E	
Maidenhead	**25**	51 31N	0	42W	
Maiduguri	**131**	12 0N	13	20 E	
Maikala Ra.	**92**	22 0N	81	0 E	
Main ~►	**42**	50 0N	8	18 E	
Maine	**36**	48 0N	0	0 E	
Maine □	**148**	45 20N	69	0W	
Mainland, Orkney, U.K.	**33**	59 0N	3	10W	
Mainland, Shetland, U.K.	**30**	60 15N	1	22W	
Mainpuri	**89**	27 18N	79	4 E	
Mainz	**42**	50 0N	8	17 E	
Maiquetía	**184**	10 36N	66	57W	
Maisí, Pta. de	**178**	20 10N	74	10W	
Maitland, N.S.W., Australia	**117**	32 33S	151	36 E	
Maitland, S. Austral., Australia	**119**	34 23S	137	40 E	
Maiz, Islas del	**179**	12 15N	83	4W	
Maizuru	**106**	35 25N	135	22 E	
Majorca, I. = Mallorca	**51**	39 30N	3	0 E	
Makarikari = Makgadikgadi Salt Pans	**136**	20 40S	25	45 E	
Makasar = Ujung Pandang	**113**	5 10S	119	20 E	

Name	Page	Lat	Lon
Makasar, Selat	113	1 0S	118 20 E
Makedhonía □	55	40 39N	22 0 E
Makena	160	20 39N	156 27W
Makeyevka	68	48 0N	38 0 E
Makgadikgadi Salt Pans	136	20 40S	25 45 E
Makhachkala	70	43 0N	47 30 E
Makkah	82	21 30N	39 54 E
Makó	59	46 14N	20 33 E
Makran Coast Range	88	25 40N	64 0 E
Makurazaki	108	31 15N	130 20 E
Makurdi	131	7 43N	8 35 E
Malabar Coast	90	11 0N	75 0 E
Malacca, Str. of	111	3 0N	101 0 E
Malad City	162	42 10N	112 20 E
Málaga	50	36 43N	4 23W
Malakal	129	9 33N	31 50 E
Malang	111	7 59S	112 45 E
Mälaren	60	59 30N	17 10 E
Malatya	81	38 25N	38 20 E
Malawi ■	137	13 0S	34 0 E
Malawi, L.	137	12 30S	34 30 E
Malay Pen.	97	7 25N	100 0 E
Malāyer	84	34 19N	48 51 E
Malaysia ■	111	5 0N	110 0 E
Malbaie, La	148	47 40N	70 10W
Malbork	58	54 3N	19 1 E
Malcolm	120	28 51S	121 25 E
Maldives ■	78	7 0N	73 0 E
Maldonado	191	35 0S	55 0W
Malebo, Pool	134	4 17S	15 20 E
Malegaon	91	20 30N	74 38 E
Mali ■	130	15 0N	2 0W
Mali Kyun	94	13 0N	98 20 E
Malin Hd.	34	55 18N	7 24W
Malindi	133	3 12S	40 5 E
Malines = Mechelen	42	51 2N	4 29 E
Mallaig	32	57 0N	5 50W
Mallorca	51	39 30N	3 0 E
Mallow	35	52 8N	8 40W
Malmédy	42	50 25N	6 2 E
Malmö	61	55 36N	12 59 E
Malmöhus län □	61	55 45N	13 30 E
Malone	151	44 50N	74 19W
Malta ■	49	35 50N	14 30 E
Malton	29	54 9N	0 48W
Maluku	113	1 0S	127 0 E
Malvern, U.K.	24	52 7N	2 19W
Malvern, U.S.A.	168	34 22N	92 50W
Malvern Hills	24	52 0N	2 19W
Malvinas, Is. = Falkland Is.	192	51 30S	59 0W
Mamers	39	48 21N	0 22 E
Mamoré ⟶	187	10 23S	65 53W
Mamou	130	10 15N	12 0W
Man	130	7 30N	7 40W
Man, I. of	28	54 15N	4 30W
Mana, Fr. Gui.	185	5 45N	53 55W
Mana, U.S.A.	160	22 3N	159 45W
Manaar, Gulf of = Mannar, G. of	90	8 30N	79 0 E
Manacapuru	185	3 16S	60 37W
Manado	113	1 29N	124 51 E
Managua	179	12 6N	86 20W
Manaos = Manaus	185	3 0S	60 0W
Manapouri	123	45 34S	167 39 E
Manaung	93	18 45N	93 40 E
Manaus	185	3 0S	60 0W
Mancha, La	50	39 10N	2 54W
Manchester, U.K.	28	53 30N	2 15W
Manchester, U.S.A.	164	42 58N	71 29W
Mandalay	93	22 0N	96 4 E
Mandale = Mandalay	93	22 0N	96 4 E
Mandurah	120	32 36S	115 48 E
Manfredónia, G. di	49	41 30N	16 10 E
Mangalore	90	12 55N	74 47 E
Mangla Dam	89	33 9N	73 44 E
Mangole	113	1 50S	125 55 E
Mangonui	122	35 1S	173 32 E
Mangyshlak P-ov.	70	44 30N	52 30 E
Manhattan	158	39 10N	96 40W
Manicoré	185	5 48S	61 16W
Manicouagan ⟶	148	49 30N	68 30W
Manila	112	14 40N	121 3 E
Manilla	116	30 45S	150 43 E
Manipur □	93	25 0N	94 0 E
Manisa	80	38 38N	27 30 E
Manistee	167	44 15N	86 20W
Manistique	150	45 59N	86 18W
Manitoba □	153	55 30N	97 0W
Manitoba, L.	153	51 0N	98 45W
Manitoulin I.	150	45 40N	82 30W
Manitowoc	167	44 8N	87 40W
Manizales	184	5 5N	75 32W
Manjil	81	36 46N	49 30 E
Manjimup	120	34 15S	116 6 E
Mankato	166	44 8N	93 59W
Manly	117	33 48S	151 17 E
Mannar, G. of	90	8 30N	79 0 E
Mannar I.	90	9 5N	79 45 E
Mannheim	42	49 28N	8 29 E
Mannum	119	34 50S	139 20 E
Manosque	37	43 49N	5 47 E
Manouane, L.	148	50 45N	70 45W
Mans, Le	39	48 0N	0 10 E
Mansel I.	146	62 0N	80 0W
Mansfield, Australia	117	37 4S	146 6 E
Mansfield, U.K.	29	53 8N	1 12W
Mansfield, U.S.A.	167	40 45N	82 30W
Manta	184	1 0S	80 40W
Mantes-la-Jolie	39	49 0N	1 41 E
Mantiqueira, Serra da	188	22 0S	44 0W
Mántova	46	45 20N	10 42 E
Mantua = Mántova	46	45 20N	10 42 E
Manu	187	12 10S	70 51W
Manukau	122	35 14S	173 13 E
Manyara, L.	135	3 40S	35 50 E
Manzanillo, Cuba	178	20 20N	77 31W
Manzanillo, Mexico	175	19 3N	104 20W
Manzhouli	98	49 35N	117 25 E
Māpimi	174	25 49N	103 51W
Maple	152	43 51N	79 31W
Maputo	137	25 58S	32 32 E
Maquinchao	192	41 15S	68 50W
Mar, Serra do	191	25 30S	49 0W
Mar Chiquita, L.	190	30 40S	62 50W
Mar del Plata	191	38 0S	57 30W
Mar Menor, L.	51	37 40N	0 45W
Marabá	188	5 20S	49 5W
Maracaibo	184	10 40N	71 37W
Maracaibo, Lago de	184	9 40N	71 30W
Maracay	184	10 15N	67 28W
Marajó, Ilha de	188	1 0S	49 30W
Maranhão = São Luís	188	2 39S	44 15W
Maranhão □	188	5 0S	46 0W
Marañón ⟶	186	4 30S	73 35W
Maraş	80	37 37N	36 53 E
Marathón	55	38 11N	23 58 E
Marbella	50	36 30N	4 57W
Marble Bar	114	21 9S	119 44 E
March	25	52 33N	0 5 E
Marché	36	46 0N	1 20 E
Marche □	47	43 22N	13 10 E
Marchena	50	37 18N	5 23W
Marches = Marche □	47	43 22N	13 10 E
Mardan	89	34 20N	72 0 E
Mardin	81	37 20N	40 43 E
Mareeba	121	16 59S	145 28 E
Margarita	175	9 20N	79 55W
Margarita I.	185	11 0N	64 0W
Margate	25	51 23N	1 24 E
Mari, A.S.S.R. □	68	56 30N	48 0 E
Maria van Diemen, C.	122	34 29S	172 40 E
Marianao	178	23 8N	82 24W
Marianna	169	30 45N	85 15W
Maribor	52	46 36N	15 40 E
Maricourt	146	61 30N	72 0W
Marie-Galante	180	15 56N	61 16W
Marienberg	41	52 30N	6 35 E
Marietta, Ga., U.S.A.	169	34 0N	84 30W
Marietta, Ohio, U.S.A.	164	39 27N	81 27W
Marília	188	22 13S	50 0W
Marín	50	42 23N	8 42W
Marinette	167	45 4N	87 40W

Maringá	**191**	23 26S	52	2W
Marion, Ill., U.S.A.	**166**	37 45N	88	55W
Marion, Ind., U.S.A.	**167**	40 35N	85	40W
Marion, Ohio, U.S.A.	**167**	40 38N	83	8W
Marken	**40**	52 26N	5	12 E
Market Drayton	**28**	52 55N	2	30W
Market Harborough	**25**	52 29N	0	55W
Market Rasen	**29**	53 24N	0	20W
Markham Mt.	**15**	83 0S	164	0 E
Marlborough	**24**	51 26N	1	44W
Marlborough □	**123**	41 45S	173	33 E
Marlborough Downs	**24**	51 25N	1	55W
Marlin	**168**	31 25N	96	50W
Marmagao	**91**	15 25N	73	56 E
Marmara, Sea of = Marmara Denizi	**80**	40 45N	28	15 E
Marmara Denizi	**80**	40 45N	28	15 E
Marmaris	**80**	36 50N	28	14 E
Marne ⟶	**39**	8 23N	18	36 E
Maroochydore	**116**	26 29S	153	5 E
Marquesas Is.	**123**	9 30S	140	0W
Marquette	**150**	46 30N	87	21W
Marrakech	**126**	31 9N	8	0W
Marree	**118**	29 39S	138	1 E
Marsabit	**133**	2 18N	38	0 E
Marseille	**37**	43 18N	5	23 E
Marseilles = Marseille	**37**	43 18N	5	23 E
Marshall, Minn., U.S.A.	**166**	44 25N	95	45W
Marshall, Mo., U.S.A.	**166**	39 8N	93	15W
Marshall, Tex., U.S.A.	**168**	32 29N	94	20W
Marshalltown	**166**	42 5N	92	56W
Marshfield	**166**	44 42N	90	10W
Martaban, G. of	**93**	16 5N	96	30 E
Martha's Vineyard	**164**	41 25N	70	35W
Martigues	**37**	43 24N	5	4 E
Martinique	**180**	14 40N	61	0W
Martinsburg	**164**	39 30N	77	57W
Martinsville, Ind., U.S.A.	**167**	39 29N	86	23W
Martinsville, Va., U.S.A.	**165**	36 41N	79	52W
Marton	**122**	40 4S	175	23 E
Marugame	**109**	34 15N	133	40 E
Maruoka	**106**	36 9N	136	16 E
Marwar	**91**	25 43N	73	45 E
Mary	**70**	37 40N	61	50 E
Maryborough = Port Laoise	**35**	53 2N	7	20W
Maryborough, Queens., Australia	**116**	25 31S	152	37 E
Maryborough, Vic., Australia	**117**	37 0S	143	44 E
Maryland □	**164**	39 10N	76	40W
Maryport	**28**	54 43N	3	30W
Marysville	**172**	39 14N	121	40W
Maryville	**165**	35 50N	84	0W
Marzūq	**127**	25 53N	13	57 E
Masan	**98**	35 11N	128	32 E
Masaya	**179**	12 0N	86	7W
Masbate, I.	**112**	12 21N	123	36 E
Mascota	**175**	20 32N	104	49W
Maseru	**137**	29 18S	27	30 E
Mashhad	**86**	36 20N	59	35 E
Masisea	**186**	8 35S	74	22W
Masjed Soleyman	**84**	31 55N	49	18 E
Mask, L.	**34**	53 36N	9	24W
Mason City	**166**	43 9N	93	12W
Masqat	**83**	23 37N	58	36 E
Massachusetts □	**164**	42 25N	72	0W
Massawa = Mitsiwa	**132**	15 35N	39	25 E
Massena	**151**	44 52N	74	55W
Massif Central	**37**	45 30N	2	21 E
Massillon	**167**	40 47N	81	30W
Mastanli = Momchilgrad	**53**	41 33N	25	23 E
Masterton	**123**	40 56S	175	39 E
Mastūrah	**82**	23 7N	38	52 E
Masuda	**108**	34 40N	131	51 E
Matachewan	**151**	47 56N	80	39W
Matadi	**134**	5 52S	13	31 E
Matagalpa	**179**	13 0N	85	58W
Matamoros, Coahuila, Mexico	**174**	25 32N	103	15W
Matamoros, Puebla, Mexico	**177**	18 2N	98	17W
Matane	**148**	48 50N	67	33W
Matanzas	**178**	23 0N	81	40W
Matapan, C. = Taínaron, Ákra	**54**	36 22N	22	27 E
Matarani	**186**	77 0S	72	10W
Matehuala	**177**	23 39N	100	39W
Mathura	**89**	27 30N	77	40 E
Matlock	**28**	53 8N	1	32W
Mato Grosso □	**188**	14 0S	55	0W
Mato Grosso, Planalto do	**188**	15 0S	59	57W
Matopo Hills	**137**	20 36S	28	20 E
Matrah	**83**	23 37N	58	30 E
Matsubara	**106**	34 33N	135	34 E
Matsudo	**107**	35 47N	139	54 E
Matsue	**109**	35 25N	133	10 E
Matsumoto	**107**	36 15N	138	0 E
Matsusaka	**106**	34 34N	136	32 E
Matsutō	**106**	36 31N	136	34 E
Matsuura	**108**	33 20N	129	49 E
Matsuyama	**109**	33 45N	132	45 E
Mattancheri	**90**	9 50N	76	15 E
Mattawa	**151**	46 20N	78	45W
Matterhorn	**44**	45 58N	7	39 E
Matucana	**186**	11 55S	76	25W
Maturín	**185**	9 45N	63	11W
Mau Ranipur	**91**	25 16N	79	8 E
Maubeuge	**38**	50 17N	3	57 E
Maudin Sun	**93**	16 0N	94	30 E
Maui	**160**	20 45N	156	20 E
Maulamyaing	**93**	16 30N	97	40 E
Mauna Kea	**160**	19 50N	155	28W
Mauna Loa	**160**	21 8N	157	10W
Maungmagan Kyunzu	**94**	14 0N	97	48 E
Mauritania ■	**126**	20 50N	10	0W
Mauritius ■	**9**	20 0S	57	0 E
Mawlaik	**93**	23 40N	94	26 E
May Pen	**180**	17 58N	77	15W
Maya ⟶	**75**	54 31N	134	41 E
Mayagüez	**180**	18 12N	67	9W
Mayerthorpe	**155**	53 57N	115	8W
Mayfield	**169**	36 45N	88	40W
Maykop	**70**	44 35N	40	25 E
Maynooth	**34**	53 22N	6	38W
Mayo	**144**	63 38N	135	57W
Mayo □	**34**	53 47N	9	7W
Mayor I.	**122**	37 16S	176	17 E
Maysville	**167**	38 39N	83	46W
Mazagán = El Jadida	**126**	33 11N	8	17W
Mazán	**186**	3 30S	73	0W
Mazar-e Sharīf	**87**	36 41N	67	0 E
Mazarredo	**192**	47 10S	66	50W
Mazatenango	**177**	14 35N	91	30W
Mazatlán	**175**	23 13N	106	25W
Mbandaka	**134**	0 1N	18	18 E
Mdina	**49**	35 51N	14	25 E
Mead, L.	**173**	36 1N	114	44W
Meadville	**164**	41 39N	80	9W
Meander River	**145**	59 2N	117	42W
Meath □	**34**	53 32N	6	40W
Meaux	**39**	48 58N	2	50 E
Mecca = Makkah	**82**	21 30N	39	54 E
Mechelen	**42**	51 2N	4	29 E
Mecklenburger Bucht	**42**	54 20N	11	40 E
Medan	**111**	3 40N	98	38 E
Medellín	**184**	6 15N	75	35W
Medford	**171**	42 20N	122	52W
Mediaş	**57**	46 9N	24	22 E
Medicine Hat	**152**	50 0N	110	45W
Medina = Al Madīnah	**82**	24 35N	39	52 E
Medina	**167**	41 9N	81	50W
Medina del Campo	**50**	41 18N	4	55W
Mediterranean Sea	**124**	35 0N	15	0 E
Medley	**152**	54 25N	110	16W
Médoc	**36**	45 10N	0	56W
Medvezhi, Ostrava	**73**	71 0N	161	0 E
Medway ⟶	**25**	51 28N	0	45 E
Meekatharra	**120**	26 32S	118	29 E
Meerut	**89**	29 1N	77	42 E
Mega	**133**	3 57N	38	19 E
Mégantic, L.	**148**	45 32N	70	53W
Mégara	**55**	37 58N	23	22 E
Meghalaya □	**93**	25 50N	91	0 E
Mei Xian	**99**	24 16N	116	6 E
Meknès	**126**	33 57N	5	33W
Mekong ⟶	**95**	9 30N	106	15 E

Melaka	**96**	2 15N	102	15 E
Melaka □	**96**	2 15N	102	15 E
Melanesia	**122**	4 0S	155	0 E
Melbourne	**117**	37 50S	145	0 E
Melchor Muzquiz	**174**	27 53N	101	31W
Melfort	**152**	52 50N	104	37W
Melilla	**126**	35 21N	2	57W
Melitopol	**68**	46 50N	35	22 E
Melo	**191**	32 20S	54	10W
Melrose	**31**	53 35N	2	44W
Melton Mowbray	**29**	52 46N	0	52W
Melun	**39**	48 32N	2	39 E
Melville	**152**	50 55N	102	50W
Melville, L.	**147**	53 30N	60	0W
Melville I., Australia	**114**	11 30S	131	0 E
Melville I., Canada	**12**	75 30N	112	0W
Melville Pen	**146**	68 0N	84	0W
Memel = Klaipeda	**68**	55 43N	21	10 E
Memphis	**169**	35 7N	90	0W
Menai Strait	**26**	53 14N	4	10W
Ménaka	**131**	15 59N	2	18 E
Menan = Chao Phraya →	**94**	13 32N	100	36 E
Menasha	**167**	44 13N	88	27W
Mende	**37**	44 31N	3	30 E
Mendip Hills	**27**	51 17N	2	40W
Mendocino	**172**	39 26N	123	50W
Mendoza	**190**	32 50S	68	52W
Menindee	**118**	32 20S	142	25 E
Menindee, L.	**118**	32 20S	142	25 E
Menominee	**150**	45 9N	87	39W
Menorca	**51**	40 0N	4	0 E
Mentawai, Kepulauan	**111**	2 0S	99	0 E
Menzies	**120**	29 40S	120	58 E
Meppel	**41**	52 42N	6	12 E
Merbein	**119**	34 10S	142	2 E
Merca	**133**	1 48N	44	50 E
Merced	**172**	37 18N	120	30W
Mercedes, Buenos Aires, Argentina	**190**	34 40S	59	30W
Mercedes, Corrientes, Argentina	**191**	29 10S	58	5W
Mercedes, San Luis, Argentina	**190**	33 40S	65	21W
Mercedes, Uruguay	**191**	33 12S	58	0W
Mere	**24**	51 5N	2	16W
Mergui Arch. = Myeik Kyunzu	**94**	11 30N	97	30 E
Mérida, Mexico	**177**	20 58N	89	37W
Mérida, Spain	**50**	38 55N	6	25W
Mérida, Venezuela	**184**	8 24N	71	8W
Mérida, Cord. de	**182**	9 0N	71	0W
Meriden	**164**	41 33N	72	47W
Meridian	**169**	32 20N	88	42W
Merowe	**129**	18 29N	31	46 E
Merredin	**120**	31 28S	118	18 E
Merrill	**156**	45 11N	89	41W
Merritt	**155**	50 10N	120	45W
Merriwa	**116**	32 6S	150	22 E
Mersey →	**28**	53 20N	2	56W
Merseyside □	**28**	53 25N	2	55W
Mersin	**80**	36 51N	34	36 E
Merthyr Tydfil	**27**	51 45N	3	23W
Méru	**39**	49 13N	2	8 E
Merville	**38**	50 38N	2	38 E
Mesa	**160**	33 20N	111	56W
Mesa, La	**173**	32 48N	117	5W
Meshed = Mashhad	**86**	36 20N	59	35 E
Mesolóngion	**54**	38 21N	21	28 E
Mesopotamia = Al Jazirah	**81**	33 30N	44	0 E
Mesquite	**173**	36 47N	114	6W
Messina, Italy	**49**	38 10N	15	32 E
Messina, S. Africa	**137**	22 20S	30	0 E
Messina, Str. di	**49**	38 5N	15	35 E
Messini	**54**	37 4N	22	1 E
Meta →	**184**	6 12N	67	28W
Metairie	**169**	29 59N	90	9W
Metán	**190**	25 30S	65	0W
Metropolis	**169**	37 10N	88	47W
Metz	**37**	49 8N	6	10 E
Meuse →	**42**	50 45N	5	41 E
Mexia	**168**	31 38N	96	32W
Mexicali	**174**	32 40N	115	29W
México, Mexico	**177**	19 20N	99	10W
México, U.S.A.	**166**	39 10N	91	55W
México □	**177**	19 20N	99	30W
Mexico ■	**174**	20 0N	100	0W
Mexico, G. of	**138**	25 0N	90	0W
Mezen →	**69**	66 11N	43	59 E
Mhow	**91**	22 33N	75	50 E
Miahuatlán	**177**	16 21N	96	36W
Miami	**170**	25 45N	80	15W
Miami Beach	**170**	25 49N	80	6W
Miāneh	**81**	37 30N	47	40 E
Mianwali	**89**	32 38N	71	28 E
Miaoli	**99**	24 37N	120	49 E
Miass	**69**	54 59N	60	6 E
Michigan □	**167**	44 40N	85	40W
Michigan, L.	**150**	44 0N	87	0W
Michigan City	**167**	41 42N	86	56W
Michikamau L.	**147**	54 20N	63	10W
Michipicoten	**150**	47 55N	84	55W
Michoacán □	**175**	19 10N	101	50W
Michurinsk	**68**	52 58N	40	27 E
Micronesia	**122**	11 0N	160	0 E
Mid Glamorgan □	**27**	51 40N	3	25W
Middelburg	**40**	51 30N	3	36 E
Middle Andaman I.	**94**	12 30N	92	30 E
Middlesboro	**165**	36 36N	83	43W
Middlesbrough	**29**	54 35N	1	14W
Middleton	**148**	44 57N	65	4W
Middletown, Conn., U.S.A.	**164**	41 37N	72	40W
Middletown, N.Y., U.S.A.	**164**	41 28N	74	28W
Middletown, Ohio, U.S.A.	**167**	39 29N	84	25W
Midland, Canada	**151**	44 45N	79	50W
Midland, Mich., U.S.A.	**167**	43 37N	84	17W
Midland, Tex., U.S.A.	**161**	32 0N	102	3W
Międzyrzec Podlaski	**58**	51 58N	22	45 E
Miercurea Ciuc	**57**	46 21N	25	48 E
Mieres	**50**	43 18N	5	48W
Migennes	**39**	47 58N	3	31 E
Mihara	**109**	34 24N	133	5 E
Miki	**109**	34 48N	134	59 E
Míkonos	**55**	37 30N	25	25 E
Mikuni-Tōge	**107**	36 50N	138	50 E
Mikura-Jima	**107**	33 52N	139	36 E
Milagro	**184**	2 11S	79	36W
Milan = Milano	**46**	45 28N	9	10 E
Milano	**46**	45 28N	9	10 E
Milâs	**80**	37 20N	27	50 E
Mildura	**119**	34 13S	142	9 E
Miles	**116**	26 40S	150	9 E
Miles City	**163**	46 24N	105	50W
Milford	**164**	38 52N	75	27W
Milford Haven	**27**	51 43N	5	2W
Milk →	**163**	48 5N	106	15W
Millau	**37**	44 8N	3	4 E
Millicent	**119**	37 34S	140	21 E
Millinocket	**148**	45 45N	68	45W
Millmerran	**116**	27 53S	151	16 E
Millom	**28**	54 13N	3	16W
Millville	**164**	39 22N	75	0W
Milne Inlet	**146**	72 30N	80	0W
Mílos	**55**	36 44N	24	25 E
Milton Keynes	**25**	52 3N	0	42W
Milwaukee	**167**	43 9N	87	58W
Milwaukie	**171**	45 27N	122	39W
Minamata	**108**	32 10N	130	30 E
Minas	**191**	34 20S	55	10W
Minas Gerais □	**188**	18 50S	46	0W
Minatitlán	**177**	17 59N	94	31W
Mindanao	**112**	8 0N	125	0 E
Mindanao Sea = Bohol Sea	**112**	9 0N	124	0 E
Minden	**168**	32 40N	93	20W
Mindoro	**112**	13 0N	121	0 E
Mindoro Strait	**112**	12 30N	120	30 E
Mine	**108**	34 12N	131	7 E
Minehead	**27**	51 12N	3	29W
Mineral Wells	**161**	32 50N	98	5W
Mingan	**148**	50 20N	64	0W
Mingenew	**120**	29 12S	115	21 E
Minho □	**50**	41 25N	8	20W
Minneapolis	**166**	44 58N	93	20W
Minnedosa	**153**	50 14N	99	50W

Minnesota □	156	46 40N	94	0W
Mino	106	35 32N	136	55 E
Mino-Kamo	106	35 23N	137	2 E
Mino-Mikawa-Kōgen	106	35 10N	137	23 E
Minorca = Menorca	51	40 0N	4	0 E
Minot	163	48 10N	101	15W
Minsk	68	53 52N	27	30 E
Mintaka Pass	89	37 0N	74	58 E
Miquelon, I.	149	47 2N	56	20W
Miraj	91	16 50N	74	45 E
Miranda do Douro	50	41 30N	6	16W
Mirpur Khas	88	25 30N	69	0 E
Mirzapur	92	25 10N	82	34 E
Mirzapur-cum-Vindhyachal = Mirzapur	92	25 10N	82	34 E
Miscou I.	148	47 57N	64	31W
Mishawaka	167	41 40N	86	8W
Mishima	107	35 10N	138	52 E
Miskitos, Cayos	179	14 26N	82	50W
Miskolc	59	48 7N	20	50 E
Misool	113	1 52S	130	10 E
Misrātah	127	32 24N	15	3 E
Mission City	154	49 10N	122	15W
Mississippi □	169	33 0N	90	0W
Mississippi →	169	29 0N	89	15W
Mississippi, Delta of the	169	29 15N	90	30W
Missoula	162	46 52N	114	0W
Missouri □	166	38 25N	92	30W
Missouri →	166	38 50N	90	8W
Mistassini L.	151	51 0N	73	30W
Mitaka	107	35 40N	139	33 E
Mitchell, Australia	116	26 29S	147	58 E
Mitchell, U.S.A.	163	43 40N	98	0W
Mitchell →	115	15 12S	141	35 E
Mitilíni	55	39 6N	26	35 E
Mito	107	36 20N	140	30 E
Mitsiwa	132	15 35N	39	25 E
Mitsukaidō	107	36 1N	139	59 E
Mittagong	117	34 28S	150	29 E
Mitú	184	1 8N	70	3W
Miura	107	35 12N	139	40 E
Miyake-Jima	107	34 0N	139	30 E
Miyako	103	39 40N	141	59 E
Miyakonojō	108	31 40N	131	5 E
Miyanojō	108	31 54N	130	27 E
Miyazaki	108	31 56N	131	30 E
Miyazu	106	35 35N	135	10 E
Miyoshi	109	34 48N	132	51 E
Mizamis = Ozamis	112	8 15N	123	50 E
Mizen Hd.	35	51 27N	9	50W
Mizoram □	93	23 30N	92	40 E
Mizunami	106	35 22N	137	15 E
Mława	58	53 9N	20	25 E
Mobara	107	35 25N	140	18 E
Moberley	166	39 25N	92	25W
Mobile	169	30 41N	88	3W
Mobutu Sese Seko, L.	132	1 30N	31	0 E
Moçâmedes = Namibe	134	15 7S	12	11 E
Moctezuma, R. →	177	21 59N	98	34W
Módena	46	44 39N	10	55 E
Modesto	172	37 43N	121	0W
Moe	117	38 12S	146	19 E
Moei →	94	17 25N	98	10 E
Moengo	185	5 45N	54	20W
Moffat	31	55 20N	3	27W
Mogadishu = Muqdisho	133	2 2N	45	25 E
Mogador = Essaouira	126	31 32N	9	42W
Mogami →	103	38 45N	140	0 E
Mogi das Cruzes	191	23 31S	46	11W
Mogilev	68	53 55N	30	18 E
Mointy	71	47 10N	73	18 E
Moisie	148	50 12N	66	1W
Mojave Desert	173	35 0N	116	30W
Mold	26	53 10N	3	10W
Moldavian S.S.R. □	68	47 0N	28	0 E
Molde	65	62 45N	7	9 E
Molfetta	49	41 12N	16	35 E
Moline	166	41 30N	90	30W
Molise □	49	41 45N	14	30 E
Mollendo	187	17 0S	72	0W
Mölndal	60	57 40N	12	3 E
Molong	117	33 5S	148	54 E
Molopo →	136	28 30S	20	13 E
Molotov = Perm	69	58 0N	57	10 E
Molucca Sea	113	4 0S	124	0 E
Moluccas = Maluku	113	1 0S	127	0 E
Mombasa	135	4 2S	39	43 E
Mombetsu	103	42 27N	142	4 E
Momchilgrad	53	41 33N	25	23 E
Mompós	184	9 14N	74	26W
Møn	61	54 57N	12	15 E
Mona, Canal de la	180	18 30N	67	45W
Monach Is.	32	57 32N	7	40W
Monaco ■	37	43 46N	7	23 E
Monaghan	34	54 15N	6	58W
Monaghan □	34	54 10N	7	0W
Monastir = Bitola	52	41 5N	21	10 E
Mönchengladbach	42	51 12N	6	23 E
Monchique	50	37 19N	8	38W
Monclova	174	26 50N	101	30W
Moncton	148	46 7N	64	51W
Monessen	164	40 9N	79	50W
Monforte	50	39 6N	7	25W
Mongalla	129	5 8N	31	42 E
Monghyr = Munger	92	25 23N	86	30 E
Mongolia ■	98	47 0N	103	0 E
Monmouth, U.K.	26	51 48N	2	43W
Monmouth, U.S.A.	166	40 50N	90	40W
Monroe, La., U.S.A.	168	32 32N	92	4W
Monroe, Mich., U.S.A.	167	41 55N	83	26W
Monroe, N.C., U.S.A.	165	35 2N	80	37W
Monrovia, Liberia	130	6 18N	10	47W
Monrovia, U.S.A.	173	34 7N	118	1W
Mons	42	50 27N	3	58 E
Mont-de-Marsan	36	43 54N	0	31W
Mont Laurier	151	46 35N	75	30W
Montague	172	41 47N	122	30W
Montana □	163	47 0N	110	0W
Montargis	39	48 0N	2	43 E
Montauban	36	44 0N	1	21 E
Montbéliard	37	47 31N	6	48 E
Montceau-les-Mines	37	46 40N	4	23 E
Montdidier	38	49 38N	2	35 E
Monte-Carlo	37	43 46N	7	23 E
Monte Caseros	191	30 10S	57	50W
Montego Bay	180	18 30N	78	0W
Montélimar	37	44 33N	4	45 E
Montemorelos	176	25 11N	99	42W
Montenegro = Crna Gora □	52	42 40N	19	20 E
Monterey	173	36 35N	121	57W
Montería	184	8 46N	75	53W
Monterrey	176	25 40N	100	30W
Montes Claros	188	16 30S	43	50W
Montevideo, Uruguay	191	34 50S	56	11W
Montevideo, U.S.A.	166	44 55N	95	40W
Montgomery = Sahiwal	89	30 45N	73	8 E
Montgomery, U.K.	26	52 34N	3	9W
Montgomery, U.S.A.	169	32 20N	86	20W
Montluçon	37	46 22N	2	36 E
Montmagny	148	46 58N	70	34W
Montmorency	148	46 53N	71	11W
Montpelier, Idaho, U.S.A.	163	42 15N	111	20W
Montpelier, Vt., U.S.A.	151	44 15N	72	38W
Montpellier	37	43 37N	3	52 E
Montréal	151	45 31N	73	34W
Montrose, U.K.	33	56 43N	2	28W
Montrose, U.S.A.	163	38 30N	107	52W
Montserrat	180	16 40N	62	10W
Monywa	93	22 7N	95	11 E
Monze, C.	88	24 47N	66	37 E
Mo'oka	107	36 26N	140	1 E
Moonta	119	34 6S	137	32 E
Moora	120	30 37S	115	58 E
Moorfoot Hills	31	55 44N	3	8W
Moorhead	156	46 51N	96	44W
Mooroopna	117	36 25S	145	22 E
Moose Jaw	152	50 24N	105	30W
Moosehead L.	148	45 34N	69	40W
Moosomin	152	50 9N	101	40W
Moosonee	140	51 17N	80	39W
Mopti	130	14 30N	4	0W
Moradabad	89	28 50N	78	50 E

Name					
Moranbah	121	22	1S	148	6 E
Moratuwa	90	6	45N	79	55 E
Morava ~►	59	48	10N	16	59 E
Moravian Hts. = Ceskomoravská Vrchovina	59	49	30N	15	40 E
Morawa	120	29	13S	116	0 E
Morawhanna	185	8	30N	59	40W
Moray Firth	33	57	50N	3	30W
Morden	153	49	15N	98	10W
Mordovian A.S.S.R.□	68	54	20N	44	30 E
Møre og Romsdal fylke □	65	62	30N	8	0 E
Morecambe	28	54	5N	2	52W
Morecambe B.	28	54	7N	3	0W
Moree	116	29	28S	149	54 E
Morehead City	165	34	46N	76	44W
Morelia	176	19	42N	101	7W
Morelos □	177	18	45N	99	0W
Morena, Sierra	50	38	20N	4	0W
Moresby I.	154	52	30N	131	40W
Morgan City	168	29	40N	91	15W
Morganton	165	35	46N	81	48W
Morgantown	164	39	39N	79	58W
Moriguchi	106	34	44N	135	34 E
Morlaix	36	48	36N	3	52W
Mornington	117	38	15S	145	5 E
Moro G.	112	6	30N	123	0 E
Morocco ■	126	32	0N	5	50W
Moroleón	177	20	8N	101	12W
Morón	178	22	8N	78	39W
Morotai	113	2	10N	128	30 E
Morrilton	168	35	10N	92	45W
Morrinhos	188	17	45S	49	10W
Morris	153	49	25N	97	22W
Morristown	165	36	18N	83	20W
Mortes, R. das ~►	188	11	45S	50	44W
Mortlake	119	38	5S	142	50 E
Mőruyá	117	35	58S	150	3 E
Morvern	30	56	38N	5	44W
Morwell	117	38	10S	146	22 E
Moscos Is.	94	14	0N	97	30 E
Moscow = Moskva	68	55	45N	37	35 E
Moscow	171	46	45N	116	59W
Mosel ~►	42	50	22N	7	36 E
Moselle = Mosel ~►	42	50	22N	7	36 E
Mosgiel	123	45	53S	170	21 E
Mosjøen	65	65	51N	13	12 E
Moskva	68	55	45N	37	35 E
Mosquera	184	2	35N	78	24W
Mosquitos, Golfo de los	179	9	15N	81	10W
Moss Vale	117	34	32S	150	25 E
Mosselbaai	136	34	11S	22	8 E
Mossman	121	16	21S	145	15 E
Mossoró	189	5	10S	37	15W
Mostaganem	127	35	54N	0	5 E
Mostar	52	43	22N	17	50 E
Mosul = Al Mawşil	81	36	15N	43	5 E
Motala	60	58	32N	16	1 E
Motherwell	31	55	48N	4	0W
Motihari	92	26	30N	84	55 E
Motueka	123	41	7S	173	1 E
Motul	177	21	6N	89	17W
Moúdhros	55	39	50N	25	18 E
Moule	180	16	20N	61	22W
Moulins	37	46	35N	3	19 E
Moultrie	170	31	11N	83	47W
Moundsville	164	39	53N	80	43W
Mount Airy	165	36	31N	80	37W
Mount Barker, S. Austral., Australia	119	35	5S	138	52 E
Mount Barker, W. Austral., Australia	120	34	38S	117	40 E
Mount Carmel	167	38	20N	87	48W
Mount Forest	151	43	59N	80	43W
Mount Gambier	119	37	50S	140	46 E
Mount Isa	115	20	42S	139	26 E
Mount Lofty Ra.	119	34	35S	139	5 E
Mount Magnet	120	28	2S	117	47 E
Mount Maunganui	122	37	40S	176	14 E
Mount Morgan	121	23	40S	150	25 E
Mount Pearl	149	47	31N	52	47W
Mount Pleasant, Mich., U.S.A.	167	43	35N	84	47W
Mount Pleasant, Tex., U.S.A.	168	33	5N	95	0W
Mount Sterling	165	38	0N	84	0W
Mount Vernon, Ill., U.S.A.	166	38	17N	88	57W
Mount Vernon, N.Y., U.S.A.	164	40	57N	73	49W
Mount Vernon, Wash., U.S.A.	171	48	25N	122	20W
Mount Whaleback	114	23	18S	119	44 E
Mountain City	172	41	54N	116	0W
Mountain View	172	37	26N	122	5W
Moura, Australia	121	24	35S	149	58 E
Moura, Brazil	185	1	32S	61	38W
Mourne ~►	34	54	45N	7	39W
Mourne Mts.	34	54	10N	6	0W
Moyale	133	3	30N	39	0 E
Mozambique ■	137	19	0S	35	0 E
Mozambique Chan.	137	20	0S	39	0 E
Mu Us Shamo	98	39	0N	109	0 E
Muaná	188	1	25S	49	15W
Muang Chiang Rai	94	19	52N	99	50 E
Muck	32	56	50N	6	15W
Mucuri	189	18	0S	39	36W
Mudanjiang	98	44	38N	129	30 E
Mudgee	117	32	32S	149	31 E
Muğla	80	37	15N	28	22 E
Mukden = Shenyang	98	41	50N	123	25 E
Mukhtuya = Lensk	74	60	48N	114	55 E
Mukinbudin	120	30	55S	118	5 E
Muktsar	89	30	30N	74	30 E
Mulchén	190	37	45S	72	20W
Mulgrave	149	45	38N	61	31W
Mulhacén	50	37	4N	3	20W
Mülheim	42	51	26N	6	53 E
Mulhouse	37	47	40N	7	20 E
Mull	30	56	27N	6	0W
Muller, Pegunungan	111	0	30N	113	30 E
Mullet Pen.	34	54	10N	10	2W
Mullewa	120	28	29S	115	30 E
Mullingar	34	53	31N	7	20W
Mullumbimby	116	28	30S	153	30 E
Multan	89	30	15N	71	36 E
Muna	113	5	0S	122	30 E
München	43	48	8N	11	33 E
Munchen-Gladbach = Mönchengladbach	42	51	12N	6	23 E
Muncie	167	40	10N	85	20W
Mundo Novo	189	11	50S	40	29W
Mungana	121	17	8S	144	27 E
Munger	92	25	23N	86	30 E
Munich = München	43	48	8N	11	33 E
Munising	150	46	25N	86	39W
Munku-Sardyk	74	51	45N	100	20 E
Münster	42	51	58N	7	37 E
Munster □	35	52	20N	8	40W
Muqdisho	133	2	2N	45	25 E
Murallón, Cuerro	192	49	48S	73	30W
Murchison ~►	120	27	45S	114	0 E
Murchison Falls = Kabarega Falls	132	2	15N	31	30 E
Murcia	51	38	20N	1	10W
Murcia □	51	37	50N	1	30W
Mureş ~►	56	46	15N	20	13 E
Mureşul = Mureş ~►	56	46	15N	20	13 E
Murfreesboro	169	35	50N	86	21W
Murgon	116	26	15S	151	54 E
Müritz See	43	53	25N	12	40 E
Murmansk	69	68	57N	33	10 E
Muroran	103	42	25N	141	0 E
Muroto	109	33	18N	134	9 E
Muroto-Misaki	109	33	15N	134	10 E
Murphysboro	166	37	50N	89	20W
Murray	169	36	40N	88	20W
Murray ~►	119	35	20S	139	22 E
Murray Bridge	119	35	6S	139	14 E
Murrumbidgee ~►	117	34	43S	143	12 E
Murrurundi	116	31	42S	150	51 E
Murtoa	119	36	35S	142	28 E
Murupara	122	38	28S	176	42 E
Murwillumbah	116	28	18S	153	27 E
Muş	81	38	45N	41	30 E
Musashino	107	35	42N	139	34 E
Muscat = Masqat	83	23	37N	58	36 E
Muscat & Oman = Oman ■	83	23	0N	58	0 E

Name	Map	Lat			Long		
Muscatine	166	41	25N	91	5W
Musgrave Ras.	114	26	0S	132	0 E
Musi →	111	2	20S	104	56 E
Muskegon	167	43	15N	86	17W
Muskegon →	167	43	25N	86	0W
Muskegon Hts.	167	43	12N	86	17W
Muskogee	168	35	50N	95	25W
Musselburgh	31	55	57N	3	3W
Muswellbrook	116	32	16S	150	56 E
Mutare	137	18	58S	32	38 E
Mutsu	103	41	5N	140	55 E
Mutsu-Wan	103	41	5N	140	55 E
Muzaffargarh	89	30	5N	71	14 E
Muzaffarnagar	89	29	26N	77	40 E
Muzaffarpur	92	26	7N	85	23 E
Mwanza	135	2	30S	32	58 E
Mweru, L.	135	9	0S	28	40 E
My Tho	95	10	29N	106	23 E
Myanaung	93	18	18N	95	22 E
Myeik Kyunzu	94	11	30N	97	30 E
Myingyan	93	21	30N	95	20 E
Myitkyina	93	25	24N	97	26 E
Mýrdalsjökull	64	63	40N	19	6W
Myrtle Point	171	43	0N	124	4W
Mysore	90	12	17N	76	41 E
Mysore □ = Karnataka □	90	13	15N	77	0 E
Naaldwijk	40	51	59N	4	13 E
Nabari	106	34	37N	136	5 E
Nablus = Nābulus	80	32	14N	35	15 E
Nābulus	80	32	14N	35	15 E
Nacogdoches	168	31	33N	94	39W
Nacozari	174	30	24N	109	39W
Nadiad	91	22	41N	72	56 E
Nadym	69	65	35N	72	42 E
Nagahama	106	35	23N	136	16 E
Nagaland □	93	26	0N	94	30 E
Nagano	107	36	40N	138	10 E
Nagaoka	105	37	27N	138	51 E
Nagappattinam	90	10	46N	79	51 E
Nagasaki	108	32	47N	129	50 E
Nagato	108	34	19N	131	5 E
Nagercoil	90	8	12N	77	26 E
Nagornyy	75	55	58N	124	57 E
Nagoya	106	35	10N	136	50 E
Nagpur	91	21	8N	79	10 E
Nahanni Butte	144	61	2N	123	31W
Nahāvand	84	34	10N	48	22 E
Naicam	152	52	30N	104	30W
Nain	147	56	34N	61	40W
Nainpur	91	22	30N	80	10 E
Nairn	33	57	35N	3	54W
Nairobi	132	1	17S	36	48 E
Naivasha	132	0	40S	36	30 E
Najafābād	85	32	40N	51	15 E
Najibabad	89	29	40N	78	20 E
Naka →	107	36	20N	140	36 E
Naka-no-Shima	104	29	51N	129	46 E
Nakama	108	33	56N	130	43 E
Nakamura	109	33	0N	133	0 E
Nakano	107	36	45N	138	22 E
Nakanojō	107	36	35N	138	51 E
Nakatsu	108	33	34N	131	15 E
Nakatsugawa	106	35	29N	137	30 E
Nakhichevan A.S.S.R. □	70	39	14N	45	30 E
Nakhodka	75	42	53N	132	54 E
Nakhon Phanom	95	17	23N	104	43 E
Nakhon Ratchasima	95	14	59N	102	12 E
Nakhon Sawan	94	15	35N	100	10 E
Nakhon Si Thammarat	96	8	29N	100	0 E
Nakina	140	50	10N	86	40W
Nakskov	61	54	50N	11	8 E
Nakuru	132	0	15S	36	4 E
Nalchik	70	43	30N	43	33 E
Nalgonda	91	17	6N	79	15 E
Nam Co	101	30	30N	90	45 E
Nam Dinh	95	20	25N	106	5 E
Nam-Phan	95	10	30N	106	0 E
Nam Tha	95	20	58N	101	30 E
Nam Tok	94	14	21N	99	4 E
Namaland	136	24	30S	17	0 E
Namangan	71	41	0N	71	40 E
Nambour	116	26	32S	152	58 E
Nambucca Heads	116	30	37S	153	0 E
Namerikawa	106	36	46N	137	20 E
Namib Desert = Namib-Woestyn	124	22	30S	15	0 E
Namib-Woestyn	124	22	30S	15	0 E
Namibe	134	15	7S	12	11 E
Namibia ■	136	22	0S	18	9 E
Nampa	171	43	34N	116	34W
Namsos	65	64	29N	11	30 E
Namur	42	50	27N	4	52 E
Nanaimo	154	49	10N	124	0W
Nanango	116	26	40S	152	0 E
Nanao	105	37	0N	137	0 E
Nanchang	99	28	42N	115	55 E
Nanching = Nanjing	99	32	2N	118	47 E
Nanching	99	32	3N	118	47 E
Nancy	37	48	42N	6	12 E
Nanda Devi	101	30	23N	79	59 E
Nandan	109	34	10N	134	42 E
Nanded	91	19	10N	77	20 E
Nandurbar	91	21	20N	74	15 E
Nanga Parbat	89	35	10N	74	35 E
Nangarhár □	87	34	20N	70	0 E
Nanjing	99	32	2N	118	47 E
Nanking = Nanching	99	32	3N	118	47 E
Nanking = Nanjing	99	32	2N	118	47 E
Nankoku	109	33	39N	133	44 E
Nanning	99	22	48N	108	20 E
Nanping	99	26	38N	118	10 E
Nantes	36	47	12N	1	33W
Nanticoke	164	41	12N	76	1W
Nanton	155	50	21N	113	46W
Nanuque	189	17	50S	40	21W
Napa	172	38	18N	122	17W
Napier	122	39	30S	176	56 E
Naples = Nápoli	49	40	50N	14	17 E
Napo →	186	3	20S	72	40W
Nápoli	49	40	50N	14	17 E
Nara, Japan	106	34	40N	135	49 E
Nara, Mali	130	15	10N	7	20W
Naracoorte	119	36	58S	140	45 E
Narasapur	92	16	26N	81	40 E
Narayanganj	92	23	40N	90	33 E
Narayanpet	91	16	45N	77	30 E
Narbonne	37	43	11N	3	0 E
Narita	107	35	47N	140	19 E
Narmada →	91	21	38N	72	36 E
Narooma	117	36	14S	150	4 E
Narrabri	116	30	19S	149	46 E
Narrandera	117	34	42S	146	31 E
Narrogin	120	32	58S	117	14 E
Narromine	116	32	12S	148	12 E
Naruto	109	34	11N	134	37 E
Narvik	64	68	28N	17	26 E
Narym	71	59	0N	81	30 E
Naser, Buheirat en	128	23	0N	32	30 E
Nashua	164	42	50N	71	25W
Nashville	169	36	12N	86	46W
Nasik	91	19	58N	73	50 E
Nasirabad	91	26	15N	74	45 E
Nassau	178	25	0N	77	20W
Nasser, L. = Naser, Buheirat en	128	23	0N	32	30 E
Nässjö	60	57	39N	14	42 E
Natal	189	5	47S	35	13W
Natal □	137	28	30S	30	30 E
Natashquan	149	50	14N	61	46W
Natchez	168	31	35N	91	25W
Natchitoches	168	31	47N	93	4W
Nathalia	117	36	1S	145	13 E
National City	173	32	39N	117	7W
Natuna Besar, Kepulauan	111	4	0N	108	15 E
Natuna Selatan, Kepulauan	111	2	45N	109	0 E
Nauru ■	122	1	0S	166	0 E
Nauta	186	4	31S	73	35W
Nautanwa	92	27	20N	83	25 E
Nautla	177	20	20N	96	50W

Navarra □	**51**	42 40N	1	40W
Navojoa	**174**	27 0N	109	30W
Navsari	**91**	20 57N	72	59 E
Nawabshah	**88**	26 15N	68	25 E
Nawalgarh	**89**	27 50N	75	15 E
Náxos	**55**	37 8N	25	25 E
Nãy Band	**87**	27 20N	52	40 E
Nayakhan	**73**	61 56N	159	0 E
Nayarit □	**175**	22 0N	105	0W
Ndélé	**129**	8 25N	20	36 E
Ndjamena	**131**	12 10N	14	59 E
Ndola	**135**	13 0S	28	34 E
Neagh, Lough	**34**	54 35N	6	25W
Near Is.	**142**	53 0N	172	0 E
Neath	**27**	51 39N	3	49W
Nebraska □	**163**	41 30N	100	0W
Nebraska City	**166**	40 40N	95	52W
Nebrodi Mts.	**49**	37 55N	14	45 E
Neches →	**168**	29 55N	93	52W
Neckar →	**42**	49 31N	8	26 E
Necochea	**190**	38 30S	58	50W
Needles, The	**24**	50 39N	1	35W
Neenah	**167**	44 10N	88	30W
Neepawa	**153**	50 15N	99	30W
Negapatam = Nagappattinam	**90**	10 46N	79	51 E
Negeri Sembilan □	**96**	2 45N	102	10 E
Negotin	**53**	44 16N	22	37 E
Negra, Pta.	**186**	6 6S	81	10W
Negro →, Argentina	**190**	41 2S	62	47W
Negro →, Brazil	**185**	3 0S	60	0W
Negros	**112**	9 30N	122	40 E
Nehbandãn	**85**	31 35N	60	5 E
Nei Monggol Zizhiqu □	**98**	42 0N	112	0 E
Neijiang	**99**	29 35N	104	55 E
Neiva	**184**	2 56N	75	18W
Nellore	**90**	14 27N	79	59 E
Nelson, Canada	**155**	49 30N	117	20W
Nelson, N.Z.	**123**	41 18S	173	16 E
Nelson, U.K.	**28**	53 50N	2	14W
Nelson →	**153**	54 33N	98	2W
Néma	**126**	16 40N	7	15W
Neman →	**68**	55 25N	21	10 E
Nemours	**39**	48 16N	2	40 E
Nemunas = Neman →	**68**	55 25N	21	10 E
Nemuro	**103**	43 20N	145	35 E
Nemuro-Kaikyõ	**103**	43 30N	145	30 E
Nenagh	**35**	52 52N	8	11W
Nenana	**142**	64 30N	149	20W
Nene →	**29**	52 38N	0	13 E
Neosho	**168**	36 56N	94	28W
Neosho →	**168**	35 59N	95	10W
Nepal ■	**92**	28 0N	84	30 E
Nephi	**162**	39 43N	111	52W
Ness, Loch	**33**	57 15N	4	30W
Netanya	**80**	32 20N	34	51 E
Netherlands ■	**41**	52 0N	5	30 E
Netherlands Antilles ■	**181**	12 15N	69	0W
Netherlands Guiana = Surinam ■	**185**	4 0N	56	0W
Nettilling L.	**146**	66 30N	71	0W
Netzahualcoyotl, Presa	**177**	17 10N	93	30W
Neuchâtel	**44**	47 0N	6	55 E
Neuchâtel, Lac de	**44**	46 53N	6	50 E
Neuquén	**190**	38 55S	68	0 E
Neuse →	**165**	35 5N	76	30W
Neusiedler See	**45**	47 50N	16	47 E
Nevada	**166**	37 51N	94	22W
Nevada □	**172**	39 20N	117	0W
Nevada, Sierra, Spain	**50**	37 3N	3	15W
Nevada, Sierra, U.S.A.	**172**	39 0N	120	30W
Nevada City	**172**	39 20N	121	0W
Nevada de Sta. Marta, Sa.	**184**	10 55N	73	50W
Nevers	**37**	47 0N	3	9 E
New Albany	**167**	38 20N	85	50W
New Amsterdam	**185**	6 15N	57	36W
New Bedford	**164**	41 40N	70	52W
New Bern	**165**	35 8N	77	3W
New Braunfels	**161**	29 43N	98	9W
New Brighton	**123**	43 29S	172	43 E
New Britain, Papua N. G.	**115**	5 50S	150	20 E
New Britain, U.S.A.	**164**	41 41N	72	47W
New Brunswick	**164**	40 30N	74	28W
New Brunswick □	**148**	46 50N	66	30W
New Caledonia = Nouvelle Calédonie	**122**	21 0S	165	0 E
New Castile = Castilla La Nueva	**50**	39 45N	3	20W
New Castle, Ind., U.S.A.	**164**	39 55N	85	23W
New Castle, Pa., U.S.A.	**164**	41 0N	80	20W
New England Ra.	**116**	30 20S	151	45 E
New Forest	**24**	50 53N	1	40W
New Glasgow	**149**	45 35N	62	36W
New Hampshire □	**164**	43 40N	71	40W
New Haven	**164**	41 20N	72	54W
New Hebrides = Vanuatu ■	**122**	15 0S	168	0 E
New Iberia	**168**	30 2N	91	54W
New Ireland	**115**	3 20S	151	50 E
New Jersey □	**164**	40 30N	74	10W
New Kensington	**164**	40 36N	79	43W
New London	**164**	41 23N	72	8W
New Mexico □	**161**	34 30N	106	0W
New Norfolk	**119**	42 46S	147	2 E
New Orleans	**169**	30 0N	90	5W
New Philadelphia	**164**	40 29N	81	25W
New Plymouth	**122**	39 4S	174	5 E
New Providence	**178**	25 25N	78	35W
New Radnor	**26**	52 15N	3	10W
New Siberian Is. = Novosibirskiye Ostrova	**72**	75 0N	142	0 E
New South Wales □	**116**	33 0S	146	0 E
New Ulm	**166**	44 15N	94	30W
New Waterford	**149**	46 13N	60	4W
New Westminster	**154**	49 13N	122	55W
New York □	**164**	42 40N	76	0W
New York City	**164**	40 45N	74	0W
New Zealand ■	**122**	40 0S	176	0 E
Newark, N.J., U.S.A.	**164**	40 41N	74	12W
Newark, N.Y., U.S.A.	**164**	43 2N	77	10W
Newark, Ohio, U.S.A.	**167**	40 5N	82	24W
Newark-on-Trent	**29**	53 6N	0	48W
Newberry, Mich., U.S.A.	**150**	46 20N	85	32W
Newberry, S.C., U.S.A.	**165**	34 17N	81	37W
Newburgh	**164**	41 30N	74	1W
Newburyport	**164**	42 48N	70	50W
Newcastle, Australia	**117**	33 0S	151	46 E
Newcastle, Canada	**148**	47 1N	65	38W
Newcastle, U.K.	**34**	54 13N	5	54W
Newcastle Emlyn	**26**	52 2N	4	29W
Newcastle-under-Lyme	**28**	53 2N	2	15W
Newcastle-upon-Tyne	**28**	54 59N	1	37W
Newfoundland □	**149**	53 0N	58	0W
Newhaven	**25**	50 47N	0	4 E
Newmarket	**25**	52 15N	0	23 E
Newnan	**170**	33 22N	84	48W
Newport, Gwent, U.K.	**27**	51 35N	3	0W
Newport, I. of W., U.K.	**25**	50 42N	1	18W
Newport, Ark., U.S.A.	**168**	35 38N	91	15W
Newport, Ky., U.S.A.	**167**	39 5N	84	23W
Newport, Oreg., U.S.A.	**171**	44 41N	124	2W
Newport, R.I., U.S.A.	**164**	41 13N	71	19W
Newport, Vt., U.S.A.	**148**	44 57N	72	17W
Newport Beach	**173**	33 40N	117	58W
Newport News	**165**	37 2N	76	30W
Newquay	**27**	50 24N	5	6W
Newry	**34**	54 10N	6	20W
Newton, Iowa, U.S.A.	**166**	41 40N	93	3W
Newton, Mass., U.S.A.	**164**	42 21N	71	10W
Newton Abbot	**27**	50 32N	3	37W
Newton Stewart	**31**	54 57N	4	30W
Newtonmore	**33**	57 4N	4	7W
Newtown	**26**	52 31N	3	19W
Newtownards	**34**	54 37N	5	40W
Ngaoundéré	**131**	7 15N	13	35 E
Ngoring Hu	**101**	34 55N	97	5 E
Nguru	**131**	12 56N	10	29 E
Nha Trang	**95**	12 16N	109	10 E
Nhill	**119**	36 18S	141	40 E
Niagara Falls, Canada	**151**	43 7N	79	5W
Niagara Falls, U.S.A.	**164**	43 5N	79	0W

Niamey . . . . **131** 13 27N 2 6 E
Nias . . . . **111** 1 0N 97 30 E
Nicaragua ■ **179** 11 40N 85 30W
Nicaragua, Lago de **179** 12 0N 85 30W
Nice . . . . **37** 43 42N 7 14 E
Nichinan . . . . **108** 31 38N 131 23 E
Nicobar Is. . . . . **8** 9 0N 93 0 E
Nicosia . . . . **80** 35 10N 33 25 E
Nicoya, Pen. de **179** 9 45N 85 40W
Nidd → **28** 54 1N 1 32W
Niederösterreich □ . . . . **45** 48 25N 15 40 E
Niedersachsen □ . . . . **42** 52 45N 9 0 E
Nieuw Nickerie **185** 6 0N 56 59W
Niger ■ . . . . **131** 13 30N 10 0 E
Niger → . . . . **131** 5 33N 6 33 E
Nigeria ■ . . . . **131** 8 30N 8 0 E
Nii-Jima . . . . **107** 34 20N 139 15 E
Niigata . . . . **103** 37 58N 139 0 E
Niihama . . . . **109** 33 55N 133 16 E
Niimi . . . . **109** 34 59N 133 28 E
Nijkerk . . . . **41** 52 13N 5 30 E
Nijmegen . . . . **41** 51 50N 5 52 E
Nikki . . . . **131** 9 58N 3 12 E
Nikkō . . . . **107** 36 45N 139 35 E
Nikolayev . . . . **68** 46 58N 32 0 E
Nikolayevsk-na-Amur . . . . . . **75** 53 8N 140 44 E
Nikolskoye . . . . **73** 55 12N 166 0 E
Nikšić . . . . **52** 42 50N 18 57 E
Nīl, Nahr en → . . . . **128** 30 10N 31 6 E
Nīl el Abyad → . . . . **129** 15 38N 32 31 E
Nīl el Azraq → . . . . **129** 15 38N 32 31 E
Nile = Nīl, Nahr en → . . . . . **128** 30 10N 31 6 E
Niles **164** 41 8N 80 40W
Nîmes . . . . **37** 43 50N 4 23 E
Nimule . . . . **129** 3 32N 32 3 E
Nīnawá . . . . **81** 36 25N 43 10 E
Nineveh = Nīnawá . . . . **81** 36 25N 43 10 E
Ningbo . . . . **99** 29 51N 121 28 E
Ningde . . . . **99** 26 38N 119 23 E
Ningpo = Ningbo . . . . **99** 29 51N 121 28 E
Ningsia Hui A.R. = Ningxia
Huizu Zizhiqu □ . . . . **98** 38 0N 106 0 E
Ningxia Huizu Zizhiqu □ . . . . **98** 38 0N 106 0 E
Niobrara → **163** 42 45N 98 0W
Nioro du Sahel **130** 15 15N 9 30W
Niort **36** 46 19N 0 29W
Nipawin **152** 53 20N 104 0W
Nipigon **150** 49 0N 88 17W
Nipigon, L. **150** 49 50N 88 30W
Niš . . . . **53** 43 19N 21 58 E
Nişāb . . . . **83** 14 25N 46 29 E
Nishinomiya . . . . **106** 34 45N 135 20 E
Nishio . . . . **106** 34 52N 137 3 E
Nishiwaki . . . . **109** 34 59N 134 58 E
Niterói **188** 22 52S 43 0W
Nith → **31** 55 20N 3 5W
Nitra . . . . **59** 48 19N 18 4 E
Nivernais . . . . **37** 47 0N 3 40 E
Nizamabad . . . . **91** 18 45N 78 7 E
Nizhne Kolymsk . . . . **73** 68 34N 160 55 E
Nizhneudinsk . . . . **74** 54 54N 99 3 E
Nizhnevartovsk . . . . **69** 60 56N 76 38 E
Nizhniy Novgorod = Gorkiy . . **68** 56 20N 44 0 E
Nizhniy Tagil . . . . **69** 57 55N 59 57 E
Nizhnyaya Tunguska → . . . . **74** 64 20N 93 0 E
Nízké Tatry . . . . **59** 48 55N 20 0 E
Nkongsamba . . . . **131** 4 55N 9 55 E
Noatak **142** 67 32N 162 59W
Nobeoka . . . . **108** 32 36N 131 41 E
Noda . . . . **107** 35 56N 139 52 E
Nogales **174** 31 20N 110 56W
Nōgata . . . . **108** 33 48N 130 44 E
Nogent-le-Rotrou . . . . **39** 48 20N 0 50 E
Noi → . . . . **94** 14 50N 100 15 E
Noirmoutier, Î. de **36** 46 58N 2 10W
Nojima-Zaki . . . . **107** 34 54N 139 53 E
Nok Kundi . . . . **88** 28 50N 62 45 E
Nome **142** 64 30N 165 24W
Nong Khae . . . . **95** 14 29N 100 53 E
Nong Khai . . . . **95** 17 50N 102 46 E

Nonoava **174** 27 28N 106 44W
Noord Brabant □ . . . . **40** 51 40N 5 0 E
Noord Holland □ . . . . **40** 52 30N 4 45 E
Noordbeveland . . . . **40** 51 35N 3 50 E
Noordoostpolder . . . . **41** 52 45N 5 45 E
Noordwijk aan Zee . . . . **40** 52 14N 4 26 E
Nootka I. **154** 49 32N 126 42W
Nord-Trøndelag fylke □ . . . . . **65** 64 20N 12 0 E
Nordaustlandet . . . . **13** 79 14N 23 0 E
Nordegg **155** 52 29N 116 5W
Nordkapp . . . . **67** 71 10N 25 44 E
Nordkinn . . . . **67** 71 8N 27 40 E
Nordland fylke □ . . . . **65** 65 40N 13 0 E
Nordrhein-Westfalen □ . . . . . . **42** 51 45N 7 30 E
Nordvik . . . . **72** 74 2N 111 32 E
Nore → **35** 52 40N 7 20W
Norfolk **165** 36 40N 76 15W
Norfolk □ . . . . **29** 52 39N 1 0 E
Norfolk I. . . . . **122** 28 58S 168 3 E
Norilsk . . . . **72** 69 20N 88 6 E
Norman **168** 35 12N 97 30W
Norman Wells **144** 65 17N 126 51W
Normandie . . . . **39** 48 45N 0 10 E
Normandin **151** 48 49N 72 31W
Normandy = Normandie . . . . . **39** 48 45N 0 10 E
Normanton . . . . **115** 17 40S 141 10 E
Norquinco **192** 41 51S 70 55W
Norristown **164** 40 9N 75 21W
Norrköping . . . . **60** 58 37N 16 11 E
Norrland □ . . . . **66** 66 50N 18 0 E
Norseman . . . . **114** 32 8S 121 43 E
Norsk . . . . **75** 52 30N 130 0 E
North Andaman I. . . . . **94** 13 15N 92 40 E
North Battleford **152** 52 50N 108 17W
North Bay **151** 46 20N 79 30W
North Bend **171** 43 28N 124 14W
North Berwick **31** 56 4N 2 44W
North C. . . . . **122** 34 23S 173 4 E
North Carolina □ **165** 35 30N 80 0W
North Channel, Br. Is. **30** 55 0N 5 30W
North Channel, Canada **150** 46 0N 83 0W
North Dakota □ **163** 47 30N 100 0W
North Downs . . . . **25** 51 17N 0 30 E
North European Plain . . . . **17** 55 0N 20 0 E
North I. . . . . **122** 38 0S 175 0 E
North Korea ■ . . . . **98** 40 0N 127 0 E
North Minch **32** 58 5N 5 55W
North Ossetian A.S.S.R. □ . . . **70** 43 30N 44 30 E
North Platte **163** 41 10N 100 50W
North Platte → **163** 41 15N 100 45W
North Pole . . . . **12** 90 0N 0 0 E
North Ronaldsay **33** 59 20N 2 30W
North Saskatchewan → **143** 53 15N 105 5W
North Sea . . . . **16** 56 0N 4 0 E
North Sentinel I. . . . . **94** 11 35N 92 15 E
North Sporades = Voríai
Sporádhes . . . . **55** 39 15N 23 30 E
North Sydney **149** 46 12N 60 15W
North Tonawanda **164** 43 5N 78 50W
North Uist **32** 57 40N 7 15W
North Vancouver **154** 49 25N 123 3W
North Walsham . . . . **29** 52 49N 1 22 E
North West Frontier □ . . . . **89** 34 0N 71 0 E
North West Highlands **32** 57 35N 5 2W
North West River **147** 53 30N 60 10W
North West Territories □ **145** 67 0N 110 0W
North York Moors **29** 54 25N 0 50W
North Yorkshire □ **28** 54 15N 1 25W
Northallerton **28** 54 20N 1 26W
Northam . . . . **120** 31 35S 116 42 E
Northam, Australia . . . . . . **120** 28 27S 114 33 E
Northampton, U.K. **25** 52 14N 0 54W
Northampton, U.S.A. **164** 42 22N 72 31W
Northampton □ **25** 52 16N 0 55W
Northcliffe . . . . **120** 34 39S 116 7 E
Northern Circars . . . . **92** 17 30N 82 30 E
Northern Ireland □ **34** 54 45N 7 0W
Northern Territory □ . . . . **114** 16 0S 133 0 E
Northfield **166** 44 30N 93 10W
Northland □ . . . . **122** 35 30S 173 30 E

Northumberland □	28	55 12N	2	0W
Northumberland Is.	121	21 30S	149	50 E
Northumberland Str.	148	46 20N	64	0W
Northwich	28	53 16N	2	30W
Norton Sd.	142	64 0N	164	0W
Norwalk	164	41 9N	73	25W
Norway ■	18	63 0N	11	0 E
Norwegian Sea	16	66 0N	1	0 E
Norwich	29	52 38N	1	17 E
Nos Kaliakra	53	43 21N	28	30 E
Noshiro	103	40 12N	140	0 E
Noss Hd.	33	58 29N	3	4W
Nossob —►	136	26 55S	20	37 E
Noteć ~►	58	52 44N	15	26 E
Notre Dame de Koartac = Koartac	146	60 55N	69	40W
Nottaway ~►	140	51 22N	78	55W
Nottingham	29	52 57N	1	10W
Nottingham □	29	53 10N	1	0W
Nouâdhibou	126	20 54N	17	0W
Nouâdhibou, Ras	126	20 50N	17	0W
Nouakchott	126	18 9N	15	58W
Noumea	122	22 17S	166	30 E
Nouveau Comptoir	140	53 0N	78	49W
Nouvelle Calédonie	122	21 0S	165	0 E
Nova Friburgo	188	22 16S	42	30W
Nova Granada	188	20 30S	49	20W
Nova Lisboa = Huambo	134	12 42S	15	54 E
Nova Scotia □	149	45 10N	63	0W
Novara	46	45 27N	8	36 E
Novaya Sibir, Ostrov	72	75 10N	150	0 E
Novaya Zemlya	69	75 0N	56	0 E
Novgorod	68	58 30N	31	25 E
Novi Pazar	52	43 12N	20	28 E
Novi Sad	52	45 18N	19	52 E
Novocherkassk	00	47 27N	40	3 E
Novokuznetsk	71	53 45N	87	10 E
Novomoskovsk	68	54 5N	38	15 E
Novorossiysk	68	44 43N	37	46 E
Novosibirsk	71	55 0N	83	5 E
Novosibirskiye Ostrova	72	75 0N	142	0 E
Nowgong	93	26 20N	92	50 E
Nowra	117	34 53S	150	35 E
Nowy Sącz	59	49 40N	20	41 E
Noyon	38	49 34N	3	0 E
Núbïya, Es Sahrâ En	129	21 30N	33	30 E
Nueces —►	161	27 50N	97	30W
Nueltin L.	145	60 30N	99	30W
Nueva Gerona	178	21 53N	82	49W
Nueva Rosita	174	27 57N	101	13W
Nuevitas	178	21 30N	77	20W
Nuevo Laredo	176	27 30N	99	30W
Nuevo Leon □	176	25 40N	100	0W
Nuhaka	122	39 3S	177	45 E
Nukey Bluff, Mt.	118	32 26S	135	29 E
Nukus	70	42 20N	59	7 E
Nulato	142	64 40N	158	10W
Nullarbor Plain	114	30 45S	129	0 E
Numan	131	9 29N	12	3 E
Numazu	107	35 7N	138	51 E
Numurkah	117	36 5S	145	26 E
Nuneaton	25	52 32N	1	29W
Nunivak	142	60 0N	166	0W
Nunspeet	41	52 21N	5	45 E
Nuoro	48	40 20N	9	20 E
Nuremburg = Nürnberg	43	49 26N	11	5 E
Nuriootpa	119	34 27S	139	0 E
Nürnberg	43	49 26N	11	5 E
Nurran, L. = Terewah, L.	116	29 52S	147	35 E
Nutak	147	57 28N	61	59W
Nuweveldberge	136	32 10S	21	45 E
Nuyts Arch.	118	32 35S	133	20 E
Nyaake	130	4 52N	7	37W
Nyainqentanglha Shan	101	30 0N	90	0 E
Nyasa, L. = Malawi, L.	137	12 30S	34	30 E
Nyíregyháza	59	47 58N	21	47 E
Nyngan	116	31 30S	147	8 E
Nysa	58	50 30N	17	22 E
Oahe L.	163	45 30N	100	25W
Oahu	160	21 30N	158	0W
Oak Hill	165	38 0N	81	7W
Oak Park	167	41 55N	87	45W
Oak Ridge	169	36 1N	84	12W
Oakengates	28	52 42N	2	29W
Oakey	116	27 25S	151	43 E
Oakham	29	52 40N	0	43W
Oakland	172	37 50N	122	18W
Oakridge	171	43 47N	122	31W
Oamaru	123	45 5S	170	59 E
Oaxaca	177	17 2N	96	40W
Oaxaca □	177	17 0N	96	30W
Ob —►	69	66 45N	69	30 E
Oba	150	49 4N	84	7W
Obama	106	35 30N	135	45 E
Oban	30	56 25N	5	30W
Obbia	133	5 25N	48	30 E
Oberhausen	42	51 28N	6	50 E
Oberon	117	33 45S	149	52 E
Oberösterreich □	45	48 10N	14	0 E
Obi, Is.	113	1 30S	127	30 E
Obihiro	103	42 56N	143	12 E
Obskaya Guba	69	69 0N	73	0 E
Ocala	170	29 11N	82	5W
Ocampo	174	28 11N	108	23W
Ocaña	184	8 15N	73	20W
Occidental, Cordillera	184	5 0N	76	0W
Ocean City	164	39 18N	74	34W
Oceanside	173	33 13N	117	26W
Ochil Hills	31	56 14N	3	40W
Oconee —►	170	31 58N	82	32W
Oconto	167	44 52N	87	53W
Ocotlán	175	20 21N	102	46W
Oda	109	35 11N	132	30 E
Ódáðahraun	64	65 5N	17	0W
Odate	103	40 16N	140	34 E
Odawara	107	35 20N	139	6 E
Odemiş	80	38 15N	28	0 E
Odense	61	55 22N	10	23 E
Oder —►	58	53 33N	14	38 E
Odessa, U.S.A.	161	31 51N	102	23W
Odessa, U.S.S.R.	68	46 30N	30	45 E
Odra —►	58	53 33N	14	38 E
Odžak	52	45 3N	18	18 E
Offaly □	35	53 15N	7	30W
Offenbach	42	50 6N	8	46 E
Oga-Hantō	103	39 58N	139	47 E
Ogaden	133	7 30N	45	30 E
Ogaki	106	35 21N	136	37 E
Ogbomosho	131	8 1N	4	11 E
Ogden	163	41 13N	112	1W
Ogdensburg	151	44 40N	75	27W
Ohio □	167	40 20N	14	10 E
Ohio —►	167	38 0N	86	0W
Ohrid	52	41 8N	20	52 E
Ohridsko, Jezero	52	41 8N	20	52 E
Oil City	164	41 26N	79	40W
Oise —►	38	49 0N	2	4 E
Oisterwijk	40	51 35N	5	12 E
Oita	108	33 14N	131	36 E
Ojos del Salado, Cerro	190	27 0S	68	40W
Oka —►	68	56 20N	43	59 E
Okawa	108	33 9N	130	21 E
Okaya	107	36 0N	138	10 E
Okayama	109	34 40N	133	54 E
Okazaki	106	34 57N	137	10 E
Okeechobee, L.	170	27 0N	80	50W
Okehampton	27	50 44N	4	1W
Okha	75	53 40N	143	0 E
Okhotsk	75	59 20N	143	10 E
Okhotsk, Sea of	77	55 0N	145	0 E
Okhotsko Kolymskoye	73	63 0N	157	0 E
Oki-no-Shima	109	32 44N	132	33 E
Oki-Shotō	109	36 5N	133	15 E
Okinawa-Jima	99	26 32N	128	0 E
Oklahoma □	161	35 20N	97	30W
Oklahoma City	161	35 25N	97	30W
Okmulgee	168	35 38N	96	0W
Oktabrsk	70	49 28N	57	25 E
Oktyabrskoy Revolyutsii, Os.	72	79 30N	97	0 E

Oktyabrskoye	**69**	62 28N	66	3 E
Okuchi	**108**	32 4N	130	37 E
Okuru	**123**	43 55S	168	55 E
Okushiri-Tō	**103**	42 15N	139	30 E
Olanchito	**179**	15 30N	86	30W
Oland	**61**	56 45N	16	38 E
Olary	**118**	32 18S	140	19 E
Olavarría	**190**	36 55S	60	20W
Old Castile = Castilla La				
Vieja	**50**	41 55N	4	0W
Old Town	**148**	45 0N	68	41W
Oldenburg	**42**	53 10N	8	10 E
Oldenzaal	**41**	52 19N	6	53 E
Oldham	**28**	53 33N	2	8W
Olds	**155**	51 50N	114	10W
Olekma →	**74**	60 22N	120	42 E
Olekminsk	**74**	60 25N	120	30 E
Olenek	**72**	68 28N	112	18 E
Olenek →	**72**	73 0N	120	10 E
Oléron, Île d'	**36**	45 55N	1	15W
Oleśnica	**58**	51 13N	17	22 E
Olifants →	**137**	24 5S	31	20 E
Ólimbos, Óros	**54**	40 6N	22	23 E
Oliveira	**188**	20 39S	44	50W
Oliver	**155**	49 13N	119	37W
Ollagüe	**187**	21 15S	68	10W
Olney	**167**	38 40N	88	0W
Olomouc	**59**	49 38N	17	12 E
Olsztyn	**58**	53 48N	20	29 E
Olt →	**57**	43 50N	24	40 E
Olympia, Greece	**54**	37 39N	21	39 E
Olympia, U.S.A.	**171**	47 0N	122	58W
Olympic Mts.	**171**	47 50N	123	45W
Olympus, Mt. = Ólimbos,				
Óros	**54**	40 6N	22	23 E
Olympus, Mt.	**171**	47 52N	123	40W
Omachi	**107**	36 30N	137	50 E
Omae-Zaki	**107**	34 36N	138	14 E
Omagh	**34**	54 36N	7	20W
Omaha	**166**	41 15N	96	0W
Omak	**171**	48 24N	119	31W
Oman ■	**83**	23 0N	58	0 E
Oman, G. of	**83**	24 30N	58	30 E
Omdurmân	**129**	15 40N	32	28 E
Ome	**107**	35 47N	139	15 E
Omeo	**117**	37 6S	147	36 E
Omihachiman	**106**	35 7N	136	3 E
Omiya	**107**	35 54N	139	38 E
Omo →	**132**	6 25N	36	10 E
Omolon →	**73**	68 42N	158	36 E
Omono-Gawa →	**103**	39 46N	140	3 E
Omsk	**71**	55 0N	73	12 E
Omura	**108**	32 56N	130	0 E
Omuta	**108**	33 0N	130	26 E
Onega	**68**	64 0N	38	10 E
Onega, L. = Onezhskoye				
Ozero	**68**	62 0N	35	30 E
Onehunga	**122**	36 55S	174	48 E
Oneida	**164**	43 5N	75	40W
Onekotan, Ostrov	**75**	49 25N	154	45 E
Onezhskoye Ozero	**68**	62 0N	35	30 E
Ongerup	**120**	33 58S	118	28 E
Ongole	**90**	15 33N	80	2 E
Onguren	**74**	53 38N	107	36 E
Onitsha	**131**	6 6N	6	42 E
Ono, Fukui, Japan	**106**	35 59N	136	29 E
Ono, Hyōgo, Japan	**109**	34 51N	134	56 E
Onoda	**108**	34 2N	131	25 E
Onomichi	**109**	34 25N	133	12 E
Onslow	**114**	21 40S	115	12 E
Onslow B.	**165**	34 20N	77	20W
Ontake-San	**106**	35 53N	137	29 E
Ontario	**173**	34 2N	117	40W
Ontario □	**140**	52 0N	88	10W
Ontario, L.	**151**	43 40N	78	0W
Oodnadatta	**118**	27 33S	135	30 E
Ooldea	**114**	30 27S	131	50 E
Oostende	**42**	51 15N	2	50 E
Oosterhout	**40**	51 39N	4	47 E
Oosterschelde	**40**	51 33N	4	0 E
Opala	**73**	51 58N	156	30 E
Opava	**58**	49 57N	17	58 E
Opelousas	**168**	30 35N	92	7W
Ophir	**142**	63 10N	156	40W
Opole	**58**	50 42N	17	58 E
Oporto = Porto	**50**	41 8N	8	40W
Opp	**169**	31 19N	86	13W
Oppland fylke □	**60**	61 15N	9	40 E
Opua	**122**	35 19S	174	9 E
Oradea	**56**	47 2N	21	58 E
Örœfajökull	**64**	64 2N	16	39W
Orai	**91**	25 58N	79	30 E
Oran, Algeria	**127**	35 45N	0	39W
Oran, Argentina	**190**	23 10S	64	20W
Orange, Australia	**117**	33 15S	149	7 E
Orange, France	**37**	44 8N	4	47 E
Orange, U.S.A.	**168**	30 10N	93	50W
Orange → = Oranje →	**136**	28 41S	16	28 E
Orange, C.	**185**	4 20N	51	30W
Orangeburg	**170**	33 35N	80	53W
Oranje →	**136**	28 41S	16	28 E
Oraşul Stalin = Braşov	**57**	45 38N	25	35 E
Orbost	**117**	37 40S	148	29 E
Orchies	**38**	50 28N	3	14 E
Ordos = Mu Us Shamo	**98**	39 0N	109	0 E
Ordu	**81**	40 55N	37	53 E
Ordzhonikidze	**70**	43 0N	44	35 E
Ore Mts. = Erzgebirge	**43**	50 25N	13	0 E
Örebro	**60**	59 20N	15	18 E
Oregon □	**171**	44 0N	121	0W
Oregon City	**171**	45 21N	122	35W
Orel	**68**	52 57N	36	3 E
Orenburg	**70**	51 45N	55	6 E
Orense	**50**	42 19N	7	55W
Orepuki	**123**	46 19S	167	46 E
Orford Ness	**24**	52 6N	1	31 E
Oriental, Cordillera	**184**	6 0N	73	0W
Orillia	**151**	44 40N	79	24W
Orinoco →	**185**	9 15N	61	30W
Orissa □	**92**	20 0N	84	0 E
Oristano	**48**	39 54N	8	35 E
Oristano, Golfo di	**48**	39 50N	8	22 E
Orizaba	**177**	18 51N	97	6W
Orkney Is.	**33**	59 0N	3	0W
Orland	**172**	39 46N	122	12W
Orlando	**170**	28 30N	81	25W
Orléanais	**39**	48 0N	2	0 E
Orléans	**39**	47 54N	1	52 E
Ormara	**88**	25 16N	64	33 E
Ormskirk	**28**	53 35N	2	53W
Örnsköldsvik	**66**	63 17N	18	40 E
Orocué	**184**	4 48N	71	20W
Oroville	**172**	39 31N	121	30W
Orsha	**68**	54 30N	30	25 E
Orsk	**70**	51 12N	58	34 E
Ortegal, C.	**50**	43 43N	7	52W
Orümïyeh	**81**	37 40N	45	0 E
Orümïyeh, Daryācheh-ye	**81**	37 50N	45	30 E
Oruro	**187**	18 0S	67	9W
Oruzgān □	**87**	33 30N	66	0 E
Oryakhovo	**53**	43 40N	23	57 E
Osage →	**166**	38 35N	91	57W
Osaka	**106**	34 40N	135	30 E
Osceola	**169**	35 40N	90	0W
Ösel = Saaremaa	**68**	58 30N	22	30 E
Osh	**71**	40 37N	72	49 E
Oshawa	**151**	43 50N	78	50W
Oshima	**107**	33 55N	132	14 E
Oshkosh	**167**	44 3N	88	35W
Oshogbo	**131**	7 48N	4	37 E
Osijek	**52**	45 34N	18	41 E
Oskaloosa	**166**	41 18N	92	40W
Oslo	**60**	59 55N	10	45 E
Osmaniye	**80**	37 5N	36	10 E
Osnabrück	**42**	52 16N	8	2 E
Osorno	**190**	40 25S	73	0W
Oss	**41**	51 46N	5	32 E
Ossa, Mt.	**119**	41 52S	146	3 E
Ostend = Oostende	**42**	51 15N	2	50 E
Östergötlands län □	**60**	58 35N	15	45 E
Östersund	**66**	63 10N	14	38 E
Østfold fylke □	**60**	59 25N	11	25 E

Ostfriesische Inseln	**42**	53 45N	7	15 E
Ostia	**46**	41 40N	12	20 E
Ostrava	**59**	49 51N	18	18 E
Ostróda	**58**	53 42N	19	58 E
Ostrofeka	**58**	53 4N	21	32 E
Ostrów Mazowiecka	**58**	52 50N	21	51 E
Ostrów Wielkopolski	**58**	51 36N	17	44 E
Ōsumi-Kaikyō	**104**	30 55N	131	0 E
Ōsumi-Shotō	**104**	30 30N	130	0 E
Oswego	**164**	43 29N	76	30W
Oswestry	**28**	52 52N	3	3W
Ōta	**107**	36 18N	139	22 E
Otago □	**123**	44 44S	169	10 E
Otake	**109**	34 12N	132	13 E
Otaki	**122**	40 45S	175	10 E
Otaru	**103**	43 10N	141	0 E
Otaru-Wan = Ishikari-Wan	**103**	43 25N	141	1 E
Otira Gorge	**123**	42 53S	171	33 E
Otoineppu	**103**	44 44N	142	16 E
Otranto	**49**	40 9N	18	28 E
Otranto, C. d'	**49**	40 7N	18	30 E
Otranto, Str. of	**52**	40 15N	18	40 E
Ōtsu	**106**	35 0N	135	50 E
Ottawa, Canada	**151**	45 27N	75	42W
Ottawa, U.S.A.	**166**	38 40N	95	6W
Ottawa → = Outaouais →	**140**	45 27N	74	8W
Ottawa Is.	**146**	59 35N	80	10W
Otter Rapids, Ont., Canada	**151**	50 11N	81	39W
Otter Rapids, Sask., Canada	**152**	55 38N	104	44W
Ottumwa	**166**	41 0N	92	25W
Otwock	**58**	52 5N	21	20 E
Ouachita →	**168**	31 38N	91	49W
Ouachita Mts.	**168**	34 50N	94	30W
Ouagadougou	**130**	12 25N	1	30W
Ouahran = Oran	**127**	35 45N	0	39W
Ouárgla	**127**	31 59N	5	16 E
Oubangi →	**131**	1 0N	17	50 E
Oudenbosch	**40**	51 35N	4	32 E
Oudtshoorn	**136**	33 35S	22	14 E
Ouessant, Île d'	**36**	48 28N	5	6W
Oujda	**127**	34 41N	1	55W
Oulu	**67**	65 1N	25	29 E
Oulujärvi	**67**	64 25N	27	15 E
Oulujoki →	**67**	65 1N	25	30 E
Ouse →	**29**	54 3N	0	7 E
Outaouais →	**140**	45 27N	74	8W
Outer Hebrides	**32**	57 30N	7	40W
Outlook	**152**	51 30N	107	0W
Outreau	**38**	50 40N	1	36 E
Ouyen	**119**	35 1S	142	22 E
Ovalle	**190**	30 33S	71	18W
Overflakkee	**40**	51 44N	4	10 E
Overijssel □	**41**	52 25N	6	35 E
Oviedo	**50**	43 25N	5	50W
Owaka	**123**	46 27S	169	40 E
Owase	**106**	34 7N	136	12 E
Owatonna	**166**	44 3N	93	10W
Owen Sound	**151**	44 35N	80	55W
Owen Stanley Range	**115**	8 30S	147	0 E
Owensboro	**167**	37 40N	87	5W
Owosso	**167**	43 0N	84	10W
Owyhee →	**171**	43 46N	117	2W
Oxford, U.K.	**25**	51 45N	1	15W
Oxford, U.S.A.	**165**	36 19N	78	36W
Oxford □	**25**	51 45N	1	15W
Oxford L.	**153**	54 51N	95	37W
Oxnard	**173**	34 10N	119	14W
Oyabe	**106**	36 47N	136	56 E
Oyama	**107**	36 18N	139	48 E
Oyana	**108**	32 32N	130	30 E
Oyo	**131**	7 46N	3	56 E
Oyonnax	**37**	46 16N	5	40 E
Ozamis	**112**	8 15N	123	50 E
Ozark	**169**	31 29N	85	39W
Ozark Plateau	**168**	37 20N	91	40W
Ozarks, L. of	**166**	38 10N	92	40W
Ozu, Ehime, Japan	**109**	33 30N	132	33 E
Ozu, Kumamoto, Japan	**108**	32 52N	130	52 E
Paarl	**136**	33 45S	18	56 E
Pabna	**92**	24 1N	89	18 E
Pacaraima, Sierra	**185**	4 0N	62	30W
Pacasmayo	**186**	7 20S	79	35W
Pachuca	**177**	20 10N	98	40W
Padang	**111**	1 0S	100	20 E
Pádova	**47**	45 24N	11	52 E
Padstow	**27**	50 33N	4	57W
Padua = Pádova	**47**	45 24N	11	52 E
Paducah	**169**	37 0N	88	40W
Pag	**52**	44 30N	14	50 E
Pagalu = Annobón	**131**	1 25S	5	36 E
Pagastikós Kólpos	**54**	39 15N	23	0 E
Page	**160**	36 57N	111	27W
Pahala	**160**	19 12N	155	25W
Pahang □	**96**	3 30N	102	45 E
Pahiatua	**122**	40 27S	175	50 E
Paignton	**27**	50 26N	3	33W
Painesville	**167**	41 42N	81	18W
Paint Hills = Nouveau Comptoir	**140**	53 0N	78	49W
Painted Desert	**160**	36 0N	111	30W
Paisley	**31**	55 51N	4	27W
Paita	**186**	5 11S	81	9W
Pak Sane	**95**	18 22N	103	39 E
Pakistan ■	**78**	30 0N	70	0 E
Pakistan, East = Bangladesh ■	**92**	24 0N	90	0 E
Pakokku	**93**	21 20N	95	0 E
Pakse	**95**	15 5N	105	52 E
Pakfïā □	**87**	33 0N	69	15 E
Palanpur	**91**	24 10N	72	25 E
Palatka	**170**	29 40N	81	40W
Palawan	**112**	9 30N	118	30 E
Palembang	**111**	3 0S	104	50 E
Palencia	**50**	42 1N	4	34W
Palermo	**48**	38 8N	13	20 E
Palestine	**168**	31 42N	95	35W
Palghat	**90**	10 46N	76	42 E
Pali	**91**	25 50N	73	20 E
Palizada	**177**	18 15N	92	5W
Palk Bay	**90**	9 30N	79	15 E
Palk Strait	**90**	10 0N	79	45 E
Palm Is.	**121**	18 40S	146	35 E
Palm Springs	**173**	33 51N	116	35W
Palma, La	**179**	8 15N	78	0W
Palma de Mallorca	**51**	39 35N	2	39 E
Palma Soriano	**178**	20 15N	76	0W
Palmas, C.	**130**	4 27N	7	46W
Palmer Land	**14**	73 0S	60	0W
Palmerston North	**122**	40 21S	175	39 E
Palmi	**49**	38 21N	15	51 E
Palmira	**184**	3 32N	76	16W
Palmyra = Tudmur	**80**	34 36N	38	15 E
Palo Alto	**172**	37 25N	122	8W
Pamirs	**71**	37 40N	73	0 E
Pamlico Sd.	**165**	35 20N	76	0W
Pampa	**161**	35 35N	100	58W
Pampas	**190**	35 0S	63	0W
Pamplona	**51**	42 48N	1	38W
Panaca	**173**	37 51N	114	23W
Panaji	**91**	15 25N	73	50 E
Panamá	**179**	9 0N	79	25W
Panama ■	**179**	8 48N	79	55W
Panamá, Golfo de	**179**	8 4N	79	20W
Panama Canal	**175**	9 10N	79	37W
Panama City	**169**	30 10N	85	41W
Panay	**112**	11 10N	122	30 E
Pančevo	**52**	44 52N	20	41 E
Pandharpur	**91**	17 41N	75	20 E
Pangfou = Bengbu	**99**	32 58N	117	20 E
Pangkalpinang	**111**	2 0S	106	0 E
Pangnirtung	**146**	66 8N	65	54W
Panjim = Panaji	**91**	15 25N	73	50 E
Panjinad Barrage	**89**	29 22N	71	15 E
Pantelleria	**48**	36 52N	12	0 E
Pánuco	**177**	22 3N	98	10W
Paoting = Baoding	**98**	38 50N	115	28 E
Paot'ou = Baotou	**98**	40 32N	110	2 E
Papien Chiang = Da →	**95**	21 15N	105	20 E
Papua, Gulf of	**115**	9 0S	144	50 E

Name	Page	Latitude	Longitude
Papua New Guinea ■	115	8 0S	145 0 E
Pará = Belém	188	1 20S	48 30W
Pará □	188	3 20S	52 0W
Paracatu	188	17 10S	46 50W
Paragua, La	185	6 50N	63 20W
Paraguay ■	191	23 0S	57 0W
Paraguay →	191	27 18S	58 38W
Paraíba = João Pessoa	189	7 10S	34 52W
Paraíba □	189	7 0S	36 0W
Parakou	131	9 25N	2 40 E
Paramaribo	185	5 50N	55 10W
Paraná	190	31 45S	60 30W
Paraná □	191	24 30S	51 0W
Paraná →	190	33 43S	59 15W
Paranaguá	191	25 30S	48 30W
Paranaíba →	188	20 6S	51 4W
Parbhani	91	19 8N	76 52 E
Parecis, Serra dos	187	13 0S	60 0W
Parent	151	47 55N	74 35W
Paria, Golfo de	180	10 20N	62 0W
Parika	185	6 50N	58 20W
Parintins	185	2 40S	56 50W
Pariparit Kyun	94	14 55S	93 45 E
Paris, France	39	48 50N	2 20 E
Paris, Tenn., U.S.A.	169	36 20N	88 20W
Paris, Tex., U.S.A.	168	33 40N	95 30W
Park Range	163	40 0N	106 30W
Parker	173	34 8N	114 16W
Parkersburg	164	39 18N	81 31W
Parkes	117	33 9S	148 11 E
Parma	46	44 50N	10 20 E
Parnaguá	188	10 10S	44 38W
Parnaíba	189	2 54S	41 47W
Parnaíba →	188	3 0S	41 50W
Parnassós	54	38 35N	22 30 E
Pärnu	68	58 28N	24 33 E
Páros	55	37 5N	25 12 E
Parral	190	36 10S	71 52W
Parramatta	117	33 48S	151 1 E
Parras	174	25 30N	102 20W
Parrett →	27	51 7N	2 58W
Parry Is.	12	77 0N	110 0W
Parry Sound	151	45 20N	80 0W
Parsons	166	37 20N	95 17W
Paruro	187	13 45S	71 50W
Parván □	87	35 0N	69 0 E
Pasadena, Calif., U.S.A.	173	34 5N	118 9W
Pasadena, Tex., U.S.A.	168	29 45N	95 14W
Pasaje	184	3 23S	79 50W
Pascagoula	169	30 21N	88 30W
Pasco	171	46 10N	119 0W
Pasco, Cerro de	186	10 45S	76 10W
Paso Robles	173	35 40N	120 45W
Passero, C.	49	36 42N	15 8 E
Passo Fundo	191	28 10S	52 20W
Pasto	184	1 13N	77 17W
Patagonia	192	45 0S	69 0W
Patan	91	23 54N	72 14 E
Patchogue	164	40 46N	73 1W
Paterson	164	40 55N	74 10W
Pathankot	89	32 18N	75 45 E
Patiala	89	30 23N	76 26 E
Patkai Bum	93	27 0N	95 30 E
Pátmos	55	37 21N	26 36 E
Patna	92	25 35N	85 12 E
Patos, Lag. dos	191	31 20S	51 0 E
Patos de Minas	188	18 35S	46 32W
Pátrai	54	38 14N	21 47 E
Patuca →	179	15 50N	84 18W
Pátzcuaro	175	19 32N	101 36W
Pau	36	43 19N	0 25W
Paulistana	189	8 9S	41 9W
Paulo Afonso	189	9 21S	38 15W
Pavia	46	45 10N	9 10 E
Pavlodar	71	52 33N	77 0 E
Pavlovo	74	63 5N	115 25 E
Pawtucket	164	41 51N	71 22W
Payette	171	44 0N	117 0W
Payne Bay = Bellin	146	60 0N	70 0W
Payne L.	146	59 30N	74 30W
Paynes Find	120	29 15S	117 42 E
Paysandú	191	32 19S	58 8W
Paz, La, Argentina	190	30 50S	59 45W
Paz, La, Bolivia	187	16 20S	68 10W
Paz, La, Mexico	174	24 10N	110 18W
Pazardzhik	53	42 12N	24 20 E
Peace →	145	59 0N	111 25W
Peace River	155	56 15N	117 18W
Peak, The	28	53 24N	1 53W
Peak Hill	116	32 47S	148 11 E
Pearl City	160	21 24N	158 0W
Pearl Harbor	160	21 20N	158 0W
Peary Land	13	82 40N	33 0W
Pebas	186	3 10S	71 46W
Pechenga	69	69 30N	31 25 E
Pechora →	69	68 13N	54 15 E
Pechorskaya Guba	69	68 40N	54 0 E
Pecos	161	31 25N	103 35W
Pecos →	161	29 42N	102 30W
Pécs	59	46 5N	18 15 E
Pedro Afonso	188	9 0S	48 10W
Pedro Juan Caballero	191	22 30S	55 40W
Peebles	31	55 40N	3 12W
Peekskill	164	41 18N	73 57W
Peel	28	54 14N	4 40W
Peel →	144	67 0N	135 0W
Pegasus Bay	123	43 20S	173 10 E
Pegu	93	17 20N	96 29 E
Pegu Yoma	93	19 0N	96 0 E
Pehuajó	190	35 45S	62 0W
Peip'ing = Beijing	98	39 55N	116 20 E
Pekalongan	111	6 53S	109 40 E
Pekan	96	3 30N	103 25 E
Pekanbaru	111	0 30N	101 15 E
Pekin	166	40 35N	89 40W
Peking = Beijing	98	39 55N	116 20 E
Peleng	113	1 20S	123 30 E
Pelly →	144	62 47N	137 19W
Pelly Bay	146	68 38N	89 50W
Peloponnes = Pelopónnisos □	54	37 10N	22 0 E
Pelopónnisos □	54	37 10N	22 0 E
Peloro, C.	49	38 15N	15 40 E
Pelorus Sound	123	40 59S	173 59 E
Pelotas	191	31 42S	52 23W
Pelvoux, Massif de	37	44 52N	6 20 E
Pematangsiantar	111	2 57N	99 5 E
Pemba	135	5 0S	39 45 E
Pembroke, Canada	151	45 50N	77 7W
Pembroke, U.K.	27	51 41N	4 57W
Pen-y-Ghent	28	54 10N	2 15W
Penas, G. de	192	47 0S	75 0W
Pench'i = Benxi	98	41 20N	123 48 E
Pendembu	130	9 7N	12 14W
Pendleton	171	45 35N	118 50W
Penetanguishene	151	44 50N	79 55W
Penguin	119	41 8S	146 6 E
Penicuik	31	55 50N	3 14W
Peninsular Malaysia □	96	4 0N	102 0 E
Pennines	28	54 50N	2 20W
Pennsylvania □	164	40 50N	78 0W
Penola	119	37 25S	140 21 E
Penonomé	179	8 31N	80 21W
Penrith, Australia	117	33 43S	150 38 E
Penrith, U.K.	28	54 40N	2 45W
Pensacola	169	30 30N	87 10W
Pensacola Mts.	14	84 0S	40 0W
Penshurst	119	37 49S	142 20 E
Penticton	155	49 30N	119 38W
Pentland Firth	33	58 43N	3 10W
Pentland Hills	31	55 48N	3 25W
Penza	68	53 15N	45 5 E
Penzance	27	50 7N	5 32W
Penzhinskaya Guba	73	61 30N	163 0 E
Peoria	166	40 40N	89 40W
Perak □	96	5 0N	101 0 E
Perche	36	48 31N	1 1 E
Pereira	184	4 49N	75 43W
Perenjori	120	29 26S	116 16 E
Pergamino	190	33 52S	60 30W
Périgueux	36	45 10N	0 42 E
Perlis □	96	6 30N	100 15 E

Perm . . . . **69** 58 0N 57 10 E
Pernambuco = Recife **189** 8 0S 35 0W
Pernambuco □ **189** 8 0S 37 0W
Pernatty Lagoon . . . . **118** 31 30S 137 12 E
Pernik . . . . **53** 42 35N 23 2 E
Peron Pen. . . . . **120** 26 0S 113 10 E
Péronne . . . . **38** 49 55N 2 57 E
Perouse Str., La . . . . **77** 45 40N 142 0 E
Perpignan . . . . **37** 42 42N 2 53 E
Perry, Iowa, U.S.A. **166** 41 48N 94 5W
Perry, Okla., U.S.A. **168** 36 20N 97 20W
Persepolis . . . . **85** 29 55N 52 50 E
Persia = Iran ■ . . . . **86** 33 0N 53 0 E
Persian Gulf = Gulf, The . . . . **85** 27 0N 50 0 E
Perth, Australia . . . . **120** 31 57S 115 52 E
Perth, Canada **151** 44 55N 76 15W
Perth, U.K. **31** 56 24N 3 27W
Perth Amboy **164** 40 31N 74 16W
Peru **167** 40 42N 86 0W
Peru ■ **186** 8 0S 75 0W
Perúgia . . . . **46** 43 6N 12 24 E
Pervouralsk . . . . **69** 56 55N 60 0 E
Pésaro . . . . **47** 43 55N 12 53 E
Pescara . . . . **47** 42 28N 14 13 E
Peshawar . . . . **89** 34 2N 71 37 E
Pesqueria ⟶ **176** 25 54N 99 11W
Petah Tiqwa . . . . **80** 32 6N 34 53 E
Petaling Jaya . . . . **96** 3 4N 101 42 E
Petaluma **172** 38 13N 122 39W
Petatlán **177** 17 31N 101 16W
Peterborough, Australia . . . . . **118** 32 58S 138 51 E
Peterborough, Canada **151** 44 20N 78 20W
Peterborough, U.K. **25** 52 35N 0 14W
Peterhead **33** 57 30N 1 49W
Peterlee **29** 54 45N 1 18W
Petersburg, Alaska, U.S.A. . . . **143** 56 50N 133 0W
Petersburg, Va., U.S.A. **164** 37 17N 77 26W
Petit Goâve **180** 18 27N 72 51W
Petitsikapau, L. **147** 54 37N 66 25W
Potlad . . . . **91** 22 30N 72 45 F
Petone . . . . **123** 41 13S 174 53 E
Petoskey **150** 45 22N 84 57W
Petrich . . . . **53** 41 24N 23 13 E
Petrolia **150** 42 54N 82 9W
Petrolina **189** 9 24S 40 30W
Petropavlovsk . . . . **71** 54 53N 69 13 E
Petropavlovsk-Kamchatskiy . . **73** 53 3N 158 43 E
Petrópolis **188** 22 33S 43 9W
Petrovaradin . . . . **52** 45 16N 19 55 E
Petrozavodsk . . . . **68** 61 41N 34 20 E
Pevek . . . . **73** 69 41N 171 19 E
Pforzheim . . . . **42** 48 53N 8 43 E
Phan Rang . . . . **95** 11 34N 109 0 E
Phangan, Ko . . . . **96** 9 45N 100 0 E
Phenix City **169** 32 30N 85 0W
Philadelphia **164** 40 0N 75 10W
Philippi . . . . **55** 41 1N 24 16 F
Philippines ■ . . . . **112** 12 0N 123 0 E
Philippopolis = Plovdiv . . . . . . **53** 42 8N 24 44 E
Phitsanulok . . . . **94** 16 50N 100 12 E
Phnom Penh . . . . **95** 11 33N 104 55 E
Phoenix **160** 33 30N 112 10W
Phoenix Is. **123** 3 30S 172 0W
Phra Chedi Sam Ong . . . . **94** 15 16N 98 23 E
Phuket . . . . **96** 7 52N 98 22 E
Piacenza . . . . **46** 45 2N 9 42 E
Piauí □ **188** 7 0S 43 0W
Picardie . . . . **38** 50 0N 2 15 E
Picardie, Plaine de . . . . **37** 50 0N 2 0 E
Picardy = Picardie . . . . **38** 50 0N 2 15 E
Picayune **169** 30 31N 89 40W
Pickering **29** 54 15N 0 46W
Picton, Australia . . . . **117** 34 12S 150 34 E
Picton, N.Z. . . . . **123** 41 18S 174 3 E
Pictou **149** 45 41N 62 42W
Pidurutalagala . . . . **90** 7 10N 80 50 E
Piedad, La **175** 20 20N 102 1W
Piedmont = Piemonte □ . . . . . **46** 45 0N 7 30 E
Piedmont Plat. **165** 34 0N 81 30W
Piedras Negras **174** 28 42N 100 31W
Piemonte □ . . . . **46** 45 0N 7 30 E

Pierre **163** 44 23N 100 20W
Pietermaritzburg . . . . **137** 29 35S 30 25 E
Pietrosul . . . . **57** 47 35N 24 43 E
Pikeville **165** 37 30N 82 30W
Pilcomayo ⟶ **190** 25 21S 57 42W
Pilsen = Plzen . . . . **43** 49 45N 13 22 E
Pimenta Bueno **187** 11 35S 61 10W
Pinang □ . . . . **96** 5 20N 100 20 E
Pinar del Río **178** 22 26N 83 40W
Pinaroo . . . . **119** 35 17S 140 53 E
Pinawa **153** 50 9N 95 50W
Pincher Creek **155** 49 30N 113 57W
Pinczów . . . . **58** 50 30N 20 35 E
Pindos Óros . . . . **54** 40 0N 21 0 E
Pindus Mts. = Pindos Óros . . . **54** 40 0N 21 0 E
Pine Bluff **168** 34 10N 92 0W
Pine Pass **155** 55 25N 122 42W
Pineville **168** 31 22N 92 30W
Ping ⟶ . . . . **94** 15 42N 100 9 E
Pingdong . . . . **99** 22 39N 120 30 E
Pingliang . . . . **99** 35 35N 106 31 E
Pingxiang . . . . **99** 22 6N 106 46 E
Piniós ⟶ . . . . **54** 37 48N 21 20 E
Pinjarra . . . . **120** 32 37S 115 52 E
Piombino . . . . **46** 42 54N 10 30 E
Piotrków Trybunalski . . . . **58** 51 23N 19 43 E
Piqua **167** 40 10N 84 10W
Piracicaba **188** 22 45S 47 40W
Piroeus = Piraiévs . . . . **55** 37 57N 23 42 E
Piraiévs . . . . **55** 37 57N 23 42 E
Pirapora **188** 17 20S 44 56W
Pírgos . . . . **54** 37 40N 21 27 E
Pirin Planina . . . . **53** 41 40N 23 30 E
Pirineos . . . . **51** 42 40N 1 0 E
Pisa . . . . **46** 43 43N 10 23 E
Pisagua **187** 19 40S 70 15W
Pisco **100** 10 0 0 70 10W
Pistóia . . . . **46** 43 57N 10 53 E
Pitcairn I. **10** 25 5S 130 5W
Piteå . . . . **67** 65 20N 21 25 E
Pitești . . . . **57** 44 52N 24 54 E
Pithiviers . . . . **39** 48 10N 2 13 E
Pitlochry **33** 56 43N 3 43W
Pitt I. **154** 53 30N 129 50W
Pittsburg, Kans., U.S.A. **166** 37 21N 94 43W
Pittsburg, Tex., U.S.A. **168** 32 59N 94 58W
Pittsburgh **164** 40 25N 79 55W
Pittsfield **164** 42 28N 73 17W
Pittsworth . . . . **116** 27 41S 151 37 E
Piura **186** 5 15S 80 38W
Placentia **149** 47 20N 54 0W
Placerville **172** 38 47N 120 51W
Placetas **178** 22 15N 79 44W
Plainfield **164** 40 37N 74 28W
Plainview **161** 34 10N 101 40W
Plaster Rock **148** 46 53N 67 22W
Plata, La **191** 35 0S 57 55W
Plata, Río de la **191** 34 45S 57 30W
Platte ⟶ **163** 39 16N 94 50W
Plattsburg **151** 44 41N 73 30W
Plauen . . . . **43** 50 29N 12 9 E
Pleasantville **164** 39 25N 74 30W
Plenty, Bay of . . . . **122** 37 45S 177 0 E
Plessisville **148** 46 14N 71 47W
Pleven . . . . **53** 43 26N 24 37 E
Płock . . . . **58** 52 32N 19 40 E
Ploiești . . . . **57** 44 57N 26 5 E
Plovdiv . . . . **53** 42 8N 24 44 E
Plymouth **27** 50 23N 4 9W
Plzen . . . . **43** 49 45N 13 22 E
Po ⟶ . . . . **47** 44 57N 12 4 E
Po Hai = Bo Hai . . . . **98** 39 0N 120 0 E
Pobeda . . . . **73** 65 12N 146 12 E
Pobedy Pik . . . . **71** 40 45N 79 58 E
Pocatello **163** 42 50N 112 25W
Pochutla **177** 15 50N 96 31W
Poços de Caldas **188** 21 50S 46 33W
Podgorica = Titograd . . . . **52** 42 30N 19 19 E
Podkamennaya
   Tunguska ⟶ . . . . **74** 61 50N 90 13 E
Point Edward **150** 43 0N 82 30W

POI

Name						
Pointe-à-Pitre	180	16	10N	61	30W
Pointe Noire	134	4	48S	11	53 E
Poissy	39	48	55N	2	0 E
Poitiers	36	46	35N	0	20 E
Poitou, Plaines et Seuil du	36	46	30N	0	1W
Pokaran	91	27	0N	71	50 E
Pola = Pula	52	44	54N	13	57 E
Poland ■	58	52	0N	20	0 E
Polden Hills	27	51	7N	2	50W
Polesye	17	52	0N	28	10 E
Polillo Is.	112	14	56N	122	0 E
Políyiros	55	40	23N	23	25 E
Pollachi	90	10	35N	77	0 E
Polotsk	68	55	30N	28	50 E
Poltava	68	49	35N	34	35 E
Polynesia	123	10	0S	162	0W
Pomona	173	34	2N	117	49W
Pompano Beach	170	26	12N	80	6W
Ponca City	168	36	40N	97	5W
Ponce	180	18	1N	66	37W
Pond Inlet	146	72	40N	77	0W
Pondicherry	90	11	59N	79	50 E
Ponnyadaung	93	22	0N	94	10 E
Ponoka	155	52	42N	113	40W
Pont-Audemer	39	49	21N	0	30 E
Ponta Grossa	191	25	7S	50	10W
Ponta Pora	188	22	20S	55	35W
Pontchartrain, L.	169	30	12N	90	0W
Pontefract	29	53	42N	1	19W
Pontevedra	50	42	26N	8	40W
Pontiac	167	42	40N	83	20W
Pontianak	111	0	3S	109	15 E
Pontine Is. = Ponziane, Isole	48	40	55N	13	0 E
Pontoise	39	49	3N	2	5 E
Pontypool	27	51	42N	3	1W
Pontypridd	27	51	36N	3	21W
Ponziane, Isole	48	40	55N	13	0 E
Poochera	118	32	43S	134	51 E
Poole	24	50	42N	1	58W
Pooley I.	154	52	45N	128	15W
Poona = Pune	91	18	29N	73	57 E
Poopó, Lago de	187	18	30S	67	35W
Popayán	184	2	27N	76	36W
Poplar Bluff	169	36	45N	90	22W
Popocatépetl, Volcán	177	19	2N	98	38W
Porcher I.	154	53	50N	130	30W
Porcupine →	142	66	35N	145	15W
Pori	67	61	29N	21	48 E
Porkkala	67	59	59N	24	26 E
Port Adelaide	119	34	46S	138	30 E
Port Alberni	154	49	40N	124	50W
Port Albert	115	38	42S	146	42 E
Port Alfred	148	48	18N	70	53W
Port Angeles	171	48	7N	123	30W
Port Antonio	180	18	10N	76	30W
Port Arthur	168	30	0N	94	0W
Port-au-Prince	180	18	40N	72	20W
Port Augusta	118	32	30S	137	50 E
Port Blair	94	11	40N	92	30 E
Port-Cartier	148	50	2N	66	50W
Port Chalmers	123	45	49S	170	30 E
Port Colborne	151	42	50N	79	10W
Port Coquitlam	154	49	15N	122	45W
Port Darwin	192	51	50S	59	0W
Port-de-Paix	180	19	50N	72	50W
Port Elgin	150	44	25N	81	25W
Port Elizabeth	136	33	58S	25	40 E
Port Erin	28	54	5N	4	45W
Port Etienne = Nouâdhibou	126	20	54N	17	0W
Port Fairy	119	38	22S	142	12 E
Port Glasgow	30	55	57N	4	40W
Port Harcourt	131	4	40N	7	10 E
Port Harrison = Inoucdjouac	146	58	25N	78	15W
Port Hawkesbury	149	45	36N	61	22W
Port Hope	151	43	56N	78	20W
Port Huron	167	43	0N	82	28W
Port Kembla	117	34	52S	150	49 E
Port Laoise	35	53	2N	7	20W
Port Lavaca	158	28	38N	96	38W
Port Lincoln	119	34	42S	135	52 E
Port Lyautey = Kenitra	126	34	15N	6	40W
Port Macquarie	116	31	25S	152	25 E
Port Morant	180	17	54N	76	19W
Port Moresby	115	9	24S	147	8 E
Port Nelson	143	57	3N	92	36W
Port Nolloth	136	29	17S	16	52 E
Port Nouveau-Québec	146	58	30N	65	59W
Port of Spain	180	10	40N	61	31W
Port Phillip B.	117	38	10S	144	50 E
Port Pirie	118	33	10S	138	1 E
Port Said = Bûr Sa'îd	128	31	16N	32	18 E
Port Simpson	154	54	30N	130	20W
Port Stanley	150	42	40N	81	10W
Port Sudán = Bûr Sûdân	129	19	32N	37	9 E
Port Talbot	27	51	35N	3	48W
Port Townsend	171	48	7N	122	50W
Portadown	34	54	27N	6	26W
Portage La Prairie	153	49	58N	98	18W
Portarlington	35	53	10N	7	10W
Porte, La	167	41	36N	86	43W
Porterville	173	36	5N	119	0W
Porthcawl	27	51	28N	3	42W
Porthmadog	26	52	55N	4	13W
Portile de Fier	56	44	42N	22	30 E
Portland, Australia	119	38	20S	141	35 E
Portland, Maine, U.S.A.	148	43	40N	70	15W
Portland, Oreg., U.S.A.	171	45	35N	122	40W
Portland, Bill of	24	50	31N	2	27W
Portland Prom.	146	58	40N	78	33W
Porto	50	41	8N	8	40W
Pôrto Alegre	191	30	5S	51	10W
Porto Empédocle	48	37	18N	13	30 E
Porto Mendes	191	24	30S	54	15W
Porto Novo	131	6	23N	2	42 E
Pôrto Seguro	189	16	26S	39	5W
Pôrto Velho	187	8	46S	63	54W
Portoferráio	46	42	50N	10	20 E
Portoscuso	48	39	12N	8	22 E
Portoviejo	184	1	7S	80	28W
Portpatrick	30	54	50N	5	7W
Portree	32	57	25N	6	11W
Portrush	34	55	13N	6	40W
Portsmouth, Domin.	180	15	34N	61	27W
Portsmouth, U.K.	25	50	48N	1	6W
Portsmouth, N.H., U.S.A.	164	43	5N	70	45W
Portsmouth, Ohio, U.S.A.	167	38	45N	83	0W
Portsmouth, Va., U.S.A.	165	36	50N	76	20W
Porttipahta	67	68	5N	26	40 E
Portugal ■	50	40	0N	7	0W
Portuguese-Guinea = Guinea-Bissau ■	130	12	0N	15	0W
Portuguese Timor ■ = Timor	113	9	0S	125	0 E
Portumna	35	53	5N	8	12W
Porvenir	192	53	10S	70	16W
Posadas	191	27	30S	55	50W
Poshan = Boshan	98	36	28N	117	49 E
Poste-de-la-Baleine	140	55	17N	77	45W
Potchefstroom	137	26	41S	27	7 E
Potenza	49	40	40N	15	50 E
Potomac →	165	38	0N	76	23W
Potosí	187	19	38S	65	50W
Potsdam, Germany	43	52	23N	13	4 E
Potsdam, U.S.A.	151	44	40N	74	59W
Pottsville	164	40	39N	76	12W
Pouce Coupé	155	55	40N	120	10W
Poughkeepsie	164	41	40N	73	57W
Poulaphouca Res.	35	53	8N	6	30W
Póvoa de Varzim	50	41	25N	8	46W
Powell, L.	163	37	25N	110	45W
Powell River	154	49	50N	124	35W
Powys □	26	52	20N	3	20W
Poyang Hu	99	29	10N	116	10 E
Poyarkovo	75	49	36N	128	41 E
Poznań	58	52	25N	16	55 E
Prachuap Khiri Khan	94	11	49N	99	48 E
Prague = Praha	58	50	5N	14	22 E
Praha	58	50	5N	14	22 E
Prainha, Amazonas, Brazil	187	7	10S	60	30W
Prainha, Pará, Brazil	185	1	45S	53	30W
Prairie du Chien	166	43	1N	91	9W
Prato	46	43	53N	11	5 E
Pratt	161	37	40N	98	45W

Name	Page	Lat	Long
Prepansko Jezero	**52**	40 55N	21 0 E
Preparis North Channel	**94**	15 12N	93 40 E
Preparis South Channel	**94**	14 36N	93 40 E
Prescott	**160**	34 35N	112 30W
Preservation Inlet	**123**	46 8S	166 35 E
Presidencia Roque Saenz Peña	**190**	26 45S	60 30W
Presidente Prudente	**188**	22 5S	51 25W
Presidio	**161**	29 30N	104 20W
Prespa, L. = Prepansko Jezero	**52**	40 55N	21 0 E
Presque Isle	**148**	46 40N	68 0W
Preston, Borders, U.K.	**28**	55 48N	2 18W
Preston, Lancs., U.K.	**21**	53 46N	2 42W
Prestonpans	**31**	55 58N	3 0W
Prestwick	**31**	55 30N	4 30W
Pretoria	**137**	25 44S	28 12 E
Préveza	**55**	38 57N	20 47 E
Prichard	**169**	30 47N	88 5W
Prilep	**52**	41 21N	21 37 E
Prince Albert	**152**	53 15N	105 50W
Prince Albert Pen.	**145**	72 30N	116 0W
Prince Albert Sd.	**145**	70 25N	115 0W
Prince Charles I.	**146**	67 47N	76 12W
Prince Edward I. □	**148**	46 20N	63 20W
Prince George	**154**	53 55N	122 50W
Prince of Wales I., Canada	**145**	73 0N	99 0W
Prince of Wales I., U.S.A.	**143**	55 30N	133 0W
Prince Patrick I.	**12**	77 0N	120 0W
Prince Rupert	**154**	54 20N	130 20W
Princess Royal I.	**154**	53 0N	128 40W
Princeton	**155**	49 27N	120 30W
Principe, I. de	**131**	1 37N	7 27 E
Principe da Beira	**187**	12 20S	64 30W
Pripet = Pripyat →	**68**	51 20N	30 9 E
Pripet Marshes = Polesye	**17**	52 0N	28 10 E
Pripyat →	**68**	51 20N	30 9 E
Pripyat Marshes = Polesye	**17**	52 0N	28 10 E
Priština	**52**	42 40N	21 13 E
Privolzhskaya Vozvyshennost	**17**	51 0N	46 0 E
Prizren	**52**	42 13N	20 45 E
Proddatur	**90**	14 45N	78 30 E
Progreso	**177**	21 17N	89 40W
Prokopyevsk	**71**	54 0N	86 45 E
Proserpine	**121**	20 21S	148 36 E
Provence	**37**	43 40N	5 46 E
Providence	**164**	41 50N	71 28W
Provo	**163**	40 16N	111 37W
Prudhoe Bay	**142**	70 20N	148 20W
Pruszków	**58**	52 9N	20 49 E
Prut →	**57**	46 3N	28 10 E
Przemyśl	**58**	49 50N	22 45 E
Przeworsk	**58**	50 6N	22 32 E
Pskov	**68**	57 50N	28 25 E
Pucallpa	**186**	8 25S	74 30W
Puebla	**177**	19 3N	98 12W
Puebla □	**177**	10 50N	98 0W
Pueblo	**163**	38 20N	104 40W
Puelches	**190**	38 5S	65 51W
Puente Alto	**190**	33 32S	70 35W
Puerto Armuelles	**179**	8 20N	82 51W
Puerto Ayacucho	**184**	5 40N	67 35W
Puerto Barrios	**177**	15 40N	88 32W
Puerto Cabello	**184**	10 28N	68 1W
Puerto Cabezas	**179**	14 0N	83 30W
Puerto Castilla	**179**	16 0N	86 0W
Puerto Cortes, C. Rica	**179**	8 55N	84 0W
Puerto Cortes, Hond.	**177**	15 51N	88 0W
Puerto Heath	**187**	12 34S	68 39W
Puerto La Cruz	**185**	10 13N	64 38W
Puerto Libertad	**174**	29 55N	112 41W
Puerto Lobos	**192**	42 0S	65 3W
Puerto Maldonado	**187**	12 30S	69 10W
Puerto Montt	**190**	41 28S	73 0W
Puerto Padre	**178**	21 13N	76 35W
Puerto Pinasco	**191**	22 36S	57 50W
Puerto Plata	**180**	19 48N	70 45W
Puerto Quepos	**179**	9 29N	84 6W
Puerto Rico ■	**180**	18 15N	66 45W
Puerto Vallarta	**175**	20 37N	105 15W
Puertollano	**50**	38 43N	4 7W
Puget Sd.	**171**	47 15N	122 30W
Púglia □	**49**	41 0N	16 30 E
Pula	**52**	44 54N	13 57 E
Pulaski, Tenn., U.S.A.	**169**	35 10N	87 0W
Pulaski, Va., U.S.A.	**165**	37 4N	80 49W
Pulicat, L.	**90**	13 40N	80 15 E
Pullman	**171**	46 49N	117 10W
Punakha	**92**	27 42N	89 52 E
Punata	**187**	17 32S	65 50W
Pune	**91**	18 29N	73 57 E
Punjab □, India	**89**	31 0N	76 0 E
Punjab □, Pakistan	**89**	30 0N	72 0 E
Puno	**187**	15 55S	70 3W
Punta Alta	**190**	38 53S	62 4W
Punta Arenas	**192**	53 10S	71 0W
Punta Gorda	**177**	16 10N	88 45W
Puntabie	**118**	32 12S	134 13 E
Puntarenas	**179**	10 0N	84 50W
Punto Fijo	**184**	11 50N	70 13W
Puquio	**186**	14 45S	74 10W
Pur →	**69**	67 31N	77 55 E
Purbeck, Isle of	**24**	50 40N	2 5W
Purmerend	**40**	52 30N	4 58 E
Purnia	**92**	25 45N	87 31 E
Pursat	**95**	12 34N	103 50 E
Purus →	**185**	3 42S	61 28W
Pusan	**98**	35 5N	129 0 E
Putao	**93**	27 28N	97 30 E
Putorana, Gory	**72**	69 0N	95 0 E
Putumayo →	**184**	3 7S	67 58W
Puy, Le	**37**	45 2N	3 53 E
Puy-de-Dôme	**37**	45 46N	2 57 E
Puyallup	**171**	47 10N	122 22W
Pwllheli	**26**	52 54N	4 26W
Pyasina →	**72**	73 30N	87 0 E
Pyatigorsk	**70**	44 2N	43 6 E
Pyinmana	**93**	19 45N	96 12 E
Pyŏngyang	**98**	39 0N	125 30 E
Pyramid I.	**172**	40 0N	119 30W
Pyrénées	**124**	42 45N	0 18 E
Qā'emshahr	**86**	36 30N	52 55 E
Qahremānshahr = Bākhtarān	**84**	34 23N	47 0 E
Qaidam Pendi	**100**	37 0N	95 0 E
Qal'at al Akhḍar	**82**	28 0N	37 10 E
Qamar, Ghubbat al	**83**	16 20N	52 30 E
Qamdo	**101**	31 15N	97 6 E
Qandahar	**87**	31 32N	65 30 E
Qasr-e Qand	**85**	26 15N	60 45 E
Qatar ■	**85**	25 30N	51 15 E
Qâyen	**86**	33 40N	59 10 E
Qazvin	**81**	36 15N	50 0 E
Qena	**128**	26 10N	32 43 E
Qeshm	**85**	26 55N	56 10 E
Qilian Shan	**100**	38 30N	96 0 E
Qingdao	**98**	36 5N	120 20 E
Qinghai □	**101**	36 0N	98 0 E
Qinghai Hu	**100**	36 40N	100 10 E
Qinhuangdao	**98**	39 56N	119 30 E
Qiqihar	**98**	47 26N	124 0 E
Qom	**86**	34 40N	51 0 E
Qomsheh	**85**	32 0N	51 55 E
Qondūz □	**87**	36 50N	68 50 E
Qu Xian	**99**	30 48N	106 58 E
Quang Ngai	**95**	15 13N	108 58 E
Quantock Hills	**27**	51 8N	3 10W
Quanzhou	**99**	24 55N	118 34 E
Quatsino	**154**	50 30N	127 40W
Queanbeyan	**117**	35 17S	149 14 E
Québec	**148**	46 52N	71 13W
Québec □	**140**	50 0N	70 0W
Queen Alexandra Ra.	**15**	85 0S	170 0 E
Queen Charlotte	**154**	53 15N	132 2W
Queen Charlotte Is.	**154**	53 20N	132 10W
Queen Charlotte Str.	**154**	51 0N	128 0W
Queen Elizabeth Is.	**138**	76 0N	95 0W
Queen Mary Land	**15**	70 0S	95 0 E
Queen Maud G.	**145**	68 15N	102 30W
Queen Maud Mts.	**15**	86 0S	160 0W

Queenscliff . . . . 117 38 16S 144 39 E
Queensland □ . . . . 115 22 0S 142 0 E
Queenstown, Australia . . . . . . 119 42 4S 145 35 E
Queenstown, N.Z. . . . . 123 45 1S 168 40 E
Quelimane . . . . 137 17 53S 36 58 E
Quelpart = Cheju Do . . . . 99 33 29N 126 34 E
Querétaro 177 20 36N 100 23W
Querétaro □ 177 21 0N 99 55W
Quesnel 154 53 0N 122 30W
Quetta . . . . 88 30 15N ●S 55 E
Quezaltenango 177 14 50N 91 30W
Quezon City . . . . 112 14 38N 121 0 E
Qui Nhon . . . . 95 13 40N 109 13 E
Quibdo 184 5 42N 76 40W
Quillabamba 186 12 50S 72 50W
Quilon . . . . 90 8 50N 76 38 E
Quilpie . . . . 116 26 35S 144 11 E
Quimper 36 48 0N 4 9W
Quincy, Calif., U.S.A. 172 39 56N 121 0W
Quincy, Fla., U.S.A. 170 30 34N 84 34W
Quincy, Ill., U.S.A. 166 39 55N 91 20W
Quincy, Mass., U.S.A. 164 42 14N 71 0W
Quintana Roo □ 177 19 40N 88 30W
Quirindi . . . . 116 31 28S 150 40 E
Quitman 170 30 49N 83 35W
Quito 184 0 15S 78 35W
Quixadá 189 4 55S 39 0W
Quorn . . . . 118 32 25S 138 0 E
Quseir . . . . 128 26 7N 34 16 E

Raahe . . . . 67 64 40N 24 28 E
Raasay 32 57 25N 6 4W
Rabat 126 34 2N 6 48W
Rabaul . . . . 115 4 24S 152 18 E
Rābigh . . . . 82 22 50N 39 5 E
Race, C. 149 46 40N 53 5W
Rach Gia . . . . 95 10 5N 105 5 E
Racibórz . . . . 58 50 7N 18 18 E
Racine 167 42 41N 87 51W
Radium Hot Springs 155 50 35N 116 2W
Radnor Forest 26 52 17N 3 10W
Radom . . . . 58 51 23N 21 12 E
Radomir . . . . 53 42 37N 23 4 E
Radstock 27 51 17N 2 25W
Radville 152 49 30N 104 15W
Rae 145 62 50N 116 3W
Rae Bareli . . . . 92 26 18N 81 20 E
Raetihi . . . . 122 39 25S 175 17 E
Rafaela 190 31 10S 61 30W
Rafḥā . . . . 82 29 35N 43 35 E
Rafsanjān . . . . 85 30 30N 56 5 E
Ragama . . . . 90 7 0N 79 50 E
Raglan . . . . 122 37 55S 174 55 E
Ragusa . . . . 49 36 56N 14 42 E
Rahaeng = Tak. . . . . 94 16 52N 99 8 E
Raichur . . . . 91 16 10N 77 20 E
Rainier, Mt. 171 46 50N 121 50W
Rainy L. 153 48 42N 93 10W
Rainy River 153 48 43N 94 29W
Raipur . . . . 92 21 17N 81 45 E
Rajahmundry . . . . 92 17 1N 81 48 E
Rajapalaiyam . . . . 90 9 25N 77 35 E
Rajasthan □ . . . . 91 26 45N 73 30 E
Rajasthan Canal . . . . 89 28 0N 72 0 E
Rajkot . . . . 91 22 15N 70 56 E
Rajshahi □ . . . . 92 25 0N 89 0 E
Raleigh 165 35 47N 78 39W
Raleigh B. 165 34 50N 76 15W
Rambouillet . . . . 39 48 40N 1 48 E
Rampur . . . . 89 28 50N 79 5 E
Ramsey 28 54 20N 4 21W
Rancagua 190 34 10S 70 50W
Ranchi . . . . 92 23 19N 85 27 E
Rangiora . . . . 123 43 19S 172 36 E
Rangoon . . . . 93 16 45N 96 20 E
Rangpur . . . . 92 25 42N 89 22 E
Raniwara . . . . 91 24 50N 72 10 E
Rankin Inlet 145 62 30N 93 0W
Rankins Springs . . . . 117 33 49S 146 14 E

Rannoch, L. 33 56 41N 4 20W
Rannoch Moor 30 56 38N 4 48W
Rapid City 163 44 0N 103 0W
Ras Dashen . . . . 132 13 8N 38 26 E
Rasa, Punta 192 40 50S 62 15W
Rasht . . . . 81 37 20N 49 40 E
Rat Is. . . . . 142 51 50N 178 15 E
Ratangarh . . . . 89 28 5N 74 35 E
Rath Luirc 35 52 21N 8 40W
Rathlin I. 34 55 18N 6 14W
Ratibor = Racibórz . . . . 58 50 7N 18 18 E
Ratlam . . . . 91 23 20N 75 0 E
Ratnagiri . . . . 91 16 57N 73 18 E
Rattray Hd. 33 57 38N 1 50W
Raub . . . . 96 3 47N 101 52 E
Raukumara Ra. . . . . 122 38 5S 177 55 E
Ravenna . . . . 47 44 28N 12 15 E
Ravenshoe . . . . 121 17 37S 145 29 E
Ravensthorpe . . . . 120 33 35S 120 2 E
Rawalpindi . . . . 89 33 38N 73 8 E
Rawlins 163 41 50N 107 20W
Ray, C. 149 47 33N 59 15W
Raymond 155 49 30N 112 35W
Razgrad . . . . 53 43 33N 26 34 E
Ré, Île de 36 46 12N 1 30W
Reading, U.K. 25 51 27N 0 57W
Reading, U.S.A. 164 40 20N 75 53W
Reay Forest 32 58 20N 4 55W
Rebun-Tō . . . . 103 45 23N 141 2 E
Recife 189 8 0S 35 0W
Reconquista 190 29 10S 59 45W
Recreo 190 29 25S 65 10W
Red ⟶ 168 31 0N 91 40W
Red Bluff 172 40 11N 122 11W
Red Cliffs . . . . 119 34 19S 142 11 E
Red Deer 155 52 20N 113 50W
Red Lake 153 51 3N 93 49W
Red Oak 166 41 0N 95 10W
Red Sea . . . . 128 25 0N 36 0 E
Red Tower Pass = Turnu
  Roşu Pasul . . . . 57 45 33N 24 17 E
Red Wing 166 44 32N 92 35W
Redcar 29 54 37N 1 4W
Redcliff 152 50 10N 110 50W
Redcliffe . . . . 116 27 12S 153 0 E
Redding 172 40 30N 122 25W
Redditch 24 52 18N 1 57W
Redlands 173 34 0N 117 11W
Redruth 27 50 14N 5 14W
Redwater 155 53 55N 113 6W
Redwood City 172 37 30N 122 15W
Ree, L. 34 53 35N 8 0W
Reedley 173 36 36N 119 27W
Regensburg . . . . 43 49 1N 12 7 E
Réggio di Calábria . . . . 49 38 7N 15 38 E
Réggio nell' Emilia . . . . 46 44 42N 10 38 E
Regina 152 50 27N 104 35W
Rehovot . . . . 80 31 54N 34 48 E
Reichenbach . . . . 43 50 36N 12 19 E
Reidsville 165 36 21N 79 40W
Reims . . . . 39 49 15N 4 0 E
Reina Adelaida, Arch. 192 52 20S 74 0W
Reindeer L. 143 57 15N 102 15W
Reliance 145 63 0N 109 20W
Remanso 189 9 41S 42 4W
Remarkable, Mt. . . . . 118 32 48S 138 10 E
Remscheid . . . . 42 51 11N 7 12 E
Rendsburg . . . . 42 54 18N 9 41 E
Renfrew, Canada 151 45 30N 76 40W
Renfrew, U.K. 31 55 52N 4 24W
Renkum . . . . 41 51 58N 5 43 E
Renmark . . . . 119 34 11S 140 43 E
Rennes 36 48 7N 1 41W
Reno 172 39 30N 119 50W
Republic 150 46 25N 87 59W
Republican ⟶ 163 39 3N 96 48W
Repulse Bay 146 66 30N 86 30W
Requena 186 5 5S 73 52W
Resht = Rasht . . . . 81 37 20N 49 40 E
Resistencia 190 27 30S 59 0W
Resolution I., Canada 146 61 30N 65 0W

Name	Page	Lat		Long	
Resolution I., N.Z.	**123**	45	40S	166	40 E
Retalhuleu	**177**	14	33N	91	46W
Réthímnon	**55**	35	18N	24	30 E
Réunion	**9**	22	0S	56	0 E
Reval = Tallinn	**68**	59	22N	24	48 E
Revelstoke	**155**	51	0N	118	10W
Revilla Gigedo, Is.	**139**	18	40N	112	0W
Rewa	**92**	24	33N	81	25 E
Rewari	**89**	28	15N	76	40 E
Rexburg	**163**	43	55N	111	50W
Rey Malabo	**131**	3	45N	8	50 E
Reykjavík	**64**	64	10N	21	57 E
Reynosa	**176**	26	5N	98	18W
Rhayader	**26**	52	19N	3	30W
Rhein ⟶	**42**	51	52N	6	20 E
Rheinland-Pfalz □	**42**	50	0N	7	0 E
Rhin = Rhein ⟶	**42**	51	52N	6	20 E
Rhine = Rhein ⟶	**42**	51	52N	6	20 E
Rhineland-Palatinate □ = Rheinland-Pfalz □	**42**	50	0N	7	0 E
Rhinelander	**150**	45	38N	89	29W
Rhode Island □	**164**	41	38N	71	37W
Rhodes = Ródhos	**55**	36	15N	28	10 E
Rhodesia = Zimbabwe ■	**137**	20	0S	30	0 E
Rhodope Mts. = Rhodopi Planina	**53**	41	40N	24	20 E
Rhodopi Planina	**53**	41	40N	24	20 E
Rhön	**42**	50	24N	9	58 E
Rhondda	**27**	51	39N	3	30W
Rhône ⟶	**37**	43	28N	4	42 E
Rhum	**32**	57	0N	6	20W
Rhyl	**26**	53	19N	3	29W
Rhymney	**27**	51	45N	3	17W
Riachão	**188**	7	20S	46	37W
Riau, Kepulauan	**111**	0	30N	104	20 E
Ribatejo □	**50**	39	15N	8	30W
Ribble ⟶	**20**	54	10N	0	00W
Ribeirão Prêto	**188**	21	10S	47	50W
Riberalta	**187**	11	0S	66	0W
Riccarton	**123**	43	32S	172	37 E
Richland	**171**	46	15N	119	15W
Richmond, Australia	**116**	20	43S	143	8 E
Richmond, N.Z.	**123**	41	20S	173	12 E
Richmond, N. Yorks., U.K.	**28**	54	24N	1	43W
Richmond, Surrey, U.K.	**25**	51	28N	0	18W
Richmond, Calif., U.S.A.	**172**	37	58N	122	21W
Richmond, Ind., U.S.A.	**167**	39	50N	84	50W
Richmond, Ky., U.S.A.	**165**	37	40N	84	20W
Richmond, Va., U.S.A.	**165**	37	33N	77	27W
Richwood	**165**	38	17N	80	32W
Ridgeway	**164**	42	56S	147	16 E
Riga	**68**	56	53N	24	8 E
Rīgestān □	**87**	30	15N	65	0 E
Rigolet	**147**	54	10N	58	23W
Rijeka	**52**	45	20N	14	21 E
Rijssen	**41**	52	19N	6	30 E
Rijswijk	**40**	52	4N	4	22 E
Rímini	**47**	44	3N	12	33 E
Rîmnicu Vîlcea	**57**	45	9N	24	21 E
Rimouski	**148**	48	27N	68	30W
Rinía	**55**	37	23N	25	13 E
Rio Branco	**187**	9	58S	67	49W
Rio Claro	**180**	10	20N	61	25W
Rio Cuarto	**190**	33	10S	64	25W
Rio de Janeiro	**188**	23	0S	43	12W
Rio de Janeiro □	**188**	22	50S	43	0W
Rio Gallegos	**192**	51	35S	69	15W
Rio Grande	**191**	32	0S	52	20W
Rio Grande ⟶	**161**	25	57N	97	9W
Rio Grande do Norte □	**189**	5	40S	36	0W
Rio Grande do Sul □	**191**	30	0S	53	0W
Rio Mulatos	**187**	19	40S	66	50W
Rio Negro	**191**	26	0S	50	0W
Rio Verde	**188**	17	50S	51	0W
Riobamba	**184**	1	50S	78	45W
Riohacha	**184**	11	33N	72	55W
Rioja, La	**190**	29	20S	67	0W
Rioja, La □	**50**	42	20N	2	20W
Ríosucio	**184**	7	27N	77	7W
Ripon	**28**	54	8N	1	31W
Rishiri-Tō	**103**	45	11N	141	15 E
Ritchies Archipelago	**94**	12	5N	94	0 E
Rivas	**179**	11	30N	85	50W
Riverhead	**164**	40	53N	72	40W
Riverside	**173**	34	0N	117	22W
Riverton	**153**	51	1N	97	0W
Riviera di Levante	**46**	44	23N	9	15 E
Riviera di Ponente	**46**	43	50N	7	58 E
Rivière-du-Loup	**148**	47	50N	69	30W
Riyadh = Ar Riyāḍ	**83**	24	41N	46	42 E
Roanne	**37**	46	3N	4	4 E
Roanoke, Ala., U.S.A.	**169**	33	9N	85	23W
Roanoke, Va., U.S.A.	**165**	37	19N	79	55W
Roanoke ⟶	**165**	35	56N	76	43W
Roanoke Rapids	**165**	36	28N	77	42W
Robinvale	**119**	34	40S	142	45 E
Roblin	**152**	51	14N	101	21W
Roboré	**187**	18	10S	59	45W
Robson, Mt.	**155**	53	10N	119	10W
Roca, C. da	**50**	38	40N	9	31W
Rocha	**191**	34	30S	54	25W
Rochdale	**28**	53	36N	2	10W
Roche-sur-Yon, La	**36**	46	40N	1	25W
Rochefort	**36**	45	56N	0	57W
Rochelle, La	**36**	46	10N	1	9W
Rochester, Minn., U.S.A.	**166**	44	1N	92	28W
Rochester, N.H., U.S.A.	**164**	43	19N	70	57W
Rochester, N.Y., U.S.A.	**164**	43	10N	77	40W
Rock Hill	**165**	34	55N	81	2W
Rock Island	**166**	41	30N	90	35W
Rock Sprs.	**163**	41	40N	109	10W
Rockall	**16**	57	37N	13	42W
Rockford	**166**	42	20N	89	0W
Rockglen	**152**	49	11N	105	57W
Rockhampton	**119**	23	22S	150	32 E
Rockingham	**120**	32	15S	115	38 E
Rockland	**148**	44	6N	69	6W
Rocky Mount	**165**	35	55N	77	4RW
Rocky Mountain House	**155**	52	22N	114	55W
Rocky Mts.	**138**	55	0N	121	0W
Ródhos	**55**	36	15N	28	10 E
Roebourne	**114**	20	44S	117	9 E
Roermond	**41**	51	12N	6	0 E
Roes Welcome Sd.	**146**	65	0N	87	0W
Rogaland fylke □	**60**	59	12N	6	20 E
Rogers	**168**	36	20N	94	5W
Rohri	**88**	27	45N	68	51 E
Rohtak	**89**	28	55N	76	43 E
Rojo, C.	**177**	21	33N	97	20W
Rolla	**166**	37	56N	91	42W
Roma, Australia	**116**	26	32S	148	49 E
Roma, Italy	**46**	41	54N	12	30 E
Romaine ⟶	**141**	50	10N	63	47W
Roman	**57**	46	57N	26	55 E
Romana, La	**180**	18	27N	68	57W
Romania ■	**57**	46	0N	25	0 E
Romans	**37**	45	3N	5	3 E
Romanzof, C.	**142**	62	0N	165	50W
Rome = Roma	**46**	41	54N	12	30 E
Rome, Ga., U.S.A.	**169**	34	20N	85	0W
Rome, N.Y., U.S.A.	**164**	43	14N	75	29W
Romilly	**39**	48	31N	3	44 E
Romney Marsh	**25**	51	0N	1	0 E
Rona	**32**	57	33N	6	0W
Rondônia □	**187**	11	0S	63	0W
Rong, Koh	**95**	10	45N	103	15 E
Ronge, La	**152**	55	6N	105	17W
Roosendaal	**40**	51	32N	4	29 E
Roraima □	**185**	2	0N	61	30W
Roraima, Mt.	**185**	5	10N	60	40W
Rosario, Argentina	**190**	33	0S	60	40W
Rosario, Brazil	**188**	3	0S	44	15W
Rosario, Mexico	**175**	22	58N	105	53W
Rosario, Paraguay	**191**	24	30S	57	35W
Rosário do Sul	**191**	30	15S	54	55W
Roscommon	**34**	53	38N	8	11W
Roscommon □	**34**	53	40N	8	15W
Roscrea	**35**	52	58N	7	50W
Roseau	**180**	15	20N	61	24W
Roseburg	**171**	43	10N	123	20W
Rosenberg	**168**	29	30N	95	48W
Rosendaël	**38**	51	3N	2	24 E

Rosetown	**152**	51 35N	107	59W
Roseville	**172**	38 46N	121	17W
Rosewood	**116**	27 38S	152	36 E
Roskilde	**61**	55 38N	12	3 E
Ross on Wye	**24**	51 55N	2	34W
Ross Sea	**15**	74 0S	178	0 E
Rossan Pt.	**34**	54 42N	8	47W
Rossland	**155**	49 6N	117	50W
Rosslare	**35**	52 17N	6	23W
Røssvatnet	**65**	65 45N	14	5 E
Rosthern	**152**	52 40N	106	20W
Rostock	**43**	54 4N	12	9 E
Rostov	**68**	47 15N	39	45 E
Roswell	**161**	33 26N	104	32W
Rosyth	**31**	56 2N	3	26W
Rother →	**25**	50 59N	0	40 E
Rotherham	**29**	53 26N	1	21W
Rothesay	**30**	55 50N	5	3W
Roto	**117**	33 0S	145	30 E
Rotorua	**122**	38 9S	176	16 E
Rotorua, L.	**122**	38 5S	176	18 E
Rotterdam	**40**	51 55N	4	30 E
Rotuma	**122**	12 25S	177	5 E
Roubaix	**37**	50 40N	3	10 E
Rouen	**38**	49 27N	1	4 E
Round Mt.	**116**	30 26S	152	16 E
Roussillon	**37**	42 30N	2	35 E
Rouyn	**151**	48 20N	79	0W
Rovaniemi	**67**	66 29N	25	41 E
Rovno	**68**	50 40N	26	10 E
Ruahine Ra.	**122**	39 55S	176	2 E
Ruapehu	**122**	39 17S	175	35 E
Rub' al Khali	**83**	18 0N	48	0 E
Rubh a' Mhail	**30**	55 55N	6	10W
Rubio	**184**	7 43N	72	22W
Rubtsovsk	**71**	51 30N	81	10 E
Rudnyy	**71**	52 57N	63	7 E
Rudolf, Ostrov	**69**	81 45N	58	30 E
Rufiji →	**135**	7 50S	39	15 E
Rufino	**190**	34 20S	62	50W
Rugby	**25**	52 23N	1	16W
Rügen	**43**	54 22N	13	25 E
Ruhr →	**42**	51 25N	6	44 E
Rukwa L.	**135**	8 0S	32	20 E
Rumania = Romania ■	**57**	46 0N	25	0 E
Rumford	**148**	44 30N	70	30W
Rumoi	**103**	43 56N	141	39W
Runcorn	**28**	53 20N	2	44W
Rupat	**111**	1 45N	101	40 E
Rupert →	**140**	51 29N	78	45W
Rupert House = Fort Rupert .	**140**	51 30N	78	40W
Ruschuk = Ruse .	**53**	43 48N	25	59 E
Ruse	**53**	43 48N	25	59 E
Russell	**152**	50 50N	101	20W
Russellville, Ala., U.S.A.	**169**	34 30N	87	44W
Russellville, Ark., U.S.A.	**168**	35 15N	93	8W
Ruston	**168**	32 30N	92	58W
Rutherglen	**31**	55 50N	4	11W
Rutland I.	**94**	11 25N	92	40 E
Ruwenzori	**132**	0 30N	29	55 E
Rwanda ■	**135**	2 0S	30	0 E
Ryan, L.	**30**	55 0N	5	2W
Ryazan	**68**	54 40N	39	40 E
Rybache	**71**	46 40N	81	20 E
Rybinsk = Andropov	**68**	58 5N	38	50 E
Ryde	**25**	50 44N	1	9W
Rye	**25**	50 57N	0	46 E
Rylstone	**117**	32 46S	149	58 E
Ryōhaku-Sanchi	**106**	36 9N	136	49 E
Ryūgasaki	**107**	35 54N	140	11 E
Rzeszów	**58**	50 5N	21	58 E
Sa Dec	**95**	10 20N	105	46 E
Saar →	**42**	49 41N	6	32 E
Saarbrücken	**42**	49 15N	6	58 E
Saaremaa	**68**	58 30N	22	30 E
Saarland □	**42**	49 15N	7	0 E
Sabadell	**51**	41 28N	2	7 E
Sabae	**106**	35 57N	136	11 E
Sabah □	**112**	6 0N	117	0 E
Sábana de la Mar	**180**	19 7N	69	24W
Sabhah	**127**	27 9N	14	29 E
Sabi →	**137**	18 50S	31	40 E
Sabinas	**174**	27 51N	101	7W
Sabinas Hidalgo, R. →	**176**	26 50N	99	35W
Sabine →	**158**	30 0N	93	35W
Sable, C., Canada	**148**	43 29N	65	38W
Sable, C., U.S.A.	**159**	25 13N	81	0W
Sable I.	**149**	44 0N	60	0W
Sabrina Coast	**15**	68 0S	120	0 E
Sabzevâr	**86**	36 15N	57	40 E
Saco	**148**	43 30N	70	27W
Sacramento	**172**	38 33N	121	30 E
Sacramento →	**172**	38 3N	121	56W
Sacramento Mts.	**161**	32 30N	105	30W
Sado, Shima	**103**	38 15N	138	30 E
Safed Koh	**87**	34 0N	70	0 E
Saffron Walden	**25**	52 2N	0	15 E
Safi	**126**	32 18N	9	20W
Saga	**108**	33 15N	130	16 E
Sagami-Nada	**107**	34 58N	139	30 E
Sagami-Wan	**107**	35 15N	139	25 E
Sagamihara	**107**	35 33N	139	25 E
Sagar	**91**	14 14N	75	6 E
Sagara	**107**	34 41N	138	12 E
Saginaw	**167**	43 26N	83	55W
Saginaw B.	**167**	43 50N	83	40W
Saglouc	**146**	62 14N	75	38W
Sagres	**50**	37 0N	8	58W
Sagua la Grande	**178**	22 50N	80	10W
Saguenay →	**148**	48 22N	71	0W
Sahara	**126**	23 0N	5	0 E
Saharanpur	**89**	29 58N	77	33 E
Saharien, Atlas	**127**	33 30N	1	0 E
Sahiwal	**89**	30 45N	73	8 E
Sahuaripa	**174**	29 3N	109	14W
Saigō	**109**	36 12N	133	20 E
Saigon = Thanh Pho Ho Chi Minh	**95**	10 58N	106	40 E
Saijō, Ehime, Japan	**109**	33 55N	133	11 E
Saijō, Hiroshima, Japan	**109**	34 25N	132	45 E
Saikhoa Ghat	**93**	27 50N	95	40 E
Saiki	**108**	32 58N	131	51 E
Saimaa	**67**	61 15N	28	15 E
Şa'in Dezh	**81**	36 40N	46	25 E
St. Abb's Head	**31**	55 55N	2	10W
St. Albans, U.K.	**25**	51 44N	0	19W
St. Albans, U.S.A.	**151**	44 49N	73	7W
St. Alban's Head	**24**	50 34N	2	3W
St. Albert	**155**	53 37N	113	32W
St. Andrews	**31**	56 20N	2	48W
St. Arnaud	**119**	36 40S	143	16 E
St. Asaph	**26**	53 15N	3	27W
St-Augustin-Saguenay	**141**	51 13N	58	38W
St. Augustine	**170**	29 52N	81	20W
St. Austell	**27**	50 20N	4	48W
St. Bee's Hd.	**28**	54 30N	3	38 E
St. Boniface	**153**	49 53N	97	5W
St. Bride's B.	**26**	51 48N	5	15W
St-Brieuc	**36**	48 30N	2	46W
St. Catharines	**151**	43 10N	79	15W
St. Charles	**166**	38 46N	90	30W
St. Christopher-Nevis ■	**180**	17 20N	62	40W
St. Cloud	**156**	45 30N	94	11W
St. Croix	**180**	17 45N	64	45W
St. David's	**26**	51 54N	5	16W
St. David's Head	**26**	51 55N	5	16W
St-Denis	**39**	48 56N	2	22 E
St-Dizier	**37**	48 40N	5	0 E
St. Elias, Mt.	**144**	60 14N	140	50W
St. Elias Mts.	**144**	60 33N	139	28W
St-Étienne	**37**	45 27N	4	22 E
St-Félicien	**151**	48 40N	72	25W
St. Gallen	**44**	47 25N	9	20 E
St. George, Australia	**116**	28 1S	148	30 E
St. George, Bermuda	**180**	32 24N	64	42W
St. Georges, Fr. Gui.	**185**	4 0N	52	0W
St. Georges, Grenada	**180**	12 5N	61	43W
St. George's Channel	**20**	52 0N	6	0W

St. Gotthard P. = San					
Gottardo, Paso del	**44**	46 33N		8 33 E
St. Helena	**125**	15 55S		5 44W
St. Helena B.	**136**	32 40S		18 10 E
St. Helens, Australia	**119**	41 20S	148	15 E
St. Helens, U.K.	**28**	53 28N		2 44W
St. Helens, U.S.A.	**171**	45 55N	122	50W
St. Helier	**36**	49 11N		2 6W
St-Hyacinthe	**151**	45 40N		72 58W
St. Ives, Cambs., U.K.	**25**	52 20N		0 5W
St. Ives, Cornwall, U.K.	**27**	50 13N		5 29W
St-Jean	**151**	45 20N		73 20W
St-Jérôme	**151**	45 47N		74 0W
St. John	**148**	45 20N		66 8W
St. John's	**149**	47 35N		52 40W
St. John's →	**170**	30 20N		81 30W
St. Johnsbury	**140**	44 25N		72 1W
St. Joseph, Mich., U.S.A.	**167**	42 5N		86 30W
St. Joseph, Mo., U.S.A.	**166**	39 46N		94 50W
St. Kilda, N.Z.	**123**	45 53S	170	31 E
St. Kilda, U.K.	**22**	57 9N		8 34W
St. Lawrence	**149**	46 54N		55 23W
St. Lawrence →	**148**	49 30N		66 0W
St. Lawrence, Gulf of	**149**	48 25N		62 0W
St. Lawrence I.	**142**	63 0N	170	0W
St. Leonard	**148**	47 12N		67 58W
St-Louis	**130**	16 8N		16 27W
St. Louis	**166**	38 40N		90 12W
St. Lucia ■	**180**	14 0N		60 50W
St. Maarten	**180**	18 0N		63 5W
St-Malo	**36**	48 39N		2 1W
St-Marc	**180**	19 10N		72 41W
St-Martin, I.	**180**	18 0N		63 0W
St. Mary Pk.	**118**	31 32S	138	34 E
St. Marys	**164**	41 27N		78 33W
St. Matthews, I. = Zadetkyi					
Kyun	**94**	10 0N		98 25 E
St. Michael's Mt.	**27**	50 7N		5 30W
St. Moritz	**44**	46 30N		9 51 E
St-Nazaire	**36**	47 17N		2 12W
St. Neots	**25**	52 14N		0 16W
St-Omer	**38**	50 45N		2 15 E
St. Pascal	**148**	47 32N		69 48W
St. Paul	**166**	44 54N		93 5W
St. Paul, I.	**149**	47 12N		60 9W
St. Petersburg	**170**	27 45N		82 40W
St-Pierre et Miquelon □	**149**	46 55N		56 10W
St-Quentin	**38**	49 50N		3 16 E
St-Raphaël	**37**	43 25N		6 46 E
St-Servan-sur-Mer	**36**	48 38N		2 0W
St. Thomas, Canada	**151**	42 45N		81 10W
St. Thomas, W. Indies	**180**	18 21N		64 55W
St-Tropez	**37**	43 17N		6 38 E
St. Vincent and the					
Grenadines ■	**180**	13 0N		61 10W
Ste-Adresse	**38**	49 31N		0 5 E
Ste Anne de Beaupré	**148**	47 2N		70 58W
Ste Marie	**180**	14 48N		61 1W
Ste-Rose	**180**	16 20N		61 45W
Ste. Rose du lac	**153**	51 4N		99 30W
Saintes	**36**	45 45N		0 37W
Saintonge	**36**	45 40N		0 50W
Saito	**108**	32 3N	131	24 E
Sajama	**187**	18 7S		69 0W
Sakai	**106**	34 30N	135	30 E
Sakaide	**109**	34 15N	133	50 E
Sakaiminato	**109**	35 38N	133	11 E
Sakakawea, L.	**163**	47 30N	102	0W
Sakata	**103**	38 55N	139	50 E
Sakhalin	**79**	51 0N	143	0 E
Sakhalinskiy Zaliv	**75**	54 0N	141	0 E
Saku	**107**	36 17N	138	31 E
Sakura	**107**	35 43N	140	14 E
Sakurai	**106**	34 30N	135	51 E
Salaberry-de-Valleyfield	**151**	45 15N		74 8W
Salado →	**190**	31 40S		60 41W
Salado, R. →	**176**	26 52N		99 19W
Salamanca, Spain	**50**	40 58N		5 39W
Salamanca, U.S.A.	**164**	42 10N		78 42W
Salamis	**55**	37 56N		23 30 E
Salcombe	**27**	50 14N		3 47W
Sale	**117**	38 6S	147	6 E
Salem, India	**90**	11 40N		78 11 E
Salem, Mass., U.S.A.	**164**	42 29N		70 53W
Salem, Oreg., U.S.A.	**171**	45 0N	123	0W
Salem, Va., U.S.A.	**165**	37 19N		80 8W
Salerno	**49**	40 40N		14 44 E
Salford	**28**	53 30N		2 17W
Salida	**163**	38 35N	106	0W
Salina, Italy	**49**	38 35N		14 50 E
Salina, U.S.A.	**161**	38 50N		97 40W
Salina Cruz	**177**	16 10N		95 12W
Salinas, Ecuador	**184**	2 10S		80 58W
Salinas, U.S.A.	**173**	36 40N	121	41W
Salinas →	**173**	36 45N	121	48W
Salinas Grandes	**190**	30 0S		65 0W
Salisbury = Harare	**137**	17 43S		31 2 E
Salisbury, U.K.	**24**	51 4N		1 48W
Salisbury, Md., U.S.A.	**165**	38 20N		75 38W
Salisbury, N.C., U.S.A.	**165**	35 20N		80 29W
Salisbury Plain	**24**	51 13N		1 50W
Salle, La	**166**	41 20N		89 6W
Salmon	**162**	45 12N	113	56W
Salmon →	**171**	45 51N	116	46W
Salmon Arm	**155**	50 40N	119	15W
Salmon River Mts.	**162**	45 0N	114	30W
Salon-de-Provence	**37**	43 39N		5 6 E
Salonica = Thessaloníki	**54**	40 38N		22 58 E
Salop = Shropshire □	**24**	52 36N		2 45W
Salt Fork →	**161**	36 37N		97 7W
Salt Lake City	**163**	40 45N	111	58W
Salta	**190**	24 57S		65 25W
Saltcoats	**30**	55 38N		4 47W
Saltillo	**174**	25 25N	101	0W
Salto	**191**	31 27S		57 50W
Salton Sea	**173**	33 20N	115	50W
Salûm	**128**	31 31N		25 7 E
Salvador	**189**	13 0S		38 30W
Salween →	**93**	16 31N		97 37 E
Salzburg	**45**	47 48N		13 2 E
Salzburg □	**45**	47 15N		13 0 E
Salzgitter	**43**	52 13N		10 22 E
Sam Neua	**95**	20 29N	104	0 E
Sama	**69**	60 12N		60 22 E
Samangán □	**87**	36 15N		68 3 E
Samar	**112**	12 0N	125	0 E
Samarkand	**70**	39 40N		66 55 E
Sāmarrā	**81**	34 12N		43 52 E
Sambalpur	**92**	21 28N		84 4 E
Sambhal	**89**	28 35N		78 37 E
Sámos	**55**	37 45N		26 50 E
Samothráki	**55**	40 28N		25 28 E
Samsun	**80**	41 15N		36 22 E
Samut Prakan	**95**	13 32N	100	40 E
Samut Sakhon	**94**	13 31N	100	13 E
Samut Songkhram →	**94**	13 24N	100	1 E
San Andreas	**172**	38 0N	120	39W
San Andres Mts.	**161**	33 0N	106	45W
San Andrés Tuxtla	**177**	18 27N		95 13W
San Angelo	**161**	31 30N	100	30W
San Antonio, Chile	**190**	33 40S		71 40W
San Antonio, U.S.A.	**161**	29 30N		98 30W
San Antonio, C., Argentina	**191**	36 15S		56 40W
San Antonio, C., Cuba	**178**	21 50N		84 57W
San Antonio de los Baños	**178**	22 54N		82 31W
San Antônio Falls	**182**	9 30S		65 0W
San Antonio Oeste	**192**	40 40S		65 0W
San Bernardino	**173**	34 7N	117	18W
San Bernardino Str.	**112**	13 0N	125	0 E
San Bernardo	**190**	33 40S		70 50W
San Blas, C.	**169**	29 40N		85 12W
San Carlos, Chile	**190**	36 10S		72 0W
San Carlos, Mexico	**174**	29 1N	100	51W
San Carlos, Nic.	**179**	11 12N		84 50W
San Carlos de Bariloche	**192**	41 10S		71 25W
San Clemente I.	**173**	32 53N	118	30W
San Cristóbal, Argentina	**190**	30 20S		61 10W
San Cristóbal, Dom. Rep.	**180**	18 25N		70 6W
San Cristóbal, Venezuela	**184**	16 50N		92 40W
San Cristóbal de las Casas	**177**	16 45N		92 38W
San Diego	**173**	32 43N	117	10W
San Felipe, Chile	**190**	32 43S		70 42W

SAN

Name	Map	Lat	Long
San Felipe, Colombia	**184**	1 55N	67 6W
San Fernando, Chile	**190**	34 30S	71 0W
San Fernando, Mexico	**174**	30 0N	115 10W
San Fernando, Trin. & Tob.	**180**	10 20N	61 30W
San Fernando, U.S.A.	**173**	34 15N	118 29W
San Fernando de Apure	**184**	7 54N	67 15W
San Francisco	**172**	37 47N	122 30W
San Francisco de Macorís	**180**	19 19N	70 15W
San Francisco del Oro	**174**	26 52N	105 51W
San Gabriel	**191**	0 36N	77 49W
San Gottardo, Paso del	**44**	46 33N	8 33 E
San Ignacio	**187**	16 20S	60 55W
San Joaquin →	**172**	37 4N	121 51W
San Jorge, Golfo	**192**	46 0S	66 0W
San Jorge, G. de	**51**	40 50N	0 55W
San José, Bolivia	**187**	17 53S	60 50W
San José, C. Rica	**179**	10 0N	84 2W
San José, U.S.A.	**172**	37 20N	121 53W
San José de Mayo	**191**	34 27S	56 40W
San José del Cabo	**175**	23 3N	109 41W
San José del Guaviare	**184**	2 35N	72 38W
San Juan, Argentina	**190**	31 30S	68 30W
San Juan, Dom. Rep.	**180**	18 49N	71 12W
San Juan, Puerto Rico	**180**	18 28N	66 8W
San Juan →	**179**	10 56N	83 42W
San Juan de los Morros	**184**	9 55N	67 21W
San Juan Mts.	**163**	38 30N	108 30W
San Julián	**192**	49 15S	67 45W
San Leandro	**172**	37 40N	122 6W
San Lorenzo	**184**	1 15N	78 50W
San Lucas, C. de	**175**	22 50N	110 0W
San Luis	**190**	33 20S	66 20W
San Luis de la Paz	**177**	21 18N	100 31W
San Luis Obispo	**173**	35 21N	120 38W
San Luis Potosí	**177**	22 9N	100 59W
San Luis Potosí □	**177**	22 30N	100 30W
San Marcos	**177**	14 59N	91 52W
San Marino ■	**47**	43 56N	12 25 E
San Mateo	**172**	37 32N	122 19W
San Matías	**187**	16 25S	58 20W
San Matías, Golfo	**192**	41 30S	64 0W
San Miguel	**177**	13 30N	88 12W
San Miguel de Tucumán	**190**	26 50S	65 20W
San Pedro →	**175**	21 45N	105 30W
San Pedro de las Colonias	**174**	25 45N	102 59W
San Pedro de Macorís	**180**	18 30N	69 18W
San Pedro Sula	**177**	15 30N	88 0W
San Rafael, Argentina	**190**	34 40S	68 21W
San Rafael, U.S.A.	**172**	37 59N	122 32W
San Roque	**190**	28 25S	58 45W
San Salvador, Bahamas	**178**	24 0N	74 40W
San Salvador, El Salv.	**177**	13 40N	89 10W
San Salvador de Jujuy	**190**	24 10S	64 48W
San Sebastián	**51**	43 17N	1 58W
San Valentín, Mte.	**192**	46 30S	73 30W
Sana'	**82**	15 27N	44 12 E
Sanandaj	**81**	35 18N	47 1 E
Sancti-Spíritus	**178**	21 52N	79 33W
Sanda	**106**	34 53N	135 14 E
Sandgate	**116**	27 18S	153 3 E
Sandomierz	**58**	50 40N	21 43 E
Sandpoint	**171**	48 20N	116 34W
Sandringham	**29**	52 50N	0 30 E
Sandstone	**120**	27 59S	119 16 E
Sandusky	**167**	41 25N	82 40W
Sandwip Chan.	**93**	22 35N	91 35 E
Sandy C.	**119**	41 25S	144 45 E
Sandy Lake	**153**	53 0N	93 15W
Sanford, Fla., U.S.A.	**170**	28 45N	81 20W
Sanford, Maine, U.S.A.	**148**	43 28N	70 47W
Sanford, N.C., U.S.A.	**165**	35 30N	79 10W
Sangay	**184**	2 0S	78 20W
Sangihe, P.	**113**	3 45N	125 30 E
Sangli	**91**	16 55N	74 33 E
Sangre de Cristo Mts.	**161**	37 0N	105 0W
Sankuru →	**134**	4 17S	20 25 E
Sano	**107**	36 19N	139 35 E
Sanok	**59**	49 35N	22 10 E
Sanquhar	**31**	55 21N	3 56W
Sanshui	**99**	23 10N	112 56 E
Santa Ana, Bolivia	**187**	13 50S	65 40W
Santa Ana, Mexico	**174**	30 33N	111 7W
Santa Ana, U.S.A.	**173**	33 48N	117 55W
Santa Bárbara, Mexico	**174**	26 48N	105 49W
Santa Bárbara, U.S.A.	**173**	34 25N	119 40W
Santa Barbara I.	**160**	33 29N	119 2W
Santa Catarina □	**191**	27 25S	48 30W
Santa Clara, Cuba	**178**	22 20N	80 0W
Santa Clara, U.S.A.	**162**	37 21N	122 0W
Santa Clotilde	**186**	2 33S	73 45W
Santa Cruz, Bolivia	**187**	17 43S	63 10W
Santa Cruz, U.S.A.	**172**	36 55N	122 1W
Santa Cruz, Is.	**122**	10 30S	166 0 E
Sta. Cruz de Tenerife	**126**	28 28N	16 15W
Santa Cruz del Sur	**178**	20 44N	78 0W
Santa Cruz do Sul	**191**	29 42S	52 25W
Santa Fe, Argentina	**190**	31 35S	60 41W
Santa Fe, U.S.A.	**161**	35 40N	106 0W
Santa Inés, I.	**192**	54 0S	73 0W
Santa Isabel = Rey Malabo	**131**	3 45N	8 50 E
Santa Lucia Range	**173**	36 0N	121 20W
Santa Maria, Brazil	**191**	29 40S	53 48W
Santa Maria, U.S.A.	**173**	34 58N	120 29W
Santa Maria da Vitória	**188**	13 24S	44 12W
Santa Maria di Leuca, C.	**49**	39 48N	18 20 E
Santa Marta	**184**	11 15N	74 13W
Santa Maura = Levkás	**54**	38 40N	20 43 E
Santa Monica	**173**	34 0N	118 30W
Santa Rosa, Argentina	**190**	36 40S	64 17W
Santa Rosa, U.S.A.	**172**	38 26N	122 43W
Santa Rosa I., Calif., U.S.A.	**173**	34 0N	120 6W
Santa Rosa I., Fla., U.S.A.	**169**	30 23N	87 0W
Santa Rosalía	**174**	27 19N	112 17W
Santana do Livramento	**191**	30 55S	55 30W
Santander	**50**	43 27N	3 51W
Santander Jiménez	**176**	24 13N	98 28W
Santarém, Brazil	**185**	2 25S	54 42W
Santarém, Portugal	**50**	39 12N	8 42W
Santiago, Brazil	**191**	29 11S	54 52W
Santiago, Chile	**190**	33 24S	70 40W
Santiago, Panama	**179**	8 0N	81 0W
Santiago de Compostela	**50**	42 52N	8 37W
Santiago de Cuba	**178**	20 0N	75 49W
Santiago de los Cabelleros	**180**	19 30N	70 40W
Santiago del Estero	**190**	27 50S	64 15W
Santiago Ixcuintla	**175**	21 50N	105 11W
Santo Amaro	**189**	12 30S	38 43W
Santo Ângelo	**191**	28 15S	54 15W
Santo Domingo	**180**	18 30N	64 54W
Santo Tomé	**191**	28 40S	56 5W
Santoña	**50**	43 29N	3 27W
Santos	**191**	24 0S	46 20W
São Borja	**191**	28 39S	56 0W
São Carlos	**188**	22 0S	47 50W
São Francisco →	**189**	10 30S	36 24W
São Francisco do Sul	**191**	26 15S	48 36W
São João del Rei	**188**	21 8S	44 15W
São José do Rio Prêto	**188**	20 50S	49 20W
São Leopoldo	**191**	29 50S	51 10W
São Lourenço	**188**	22 7S	45 3W
São Luís	**188**	2 39S	44 15W
São Paulo	**191**	23 32S	46 37W
São Paulo □	**188**	22 0S	49 0W
São Paulo de Olivença	**184**	3 27S	68 48W
São Roque, C. de	**189**	5 30S	35 16W
São Tomé	**131**	0 10N	6 39 E
São Tomé & Príncipe ■	**131**	0 12N	6 39 E
São Vicente, Cabo de	**50**	37 0N	9 0W
Saône →	**37**	45 44N	4 50 E
Sapporo	**103**	43 0N	141 21 E
Sapulpa	**168**	36 0N	96 0W
Saqqez	**81**	36 15N	46 20 E
Sar Planina	**52**	42 10N	21 0 E
Saragossa = Zaragoza	**51**	41 39N	0 53W
Sarajevo	**52**	43 52N	18 26 E
Saranac Lake	**151**	44 20N	74 10W
Sarangani B.	**112**	6 0N	125 13 E
Saransk	**68**	54 10N	45 10 E
Sarapul	**69**	56 28N	53 48 E
Sarasota	**165**	27 20N	82 30W
Saratoga Springs	**164**	43 5N	73 47W
Saratov	**68**	51 30N	46 2 E

Sarawak □ 111   2   0N 113   0 E
Sardegna . . . . 48 39 57N   9   0 E
Sardinia = Sardegna . . . . 48 39 57N   9   0 E
Sargodha . . . . 89 32 10N   72 40 E
Sarh 131   9   5N   18 23 E
Sārī . . . . 86 36 30N   53   4 E
Sarina . . . . 121 21 22S 149 13 E
Sarmiento 192 45 35S   69   5W
Sarnia 150 42 58N   82 23W
Saronikós Kólpos . . . . 55 37 45N   23 45 E
Sarre = Saar → . . . . 42 49 41N   6 32 E
Sarre, La 151 48 45N   79 15W
Sarthe → 36 47 33N   0 31W
Sasaram . . . . 92 24 57N   84   5 E
Sasebo . . . . 108 33 10N 129 43 E
Saskatchewan □ 152 54 40N 106   0W
Saskatchewan → 152 53 37N 100 40W
Saskatoon 152 52 10N 106 38W
Sassandra 130   5   0N   6   8W
Sássari . . . . 48 40 44N   8 33 E
Sata-Misaki . . . . 108 30 59N 130 40 E
Satara . . . . 91 17 44N   73 58 E
Satmala Hills . . . . 91 20 15N   74 40 E
Satna . . . . 92 24 35N   80 50 E
Satpura Ra. . . . . 91 21 25N   76 10 E
Sattahip . . . . 95 12 41N 100 54 E
Satu Mare . . . . 56 47 46N   22 55 E
Sauðarkrókur 64 65 45N   19 40W
Saudi Arabia ■ . . . . 82 26   0N   44   0 E
Sault Ste. Marie, Canada 150 46 30N   84 20W
Sault Ste. Marie, U.S.A. 150 46 27N   84 22W
Saumur. 36 47 15N   0   5W
Sava → . . . . 52 44 50N   20 26 E
Savanna la Mar 180 18 10N   78 10W
Savannah. 170 32   4N   81   4W
Savannah → 170 32   2N   80 53W
Davannakhet . . . . 95 16 30N 104 49 E
Savoie □ . . . . 37 45 26N   6 35 E
Savona . . . . 46 44 19N   8 29 E
Sawankhalok . . . . 94 17 19N   99 50 E
Sawara . . . . 107 35 55N 140 30 E
Sawatch Mts. 163 38 30N 106 30W
Sawu, I. . . . . 113 10 35S 121 50 E
Sawu Sea 113   9 30S 121 50 E
Saxony, Lower =
   Niedersachsen □ . . . . 42 52 45N   9   0 E
Sayan, Zapadnyy . . . . 77 52 30N   94   0 E
Saydā . . . . 80 33 35N   35 25 E
Sayhut . . . . 83 15 12N   51 10 E
Sayula 175 19 52N 103 36W
Sazan . . . . 52 40 30N   19 20 E
Scafell Pikes 28 54 26N   3 14W
Scalloway 30 60   9N   1 16W
Scandinavia . . . . 16 64   0N   12   0 E
Scapa Flow 33 58 52N   3   6W
Scarborough 29 54 17N   0 24W
Schaffhausen . . . . 44 47 42N   8 39 E
Schefferville. 146 54 48N   66 50W
Schelde → . . . . 42 51 15N   4 16 E
Schenectady 164 42 50N   73 58W
Scheveningen . . . . 40 52   6N   4 16 E
Schiedam . . . . 40 51 55N   4 25 E
Schiermonnikoog . . . . 41 53 30N   6 15 E
Schleswig-Holstein □ . . . . 42 54 10N   9 40 E
Schouten I. . . . . 119 42 20S 148 20 E
Schouten Is. 113   1   0S 136   0 E
Schouwen . . . . 40 51 43N   3 45 E
Schreiber 150 48 45N   87 20W
Schwäbische Alb . . . . 42 48 30N   9 30 E
Schwarzwald . . . . 42 48   0N   8   0 E
Schwerin . . . . 43 53 37N   11 22 E
Schwyz . . . . 44 47   2N   8 39 E
Scilly, Isles of. 20 49 55N   6 15W
Scone, Australia . . . . 116 32   5S 150 52 E
Scone, U.K. 31 56 25N   3 26W
Scoresbysund. 13 70 20N   23   0W
Scotia Sea 14 56   5S   56   0W
Scotland □ 23 57   0N   4   0W
Scottsbluff 163 41 55N 103 35W
Scottsdale . . . . 119 41   9S 147 31 E
Scranton 164 41 22N   75 41W

Scunthorpe 29 53 35N   0 38W
Scutari = Üsküdar . . . . 80 41   0N   29   5 E
Seaforth 150 43 35N   81 25W
Searcy 168 35 15N   91 45W
Seascale 28 54 24N   3 29W
Seattle 171 47 41N 122 15W
Sebastián Vizcaíno, B. 174 28   0N 114 30W
Sebastopol = Sevastopol . . . . 68 44 35N   33 30 E
Sebring 170 27 30N   81 26W
Sebta = Ceuta 126 35 52N   5 18W
Sebuku, Teluk 111   4   0N 118 10 E
Sechura, Desierto de 186   6   0S   80 30W
Seclin . . . . 38 50 33N   3   2 E
Sedalia 166 38 40N   93 18W
Segamat 96   2 30N 102 50 E
Ségou 130 13 30N   6 16W
Segovia = Coco → 179 15   0N   83   0W
Segovia 50 40 57N   4 10W
Séguéla 130   7 55N   6 40W
Segura → 51 38   6N   0 54W
Seine → . . . . 38 49 26N   0 26 E
Seistan . . . . 85 30 50N   61   0 E
Seki . . . . 106 35 29N 136 55 E
Sekondi-Takoradi 130   4 58N   1 45W
Selangor □ 96   3 10N 101 30 E
Selby 29 53 47N   1   5W
Sélibabi 130 15 10N   12 15W
Selkirk, Canada 153 50 10N   96 55W
Selkirk, U.K. 31 55 33N   2 50W
Selkirk Mts. 155 51 15N 117 40W
Selma, Ala., U.S.A. 169 32 30N   87   0W
Selma, Calif., U.S.A. 173 36 39N 119 39W
Selsey Bill 24 50 44N   0 47W
Selvas 187   6 30S   67   0W
Semarang 111   7   0S 110 26 E
Seminole 168 35 15N   96 45W
Semipalatinsk . . . . 71 50 30N   80 10 E
Semnān . . . . 86 35 55N   53 25 E
Semnān □ . . . . 86 36   0N   54   0 E
Sendai, Kagoshima, Japan . . 108 31 50N 130 20 E
Sendai, Miyagi, Japan . . . . . . 103 38 15N 140 53 E
Senegal ■ 130 14 30N   14 30W
Senegal → 126 15 48N   16 32W
Senge Khambab =
   Indus → . . . . 88 24 20N   67 47 E
Senhor-do-Bonfim 189 10 30S   40 10W
Senja I. . . . . 64 69 15N   17 30 E
Senlis . . . . 39 49 13N   2 35 E
Sennâr . . . . 129 13 30N   33 35 E
Senneterre 151 48 25N   77 15W
Sens . . . . 39 48 11N   3 15 E
Senta . . . . 52 45 55N   20   3 E
Seoul = Sôul . . . . 98 37 31N 126 58 E
Sept-Îles 148 50 13N   66 22W
Seram 113   3 10S 129   0 E
Seram Sea 113   2 30S 128 30 E
Seremban 96   2 43N 101 53 E
Serena, La 190 29 55S   71 10W
Sereth = Siret → . . . . 56 47 58N   26   5 E
Sergipe □ 189 10 30S   37 30W
Sérifos . . . . 55 37   9N   24 30 E
Serny Zavod . . . . 70 39 59N   58 50 E
Serov . . . . 69 59 29N   60 35 E
Serowe . . . . 137 22 25S   26 43 E
Serpukhov . . . . 68 54 55N   37 28 E
Serra do Navio 185   0 59N   52   3W
Sérrai . . . . 55 41   5N   23 31 E
Sesheke . . . . 134 17 29S   24 13 E
Setana . . . . 103 42 26N 139 51 E
Sète . . . . 37 43 25N   3 42 E
Sétif . . . . 127 36   9N   5 26 E
Seto . . . . 106 35 14N 137   6 E
Setonaikai . . . . 109 34 20N 133 30 E
Settle 28 54   5N   2 18W
Setúbal 50 38 30N   8 58W
Sevastopol . . . . 68 44 35N   33 30 E
Seven Sisters 154 54 56N 128 10W
Severn →, Canada 140 56   2N   87 36W
Severn →, U.K. 24 51 35N   2 38W
Severnaya Zemlya . . . . 72 79   0N 100   0 E
Severodvinsk . . . . 69 64 27N   39 58 E

Sevilla **50** 37 23N 6 0W
Seville = Sevilla **50** 37 23N 6 0W
Seward **142** 60 6N 149 26W
Seward Pen. **142** 65 0N 164 0W
Seychelles ■ . . . . **78** 5 0S 56 0 E
Seyðisfjörður **64** 65 16N 14 0W
Seymour . . . . **117** 37 0S 145 10 E
Seyne-sur-Mer, La . . . . **37** 43 7N 5 52 E
Sézanne . . . . **39** 48 40N 3 40 E
Sfax . . . . **127** 34 49N 10 48 E
Sfîntu Gheorghe . . . . **57** 45 52N 25 48 E
Shaanxi □ . . . . **99** 35 0N 109 0 E
Shaba □ . . . . **135** 8 0S 25 0 E
Shache . . . . **100** 38 20N 77 10 E
Shaftesbury **24** 51 0N 2 12W
Shahdād . . . . **85** 30 30N 57 40 E
Shakhty . . . . **68** 47 40N 40 16 E
Shamo = Gobi . . . . **98** 44 0N 111 0 E
Shamokin **164** 40 47N 76 33W
Shan □ . . . . **93** 21 30N 98 30 E
Shandong □ . . . . **99** 36 0N 118 0 E
Shanghai . . . . **99** 31 15N 121 26 E
Shangqiu . . . . **99** 34 26N 115 36 E
Shangrao . . . . **99** 28 25N 117 59 E
Shangshui . . . . **99** 33 42N 114 35 E
Shannon ─► **35** 52 35N 9 30W
Shansi = Shanxi □ . . . . **98** 37 0N 112 0 E
Shantou . . . . **99** 23 18N 116 40 E
Shantung = Shandong □ . . . . **99** 36 0N 118 0 E
Shanxi □ . . . . **98** 37 0N 112 0 E
Shaoguan . . . . **99** 24 48N 113 35 E
Shaoxing . . . . **99** 30 0N 120 35 E
Shaoyang . . . . **99** 27 14N 111 25 E
Shap **28** 54 32N 2 40W
Sharjah = Ash Shāriqah . . . . **85** 25 23N 55 26 E
Shark B. . . . . **120** 25 55S 113 32 E
Sharon **164** 41 18N 80 30W
Shashi . . . . **99** 30 25N 112 14 E
Shasta, Mt. **172** 41 30N 122 12W
Shasta L. **172** 40 50N 122 15W
Shaunavon **152** 49 35N 108 25W
Shawano **167** 44 45N 88 38W
Shawinigan **151** 46 35N 72 50W
Shawnee **168** 35 15N 97 0W
Shcherbakov = Andropov . . . **68** 58 5N 38 50 E
Shebele, Wabi ─► . . . . **133** 2 0N 44 0 E
Sheboygan **167** 43 46N 87 45W
Sheerness . . . . **24** 51 26N 0 47 E
Sheffield **28** 53 23N 1 28W
Shekhupura . . . . **89** 31 42N 73 58 E
Shelburne **148** 43 47N 65 20W
Shelby, Mont., U.S.A. **163** 48 30N 111 52W
Shelby, N.C., U.S.A. **165** 35 18N 81 34W
Shelbyville, Ind., U.S.A. **167** 39 30N 85 42W
Shelbyville, Tenn., U.S.A. **169** 35 30N 86 25W
Shelikhova, Zaliv . . . . **73** 59 30N 157 0 E
Shellharbour . . . . **117** 34 31S 150 51 E
Shelton **171** 47 15N 123 6W
Shenandoah **166** 40 50N 95 25W
Shensi = Shaanxi □ . . . . **99** 35 0N 109 0 E
Shenyang . . . . **98** 41 50N 123 25 E
Shepparton . . . . **117** 36 23S 145 26 E
Sheppey, I. of . . . . **24** 51 23N 0 50 E
Sherborne **27** 50 56N 2 31W
Sherbrooke **148** 45 28N 71 57W
Sheridan **163** 44 50N 107 0W
Sherman **168** 33 40N 96 35W
Sherridon **152** 55 8N 101 5W
Sherwood Forest **29** 53 5N 1 5W
Shetland Is. **30** 60 30N 1 30W
Shibām . . . . **83** 16 0N 48 36 E
Shibata . . . . **103** 37 57N 139 20 E
Shibetsu . . . . **103** 44 10N 142 23 E
Shibukawa . . . . **107** 36 29N 139 0 E
Shibushi-Wan . . . . **108** 31 24N 131 8 E
Shiel, L. **32** 56 48N 5 32W
Shihchiachuangi =
Shijiazhuang . . . . **98** 38 2N 114 28 E
Shijiazhuang . . . . **98** 38 2N 114 28 E
Shikarpur . . . . **88** 27 57N 68 39 E
Shikine-Jima . . . . **107** 34 19N 139 13 E

Shikoku . . . . **109** 33 30N 133 30 E
Shikoku □ . . . . **109** 33 30N 133 30 E
Shikoku-Sanchi . . . . **109** 33 30N 133 30 E
Shillong . . . . **93** 25 35N 91 53 E
Shimabara . . . . **108** 32 48N 130 20 E
Shimada . . . . **107** 34 49N 138 10 E
Shimizu . . . . **107** 35 0N 138 30 E
Shimo-Jima . . . . **108** 32 15N 130 7 E
Shimo-Koshiki-Jima . . . . **108** 31 40N 129 43 E
Shimoda . . . . **107** 34 40N 138 57 E
Shimodate . . . . **107** 36 20N 139 55 E
Shimoga . . . . **90** 13 57N 75 32 E
Shimonoseki . . . . **108** 33 58N 131 0 E
Shin, L. **33** 58 7N 4 30W
Shin-Tone ─► . . . . **107** 35 44N 140 51 E
Shinano ─► . . . . **105** 36 50N 138 30 E
Shingū . . . . **106** 33 40N 135 55 E
Shinji Ko . . . . **109** 35 26N 132 57 E
Shinjō . . . . **103** 38 46N 140 18 E
Shinminato . . . . **106** 36 47N 137 4 E
Shinshiro . . . . **106** 34 54N 137 30 E
Shio-no-Misaki . . . . **106** 33 25N 135 45 E
Shiogama . . . . **103** 38 19N 141 1 E
Shiojiri . . . . **107** 36 6N 137 58 E
Shipka . . . . **53** 42 46N 25 33 E
Shirane-San, Gumma, Japan . **107** 36 48N 139 22 E
Shirane-San, Yamanashi,
Japan . . . . **107** 35 42N 138 9 E
Shīrāz . . . . **85** 29 42N 52 30 E
Shire ─► . . . . **137** 17 42S 35 19 E
Shiriya-Zaki . . . . **103** 41 25N 141 30 E
Shivpuri . . . . **91** 25 26N 77 42 E
Shizuoka . . . . **107** 35 0N 138 24 E
Shkoder = Shkodra . . . . **52** 42 6N 19 20 E
Shkodra . . . . **52** 42 6N 19 20 E
Shkumbini ─► . . . . **52** 41 5N 19 50 E
Shō-Gawa ─► . . . . **106** 36 47N 137 4 E
Shōbara . . . . **109** 34 51N 133 1 E
Shoeburyness . . . . **24** 51 31N 0 49 E
Sholapur = Solapur . . . . **91** 17 43N 75 56 E
Shoshone **172** 43 0N 114 27W
Shreveport **168** 32 30N 93 50W
Shrewsbury **28** 52 42N 2 45W
Shrirampur . . . . **92** 22 44N 88 21 E
Shropshire □ **24** 52 36N 2 45W
Shuangyashan . . . . **98** 46 37N 131 22 E
Siahan Range . . . . **88** 27 30N 64 40 E
Sialkot . . . . **89** 32 32N 74 30 E
Siam = Thailand ■ . . . . **95** 16 0N 102 0 E
Sian = Xi'an . . . . **99** 34 15N 109 0 E
Siberia . . . . **77** 60 0N 100 0 E
Siberut . . . . **111** 1 30S 99 0 E
Sibi . . . . **88** 29 30N 67 54 E
Sibiu . . . . **57** 45 45N 24 9 E
Sichuan □ . . . . **99** 31 0N 104 0 E
Sicilia . . . . **49** 37 30N 14 30 E
Sicily = Sicilia . . . . **49** 37 30N 14 30 E
Sicuani **187** 14 21S 71 10W
Sidi-bel-Abbès **127** 35 13N 0 39W
Sidlaw Hills **31** 56 32N 3 10W
Sidley, Mt. **15** 77 2S 126 2W
Sidmouth **27** 50 40N 3 13W
Sidney **154** 48 39N 123 24W
Sidon = Saydā . . . . **80** 33 35N 35 25 E
Sidra, G. of = Surt, Khalīj . . . . **127** 31 40N 18 30 E
Siedlce . . . . **58** 52 10N 22 20 E
Siena . . . . **46** 43 20N 11 20 E
Sierra Blanca Pk. **161** 33 20N 105 54W
Sierra Leone ■ **130** 9 0N 12 0W
Sífnos . . . . **55** 37 0N 24 45 E
Siglufjörður **64** 66 12N 18 55W
Sihanoukville = Kompong
Som . . . . **95** 10 38N 103 30 E
Siirt . . . . **81** 37 57N 41 55 E
Sikar . . . . **89** 27 33N 75 10 E
Sikeston **169** 36 52N 89 35W
Sikhote Alin, Khrebet . . . . **75** 46 0N 136 0 E
Síkinos . . . . **55** 36 40N 25 8 E
Sikkim □ . . . . **92** 27 50N 88 30 E
Silchar . . . . **93** 24 49N 92 48 E
Silesia = Slask . . . . **58** 51 0N 16 30 E

Siling Co. **101** 31 50N 89 20 E
Silloth **28** 54 53N 3 25W
Simcoe **151** 42 50N 80 20W
Simenga . . . . **74** 62 42N 108 25 E
Simeulue . . . . **111** 2 45N 95 45 E
Simferopol . . . . **68** 44 55N 34 3 E
Simi Valley **173** 34 16N 118 47W
Simla. . . . . **89** 31 2N 77 9 E
Simplon Pass . . . . **44** 46 15N 8 0 E
Simushir, Ostrov . . . . **75** 46 50N 152 30 E
Sinai = Es Sīnā'. . . . . **128** 29 0N 34 0 E
Sinaloa **174** 25 50N 108 20W
Sinaloa □. **174** 25 0N 107 30W
Sincelejo **184** 9 18N 75 24W
Sinclair Mills **155** 54 5N 121 40W
Sind □ . . . . **88** 26 0N 69 0 E
Sind Sagar Doab . . . . **89** 32 0N 71 30 E
Singa . . . . **129** 13 10N 33 57 E
Singapore ■ . . . . **96** 1 17N 103 51 E
Singapore, Straits of. . . . . **96** 1 15N 104 0 E
Singkaling Hkamti . . . . **92** 26 0N 95 39 E
Singleton . . . . **117** 32 33S 151 0 E
Singora = Songkhla. . . . . **97** 7 13N 100 37 E
Sinkiang Uighur = Xinjiang
  Uygur Zizhiqu □ . . . . **100** 42 0N 86 0 E
Sioux City **166** 42 32N 96 25W
Sioux Falls **166** 43 35N 96 40W
Sioux Lookout **153** 50 10N 91 50W
Siping . . . . **98** 43 8N 124 21 E
Sipora . . . . **111** 2 18S 99 40 E
Siracusa . . . . **49** 37 4N 15 17 E
Sirajganj . . . . **92** 24 25N 89 47 E
Siret → . . . . **57** 47 58N 26 5 E
Síros . . . . **55** 37 28N 24 57 E
Sitapur . . . . **92** 27 38N 80 45 E
Sitka **143** 57 9N 135 20W
Sittard . . . . **41** 51 0N 5 52 E
Sivas . . . . **80** 39 43N 36 58 E
Siverek . . . . **81** 37 50N 39 19 E
Sivrihisar . . . . **80** 39 30N 31 35 E
Sīwa . . . . **128** 29 11N 25 31 E
Siwalik Range . . . . **92** 28 0N 83 0 E
Sizewell . . . . **24** 52 13N 1 38 E
Sjumen = Kolarovgrad . . . . . . **53** 43 18N 26 55 E
Skadarsko Jezero. . . . . **52** 42 10N 19 20 E
Skagerrak . . . . **60** 57 30N 9 0 E
Skagway **143** 59 23N 135 20W
Skaraborgs län □ . . . . **60** 58 20N 13 30 E
Skeena → **154** 54 9N 130 5W
Skegness . . . . **29** 53 9N 0 20 E
Skollofto - ► . . . . **66** 65 30N 18 30 E
Skellefteå . . . . **67** 64 45N 20 58 E
Skerries, The **26** 53 27N 4 40W
Skiddaw **28** 54 39N 3 9W
Skien . . . . **60** 59 12N 9 35 E
Skierniewice . . . . **58** 51 58N 20 10 E
Skikda . . . . **127** 36 50N 6 58 E
Skipton **28** 53 57N 2 1W
Skíros . . . . **55** 38 55N 24 34 E
Skopje . . . . **52** 42 1N 21 32 E
Skowhegan **148** 44 49N 69 40W
Skull **35** 51 32N 9 40W
Skye **32** 57 15N 6 10W
Skyros = Skíros . . . . **55** 38 55N 24 34 E
Slaney → **35** 52 52N 6 45W
Slask . . . . **58** 51 0N 16 30 E
Slave → **145** 61 18N 113 39W
Slave Coast . . . . . : . . . . **124** 6 0N 2 30 E
Sleaford **29** 53 0N 0 22W
Sliedrecht . . . . **40** 51 50N 4 45 E
Slieve Aughty **35** 53 4N 8 30W
Slieve Bloom **35** 53 4N 7 40W
Slieve Donard **34** 54 10N 5 57W
Slieve Mish **35** 52 12N 9 50W
Slievenamon **35** 52 25N 7 37W
Sligo **34** 54 17N 8 28W
Sligo □ **34** 54 10N 8 35W
Sliven . . . . **53** 42 42N 26 19 E
Slovakian Ore Mts. =
  Slovenské Rudohorie. . . . . . **59** 48 45N 20 0 E
Slovenia = Slovenija □ . . . . . . **52** 45 58N 14 30 E

Slovenija □ . . . . **52** 45 58N 14 30 E
Slovenské Rudohorie. . . . . **59** 48 45N 20 0 E
Słupsk . . . . **58** 54 30N 17 3 E
Slyne Hd. **34** 53 25N 10 10W
Smara **126** 32 9N 8 16W
Smithers **154** 54 45N 127 10W
Smithfield **165** 35 31N 78 16W
Smiths Falls **151** 44 55N 76 0W
Smithton . . . . **119** 40 53S 145 6 E
Smolensk . . . . **68** 54 45N 32 0 E
Smolikas, Óros . . . . **54** 40 9N 20 58 E
Smyrna = İzmir . . . . **80** 38 25N 27 8 E
Snœfell, Iceland **64** 64 48N 15 34W
Snœfell, U.K. **28** 54 18N 4 26W
Snœfellsjökull **64** 64 49N 23 46W
Snake → **171** 46 12N 119 2W
Sneek . . . . **41** 53 2N 5 40 E
Snowdon **26** 53 4N 4 8W
Snowdrift **145** 62 24N 110 44W
Snowy Mts. . . . . **117** 36 30S 148 20 E
Sobat → . . . . **129** 8 32N 32 40 E
Sobral **177** 3 50S 40 20W
Soch'e = Shache . . . . **100** 38 20N 77 10 E
Sochi . . . . **70** 43 35N 39 40 E
Société, Is. de la **123** 17 0S 151 0W
Society Is. = Société, Is. de
  la **123** 17 0S 151 0W
Socorro **161** 34 4N 106 54W
Socotra . . . . **78** 12 30N 54 0 E
Söderhamn . . . . **60** 61 18N 17 10 E
Södermanlands län □ . . . . **60** 59 10N 16 30 E
Södertälje . . . . **60** 59 12N 17 39 E
Sodo . . . . **132** 7 0N 37 41 E
Sofala . . . . **137** 33 4S 149 43 E
Sofia = Sofiya . . . . **53** 42 45N 23 20 E
Sofiya . . . . **53** 42 45N 23 20 E
Øygn og Fjordane fylke □ . . . . . **60** 01 10N 0 0 E
Soissons . . . . **39** 49 25N 3 19 E
Sōja . . . . **109** 34 40N 133 45 E
Söke . . . . **80** 37 48N 27 28 E
Sol Iletsk . . . . **70** 51 10N 55 0 E
Solapur . . . . **91** 17 43N 75 56 E
Soledad, Colombia **184** 10 55N 74 46W
Soledad, Venezuela **185** 8 10N 63 34W
Solent, The **24** 50 45N 1 25W
Solesmes . . . . **38** 50 10N 3 30 E
Solikamsk . . . . **69** 59 38N 56 50 E
Solimões → =
  Amazonas → **185** 0 5S 50 0W
Sóller . . . . **51** 39 46N 2 43 E
Sololá . . . . **177** 14 49N 91 10 E
Solomon Is. ■ . . . . **122** 6 0S 155 0 E
Solţānābād . . . . **86** 36 29N 58 5 E
Solway Firth **31** 54 45N 3 38W
Somali Rep ■ . . . . **133** 7 0N 47 0 F
Sombor . . . . **52** 45 46N 19 9 E
Sombrerete **175** 23 38N 103 39W
Somerset, Bermuda **180** 32 16N 64 55W
Somerset, U.S.A. **169** 37 5N 84 40W
Somerset □ **27** 51 9N 3 0W
Somerset I. **145** 73 30N 93 0W
Somme □ . . . . **36** 50 0N 2 20 E
Somport, Puerto de **51** 42 48N 0 31W
Søndre Strømfjord **147** 66 59N 50 40W
Songkhla . . . . **97** 7 13N 100 37 E
Sonora □ **174** 29 20N 110 40W
Soochow = Suzhou . . . . **99** 31 19N 120 38 E
Sop's Arm **149** 49 46N 56 56W
Sør-Rondane . . . . **14** 72 0S 25 0 E
Sør-Trøndelag fylke □ . . . . **65** 63 0N 10 0 E
Sorata **187** 15 50S 68 40W
Sorel **151** 46 0N 73 10W
Soria **51** 41 43N 2 32W
Sorocaba **191** 23 31S 47 27W
Sørøya . . . . **67** 70 40N 22 30 E
Sorsogon . . . . **112** 13 0N 124 0 E
Sosnowiec . . . . **58** 50 20N 19 10 E
Sotteville-lès-Rouen . . . . **38** 49 24N 1 5 E
Sŏul . . . . **98** 37 31N 126 58 E
Souris, Man., Canada **153** 49 40N 100 20W
Souris, P.E.I., Canada **149** 46 21N 62 15W

South Africa, Rep. of ■ ...... **136** 32 0S 17 0 E
South Auckland & Bay of
  Plenty □ .... **122** 38 30S 177 0 E
South Australia □ .... **118** 32 0S 139 0 E
South Bend **167** 41 38N 86 20W
South Carolina □ **165** 33 45N 81 0W
South Charleston **165** 38 20N 81 40W
South China Sea .... **77** 10 0N 113 0 E
South Dakota □ **163** 45 0N 100 0W
South Downs **25** 50 53N 0 10W
South Georgia **183** 54 30S 37 0W
South Glamorgan □ **27** 51 30N 3 20W
South Haven **167** 42 22N 86 20W
South Island .... **123** 44 0S 170 0 E
South Korea ■ .... **98** 36 0N 128 0 E
South Orkney Is. **14** 63 0S 45 0W
South Platte ⟶ **163** 41 7N 100 42W
South Pole .... **14** 90 0S 0 0 E
South Porcupine **151** 48 30N 81 12W
South Ronaldsay **33** 58 46N 2 58W
South Sandwich Is. **14** 57 0S 27 0W
South Sentinel I. .... **94** 11 1N 92 16 E
South Shetland Is. **14** 62 0S 59 0W
South Shields **28** 54 59N 1 26W
South Taranaki Bight .... **122** 39 40S 174 5 E
South Uist **32** 57 20N 7 15W
South West Africa =
  Namibia ■ .... **136** 22 0S 18 9 E
South West Cape .... **123** 47 16S 167 31 E
South Yemen ■ .... **83** 15 0N 48 0 E
South Yorkshire □ **29** 53 30N 1 20W
Southampton **25** 50 54N 1 23W
Southampton I. **146** 64 30N 84 0W
Southend-on-Sea .... **25** 51 32N 0 42 E
Southern Alps .... **123** 43 41S 170 11 E
Southern Cross .... **120** 31 12S 119 15 E
Southern Indian L. **143** 57 10N 98 30W
Southern Uplands **31** 55 30N 3 3W
Southland □ .... **123** 45 51S 168 13 E
Southport, Australia ...... **116** 27 58S 153 25 E
Southport, U.K. **28** 53 38N 3 1W
Southwold .... **25** 52 19N 1 41 E
Sovetskaya Gavan .... **75** 48 50N 140 0 E
Soviet Union ■ = Union of
  Soviet Socialist
  Republics ■ .... **79** 60 0N 100 0 E
Sōya-Kaikyō = Perouse Str.,
  La .... **77** 45 40N 142 0 E
Spain ■ **50** 40 0N 5 0W
Spalding **29** 52 47N 0 9W
Spandau .... **43** 52 35N 13 7 E
Spanish Fork **163** 40 10N 111 37W
Spanish Town **180** 18 0N 76 57W
Sparks **172** 39 30N 119 45W
Sparta = Spárti .... **54** 37 5N 22 25 E
Sparta................ **166** 43 55N 90 47W
Spartanburg **165** 35 0N 82 0W
Spárti .... **54** 37 5N 22 25 E
Spartivento, C., Calabria, Italy **49** 37 56N 16 4 E
Spartivento, C., Sard., Italy ... **48** 38 52N 8 50 E
Spassk-Dalniy........... **75** 44 40N 132 48 E
Speightstown **180** 13 15N 59 39W
Spence Bay............ **145** 69 32N 93 32W
Spencer **166** 43 5N 95 19W
Spencer G. .... **119** 34 0S 137 20 E
Spenser Mts. .... **123** 42 15S 172 45 E
Sperrin Mts. **34** 54 50N 7 0W
Spessart.............. **42** 50 10N 9 20 E
Spey ⟶ **33** 57 26N 3 25W
Spézia, La .... **46** 44 8N 9 50 E
Spinazzola .... **49** 40 58N 16 5 E
Spithead **25** 50 43N 1 5W
Spitzbergen = Svalbard ..... **13** 78 0N 17 0 E
Split................. **52** 43 31N 16 26 E
Splügenpass .... **44** 46 30N 9 20 E
Spokane.............. **171** 47 45N 117 25W
Sporyy Navolok, Mys .... **69** 75 50N 68 40 E
Spratly, I. .... **112** 8 20N 112 0 E
Spring Mts. **173** 36 20N 115 43W
Springfield, Ill., U.S.A. **166** 39 48N 89 40W
Springfield, Mass., U.S.A..... **164** 42 8N 72 37W

Springfield, Mo., U.S.A....... **168** 37 15N 93 20W
Springfield, Ohio, U.S.A. **167** 39 58N 83 48W
Springfield, Oreg., U.S.A. **171** 44 2N 123 0W
Springfield, Tenn., U.S.A. **169** 36 35N 86 55W
Springfield, Vt., U.S.A. **164** 43 20N 72 30W
Springhill **148** 45 40N 64 4W
Springs............... **137** 26 13S 28 25 E
Springwood .... **117** 33 41S 150 33 E
Spurn Hd. .... **29** 53 34N 0 8 E
Squamish............. **154** 49 45N 123 10W
Sredinnyy Khrebet .... **73** 57 0N 160 0 E
Srednekolymsk .... **73** 67 27N 153 40 E
Sremska Mitrovica .... **52** 44 59N 19 33 E
Srepok ⟶ .... **95** 13 33N 106 16 E
Sretensk .... **74** 52 10N 117 40 E
Sri Lanka ■ .... **90** 7 30N 80 50 E
Srinagar .... **89** 34 5N 74 50 E
Stadskanaal .... **41** 53 4N 6 55 E
Staffa **30** 56 26N 6 21W
Stafford **28** 52 49N 2 9W
Stafford □ **28** 52 53N 2 10W
Staines **25** 51 26N 0 30W
Stalingrad = Volgograd ..... **68** 48 40N 44 25 E
Stalino = Donetsk......... **68** 48 0N 37 45 E
Stalinogorsk =
  Novomoskovsk .... **68** 54 5N 38 15 E
Stalybridge **28** 53 29N 2 4W
Stamford, U.K. **25** 52 39N 0 29W
Stamford, U.S.A. **164** 41 5N 73 30W
Stanislav = Ivano-Frankovsk . **68** 48 40N 24 40 E
Stanley, Canada **152** 55 24N 104 22W
Stanley, Falk. Is. **192** 51 40S 59 51W
Stanovoy Khrebet......... **75** 55 0N 130 0 E
Stanthorpe .... **116** 28 36S 151 59 E
Stara Planina .... **53** 43 15N 23 0 E
Stara Zagora .... **53** 42 26N 25 39 E
Starkville **169** 33 26N 88 48W
Start Pt. **27** 50 13N 3 38W
State College........... **164** 40 47N 77 49W
Staten, I. = Estados, I. de los . **192** 54 40S 64 30W
Statesboro **170** 32 26N 81 46W
Statesville **165** 35 48N 80 51W
Staunton.............. **165** 38 7N 79 4W
Stavanger .... **60** 58 57N 5 40 E
Staveren.............. **40** 52 53N 5 22 E
Stavropol .... **70** 45 5N 42 0 E
Stawell .... **119** 37 5S 142 47 E
Steenwijk .... **41** 52 47N 6 7 E
Stefanie L. = Chew Bahir .... **132** 4 40N 36 50 E
Steiermark □ .... **45** 47 26N 15 0 E
Steinbach **153** 49 32N 96 40W
Steinkjer .... **65** 63 59N 11 31 E
Stellarton **149** 45 32N 62 30W
Stephenville........... **149** 48 31N 58 35W
Stereá Ellas □ .... **54** 38 50N 22 0 E
Sterling, Colo., U.S.A. **163** 40 40N 103 15W
Sterling, Ill., U.S.A. **166** 41 45N 89 45W
Sterlitamak............ **71** 53 40N 56 0 E
Stettin = Szczecin .... **58** 53 27N 14 27 E
Stettler **155** 52 19N 112 40W
Steubenville........... **164** 40 21N 80 39W
Stevens Port **166** 44 32N 89 34W
Stewart **144** 63 19N 139 26W
Stewart I. .... **123** 46 58S 167 54 E
Stikine ⟶ **144** 56 40N 132 30W
Stillwater, Minn., U.S.A. **166** 45 3N 92 47W
Stillwater, Okla., U.S.A. **168** 36 5N 97 3W
Stillwater Ra. **172** 39 45N 118 6W
Stip .... **53** 41 42N 22 10 E
Stirling **31** 56 7N 3 57W
Stirling Ra. .... **120** 34 23S 118 0 E
Stockholm .... **60** 59 20N 18 3 E
Stockholms län □ .... **60** 59 30N 18 20 E
Stockport **28** 53 25N 2 11W
Stockton **172** 38 0N 121 20W
Stockton-on-Tees **29** 54 34N 1 20W
Stoke-on-Trent **28** 53 1N 2 11W
Stonehaven **33** 56 58N 2 11W
Stonehenge **24** 51 9N 1 45W
Stonewall **153** 50 10N 97 19W
Stora Lulevatten .... **66** 67 10N 19 30 E

Storavan	**66**	65 45N	18	10 E
Store Bœlt	**61**	55 20N	11	0 E
Storm B.	**119**	43 10S	147	30 E
Storm Lake	**166**	42 35N	95	11W
Stornoway	**32**	58 12N	6	23W
Storsjön	**66**	63 12N	14	18 E
Storuman	**66**	65 5N	17	10 E
Stour →,				
Hereford & Worcs., U.K.	**24**	52 25N	2	13W
Stour →, Kent, U.K.	**25**	51 15N	1	20 E
Stour →, Suffolk, U.K.	**25**	51 55N	1	5 E
Stourbridge	**24**	52 28N	2	8W
Stowmarket	**25**	52 11N	1	0 E
Strabane	**34**	54 50N	7	28W
Stralsund	**43**	54 17N	13	5 E
Ctrangford, L.	**34**	54 30N	5	37W
Stranraer	**30**	54 54N	5	0W
Strasbourg	**37**	48 35N	7	42 E
Stratford, Canada	**151**	43 23N	81	0W
Stratford, N.Z.	**122**	39 20S	174	19 E
Stratford-on-Avon	**24**	52 12N	1	42W
Strath Spey	**33**	57 15N	3	40W
Strathalbyn	**119**	35 13S	138	53 E
Strathclyde □	**30**	56 0N	4	50W
Strathmore	**33**	56 40N	3	4W
Strathy Pt.	**33**	58 35N	4	0W
Streaky B.	**118.**	32 51S	134	18 E
Streator	**167**	41 9N	88	52W
Strómboli	**49**	38 48N	15	12 E
Stromeferry	**32**	57 20N	5	33W
Stromness	**33**	58 58N	3	18W
Stronsay	**33**	59 8N	2	38W
Stroud	**24**	51 44N	2	12W
Strumica	**53**	41 28N	22	41 E
Stuart L.	**154**	54 30N	124	30W
Stung Treng	**95**	13 31N	105	58 E
Sturgeon Bay	**167**	44 52N	87	20W
Sturgeon Falls	**151**	46 25N	79	57W
Stuttgart, Germany	**42**	48 46N	9	10 E
Stuttgart, U.S.A.	**168**	34 30N	91	33W
Styria = Steiermark □	**45**	47 26N	15	0 E
Suakin	**129**	19 8N	37	20 E
Subotica	**52**	46 6N	19	49 E
Suchitoto	**177**	13 56N	89	0W
Suchou = Suzhou	**99**	31 19N	120	38 E
Süchow = Xuzhou	**99**	34 18N	117	10 E
Sucre	**187**	19 0S	65	15W
Sudan ■	**129**	15 0N	30	0 E
Sudbury, Canada	**151**	46 30N	81	0W
Sudbury, U.K.	**25**	52 2N	0	44 E
Sudetan Mts. = Sudety	**58**	50 20N	16	45 E
Sudety	**58**	50 20N	16	45 E
Suez = El Suweis	**128**	29 58N	32	31 E
Suez Canal = Suweis, Qanâl				
es	**128**	31 0N	32	20 E
Suffolk	**165**	36 47N	76	33W
Suffolk □	**25**	52 16N	1	0 E
Sugluk = Saglouc	**146**	62 14N	75	38W
Suhbaatar	**98**	50 17N	106	10 E
Suir →	**35**	52 15N	7	10W
Suita	**106**	34 45N	135	32 E
Sukhona →	**68**	60 30N	45	0 E
Sukhumi	**70**	43 0N	41	0 E
Sukkertoppen	**147**	65 26N	52	55W
Sukkur	**88**	27 42N	68	54 E
Sukkur Barrage	**88**	27 40N	68	50 E
Sukumo	**109**	32 56N	132	44 E
Sulaiman Range	**89**	30 30N	69	50 E
Sulawesi □	**113**	2 0S	120	0 E
Sulina	**57**	45 10N	29	40 E
Sulitjelma	**66**	67 9N	16	3 E
Sullana	**186**	4 52S	80	39W
Sullivan	**167**	39 5N	87	26W
Sullivan I. = Lambi Kyun	**96**	10 50N	98	20 E
Sulphur Springs	**168**	33 5N	95	36W
Sulu Arch.	**112**	6 0N	121	0 E
Sulu Sea	**112**	8 0N	120	0 E
Suluq	**128**	31 44N	20	14 E
Sumatera □	**111**	0 40N	100	20 E
Sumatra = Sumatera □	**111**	0 40N	100	20 E
Sumba	**113**	9 45S	119	35 E
Sumbawa	**113**	8 26S	117	30 E
Sumburgh Hd.	**30**	59 52N	1	17W
Summerland	**155**	49 32N	119	41W
Summerside	**148**	46 24N	63	47W
Sumoto	**109**	34 21N	134	54 E
Sumter	**165**	33 55N	80	22W
Sumy	**68**	50 57N	34	50 E
Sunbury, Australia	**117**	37 35S	144	44 E
Sunbury, U.S.A.	**164**	40 50N	76	46W
Sunda, Selat	**111**	6 20S	105	30 E
Sundarbans, The	**92**	22 0N	89	0 E
Sunderland	**28**	54 54N	1	22W
Sundsvall	**66**	62 23N	17	17 E
Sungei Patani	**96**	5 38N	100	29 E
Sungei Siput	**96**	4 51N	101	6 E
Sungurlu	**80**	40 12N	34	21 E
Sunnyside	**171**	46 24N	120	2W
Sunnyvale	**172**	37 23N	122	2W
Suntar	**74**	62 15N	117	30 E
Suō-Nada	**108**	33 50N	131	30 E
Superior	**150**	46 45N	92	5W
Superior, L.	**150**	47 40N	87	0W
Suphan Daği	**81**	38 54N	42	48 E
Sūr	**80**	22 34N	59	32 E
Surabaja = Surabaya	**111**	7 17S	112	45 E
Surabaya	**111**	7 17S	112	45 E
Surakarta	**111**	7 35S	110	48 E
Surat	**91**	21 12N	72	55 E
Surat Thani	**96**	9 6N	99	20 E
Suratgarh	**89**	29 18N	73	55 E
Surgut	**69**	61 14N	73	20 E
Surin	**95**	14 50N	103	34 E
Surinam ■	**185**	4 0N	56	0W
Surrey □	**25**	51 16N	0	30W
Surt	**127**	31 11N	16	39 E
Surt, Khalīj	**127**	31 40N	18	30 E
Suruğa-Wan	**107**	34 45N	138	30 E
Susaki	**109**	33 22N	133	17 E
Susanville	**172**	40 28N	120	40W
Susquehanna →	**164**	39 33N	76	5W
Sutherland Falls	**123**	44 48S	167	46 E
Sutlej →	**89**	29 23N	71	3 E
Sutton-in-Ashfield	**29**	53 7N	1	20W
Suva	**122**	18 6S	178	30 E
Suwa	**107**	36 2N	138	8 E
Suwa-Ko	**107**	36 3N	138	5 E
Suwannee →	**170**	29 18N	83	9W
Suwanose-Jima	**104**	29 38N	129	43 E
Suweis, Qanâl es	**128**	31 0N	32	20 E
Suzaka	**107**	36 39N	138	19 E
Suzhou	**99**	31 19N	120	38 E
Suzu-Misaki	**105**	37 31N	137	21 E
Svalbard	**13**	78 0N	17	0 E
Svartenhuk Halvø	**146**	71 50N	54	30W
Svendborg	**61**	55 4N	10	35 E
Sverdlovsk	**69**	56 50N	60	30 E
Sverdrup Is.	**12**	79 0N	97	0W
Svishtov	**53**	43 36N	25	23 E
Svobodnyy	**75**	51 20N	128	0 E
Swabian Alps =				
Schwäbische Alb	**42**	48 30N	9	30 E
Swakopmund	**136**	22 37S	14	30 E
Swale →	**28**	54 5N	1	20W
Swan Hill	**117**	35 20S	143	33 E
Swan Hills	**155**	54 42N	115	24W
Swan Islands	**178**	17 22N	83	57W
Swan River	**152**	52 10N	101	16W
Swanage	**24**	50 36N	1	59W
Swansea	**27**	51 37N	3	57W
Swartberge	**136**	33 20S	22	0 E
Swatow = Shantou	**99**	23 18N	116	40 E
Swaziland ■	**137**	26 30S	31	30 E
Sweden ■	**66**	57 0N	15	0 E
Sweetwater	**161**	32 30N	100	28W
Swift Current	**152**	50 20N	107	45W
Swindon	**24**	51 33N	1	47W
Switzerland ■	**44**	46 30N	8	0 E
Swords	**34**	53 27N	6	15W
Sydney, Australia	**117**	33 53S	151	10 E
Sydney, Canada	**149**	46 7N	60	7W
Sydney Mines	**149**	46 18N	60	15W

Name				
Sydprøven	**147** 60 30N	45 35W
Sydra G. of = Surt, Khalīj	**127** 31 40N	18 30 E
Syktyvkar	**69** 61 45N	50 40 E
Sylacauga	**169** 33 10N	86 15W
Sylhet	**92** 24 54N	91 52 E
Sylvan Lake	**155** 52 20N	114 3W
Syracuse	**164** 43 4N	76 11W
Syrdarya →	**71** 46 3N	61 0 E
Syria ■	**80** 35 0N	38 0 E
Syrian Desert	**76** 31 0N	40 0 E
Syzran	**68** 53 12N	48 30 E
Szczecin	**58** 53 27N	14 27 E
Szechwan = Sichuan □	**99** 31 0N	104 0 E
Szeged	**59** 46 16N	20 10 E
Székesfehérvár	**59** 47 15N	18 25 E
Szolnok	**59** 47 10N	20 15 E
Szombathely	**59** 47 14N	16 38 E
Tabacal	**190** 23 15S	64 15W
Tābah	**82** 26 55N	42 38 E
Tabasco □	**177** 18 0N	92 40W
Taber	**155** 49 47N	112 8W
Tablas	**112** 12 25N	122 2 E
Table Mt.	**136** 34 0S	18 22 E
Table Top, Mt.	**121** 23 24S	147 11 E
Tabora	**135** 5 2S	32 50 E
Tabrīz	**81** 38 7N	46 20 E
Tabūk	**82** 28 23N	36 36 E
Tachibana-Wan	**108** 32 45N	130 7 E
Tachikawa	**107** 35 42N	139 25 E
Tacna	**187** 18 0S	70 20W
Tacoma	**171** 47 15N	122 30W
Tacuarembó	**191** 31 45S	56 0W
Tademaït, Plateau du	**127** 28 30N	2 30 E
Tadoussac	**148** 48 11N	69 42W
Tadzhik S.S.R. □	**71** 35 30N	70 0 E
Taegu	**98** 35 50N	128 37 E
Taejŏn	**98** 36 20N	127 28 E
Taganrog	**68** 47 12N	38 50 E
Tagish	**144** 60 19N	134 16W
Tagua, La	**184** 0 3N	74 40W
Tagus = Tajo →	**50** 38 40N	9 24W
Tahiti	**123** 17 37S	149 27W
Tahoua	**131** 14 57N	5 16 E
Taibei	**99** 25 4N	121 29 E
T'aichung = Taizhong	**99** 24 12N	120 35 E
Taidong	**99** 22 43N	121 9 E
Taihape	**122** 39 41S	175 48 E
Tailem Bend	**119** 35 12S	139 29 E
Taimyr = Taymyr, Poluostrov .	**72** 75 0N	100 0 E
Tain	**33** 57 49N	4 4W
Tainan	**99** 23 17N	120 18 E
Taïnaron, Ákra	**54** 36 22N	22 27 E
T'aipei = Taibei	**99** 25 4N	121 29 E
Taiping	**96** 4 51N	100 44 E
Taisha	**109** 35 24N	132 40 E
Taitao, Pen. de	**192** 46 30S	75 0W
Taiwan ■	**99** 23 30N	121 0 E
Taiyuan	**98** 37 52N	112 33 E
Taizhong	**99** 24 12N	120 35 E
Ta'izz	**83** 13 35N	44 2 E
Tajimi	**106** 35 19N	137 8 E
Tajo →	**50** 38 40N	9 24W
Tak	**94** 16 52N	99 8 E
Takachiho	**108** 32 42N	131 18 E
Takada	**105** 37 7N	138 15 E
Takahashi	**109** 34 51N	133 39 E
Takamatsu	**109** 34 20N	134 5 E
Takaoka	**106** 36 47N	137 0 E
Takapuna	**122** 36 47S	174 47 E
Takasago	**109** 34 45N	134 48 E
Takasaki	**107** 36 20N	139 0 E
Takatsuki	**106** 34 51N	135 37 E
Takawa	**108** 33 38N	130 51 E
Takayama	**106** 36 18N	137 11 E
Takayama-Bonchi	**106** 36 0N	137 18 E
Takefu	**106** 35 50N	136 10 E
Takehara	**109** 34 21N	132 55 E
Taketa	**108** 32 58N	131 24 E
Takhār □	**87** 36 40N	70 0 E
Takla Landing	**154** 55 30N	125 50W
Takla Makan	**76** 39 0N	83 0 E
Taku	**108** 33 18N	130 3 E
Talara	**186** 4 38S	81 18 E
Talaud, Kepulauan	**113** 4 30N	127 10 E
Talca	**190** 35 28S	71 40W
Talcahuano	**190** 36 40S	73 10W
Talesh, Kūhhā-ye	**81** 39 0N	48 30 E
Talguppa	**90** 14 10N	74 45 E
Taliabu	**113** 1 45S	125 0 E
Talkeetna	**142** 62 20N	150 9W
Tall 'Afar	**81** 36 22N	42 27 E
Talladega	**169** 33 28N	86 2W
Tallahassee	**170** 30 25N	84 15W
Tallangatta	**117** 36 15S	147 19 E
Tallinn	**68** 59 22N	24 48 E
Tallulah	**168** 32 25N	91 12W
Tamale	**130** 9 22N	0 50W
Tamana	**108** 32 58N	130 32 E
Tamano	**109** 34 29N	133 59 E
Tamanrasset	**127** 22 50N	5 30 E
Tamar →	**27** 50 33N	4 15W
Tamaulipas □	**176** 24 0N	98 45W
Tambellup	**120** 34 4S	117 37 E
Tambov	**68** 52 45N	41 28 E
Tamgak, Mts.	**127** 19 12N	8 35 E
Tamil Nadu □	**90** 11 0N	77 0 E
Tammerfors = Tampere	**67** 61 30N	23 50 E
Tamo Abu, Pegunungan	**111** 3 10N	115 0 E
Tampa	**170** 27 57N	82 38W
Tampa B.	**170** 27 40N	82 40W
Tampere	**67** 61 30N	23 50 E
Tampico	**177** 22 20N	97 50W
Tamrah	**83** 20 24N	45 25 E
Tamsagbulag	**98** 47 14N	117 21 E
Tamworth, Australia	**116** 31 7S	150 58 E
Tamworth, U.K.	**24** 52 38N	1 41W
Tana →, Kenya	**133** 2 32S	40 31 E
Tana →, Norway	**67** 70 30N	28 23 E
Tana, L.	**132** 13 5N	37 30 E
Tanabe	**106** 33 44N	135 22 E
Tanana	**142** 65 10N	152 15W
Tananarive = Antananarivo .	**137** 18 55S	47 31 E
Tanba-Sanchi	**106** 35 7N	135 48 E
Tandil	**190** 37 15S	59 6W
Tando Adam	**88** 25 45N	68 40 E
Tane-ga-Shima	**104** 30 30N	131 0 E
Tanen Tong Dan	**93** 16 30N	98 30 E
Tanezrouft	**127** 23 9N	0 11 E
Tanga	**135** 5 5S	39 2 E
Tanganyika, L.	**135** 6 40S	30 0 E
Tanger	**126** 35 50N	5 49W
Tanggula Shan	**101** 32 40N	92 10 E
Tangier = Tanger	**126** 35 50N	5 49W
Tangshan	**98** 39 38N	118 10 E
Tanimbar, Kepulauan	**113** 7 30S	131 30 E
Taniyama	**108** 31 31N	130 31 E
Tanjore = Thanjavur	**90** 10 48N	79 12 E
Tannu Ola	**74** 51 0N	94 0 E
Tanout	**131** 14 50N	8 55 E
Tanta	**128** 30 45N	30 57 E
Tantung = Dandong	**98** 40 10N	124 20 E
Tanunda	**119** 34 30S	139 0 E
Tanzania ■	**135** 6 40S	34 0 E
Tapa Shan = Daba Shan	**99** 32 0N	109 0 E
Tapachula	**177** 14 54N	92 17W
Tapajós →	**185** 2 24S	54 41W
Tapanui	**123** 45 56S	169 18 E
Tapi →	**91** 21 8N	72 41 E
Tara →	**71** 56 42N	74 36 E
Tarabagatay, Khrebet	**71** 48 0N	83 0 E
Tarābulus, Lebanon	**80** 34 31N	35 50 E
Tarābulus, Libya	**127** 32 49N	13 7 E
Taranaki □	**122** 39 5S	174 51 E
Táranto	**49** 40 30N	17 11 E
Táranto, G. di	**49** 40 0N	17 15 E
Tarapoto	**186** 6 30S	76 20W
Tarare	**37** 45 54N	4 26 E
Tararua Range	**123** 40 45S	175 25 E
Tarauacá	**187** 8 6S	70 48W

Tarbela Dam	**89**	34	8N	72	52 E
Tarbert	**32**	57	54N	6	49W
Tarbes	**36**	43	15N	0	3 E
Tarcoola	**118**	30	44 S	134	36 E
Taree	**116**	31	50 S	152	30 E
Tarfaya	**126**	27	55N	12	55W
Tarifa	**50**	36	1N	5	36W
Tarija	**187**	21	30 S	64	40W
Tarim ⟶	**100**	41	5N	86	40 E
Tarim Pendi	**100**	40	0N	84	0 E
Tarko Sale	**69**	64	55N	77	50 E
Tarn ⟶	**36**	44	5N	1	6 E
Tarnobrzeg	**58**	50	35N	21	41 E
Tarnów	**58**	50	3N	21	0 E
Tarragona	**51**	41	5N	1	17 E
Tarrasa	**51**	41	34N	2	1 E
Tarsus	**80**	36	58N	34	55 E
Tartagal	**190**	22	30 S	63	50W
Tarjūs	**80**	34	55N	35	55 E
Tarumizu	**108**	31	29N	130	42 E
Tarutao, Ko	**96**	6	33N	99	40 E
Taschereau	**151**	48	40N	78	40W
Tashi Chho Dzong =					
Thimphu	**92**	27	31N	89	45 E
Tashkent	**71**	41	20N	69	10 E
Tasman B.	**123**	40	59 S	173	25 E
Tasman Mts.	**123**	41	3 S	172	25 E
Tasman Sea	**122**	36	0 S	160	0 E
Tasmania □	**119**	42	0 S	146	30 E
Tatabánya	**59**	47	32N	18	25 E
Tatarsk	**71**	55	14N	76	0 E
Tateshina-Yama	**107**	36	8N	138	11 E
Tateyama	**107**	35	0N	139	50 E
Tatra = Tatry	**59**	49	20N	20	0 E
Tatry	**59**	49	20N	20	0 E
Tatsuno	**109**	34	52N	134	33 E
Tat'ung = Datong	**98**	40	6N	113	18 E
Taubaté	**191**	23	0 S	45	36W
Tauern	**45**	47	15N	12	40 E
Taumarunui	**122**	38	53 S	175	15 E
Taunggyi	**93**	20	50N	97	0 E
Taungup Taunggya	**93**	18	20N	93	40 E
Taunton, U.K.	**27**	51	1N	3	7W
Taunton, U.S.A.	**164**	41	54N	71	6W
Taunus	**42**	50	15N	8	20 E
Taupo	**122**	38	41 S	176	7 E
Taupo, L.	**122**	38	46 S	175	55 E
Tauranga	**122**	37	42 S	176	11 E
Taurus Mts. = Toros Daglari	**80**	37	0N	35	0 E
Taverny	**39**	49	2N	2	13 E
Tavistock	**27**	50	33N	4	9W
Tavoy	**94**	14	2N	98	12 E
Tawas City	**167**	44	16N	83	31W
Tay ⟶	**33**	56	37N	3	38W
Tayabamba	**186**	8	15 S	77	16W
Taylor Mt.	**161**	35	16N	107	36W
Taymā	**82**	27	35N	38	45 E
Taymyr, Poluostrov	**72**	75	0N	100	0 E
Tayshet	**74**	55	58N	98	1 E
Tayside □	**31**	56	25N	3	30W
Taz ⟶	**69**	67	32N	78	40 E
Tbilisi	**70**	41	43N	44	50 E
Tchad ■ = Chad ■	**131**	15	0N	17	15 E
Tchad, L.	**131**	13	30N	14	30 E
Tch'eng-tou = Chengdu	**99**	30	38N	104	2 E
Tch'ong-k'ing = Chongqing	**99**	29	35N	106	25 E
Te Anau, L.	**123**	45	15 S	167	45 E
Te Kuiti	**122**	38	20 S	175	11 E
Tecuala	**175**	22	23N	105	27W
Tefé	**185**	3	25 S	64	50W
Tegal	**111**	6	52 S	109	8 E
Tegucigalpa	**179**	14	5N	87	14W
Tehachapi Mts.	**173**	35	0N	118	40W
Tehrān	**86**	35	44N	51	30 E
Tehuacán	**177**	18	27N	97	23W
Tehuantepec	**177**	16	21N	95	13W
Tehuantepec, G. de	**177**	16	0N	94	50W
Tehuantepec, Istmo de	**177**	17	0N	94	30W
Teifi ⟶	**26**	52	4N	4	14W
Teignmouth	**27**	50	33N	3	30W
Tejo ⟶	**50**	38	40N	9	24W
Tekax	**177**	20	12N	89	17W
Tekeli	**71**	44	50N	79	0 E
Tekirdağ	**80**	40	58N	27	30 E
Tel Aviv-Yafo	**80**	32	4N	34	48 E
Tela	**179**	15	40N	87	28W
Telanaipura = Jambi	**111**	1	38 S	103	30 E
Telegraph Cr. ⟶	**144**	58	0N	131	10W
Telemark fylke □	**60**	59	25N	8	30 E
Teles Pires ⟶	**187**	7	21 S	58	3W
Telford	**28**	52	42N	2	31W
Tell City	**167**	38	0N	86	44W
Teme ⟶	**24**	52	23N	2	15W
Temerloh	**96**	3	27N	102	25 E
Temirtau	**71**	50	5N	72	56 E
Temora	**117**	34	30 S	147	30 E
Temosachic	**174**	28	57N	107	51W
Temple	**158**	31	5N	97	22W
Temuco	**190**	38	45 S	72	40W
Temuka	**123**	44	14 S	171	17 E
Tenali	**91**	16	15N	80	35 E
Tenancingo	**177**	19	0N	99	33W
Tenango	**177**	19	7N	99	33W
Tenby	**27**	51	40N	4	42W
Tenerife	**126**	28	15N	16	35W
Teng Xian	**99**	35	5N	117	10 E
Tennessee □	**169**	36	0N	86	30W
Tennessee ⟶	**169**	37	4N	88	34W
Tenri	**106**	34	39N	135	49 E
Tenryū	**107**	34	52N	137	49 E
Tenryū-Gawa ⟶	**107**	35	39N	137	48 E
Tenterfield	**116**	29	0 S	152	0 E
Teófilo Otoni	**189**	17	50 S	41	30W
Tepic	**175**	21	30N	104	54W
Terang	**119**	38	15 S	142	55 E
Terek ⟶	**70**	44	0N	47	30 E
Terengganu □	**96**	4	55N	103	0 E
Teresina	**188**	5	9 S	42	45W
Terewah, L.	**116**	29	52 S	147	35 E
Termez	**70**	37	15N	67	15 E
Términos, L. de	**177**	18	37N	91	33W
Terneuzen	**40**	51	20N	3	50 E
Terni	**46**	42	34N	12	38 E
Terrace	**154**	54	30N	128	35W
Terre Haute	**167**	39	28N	87	24W
Terrell	**168**	32	44N	96	19W
Terschelling	**40**	53	25N	5	20 E
Teruel	**51**	40	22N	1	8W
Teshio	**103**	44	53N	141	44 E
Teslin	**144**	60	10N	132	43W
Test ⟶	**24**	51	7N	1	30W
Tete	**137**	16	13 S	33	33 E
Teteven	**53**	42	50N	24	17 E
Tétouan	**126**	35	35N	5	21W
Tetuán = Tétouan	**126**	35	35N	5	21W
Teuco ⟶	**190**	25	35 S	60	11W
Teutoburger Wald	**42**	52	5N	8	20 E
Tevere ⟶	**46**	41	44N	12	14 E
Tewkesbury	**24**	51	59N	2	8W
Toxarkana, Ark., U.S.A.	**168**	33	25N	94	0W
Texarkana, Tex., U.S.A.	**168**	33	25N	94	3W
Texas □	**161**	31	40N	98	30W
Texel	**40**	53	5N	4	50 E
Teziutlán	**177**	19	49N	97	21W
Tezpur	**93**	26	40N	92	45 E
Thabana Ntlenyana	**137**	29	30 S	29	16 E
Thailand ■	**95**	16	0N	102	0 E
Thailand, G. of	**95**	11	30N	101	0 E
Thal Desert	**89**	31	10N	71	30 E
Thame ⟶	**24**	51	35N	1	8W
Thames ⟶	**122**	37	7 S	175	34 E
Thames ⟶	**25**	51	30N	0	35 E
Thane	**91**	19	12N	72	59 E
Thanh Hoa	**95**	19	48N	105	46 E
Thanh Pho Ho Chi Minh	**95**	10	58N	106	40 E
Thanjavur	**90**	10	48N	79	12 E
Thar Desert	**89**	28	0N	72	0 E
Thásos	**55**	40	40N	24	40 E
Thaungdut	**93**	24	30N	94	40 E
Thazi	**93**	21	0N	96	5 E
The Dalles	**171**	45	40N	121	11W
The Grenadines, Is.	**180**	12	40N	61	20W

The Hague = 's-Gravenhage . **40** 52 7N 4 17 E
The Macumba —▸ .... **118** 27 52S 137 12 E
The Neales —▸ .... **118** 28 8S 136 47 E
The Pas **152** 53 45N 101 15W
The Rock .... **117** 35 15S 147 2 E
The Warburton —▸ .... **118** 28 4S 137 28 E
Thebes = Thívai .... **55** 38 19N 23 19 E
Thermaïkos Kólpos .... **54** 40 15N 22 45 E
Thermopolis **163** 43 35N 108 10W
Thessalía □ .... **54** 39 30N 22 0 E
Thessalon **150** 46 20N 83 30W
Thessaloníki .... **54** 40 38N 22 58 E
Thessaly = Thessalía □ ..... **54** 39 30N 22 0 E
Thetford Mines **148** 46 8N 71 18W
Thicket Portage............ **153** 55 19N 97 42W
Thies **130** 14 50N 16 51W
Thimphu .... **92** 27 31N 89 45 E
Thionville .... **37** 49 20N 6 10 E
Thíra .... **55** 36 23N 25 27 E
Thirsk **29** 54 15N 1 20W
Thisted .... **61** 56 58N 8 40 E
Thívai .... **55** 38 19N 23 19 E
Thomaston................ **170** 32 54N 84 20W
Thomasville, Ga., U.S.A. **170** 30 50N 84 0W
Thomasville, N.C., U.S.A. **165** 35 55N 80 4W
Thon Buri .... **94** 13 43N 100 29 E
Thornaby on Tees **29** 54 36N 1 19W
Thrace = Thráki □ .... **55** 41 9N 25 30 E
Thráki □ .... **55** 41 9N 25 30 E
Three Hills **155** 51 43N 113 15W
Three Hummock I. .... **119** 40 25S 144 55 E
Thule **13** 77 40N 69 0W
Thundelarra.............. **120** 28 53S 117 7 E
Thunder B................ **150** 45 0N 83 20W
Thunder Bay **150** 48 20N 89 15W
Thüringer Wald .... **43** 50 35N 11 0 E
Thurles **35** 52 40N 7 53W
Thursday I................ **115** 10 30S 142 3 E
Thurso **33** 58 34N 3 31W
Tian Shan .... **100** 43 0N 84 0 E
Tianjin .... **98** 39 8N 117 10 E
Tianshui .... **99** 34 32N 105 40 E
Tiber = Tevere —▸ .... **46** 41 44N 12 14 E
Tibesti.................. **127** 21 0N 17 30 E
Tibet = Xizang □ .... **101** 32 0N 88 0 E
Tibooburra............... **118** 29 26S 142 1 E
Ticul **177** 20 24N 89 32W
Tiel .... **40** 51 53N 5 26 E
Tien Shan .... **76** 42 0N 80 0 E
Tien-tsin = Tianjin .... **98** 39 8N 117 10 E
T'ienching = Tianjin .... **98** 39 8N 117 10 E
Tientsin = Tianjin .... **98** 39 8N 117 10 E
Tierra de Campos.......... **50** 42 10N 4 50W
Tierra del Fuego □ **192** 54 0S 67 45W
Tiffin **167** 41 8N 83 10W
Tiflis = Tbilisi .... **70** 41 43N 44 50 E
Tifton **170** 31 28N 83 32W
Tignish **148** 46 58N 64 2W
Tigris = Dijlah, Nahr —▸ .... **81** 31 0N 47 25 E
Tijuana **174** 32 32N 117 1W
Tiksi .... **72** 71 40N 128 45 E
Tilburg .... **40** 51 31N 5 6 E
Tilbury .... **25** 51 27N 0 24 E
Tillsonburg............... **151** 42 53N 80 44W
Tílos .... **55** 36 27N 27 27 E
Timaru .... **123** 44 23S 171 14 E
Timbuktu = Tombouctou **130** 16 50N 3 0W
Timişoara .... **56** 45 43N 21 15 E
Timmins **151** 48 28N 81 25W
Timor .... **113** 9 0S 125 0 E
Timor Sea................ **113** 10 0S 127 0 E
Tinaca Pt................ **112** 5 30N 125 25 E
Tindouf................. **126** 27 42N 8 10W
Tinnevelly = Tirunelveli ..... **90** 8 45N 77 45 E
Tinogasta **190** 28 5S 67 32W
Tínos................... **55** 37 33N 25 8 E
Tioman, Pulau .... **96** 2 50N 104 10 E
Tipperary **35** 52 28N 8 10W
Tipperary □ **35** 52 37N 7 55W
Tipton **24** 52 32N 2 4W
Tirana .... **52** 41 18N 19 49 E

Tiraspol .... **68** 46 55N 29 35 E
Tire .... **80** 38 5N 27 50 E
Tirebolu .... **81** 40 58N 38 45 E
Tiree **30** 56 31N 6 55W
Tîrgu Mureş.............. **57** 46 31N 24 38 E
Tirol □.................. **45** 47 3N 10 43 E
Tiruchchirappalli .... **90** 10 45N 78 45 E
Tirunelveli .... **90** 8 45N 77 45 E
Tisa —▸ .... **59** 45 15N 20 17 E
Tisdale **152** 52 50N 104 0W
Titicaca, L.............. **187** 15 30S 69 30W
Titograd .... **52** 42 30N 19 19 E
Titov Veles.............. **53** 41 46N 21 47 E
Titovo Užice............. **52** 43 55N 19 50 E
Tiverton **27** 50 54N 3 30W
Tívoli .... **46** 41 58N 12 45 E
Tizimín **177** 21 9N 88 9W
Tjirebon = Cirebon .... **111** 6 45S 108 32 E
Tlaxcala □ **177** 19 25N 98 10W
Tlaxiaco **177** 17 18N 97 40W
Tlemcen **127** 34 52N 1 21W
To-Shima .... **107** 34 31N 139 17 E
Toamasina............... **137** 18 10S 49 25 E
Toba Kakar .... **88** 31 30N 69 0 E
Tobago................. **180** 11 10N 60 30W
Tobermory **30** 56 37N 6 4W
Tobolsk .... **69** 58 15N 68 10 E
Tobruk = Tubruq .... **128** 32 7N 23 55 E
Tocantins —▸ .... **188** 1 45S 49 10 E
Toccoa **165** 34 32N 83 17W
Tochigi .... **107** 36 25N 139 45 E
Tocopilla **190** 22 5S 70 10W
Todos Santos **175** 23 27N 110 13W
Tōgane .... **107** 35 33N 140 22 E
Togliatti .... **68** 53 32N 49 24 E
Togo ■ .... **130** 6 15N 1 35 E
Tōhoku □ .... **103** 39 50N 141 45 E
Tōjō................... **109** 34 53N 133 16 E
Tokai .... **106** 35 2N 136 55 E
Tokaj.................. **58** 48 8N 21 27 E
Tokara Kaikyō .... **104** 30 0N 130 0 E
Tokat.................. **80** 40 22N 36 35 E
Tokelau Is............... **123** 9 0S 171 45W
Toki .... **106** 35 18N 137 8 E
Tokoname .... **106** 34 53N 136 51 E
Tokorozawa.............. **107** 35 47N 139 28 E
Tokushima .... **109** 34 4N 134 34 E
Tokuyama .... **108** 34 3N 131 50 E
Tōkyō .... **107** 35 45N 139 45 E
Tōkyō-Wan .... **107** 35 25N 139 47 E
Tolbukhin .... **53** 43 37N 27 49 E
Toledo, Spain **50** 39 50N 4 2W
Toledo, U.S.A............ **167** 41 37N 83 33W
Tolga .... **127** 34 40N 5 22 E
Tolima, Vol. **184** 4 40N 75 19W
Toluca **177** 19 20N 99 40W
Tomakomai .... **103** 42 38N 141 36 E
Tombigbee —▸ **169** 31 4N 87 58W
Tombouctou **130** 16 50N 3 0W
Tomini, Teluk .... **113** 0 10S 122 0 E
Tomsk.................. **71** 56 30N 85 5 E
Tonalá **177** 16 4N 93 45W
Tonantins **184** 2 45S 67 45W
Tonbridge .... **25** 51 12N 0 18 E
Tong Xian .... **98** 39 55N 116 35 E
Tonga ■ **123** 19 50S 174 30W
Tongchuan .... **99** 35 6N 109 3 E
Tonghua................ **98** 41 42N 125 58 E
Tongking, G. of .... **95** 20 0N 108 0 E
Tongue................ **33** 58 29N 4 25W
Tongue —▸ **152** 46 24N 105 52W
Tonk .... **91** 26 6N 75 54 E
Tonkin = Bac Phan .... **95** 22 0N 105 0 E
Tonlé Sap............... **95** 13 0N 104 0 E
Tonopah................ **172** 38 4N 117 12W
Tonoshō .... **109** 34 29N 134 11 E
Tooele **162** 40 30N 112 20W
Toowoomba .... **116** 27 32S 151 56 E
Topeka **166** 39 3N 95 40W
Toppenish **171** 46 27N 120 16W
Torbay **27** 50 26N 3 31W
Torino .... **46** 45 4N 7 40 E

TUL

Name	Pg	°	′		°	′	
Tormes ~→	50	41	18N		6	29W	
Torne älv ~→	67	65	50N		24	12 E	
Torneå = Tornio	67	65	50N		24	12 E	
Torneträsk	66	68	24N		19	15 E	
Tornio	67	65	50N		24	12 E	
Toro, Cerro del	190	29	10S		69	50W	
Toronto, Australia	117	33	0S		151	30 E	
Toronto, Canada	151	43	39N		79	20W	
Toros Daglari	80	37	0N		35	0 E	
Torquay	27	50	27N		3	31W	
Torre Annunziata	49	40	45N		14	26 E	
Tôrre de Moncorvo	50	41	12N		7	8W	
Torremolinos	50	36	38N		4	30W	
Torrens, L.	119	31	0S		137	50 E	
Torreón	174	25	33N		103	26W	
Torres Vedras	50	39	5N		9	15W	
Torridge ~→	27	50	51N		4	10W	
Torrington	164	41	50N		73	9W	
Tortosa	51	40	49N		0	31 E	
Tortosa, C.	51	40	41N		0	52 E	
Toruń	58	53	0N		18	39 E	
Tory I.	34	55	17N		8	12W	
Tosa-Shimizu	109	32	52N		132	58 E	
Tosa-Wan	109	33	15N		133	30 E	
Toscana	46	43	30N		11	5 E	
Tostado	190	29	15S		61	50W	
Tosu	109	33	22N		130	31 E	
Totnes	27	50	26N		3	41W	
Totonicapán	177	14	58N		91	12W	
Tottori	109	35	30N		134	15 E	
Toubkal, Djebel.	126	31	0N		8	0W	
Touggourt	127	33	6N		6	4 E	
Toulon	37	43	10N		5	55 E	
Toulouse	36	43	37N		1	27 E	
Toungoo	93	19	0N		96	30 E	
Touraine	36	47	20N		0	30 E	
Tourane = Da Nang	93	16	4N		108	13 E	
Tourcoing	38	50	42N		3	10 E	
Tournai	42	50	35N		3	25 E	
Tours	36	47	22N		0	40 E	
Townsville	121	19	15S		146	45 E	
Towson	164	39	26N		76	34W	
Toyama	106	36	40N		137	15 E	
Toyama-Wan	105	37	0N		137	30 E	
Toyohashi	106	34	45N		137	25 E	
Toyokawa	106	34	48N		137	27 E	
Toyonaka	106	34	50N		135	28 E	
Toyooka	109	35	35N		134	48 E	
Toyota	106	35	3N		137	7 E	
Tozeur	127	33	56N		8	8 E	
Trabzon	81	41	0N		39	45 E	
Tracy	172	37	46N		121	27W	
Trafalgar, C.	50	36	10N		6	2W	
Trail	155	49	5N		117	40W	
Tralee	35	52	16N		9	42W	
Tralee B.	35	52	17N		9	55W	
Tran Ninh, Cao Nguyen	95	19	30N		103	10 E	
Trangan	113	6	40S		134	20 E	
Trangie	116	32	4S		148	0 E	
Transantarctic Mts.	15	85	0S		170	0W	
Transcona	153	49	55N		97	0W	
Transilvania	57	46	19N		25	0 E	
Transkei	137	32	15S		28	15 E	
Transvaal □	137	25	0S		29	0 E	
Transylvania = Transilvania	57	46	19N		25	0 E	
Transylvanian Alps	17	45	30N		25	0 E	
Trápani	48	38	1N		12	30 E	
Traralgon	117	38	12S		146	34 E	
Trasimeno, L.	46	43	10N		12	5 E	
Travers, Mt.	123	42	1S		172	45 E	
Traverse City	167	44	45N		85	39W	
Travnik	52	44	17N		17	39 E	
Tredegar	27	51	47N		3	16W	
Tregaron	26	52	14N		3	56W	
Treinta y Tres	191	33	16S		54	17W	
Trelew	192	43	10S		65	20W	
Trenque Lauquen	190	36	5S		62	45W	
Trent ~→	29	53	33N		0	44W	
Trentino-Alto Adige □	47	46	30N		11	0 E	
Trento	47	46	5N		11	8 E	
Trenton, Canada	151	44	10N		77	34W	
Trenton, Mo., U.S.A.	166	40	5N		93	37W	
Trenton, N.J., U.S.A.	164	40	15N		74	41W	
Tréport, Le	38	50	3N		1	20 E	
Tres Arroyos	190	38	26S		60	20W	
Três Lagoas	188	20	50S		51	43W	
Tres Montes, C.	192	46	50S		75	30W	
Tres Puntas, C.	192	47	0S		66	0W	
Treviso	47	45	40N		12	15 E	
Trichinopoly = Tiruchchirappalli	90	10	45N		78	45 E	
Trichur	90	10	30N		76	18 E	
Trier	42	49	45N		6	37 E	
Trieste	47	45	39N		13	45 E	
Tríkkala	54	39	34N		21	47 E	
Trincomalee	90	8	38N		81	15 E	
Trinidad, Bolivia	187	14	46S		64	50W	
Trinidad, Colombia	184	5	25N		71	40W	
Trinidad, Cuba	178	21	48N		80	0W	
Trinidad, Uruguay	191	33	30S		56	50W	
Trinidad, U.S.A.	163	37	15N		104	30W	
Trinidad & Tobago ■	180	10	30N		61	20W	
Trinity ~→	168	30	30N		95	0W	
Trinity Mts.	172	40	20N		118	50W	
Tripoli = Tarābulus, Lebanon.	80	34	31N		35	50 E	
Tripoli = Tarābulus, Libya....	127	32	49N		13	7 E	
Trípolis	54	37	31N		22	25 E	
Tripura □	93	24	0N		92	0 E	
Trivandrum	90	8	41N		77	0 E	
Trois-Riviéres	151	46	25N		72	34W	
Troitsk	71	54	10N		61	35 E	
Trollhättan	60	58	17N		12	20 E	
Tromsø	66	69	40N		18	56 E	
Trondheim	65	63	36N		10	25 E	
Trossachs, The	31	56	14N		4	24W	
Trotternish	32	57	32N		6	15W	
Trouville	38	49	21N		0	5 E	
Trowbridge	24	51	18N		2	12W	
Troy, Ala., U.S.A.	169	31	50N		85	58W	
Troy, N.Y., U.S.A.	164	42	45N		73	39W	
Troyes	39	48	19N		4	3 E	
Trucial States = United Arab Emirates ■	85	23	50N		54	0 E	
Trujillo, Hond.	179	16	0N		86	0W	
Trujillo, Peru	186	8	6S		79	0W	
Trujillo, Venezuela	184	9	22N		70	38W	
Trundle	117	32	53S		147	35 E	
Trung-Phan	95	16	0N		108	0 E	
Truro, Canada	149	45	21N		63	14W	
Truro, U.K.	27	50	17N		5	2W	
Tselinograd	71	51	10N		71	30 E	
Tsinan = Jinan	98	36	38N		117	1 E	
Tsinghai = Qinghai □	101	36	0N		98	0 E	
Tsingtao = Qingdao	98	36	5N		120	20 E	
Tsu	106	34	45N		136	25 E	
Tsuchiura	107	36	5N		140	15 E	
Tsugaru-Kaikyō	103	41	35N		141	0 E	
Tsukumi	108	33	4N		131	52 E	
Tsukushi-Sanchi	108	33	25N		130	30 E	
Tsuruga	106	35	45N		136	2 E	
Tsurugi-San	109	33	51N		134	6 E	
Tsuruoka	103	38	44N		139	50 E	
Tsushima, Gifu, Japan	106	35	10N		136	43 E	
Tsushima, Nagasaki, Japan	104	34	20N		129	20 E	
Tuamotu Arch.	123	17	0S		144	0W	
Tubarão	191	28	30S		49	0W	
Tubruq	128	32	7N		23	55 E	
Tubuai Is.	123	25	0S		150	0W	
Tucacas	184	10	48N		68	19W	
Tucson	160	32	14N		110	59W	
Tucumcari	161	35	12N		103	45W	
Tucupita	185	9	2N		62	3W	
Tucuruí	188	3	42S		49	44W	
Tudmur	80	34	36N		38	15 E	
Tuktoyaktuk	144	69	27N		133	2W	
Tula, Mexico	177	23	0N		99	43W	
Tula, U.S.S.R.	68	54	13N		37	38 E	
Tulare	173	36	15N		119	26W	
Tulcán	184	0	48N		77	43W	
Tullahoma	169	35	23N		86	12W	
Tullamore	35	53	17N		7	30W	
Tully	121	17	56S		145	55 E	

73

Name	Page	Lat	Long
Tulsa	168	36 10N	96 0W
Tulua	184	4 6N	76 11W
Tuma →	179	13 6N	84 35W
Tumaco	184	1 50N	78 45W
Tumatumari	185	5 20N	58 55W
Tumbarumba	117	35 44S	148 0 E
Túmbes	186	3 37S	80 27W
Tumkur	90	13 18N	77 6 E
Tummel, L.	33	56 43N	3 55W
Tummo	127	22 45N	14 8 E
Tump	88	26 7N	62 16 E
Tumucumaque, Serra	188	2 0N	55 0W
Tumut	117	35 16S	148 13 E
Tunbridge Wells	25	51 7N	0 16 E
Tundzha →	53	41 40N	26 35 E
Tunis	127	36 50N	10 11 E
Tunisia ■	127	33 30N	9 10 E
Tunja	184	5 33N	73 25W
Tunxi	99	29 42N	118 25 E
Tupelo	169	34 15N	88 42W
Tupiza	187	21 30S	65 40W
Tupper L.	151	44 18N	74 30W
Tuque, La.	151	47 30N	72 50W
Túquerres	184	1 5N	77 37W
Tura	92	25 30N	90 16 E
Turayf	82	31 41N	38 39 E
Turfan = Turpan	100	43 58N	89 10 E
Turfan Depression = Turpan Hami	100	42 40N	89 25 E
Tŭrgovishte	53	43 17N	26 38 E
Turgutlu	80	38 30N	27 48 E
Turin = Torino	46	45 4N	7 40 E
Turkana, L.	132	3 30N	36 5 E
Turkestan	71	43 17N	68 16 E
Turkey ■	80	39 0N	36 0 E
Turkmen S.S.R. □	70	39 0N	59 0 E
Turks Is.	180	21 20N	71 20W
Turku	67	60 30N	22 19 E
Turlock	172	37 30N	120 55W
Turnagain, C.	122	40 28S	176 38 E
Turnhout	42	51 19N	4 57 E
Tŭrnovo	53	43 5N	25 41 E
Turnu Rosu Pasul	57	45 33N	24 17 E
Turnu-Severin	56	44 39N	22 41 E
Turpan	100	43 58N	89 10 E
Turpan Hami	100	42 40N	89 25 E
Turukhansk	74	65 21N	88 5 E
Tuscaloosa	169	33 13N	87 31W
Tuscany = Toscana	46	43 30N	11 5 E
Tuskegee	169	32 24N	85 39W
Tutrakan	53	44 2N	26 40 E
Tuvalu ■	122	8 0S	178 0 E
Tuxpan	177	20 57N	97 24W
Tuxtla Gutiérrez	177	16 45N	93 7W
Tuy Hoa	95	13 5N	109 10 E
Tuyen Hoa	95	17 50N	106 10 E
Tuz Gölü	80	38 45N	33 30 E
Ţūz Khurmātū	81	34 56N	44 38 E
Tuzla	52	44 34N	18 41 E
Tweed →	31	55 42N	2 10W
Tweed Heads	116	28 10S	153 31 E
Twin Falls	172	42 30N	114 30W
Two Harbors	156	47 1N	91 40W
Tyler	168	32 18N	95 18W
Tyne →	28	54 58N	1 28W
Tyne & Wear □	28	54 55N	1 35W
Tynemouth	28	55 1N	1 27W
Tyrol = Tirol □	45	47 3N	10 43 E
Tyrrhenian Sea	48	40 0N	12 30 E
Tyumen	69	57 11N	65 29 E
Tzukong = Zigong	99	29 15N	104 48 E
Uaupés	184	0 8S	67 5W
Ubangi = Oubangi →	131	1 0N	17 50 E
Ube	108	33 56N	131 15 E
Uberaba	188	19 50S	47 55W
Uberlândia	188	19 0S	48 20W
Ubon Ratchathani	95	15 15N	104 50 E
Ucayali →	186	4 30S	73 30W
Uchi Lake	153	51 5N	92 35W
Uchiura-Wan	103	42 25N	140 40 E
Uchur →	75	58 48N	130 35 E
Udaipur	91	24 36N	73 44 E
Uddevalla	60	58 21N	11 55 E
Údine	47	46 5N	13 10 E
Udmurt A.S.S.R. □	69	57 30N	52 30 E
Udon Thani	95	17 29N	102 46 E
Ueda	107	36 24N	138 16 E
Uelen	73	66 10N	170 0W
Uelzen	43	53 0N	10 33 E
Ueno	106	34 45N	136 8 E
Ufa	69	54 45N	55 55 E
Uganda ■	132	2 0N	32 0 E
Uinta Mts.	163	40 45N	110 30W
Uithuizen	41	53 24N	6 41 E
Uji	106	34 53N	135 48 E
Ujjain	91	23 9N	75 43 E
Ujpest	59	47 32N	19 6 E
Ujung Pandang	113	5 10S	119 20 E
Ukiah	172	39 10N	123 9W
Ukrainian S.S.R. □	68	49 0N	32 0 E
Ulaanbaatar	98	47 55N	106 53 E
Ulan Bator = Ulaanbaatar	98	47 55N	106 53 E
Ulan Ude	74	51 45N	107 40 E
Ulcinj	52	41 58N	19 10 E
Ulhasnagar	91	19 15N	73 10 E
Ulladulla	117	35 21S	150 29 E
Ullapool	32	57 54N	5 10W
Ullswater	28	54 35N	2 52W
Ulm	42	48 23N	10 0 E
Ulster □	34	54 35N	6 30W
Ulverston	28	54 13N	3 7W
Ulverstone	119	41 11S	146 11 E
Ulyanovsk	68	54 20N	48 25 E
Ulyasutay	100	47 56N	97 28 E
Umbrella Mts	123	45 35S	169 5 E
Umbria □	46	42 53N	12 30 E
Ume älv →	66	63 45N	20 20 E
Umeå	66	63 45N	20 20 E
Umm al Qaywayn	85	25 30N	55 35 E
Umm Lajj	82	25 0N	37 23 E
Umnak	142	53 20N	168 20W
Umpang	94	16 3N	98 54 E
Umtata	137	31 36S	28 49 E
Unalaska	142	53 40N	166 40W
Ungava B.	146	59 30N	67 30W
Ungava Pen.	146	60 0N	74 0W
União da Vitória	191	26 13S	51 5W
Unimak	142	55 0N	164 0W
Union City	169	36 25N	89 0W
Union of Soviet Socialist Republics ■	79	60 0N	100 0 E
Uniontown	164	39 54N	79 45W
United Arab Emirates ■	85	23 50N	54 0 E
United Kingdom ■	18	55 0N	3 0W
United States of America ■	139	37 0N	96 0W
Unity	152	52 30N	109 5W
Unnao	92	26 35N	80 30 E
Unst	30	60 50N	0 55W
Uozu	106	36 48N	137 24 E
Upata	185	8 1N	62 24W
Upper Austria = Oberösterreich □	45	48 10N	14 0 E
Upper Hutt	123	41 8S	175 5 E
Upper Taimyr →	72	74 15N	99 48 E
Upper Volta ■ = Burkina Faso ■	130	12 0N	1 0W
Uppsala	60	59 53N	17 38 E
Uppsala län □	60	60 0N	17 30 E
Ur	84	30 55N	46 25 E
Uracara	185	2 20S	57 50W
Urakawa	103	42 9N	142 47 E
Ural →	70	47 0N	51 48 E
Ural Mts. = Uralskie Gory	69	60 0N	59 0 E
Uralsk	70	51 20N	51 20 E
Uralskie Gory	69	60 0N	59 0 E
Uranium City	145	59 34N	108 37W
Urawa	107	35 50N	139 40 E
Urbana, Ill., U.S.A.	167	40 7N	88 12W
Urbana, Ohio, U.S.A.	167	40 9N	83 44W

Urbana, La 184 7 8N 66 56W
Urcos 187 13 40S 71 38W
Ures 174 29 26N 110 24W
Urfa .... 81 37 12N 38 50 E
Urgench .... 70 41 40N 60 41 E
Uribia 184 11 43N 72 16W
Urk .... 41 52 39N 5 36 E
Urmia = Orūmīyeh .... 81 37 40N 45 0 E
Urmia, L. = Orūmīyeh,
   Daryāčheh-ye .... 81 37 50N 45 30 E
Uruapan 175 19 30N 102 0W
Uruçuí 188 7 20S 44 28W
Uruguaiana 191 29 50S 57 0W
Uruguay ■ 191 32 30S 56 30W
Uruguay ⟶ 191 34 12S 58 18W
Ürümchi = Ürümqi .... 100 43 45N 87 45 E
Ürümqi .... 100 43 45N 87 45 E
Urup, Os. .... 75 46 0N 151 0 E
Usa .... 108 33 31N 131 21 E
Uşak .... 80 38 43N 29 28 E
Usfan .... 82 21 58N 39 27 E
Ushant = Ouessant, Île d' .. 36 48 28N 5 6W
Ushibuka .... 108 32 11N 130 1 E
Ushuaia 192 54 50S 68 23W
Usk ⟶ 26 51 37N 2 56W
Üsküdar .... 80 41 0N 29 5 E
Usolye Sibirskoye .... 74 52 48N 103 40 E
Uspenskiy .... 71 48 41N 72 43 E
Ussuriysk .... 75 43 48N 131 59 E
Ust-Aldan = Batamay .... 74 63 30N 129 15 E
Ust-Ilimsk .... 74 58 3N 102 39 E
Ust-Kamchatsk .... 73 56 10N 162 28 E
Ust-Kamenogorsk .... 71 50 0N 82 36 E
Ust Maya .... 75 60 30N 134 28 E
Ust Olenek .... 72 73 0N 119 48 E
Ust Port .... 69 69 40N 84 26 E
Ust Urt = Ustyurt, Plato .... 70 44 0N 55 0 E
Ust Vorkuta .... 69 67 24N 64 0 E
Ustí nad Labem .... 58 50 41N 14 3 E
Ustica .... 48 38 42N 13 10 E
Ustinov .... 69 56 51N 53 14 E
Ustyurt, Plato .... 70 44 0N 55 0 E
Usu .... 100 44 27N 84 40 E
Usuki .... 108 33 8N 131 49 E
Usumbura = Bujumbura ..... 135 3 16S 29 18 E
Utah □ 163 39 30N 111 30W
Utah, L. 163 40 10N 111 58W
Uthai Thani .... 94 15 22N 100 3 E
Utica 164 43 5N 75 18W
Uto .... 108 32 41N 130 40 E
Utrecht .... 40 52 5N 5 8 E
Utrecht □ .... 40 52 6N 5 7 E
Utrera 50 37 12N 5 48W
Utsunomiya .... 107 36 30N 139 50 E
Uttar Pradesh □ .... 92 27 0N 80 0 E
Uttoxeter 28 52 53N 1 50W
Uusikaupunki .... 66 60 47N 21 25 E
Uvalde 161 29 15N 99 48W
Uvs Nuur .... 74 50 20N 92 30 E
Uwajima .... 109 33 10N 132 35 E
Uzbek S.S.R. □ .... 70 41 30N 65 0 E

Vaal ⟶ .... 137 29 4S 23 38 E
Vaals .... 41 50 46N 6 1 E
Vaasa .... 67 63 6N 21 38 E
Vác .... 58 47 49N 19 10 E
Vach ⟶ .... 69 60 45N 76 45 E
Vadodara .... 91 22 20N 73 10 E
Vadsø .... 67 70 3N 29 50 E
Váh ⟶ .... 59 47 55N 18 0 E
Vaigach .... 69 70 10N 59 0 E
Val d'Or 151 48 7N 77 47W
Valahia .... 57 44 35N 25 0 E
Valcheta 192 40 40S 66 8W
Valdés, Pen. 192 42 30S 63 45W
Valdez 142 61 14N 146 17W
Valdivia 190 39 50S 73 14W
Valdosta 170 30 50N 83 20W
Valence .... 37 44 57N 4 54 E
Valencia, Spain 51 39 27N 0 23W
Valencia, Venezuela 184 10 11N 68 0W
Valencia □ 51 39 20N 0 40W
Valencia, Albufera de 51 39 20N 0 27W
Valencia, G. de .... 51 39 30N 0 20 E
Valencia de Alcántara 50 39 25N 7 14W
Valenciennes .... 38 50 20N 3 34 E
Valentia I. 35 51 54N 10 22W
Valera 184 9 19N 70 37W
Valkenswaard .... 41 51 21N 5 29 E
Valladolid, Mexico 177 20 41N 88 12W
Valladolid, Spain. 50 41 38N 4 43W
Valle d'Aosta □ .... 46 45 45N 7 22 E
Valle de la Pascua 184 9 13N 66 0W
Valle de Santiago 177 20 23N 101 12W
Vallooas 50 40 23N 3 41W
Vallejo 172 38 12N 122 15W
Valletta .... 49 35 54N 14 30 E
Valley City 163 46 57N 98 0W
Valley View 155 40 39N 76 33W
Valona = Vlóra .... 52 40 32N 19 28 E
Valparaíso, Chile 190 33 2S 71 40W
Valparaíso, Mexico. 175 22 46N 103 34W
Valsad .... 91 20 40N 72 58 E
Van .... 81 38 30N 43 20 E
Van, L. = Van Gölü .... 81 38 30N 43 0 E
Van Buren, Canada 148 47 10N 67 55W
Van Buren, U.S.A. 168 35 28N 94 18W
Van Gölü .... 81 38 30N 43 0 E
Van Wert 167 40 52N 84 31W
Vancouver, Canada 154 49 15N 123 10W
Vancouver, U.S.A. 171 45 44N 122 41W
Vancouver I. 154 49 50N 126 0W
Vandalia 166 38 57N 89 4W
Vanderhoof 154 54 0N 124 0W
Vänern .... 60 58 47N 13 30 E
Vâñier 151 45 27N 75 40W
Vankarem .... 73 67 51N 175 50 E
Vännäs .... 66 63 58N 19 48 E
Vannec 36 47 40N 2 47W
Vanua Levu .... 122 16 33S 179 15 E
Vanuatu ■ .... 122 15 0S 168 0 E
Varanasi .... 92 25 22N 83 0 E
Varangerfjorden .... 67 70 3N 29 25 E
Varaždin .... 52 46 20N 16 20 E
Vardak □ .... 87 34 0N 68 0 E
Vardø .... 67 70 23N 31 5 E
Vârmland .... 60 60 0N 13 30 E
Varna .... 53 43 13N 27 56 E
Vascongadas 50 42 50N 2 45W
Västerås .... 60 59 37N 16 38 E
Västmanlands län □ .... 60 59 45N 16 20 E
Vatnajökull 64 64 30N 16 48W
Vatra-Dornei .... 57 47 22N 25 22 E
Vättern .... 60 58 25N 14 30 E
Vaygach, Ostrov .... 69 70 0N 60 0 E
Veendam .... 41 53 5N 6 52 E
Vega, La 180 19 20N 70 30W
Veghel .... 41 51 37N 5 32 E
Vegreville 155 53 30N 112 5W
Vela, La 184 11 27N 69 34W
Vellore .... 90 12 57N 79 10 E
Venado Tuerto 190 33 50S 62 0W
Vendôme .... 39 47 47N 1 3 E
Véneto □ .... 47 45 40N 12 0 E
Venézia .... 47 45 27N 12 20 E
Venézia, Golfo di .... 47 45 20N 13 0 E
Venezuela ■ 184 8 0N 65 0W
Venezuela, Golfo de 184 11 30N 71 0W
Vengurla .... 91 15 53N 73 45 E
Venice = Venézia .... 47 45 27N 12 20 E
Venlo .... 41 51 22N 6 11 E
Venraij .... 41 51 31N 6 0 E
Ventnor 24 50 35N 1 12W
Ventoux .... 37 44 10N 5 17 E
Ventura 173 34 16N 119 18W
Veracruz 177 19 10N 96 10W
Veracruz □ 177 19 20N 96 40W
Verde, R. ⟶ 175 15 59N 97 50W
Verdun .... 37 49 12N 5 24 E
Vereeniging .... 137 26 38S 27 57 E

Name							
Verkhoyansk	72	67	35N	133	25 E
Verkhoyanskiy Khrebet	72	66	0N	129	0 E
Vermilion	152	53	20N	110	50W
Vermont □	164	43	40N	72	50W
Verneuil-sur-Avre	39	48	45N	0	55 E
Vernon, Canada	155	50	20N	119	15W
Vernon, France	39	49	5N	1	30 E
Vernon, U.S.A.	161	34	10N	99	20W
Verona	46	45	27N	11	0 E
Versailles	39	48	48N	2	8 E
Vert, C.	130	14	45N	17	30W
Verviers	42	50	37N	5	52 E
Vest-Agder fylke □	60	58	30N	7	15 E
Vesterålen	64	68	45N	15	0 E
Vestfjorden	64	67	55N	14	0 E
Vestfold fylke □	60	59	15N	10	0 E
Vestspitsbergen	13	78	40N	17	0 E
Vesuvio	49	40	50N	14	22 E
Vesuvius, Mt. = Vesuvio	49	40	50N	14	22 E
Viacha	187	16	39S	68	18W
Viborg	61	56	27N	9	23 E
Vicenza	47	45	32N	11	31 E
Vichy	37	46	9N	3	26 E
Vicksburg	169	32	22N	90	56W
Victor Harbor	119	35	30S	138	37 E
Victoria, Canada	154	48	30N	123	25W
Victoria, Chile	190	38	13S	72	20W
Victoria, U.S.A.	158	28	50N	97	0W
Victoria □	117	37	0S	144	0 E
Victoria, L.	132	1	0S	33	0 E
Victoria de las Tunas	178	20	58N	76	59W
Victoria Falls	137	17	58S	25	52 E
Victoria I.	145	71	0N	111	0W
Victoria Ld.	15	75	0S	160	0 E
Victoriaville	148	46	4N	71	56W
Vidalia	170	32	13N	82	25W
Vidin	53	43	59N	22	50 E
Viedma	192	40	50S	63	0W
Vienna = Wien	45	48	12N	16	22 E
Vienne	37	45	31N	4	53 E
Vienne →	36	47	13N	0	5 E
Vientiane	95	17	58N	102	36 E
Vientos, Paso de los	180	20	0N	74	0W
Vietnam ■	95	19	0N	106	0 E
Vigo	50	42	12N	8	41W
Vijayawada	92	16	31N	80	39 E
Vila Real de Santo António	50	37	10N	7	28W
Vilhelmina	66	64	35N	16	39 E
Vilhena	187	12	40S	60	5W
Villa Bella	187	10	25S	65	22W
Villa Bens = Tarfaya	126	27	55N	12	55W
Villa Cisneros = Dakhla	126	23	50N	15	53W
Villa Dolores	190	31	58S	65	15W
Villa María	190	32	20S	63	10W
Villa Montes	187	21	10S	63	30W
Villaguay	190	32	0S	59	0W
Villahermosa	177	17	59N	92	55W
Villanueva de la Serena	50	38	59N	5	50W
Villarreal	51	39	55N	0	3W
Villarrica	191	39	15S	72	15W
Villazón	187	22	0S	65	35W
Ville Platte	168	30	45N	92	17W
Villefranche-sur-Saône	37	45	59N	4	43 E
Villers-Cotterêts	39	49	15N	3	4 E
Vilnius	68	54	38N	25	19 E
Vilskutskogo, Proliv	72	78	0N	103	0 E
Vilyuy →	74	64	24N	126	26 E
Vilyuysk	74	63	40N	121	35 E
Viña del Mar	190	33	0S	71	30W
Vincennes	167	38	42N	87	29W
Vindhya Ra.	91	22	50N	77	0 E
Vinh	95	18	45N	105	38 E
Vinita	168	36	40N	95	12W
Vinkovci	52	45	19N	18	48 E
Vinnitsa	68	49	15N	28	30 E
Viramgam	91	23	5N	72	0 E
Virden	153	49	50N	100	56W
Vire	36	48	50N	0	53W
Vírgenes, C.	192	52	19S	68	21W
Virgin →	173	36	50N	114	10W
Virgin Is.	180	18	40N	64	30W
Virginia	156	47	30N	92	32W
Virginia □	165	37	45N	78	0W
Virginia Beach	165	36	54N	75	58W
Visalia	173	36	25N	119	18W
Visby	60	57	37N	18	18 E
Viscount Melville Sd.	145	74	10N	108	0W
Višegrad	52	43	47N	19	17 E
Vishakhapatnam	92	17	45N	83	20 E
Vistula = Wisła →	58	54	22N	18	55 E
Vitebsk	68	55	10N	30	15 E
Viti Levu	122	17	30S	177	30 E
Vitim →	74	59	26N	112	34 E
Vitória, Brazil	189	20	20S	40	22W
Vitória, Spain	50	42	50N	2	41W
Vitória da Conquista	189	14	51S	40	51W
Vizianagaram	92	18	6N	83	30 E
Vlaardingen	40	51	55N	4	21 E
Vladimir	68	56	15N	40	30 E
Vladivostok	75	43	10N	131	53 E
Vlieland	40	53	16N	4	55 E
Vlissingen	40	51	26N	3	34 E
Vlóra	52	40	32N	19	28 E
Vltava →	59	50	21N	14	30 E
Vogelkop	113	1	25S	133	0 E
Vogels Berg, mt.	42	50	37N	9	30 E
Vohimena, Tanjon' i	137	25	36S	45	8 E
Voi	133	3	25S	38	32 E
Volendam	40	52	30N	5	4 E
Volga →	68	48	30N	46	0 E
Volga Hts. = Privolzhskaya Vozvyshennost	17	51	0N	46	0 E
Volgograd	68	48	40N	44	25 E
Vollenhove	41	52	40N	5	58 E
Vologda	68	59	10N	40	0 E
Vólos	54	39	24N	22	59 E
Volsk	68	52	5N	47	22 E
Volta →	130	5	46N	0	41 E
Volta, L.	130	7	30N	0	15 E
Volta Redonda	188	22	31S	44	5W
Voorburg	40	52	5N	4	24 E
Vopnafjörður	64	65	45N	14	40W
Vorlai Sporádhes	55	39	15N	23	30 E
Voronezh	68	51	40N	39	10 E
Voroshilovgrad	68	48	38N	39	15 E
Vosges	37	48	20N	7	10 E
Vostochnyy Sayan	74	54	0N	96	0 E
Vrangelya, Ostrov	73	71	0N	180	0 E
Vranje	53	42	34N	21	54 E
Vratsa	53	43	13N	23	30 E
Vršac	52	45	8N	21	18 E
Vught	40	51	38N	5	20 E
Vulcan	155	50	25N	113	15W
Vyborg	68	60	43N	28	47 E
Vychegda →	69	61	18N	46	36 E
Vychodné Beskydy	59	49	30N	22	0 E
Wa	130	10	7N	2	25W
Waal →	41	51	59N	4	30 E
Waalwijk	40	51	42N	5	4 E
Wabash	167	40	48N	85	46W
Wabash →	167	37	46N	88	2W
Wąbrzeźno	58	53	16N	18	57 E
Waco	168	31	33N	97	5W
Wād Medanî	129	14	28N	33	30 E
Waddenzee	40	53	6N	5	10 E
Waddington, Mt.	154	51	23N	125	15W
Waddinxveen	40	52	2N	4	40 E
Wadena	152	51	57N	103	47W
Wadi Halfa	129	21	53N	31	19 E
Wageningen	41	51	58N	5	40 E
Wager Bay	146	65	56N	90	49W
Wagga Wagga	117	35	7S	147	24 E
Wagin	120	33	17S	117	25 E
Waigeo	113	0	20S	130	40 E
Waihi	122	37	23S	175	52 E
Waikerie	119	34	9S	140	0 E
Waikokopu	122	39	3S	177	52 E
Waimate	123	44	45S	171	3 E
Wainwright, Canada	152	52	50N	110	50W

Wainwright, U.S.A. **142** 70 39N 160 1W
Waipara . . . . **123** 43 3S 172 46 E
Waipu . . . . **122** 35 59S 174 29 E
Waipukurau . . . . **122** 40 1S 176 33 E
Wairoa . . . . **122** 39 3S 177 25 E
Waitara . . . . **122** 38 59S 174 15 E
Wajima . . . . **105** 37 30N 137 0 E
Wajir . . . . **133** 1 42N 40 5 E
Wakasa-Wan . . . . **106** 35 40N 135 30 E
Wakatipu, L. . . . . **123** 45 5S 168 33 E
Wakayama . . . . **106** 34 15N 135 15 E
Wakefield, N.Z. . . . . **123** 41 24S 173 5 E
Wakefield, U.K. **28** 53 41N 1 31W
Wakkanai . . . . **103** 45 28N 141 35 E
Wałbrzych . . . . **58** 50 45N 16 18 E
Walcha . . . . **116** 30 55S 151 31 E
Walcheren . . . . **40** 51 30N 3 35 E
Wales □ **26** 52 30N 3 30W
Walgett . . . . **116** 30 0S 148 5 E
Walkerton **151** 44 10N 81 10W
Walla Walla **171** 46 3N 118 25W
Wallaceburg **150** 42 34N 82 23W
Wallachia = Valahia . . . . **57** 44 35N 25 0 E
Wallangarra . . . . **116** 28 56S 151 58 E
Wallaroo . . . . **119** 33 56S 137 39 E
Wallasey **28** 53 26N 3 2W
Wallerawang . . . . **117** 33 25S 150 4 E
Wallis & Futuna **122** 13 18S 176 10W
Wallowa, Mts. **171** 45 20N 117 30W
Wallsend, Australia . . . . **117** 32 55S 151 40 E
Wallsend, U.K. **28** 54 59N 1 30W
Walney, Isle of **28** 54 5N 3 15W
Walpole . . . . **120** 34 58S 116 44 E
Walsall **24** 52 36N 1 59W
Walvis Bay . . . . **136** 23 0S 14 28 E
Wana . . . . **88** 32 20N 69 32 E
Wanaka I . . . . **123** 44 33S 169 7 E
Wang Saphung . . . . **95** 17 18N 101 46 E
Wanganui . . . . **122** 39 56S 175 3 E
Wangaratta . . . . **117** 36 21S 146 19 E
Wanxian . . . . **99** 30 42N 108 20 E
Warabi . . . . **107** 35 49N 139 41 E
Warangal . . . . **91** 17 58N 79 35 E
Warburton . . . . **117** 37 47S 145 42 E
Wardha . . . . **91** 20 45N 78 39 E
Wardha ➝ . . . . **91** 19 57N 79 11 E
Warialda . . . . **116** 29 29S 150 33 E
Warley **24** 52 30N 2 0W
Warner Mts. **172** 41 30N 120 20W
Waroona . . . . **120** 32 50S 115 58 E
Warracknabeal . . . . **119** 36 9S 142 26 E
Warragul . . . . **117** 38 10S 145 58 E
Warrego ➝ . . . . **116** 30 24S 145 21 E
Warrego Ra. . . . . **121** 24 58S 146 0 E
Warren, Australia . . . . **116** 31 42S 147 51 E
Warren, Ark., U.S.A. **168** 33 35N 92 3W
Warren, Mich., U.S.A. **167** 42 31N 83 2W
Warren, Ohio, U.S.A. **164** 41 18N 80 52W
Warren, Pa., U.S.A. **164** 41 52N 79 10W
Warrenpoint **34** 54 7N 6 15W
Warrensburg **166** 38 45N 93 45W
Warrington, U.K. **28** 53 25N 2 38W
Warrington, U.S.A. **169** 30 22N 87 16W
Warrnambool . . . . **119** 38 25S 142 30 E
Warsaw = Warszawa . . . . **58** 52 13N 21 0 E
Warszawa . . . . **58** 52 13N 21 0 E
Warta ➝ . . . . **58** 52 35N 14 39 E
Warthe = Warta ➝ . . . . **58** 52 35N 14 39 E
Warwick, Australia . . . . **116** 28 10S 152 1 E
Warwick, U.K. **24** 52 17N 1 36W
Warwick, U.S.A. **164** 41 43N 71 25W
Warwick □ **24** 52 20N 1 30W
Wasatch Ra. **163** 40 30N 111 15W
Wasco **173** 35 37N 119 16W
Wash, The . . . . **29** 52 58N 0 20 E
Washim . . . . **91** 20 3N 77 0 E
Washington, D.C., U.S.A. **165** 38 52N 77 0W
Washington, Ind., U.S.A. **167** 38 40N 87 8W
Washington, Mo., U.S.A. **166** 38 35N 91 1W
Washington, Pa., U.S.A. **164** 40 10N 80 20W
Washington □ **171** 47 45N 120 30W

Wassenaar . . . . **40** 52 8N 4 24 E
Waterbury **164** 41 32N 73 0W
Waterford **35** 52 16N 7 8W
Waterford □ **35** 52 10N 7 40W
Waterloo, Canada **151** 43 30N 80 32W
Waterloo, U.S.A. **166** 42 27N 92 20W
Watertown, N.Y., U.S.A. **151** 43 58N 75 57W
Watertown, Wis., U.S.A. **167** 43 15N 88 45W
Waterville **148** 44 35N 69 40W
Watling I. = San Salvador **178** 24 0N 74 40W
Watrous **152** 51 40N 105 25W
Watson Lake **144** 60 6N 128 49W
Watsonville **173** 36 55N 121 49W
Watubela, Kepulauan . . . . **113** 4 28S 131 35 E
Wauchope . . . . **116** 31 28S 152 45 E
Waukegan **167** 42 22N 87 54W
Waukesha **167** 43 0N 88 15W
Wausau **166** 44 57N 89 40W
Wauwatosa **167** 43 6N 87 59W
Waveney ➝ . . . . **25** 52 24N 1 20 E
Wâw . . . . **129** 7 45N 28 1 E
Waxahachie **168** 32 22N 96 53W
Waycross **170** 31 12N 82 25W
Waynesboro, Pa., U.S.A. **164** 39 46N 77 32W
Waynesboro, Va., U.S.A. **165** 38 4N 78 57W
Waynesville **165** 35 31N 83 0W
Wazirabad . . . . **89** 32 30N 74 8 E
Weald, The . . . . **25** 51 7N 0 9 E
Webo = Nyaake **130** 4 52N 7 37W
Weddell Sea **14** 72 30S 40 0W
Wedderburn . . . . **117** 36 26S 143 33 E
Wee Waa . . . . **116** 30 11S 149 26 E
Weert . . . . **41** 51 15N 5 43 E
Weesp . . . . **40** 52 18N 5 2 E
Weifang . . . . **98** 36 47N 119 10 E
Weiser **171** 44 10N 117 0W
Walbaum Hill . . . . **118** 27 21S 134 6 E
Welch **165** 37 29N 81 36W
Welland **151** 43 0N 79 15W
Welland ➝ **29** 52 43N 0 10W
Wellingborough **25** 52 18N 0 41W
Wellington, Australia . . . . **116** 32 35S 148 59 E
Wellington, N.Z. . . . . **123** 41 19S 174 46 E
Wellington, Salop, U.K. **28** 52 42N 2 31W
Wellington, Somerset, U.K. **27** 50 58N 3 13W
Wellington □ . . . . **123** 40 8S 175 36 E
Wellington, I. **192** 49 30S 75 0W
Wells, Norfolk, U.K. . . . . **29** 52 57N 0 51 E
Wells, Somerset, U.K. **27** 51 12N 2 39W
Wells, U.S.A. **172** 41 8N 115 0W
Wollovillo, N.Y., U.S.A. **164** 42 9N 77 53W
Wellsville, Ohio, U.S.A. **164** 40 36N 80 40W
Welshpool **26** 52 40N 3 9W
Wem **28** 52 52N 2 45W
Wenatchee **171** 47 30N 120 17W
Wenchow = Wenzhou . . . . **99** 28 0N 120 38 E
Wensleydale **28** 54 18N 2 0W
Wentworth . . . . **119** 34 2S 141 54 E
Wenzhou . . . . **99** 28 0N 120 38 E
Werribee . . . . **117** 37 54S 144 40 E
Werris Creek . . . . **116** 31 18S 150 38 E
Weser ➝ . . . . **42** 53 33N 8 30 E
West Bengal □ . . . . **92** 23 0N 88 0 E
West Bromwich **24** 52 32N 2 1W
West Falkland **192** 51 40S 60 0W
West Frankfort **166** 37 56N 89 0W
West Germany ■ . . . . **42** 52 0N 9 0 E
West Glamorgan □ **27** 51 40N 3 55W
West Memphis **169** 35 5N 90 11W
West Midlands □ **24** 52 30N 1 55W
West Palm Beach **170** 26 44N 80 3W
West Schelde ➝ =
Westerschelde ➝ . . . . **40** 51 25N 3 25 E
West Siberian Plain . . . . **76** 62 0N 75 0 E
West Sussex □ **25** 50 55N 0 30W
West Virginia □ **165** 39 0N 81 0W
West Yorkshire □ **28** 53 45N 1 40W
Western Australia □ . . . . **114** 25 0S 118 0 E
Western Ghats . . . . **90** 14 0N 75 0 E
Western Isles □ **32** 57 30N 7 10W
Western Sahara ■ **126** 25 0N 13 0W

Name	Map	Lat°	Lat'	N/S	Long°	Long'	E/W
Western Samoa ■	123	14	0S	172	0W
Westerschelde →~	40	51	25N	3	25 E
Westerwald	42	50	39N	8	0 E
Westfriesche Eilanden	40	53	20N	5	10 E
Westland □	123	43	33S	169	59 E
Westland Bight	123	42	55S	170	5 E
Westlock	155	54	9N	113	55W
Westmeath □	34	53	30N	7	30W
Westminster	164	39	34N	77	1W
Weston	165	39	3N	80	29W
Weston-super-Mare	27	51	20N	2	59W
Westport	123	41	46S	171	37 E
Westray	33	59	18N	3	0W
Wetar	113	7	30S	126	30 E
Wetaskiwin	155	52	55N	113	24W
Wewaka	168	35	10N	96	35W
Wexford	35	52	20N	6	28W
Wexford □	35	52	20N	6	25W
Weyburn	152	49	40N	103	50W
Weymouth	27	50	36N	2	28W
Whakatane	122	37	57S	177	1 E
Whale Cove	145	62	11N	92	36W
Whalsay	30	60	22N	1	0W
Whangamomona	122	39	8S	174	44 E
Whangarei	122	35	43S	174	21 E
Wharfe →~	29	53	55N	1	30W
Wheeler Pk.	172	38	57N	114	15W
Wheeling	164	40	2N	80	41W
Whernside	28	54	14N	2	24W
Whitby	29	54	29N	0	37W
Whitchurch	28	52	58N	2	42W
White →~, Ark., U.S.A.	168	33	53N	91	3W
White →~, Ind., U.S.A.	167	38	25N	87	45W
White →~, S. Dak., U.S.A.	163	43	45N	99	30W
White Cliffs	118	30	50S	143	10 E
White Mts.	157	44	15N	71	15W
White Nile = Nîl el Abyad →~	129	15	38N	32	31 E
White Russia = Byelorussian S.S.R. □	68	53	30N	27	0 E
White Sea = Beloye More	69	66	30N	38	0 E
Whitecliffs	123	43	26S	171	55 E
Whitehaven	28	54	33N	3	35W
Whitehorse	144	60	43N	135	3W
Whitney, Mt.	173	36	35N	118	14W
Whitstable	25	51	21N	1	2 E
Whitsunday I.	121	20	15S	149	4 E
Whittier	142	60	46N	148	48W
Whyalla	118	33	2S	137	30 E
Wichita	158	37	40N	97	20W
Wichita Falls	161	33	57N	98	30W
Wick	33	58	26N	3	5W
Wickepin	120	32	50S	117	30 E
Wicklow	35	53	0N	6	2W
Wicklow □	35	52	59N	6	25W
Wicklow Mts.	35	53	0N	6	30W
Widnes	28	53	22N	2	44W
Wieluń	58	51	15N	18	34 E
Wien	45	48	12N	16	22 E
Wiesbaden	42	50	7N	8	17 E
Wigan	28	53	33N	2	38W
Wight, I. of	25	50	40N	1	20W
Wigtown	31	54	52N	4	27W
Wigtown B.	31	54	46N	4	15W
Wilcannia	118	31	30S	143	26 E
Wildwood	164	38	59N	74	46W
Wilhelmshaven	42	53	30N	8	9 E
Wilkes Barre	164	41	15N	75	52W
Wilkes Sub-Glacial Basin	15	75	0S	130	0 E
Wilkie	152	52	27N	108	42W
Willamina	171	45	9N	123	32W
Willemstad	181	12	5N	69	0W
Williams L.	154	51	48N	90	45W
Williamsburg	165	37	17N	76	44W
Williamson	165	37	46N	82	17W
Williamsport	164	41	18N	77	1W
Williamstown	117	37	51S	144	52 E
Williston	163	48	10N	103	35W
Willits	172	39	28N	123	17W
Willmar	156	45	5N	95	0W
Wilmette	167	42	6N	87	44W
Wilmington, Del., U.S.A.	164	39	45N	75	32W
Wilmington, N.C., U.S.A.	165	34	14N	77	54W
Wilson	165	35	44N	77	54W
Wilsons Promontory	117	38	55S	146	25 E
Wilton	24	51	5N	1	52W
Wiltshire □	24	51	20N	2	0W
Wiluna	120	26	36S	120	14 E
Wimereux	38	50	45N	1	37 E
Winchester, U.K.	25	51	4N	1	19W
Winchester, Ind., U.S.A.	167	40	10N	84	56W
Winchester, Ky., U.S.A.	165	38	0N	84	8W
Winchester, Va., U.S.A.	164	39	14N	78	8W
Wind River Range	163	43	0N	109	30W
Windermere	28	54	24N	2	56W
Windermere, L.	28	54	20N	2	57W
Windhoek	136	22	35S	17	4 E
Windsor, Australia	117	33	37S	150	50 E
Windsor, Nfld., Canada	149	48	57N	55	40W
Windsor, Ont., Canada	150	42	18N	83	0W
Windsor, U.K.	25	51	28N	0	36W
Windward Is.	181	13	0N	63	0W
Windward Passage = Vientos, Paso de los	180	20	0N	74	0W
Winisk →~	140	55	17N	85	5W
Winkler	153	49	10N	97	56W
Winnemucca	172	41	0N	117	45W
Winnfield	168	31	57N	92	38W
Winnipeg	153	49	54N	97	9W
Winnipeg, L.	153	52	0N	97	0W
Winnipegosis L.	153	52	30N	100	0W
Winona	166	44	2N	91	39W
Winooski	151	44	31N	73	11W
Winschoten	41	53	9N	7	3 E
Winslow	161	35	2N	110	41W
Winston-Salem	165	36	7N	80	15W
Winter Haven	170	28	0N	81	42W
Winter Park	170	28	34N	81	19W
Winterswijk	41	51	58N	6	43 E
Winterthur	44	47	30N	8	44 E
Wirral	28	53	25N	3	0W
Wisbech	29	52	39N	0	10 E
Wisconsin □	166	44	30N	90	0W
Wisconsin →~	166	43	0N	91	15W
Wisconsin Rapids	166	44	25N	89	50W
Wishaw	31	55	46N	3	55W
Wisła →~	58	54	22N	18	55 E
Witham →~	29	53	3N	0	8W
Withernsea	29	53	43N	0	2 E
Witney	24	51	47N	1	29W
Włocławek	58	52	40N	19	3 E
Wodonga	117	36	5S	146	50 E
Wokam	113	5	45S	134	28 E
Woking	25	51	18N	0	33W
Wolin	58	53	50N	14	37 E
Wollaston L.	145	58	7N	103	10W
Wollaston Pen.	145	69	30N	115	0W
Wollongong	117	34	25S	150	54 E
Wolverhampton	24	52	35N	2	6W
Wondai	116	26	20S	151	49 E
Wŏnsan	98	39	11N	127	27 E
Wonthaggi	117	38	37S	145	37 E
Woodburn	116	29	6S	153	23 E
Woodenbong	116	28	24S	152	39 E
Woodend	117	37	20S	144	33 E
Woodland	172	38	40N	121	50W
Woods, L. of the	153	49	15N	94	45W
Woodstock, N.B., Canada	148	46	11N	67	37W
Woodstock, Ont., Canada	151	43	10N	80	45W
Woolgoolga	116	30	6S	153	11 E
Woomera	118	31	30S	137	10 E
Woonsocket	164	42	0N	71	30W
Wooroloo	120	31	48S	116	18 E
Worcester, U.K.	24	52	12N	2	12W
Worcester, U.S.A.	164	42	14N	71	49W
Workington	28	54	39N	3	34W
Worksop	29	53	19N	1	9W
Wormerveer	40	52	30N	4	46 E
Worms	42	49	37N	8	21 E
Worthing	25	50	49N	0	21W
Worthington	166	43	35N	95	36W
Wou-han = Wuhan	99	30	31N	114	18 E